FREE INTERNET ACCESS AS A HUMAN RIGHT

Merten Reglitz proposes a new human right that ensures internet access for those who cannot afford it and protects that right from arbitrary interferences by those who would exploit it for harm. The first part of the book justifies the claim for this new right by showing how internet access is vital for the enjoyment of human rights around the globe. In the second part, Reglitz specifies the content of this right, assessing today's standard threats to internet access. He recommends a minimum international standard of connectivity and explains how states have misused the internet. He documents how private companies already manipulate both internet access and content to maximise profit, and how lack of rights enforcement allows people to harm others online. The book establishes that a new human right to free internet access is essential to secure its role for the benefit and progress, not detriment, of humanity.

Merten Reglitz is Associate Professor of Philosophy at the University of Birmingham.

Free Internet Access as a Human Right

MERTEN REGLITZ
University of Birmingham

Shaftesbury Road, Cambridge CB2 8EA, United Kingdom

One Liberty Plaza, 20th Floor, New York, NY 10006, USA

477 Williamstown Road, Port Melbourne, VIC 3207, Australia

314–321, 3rd Floor, Plot 3, Splendor Forum, Jasola District Centre, New Delhi – 110025, India

103 Penang Road, #05–06/07, Visioncrest Commercial, Singapore 238467

Cambridge University Press is part of Cambridge University Press & Assessment, a department of the University of Cambridge.

We share the University's mission to contribute to society through the pursuit of education, learning and research at the highest international levels of excellence.

www.cambridge.org
Information on this title: www.cambridge.org/9781009520553

DOI: 10.1017/9781009520508

© Merten Reglitz 2024

This publication is in copyright. Subject to statutory exception and to the provisions of relevant collective licensing agreements, no reproduction of any part may take place without the written permission of Cambridge University Press & Assessment.

When citing this work, please include a reference to the DOI 10.1017/9781009520508

First published 2024

A catalogue record for this publication is available from the British Library

Library of Congress Cataloging-in-Publication Data
NAMES: Reglitz, Merten, author.
TITLE: Free Internet access as a human right / Merten Reglitz.
DESCRIPTION: Cambridge, United Kingdom ; New York, NY : Cambridge University Press, 2024. | Includes bibliographical references and index.
IDENTIFIERS: LCCN 2024009586 (print) | LCCN 2024009587 (ebook) | ISBN 9781009520553 (hardback) | ISBN 9781009520508 (ebook)
SUBJECTS: LCSH: Right to Internet access. | Internet – Access control – Law and legislation. | Internet governance – Law and legislation. | Freedom of information.
CLASSIFICATION: LCC K3240 .R4379 2024 (print) | LCC K3240 (ebook) | DDC 343.09/944–dc23/eng/20240310
LC record available at https://lccn.loc.gov/2024009586
LC ebook record available at https://lccn.loc.gov/2024009587

ISBN 978-1-009-52055-3 Hardback
ISBN 978-1-009-52051-5 Paperback

Cambridge University Press & Assessment has no responsibility for the persistence or accuracy of URLs for external or third-party internet websites referred to in this publication and does not guarantee that any content on such websites is, or will remain, accurate or appropriate.

To my parents, Winfried and Jutta, and my wife, Kristin.

Contents

Acknowledgements		*page* ix
	Introduction	1
	PART I JUSTIFICATIONS	15
1	Human Rights as Protections of a Minimally Decent Human Life	17
2	Derivative Rights and Linkage Arguments for Rights	48
3	Internet Access and Civil and Political Human Rights	71
4	Internet Access and Socio-economic Human Rights	106
	PART II OBLIGATIONS Introduction to Part II	139
5	Poverty as a Standard Threat	143
6	States as Standard Threats	186
7	Private Companies as Standard Threats	230
8	Other Internet Users as Standard Threats	278
	Conclusion	322
Bibliography		337
Index		367

Acknowledgements

The roots of this project go back a while. I had just started my postdoctoral fellowship at the Goethe University Frankfurt when I was asked by Roberto Parra and Victor Peralta Del Riego to give a keynote lecture as part of the Semana de Desarrollo Humano on the topic of 'social media and human rights' at the Universidad del Caribe, Mexico, in April 2014. I thank them for this crucial invitation. Discussing this topic with students and colleagues in Cancún, I was first confronted with the question of what a lack of internet access means for people's opportunities, and what should be done about it. During my postdoctoral fellowship, I pursued research on different topics. However, after I took up a post as lecturer in the Department of Philosophy at the University of Birmingham, my mentor Heather Widdows encouraged me to continue my initial investigations on the problems of digital exclusion and the moral relevance of the internet. Upon acceptance of my 2019 article 'The Human Right to Free Internet Access', the press office of the University of Birmingham contacted me about writing a press release on the forthcoming publication of my first research on this topic. As a philosopher, I was not used to informing the press of my publications. Within two days of the notice being released, about 200 websites globally reported on the publication of the article. As it happened, not a week later, Jeremy Corbyn's Labour campaign for the upcoming 2019 UK parliamentary elections pledged to nationalise the UK's broadband infrastructure, and to provide free full-fibre broadband to all households by 2030. This led to a flurry of invitations to radio interviews with BBC World Radio, LBC Radio, Deutschlandfunk Radio Germany, and the *Daily Mail*'s podcast 'The Daily Show'. All these responses indicated that the topic I was working on was of interest not only within the UK, but also around the world, and this provided further encouragement to expand my research on it, which is now culminating in this book.

Throughout the years, I have received helpful comments on earlier drafts of parts of the book or already published articles on this topic. In this respect, I would like to thank Daniel Edward Callies, Thomas Christiano, Beth Kahn, James Lewis, Jonathan Parry, Wouter Peeters, Heather Widdows, and Jeremy Williams. The final version of the book has tremendously benefited from two manuscript workshops. I would especially like to thank Julian Culp for the workshop at the American University Paris, France, in May 2023, and Darrel Moellendorf and Ellen Niess for organising the workshop at the Goethe University Frankfurt, Germany, in October 2023. I am extremely grateful to the participants of these workshops (in Paris: Fatima Aziz, Julian Culp, Oliver Feltham, Philip Golub, Claudia Roda, Sharon Weill, Zona Zaric; and in Frankfurt: Julio Cáceda Adrianzen, Dimitrios Efthymiou, Maria Paola Ferretti, Calos Gálvez Bermúdez, Eszter Kollár, Darrel Moellendorf, Cain Shelley, and Lukas Sparenborg) for their invaluable feedback. Eszter Kollár and Adam Henschke both hosted me for research visits at the Catholic University of Leuven and Twente University, Enschede, which greatly helped me make progress on completing this manuscript. I would also like to acknowledge and thank the British Academy for awarding me a Small Grant that allowed me to undertake activities (such as the research visit to Enschede and both manuscript workshops) that were crucial for finalising the book. Moreover, a sincere thanks to the editors of the forthcoming *Routledge Handbook for Philosophy of Human Rights*, Kerri Woods and Jesse Tomalty, for inviting me to contribute a chapter to this edited collection, and for organising a workshop to discuss chapter drafts in Leeds in May 2023. The discussion of my ideas during this workshop provided very detailed feedback on my work and I am grateful to all participants for their comments.

Finally, and most importantly, this book would have never come about without the love and support of those closest to me. I thank my parents for introducing me to universal moral values when raising me. With all my heart, I thank my wife Kristin for her unwavering love, support, encouragement, constructive philosophical feedback on all parts and aspects of my research, and for her belief in me throughout the entirety of this project – especially at the times when I had little confidence myself. With my father-in-law, Art Held, I have discussed many of the technological details of the internet and my ideas for this book. I have benefited enormously from his expertise and insightful feedback, for which I am grateful too. Without Eszter Kollár, Darrel Moellendorf, Wouter Peeters, and Heather Widdows I would not have been able to develop as a philosopher or write this book, and I thank them very much their mentorship, their friendship, and their invaluable feedback throughout the years.

Some passages in Chapter 3 are taken from my paper 'The Human Right to Free Internet Access', *Journal of Applied Philosophy* 37(2) (2020): 314–331. Significant sections of Chapter 4 have been published as part of my paper 'The Socio-Economic Argument for the Human Right to Internet Access', *Politics, Philosophy & Economics* 22(4) (2023): 441–469. All passages are reused with permission.

Introduction

What was life like before the internet? Remember (or, if you cannot, imagine) what people had to do to obtain information about something they wanted to know. How did they get their news? How did they interact with public services? How did they communicate with family and friends – especially those far away? What options did they have to express their views to their fellow citizens and those who ruled over them? How did they entertain themselves? How did they shop? But also: how could other people know about a person's most intimate interests or thoughts? How could governments know what people were talking about in private with their friends? And what power did individuals have to misinform others by spreading rumours or lies? Whether we think that we are overall better off or not for having it around, it is certain that the internet has changed all these things (and most aspects of life) for everyone who can access and use it.

In fact, the internet has fundamentally changed people's opportunities to enjoy and exercise some of their most important possessions: their human rights. This is unsurprising if we consider two things. First, the internet permits the creation, transmission, recording, and searching of information in unprecedented ways. Second, all human rights rely on information. Either they are directly about information (e.g. the rights to free information, education, free speech, to take part in cultural life, or to enjoy the benefits of scientific progress and its applications) or information is essential for them (e.g. health, security of person, political participation, freedom of thought, conscience, and religion, and for the prevention of threats to liberty, and freedom from torture by holding to account those who hold power). In the latter case, we need information, for example, to know how to stay or become healthy, to know and avoid threats to our safety, to form religious beliefs, to hold those to account who abuse their power. Today, whether one has internet access or not naturally matters for how well we can make use of our human rights. The Human Rights Council of the United Nations (UN) generally agreed with this diagnosis when it asserted that the internet 'has become an indispensable tool for realizing a range of human rights, combating inequality, and accelerating development and human progress' (UN 2011a: 22). However, contrary to some reports that appeared in the global press after its General Assembly had passed a non-binding resolution on *The Promotion, Protection, and Enjoyment of Human Rights on the Internet* (UN 2016) in 2016, the UN has not recognised a stand-alone human right to the internet as such.

This is essentially why this book makes the argument that public authorities should recognise free access to the internet as a new human right itself. By 'free' I mean two things: internet access should be provided free of charge for those unable to afford it; and it should be free from arbitrary interference (i.e. unjustifiable obstructions and control) by others. As will become clear, the argument that free internet access ought to be a human right also implies the demand that certain uses of the internet are free (i.e. unobstructed and uncompromised). That is because, even though internet access deserves special protection as a human right since it has become practically indispensable for our existing human rights, it is alone insufficient for enjoying these rights. Rather, people must be able to access *and* use the internet to make use of and protect their human rights using online means. However, because free access is prior to use, and because the importance of free internet access implies the importance of free internet use, the new human right that this book argues for is called the human right to free internet access.

As we will see throughout the book, the stakes are high. If people are not able to access the internet, they face political, social, and cultural disadvantage and exclusion. Many of those digitally excluded are also denied important means for utilising at least to some degree some of their most essential human rights (e.g. education and medical care) when they currently cannot do so at all. Problematically, according to estimates of the UN's International Telecommunications Union (ITU), 33 per cent of humanity (or 2.6 billion people) were still offline in 2023 (ITU 2023a: 1). Moreover, if people cannot access and use the internet freely, they are in danger of being monitored, manipulated, threatened, or targeted by others such as their government, profit-seeking companies, or other internet users. If the internet is used to frustrate their legitimate interests, people cannot enjoy many of their most basic rights without having to put themselves at risk. In the worst case, their internet use can even lead to their imprisonment or death. In 2022, the non-governmental organisation (NGO) Freedom House studied internet freedom in seventy countries that are home to 89 per cent of global internet users. It found that for more than 70 per cent of them the internet is either 'not free' or only 'partially free' (Freedom House 2022: 5), meaning that most internet users worldwide face some form of negative repercussions for accessing and using the internet for legitimate purposes. It was unimaginable not too long ago, but today a person's message sent via the internet can capture the attention of millions, a video or post shared online can spark a social movement and change at societal level, and people can join together with others across the globe to promote political causes. On the other hand, though, a government can find out about a citizen's most private beliefs by accessing their online search history or emails, private companies can tailor prices individually to consumers based on what they know about their interests, the police can identify and arrest homosexuals by surveilling online dating platforms, and oppressive regimes can identify their opponents domestically and abroad by monitoring what thoughts people express online. In this context, a new human right to internet access would give people an enforceable entitlement or (where this right is not respected) at least a strong argumentative resource to demand that they are guaranteed unrestricted access to and use of the internet.

What is the internet? When looking for a suitable definition, we can consult (as many people looking for information do) Wikipedia. Wikipedia is a fitting source for our purposes because it is itself something that has been made possible by the internet as the result of the online collaboration of thousands of contributors. According to Wikipedia – the self-described 'largest and most-read reference work in history' (Wikipedia 2021) – the internet

> Is the global system of interconnected computer networks that uses the Internet protocol suite (TCP/IP) to communicate between networks and devices. It is a *network of networks* that consists of private, public, academic, business, and government networks of local to global scope, linked by a broad array of electronic, wireless, and optical networking technologies. The Internet carries a vast range of information resources and services, such as the interlinked hypertext documents and applications of the World Wide Web (WWW), electronic mail, telephony, and file sharing. (Wikipedia 2023a)

The internet has been called many things. Some have argued it is the greatest invention of all time (Weinberg 2012). Some have said it has been less transformative than the washing machine (Skidelsky 2010). Others have argued that it has finally enabled humankind globally to realise one of our very species-specific activities, namely, to communicate and exchange things and ideas with people far away (Smith 2022: 77). Whatever else we make of it, the development of this information communication technology (ICT) can certainly be considered a watershed moment in the social evolution of humanity, just as were the invention of the written word, the printing press, or electricity. The internet, however, is more than just another technical invention or mass medium. Unlike books, newspapers, TV programmes, and radio stations that were previous innovations in how people communicated information, the internet presents another step in human development for at least two reasons. First, it makes the information it is used to transmit individually searchable. Given how much information there is in this world, this is something extraordinarily useful. Second, it allows individuals, with only insignificant costs or technical knowledge, to become senders of information and creators of content that can potentially reach all around the globe and vast numbers of people (Dutton 2023). No other medium has therefore increased the informational and communicative power of individual human beings as the internet. With this increase in power come enormous opportunities for both empowerment and oppression. The human right to free internet access wants to ensure that the internet is used for the former, not the latter.

As is the case with all technologies, the internet does not inevitably have good or bad consequences. Like television and radio programmes or newspapers, it can be used to promote vital universal interests and human progress, or to harm and control people. At the beginning of the twenty-first century, there was widespread optimism about the empowering capacities of the internet. In 2000, Bill Clinton famously argued that attempting to constrain the internet's global power to expand opportunities for free speech was like 'trying to nail Jello to the wall' (Allen-Ebrahimian 2016). However, by 2011 critics of this 'cyber-utopianism' such as Evgeny Mozorov (2011) had warned that autocrats were employing the internet not to liberate, but to oppress their subjects by using it to spread false information and to monitor populations for signs of dissent. Since at least the middle of the second decade of the twenty-first century, there has also been growing awareness and concern about how private companies profit from gathering unprecedented personal information about their users. This knowledge, though, cannot only be used to sell advertising products and services, but also to target individuals with misinformation or politically divisive messages (Zuboff 2019). Against any form of positive or negative 'techno-determinism' (i.e. the belief that a technology inevitably will have good or bad effects), though, a realistic assessment of the internet's effects on human rights must conclude that its effects depend on how it is used, on how public authorities regulate its use, and whether governments themselves are misusing the possibilities it offers. Whether they do in turn crucially depends on public pressure and on what uses of the internet citizens allow their governments to get away with.

What seems certain is that humanity is extremely unlikely to abandon the internet.[1] Given its usefulness for most aspects of people's lives, 'we couldn't kill the Internet if we tried' (Ohm 2016). The real question then is not whether the internet is good or bad, but rather how we shape it. The answer to this question is of momentous importance. But in the current 'absence of a shared global vision' for the internet (Freedom House 2021: 2), the competition for political global dominance between democracies and autocracies also produces rivalling visions for how the internet should be used. Despite the UN demand that 'rights that people have offline must also be protected online' (UN 2016: 2), autocratic states such as China and Russia use the internet to establish *digital authoritarianism* by using it to keep their subjects in check. To gain political influence and economic profit, these digital autocracies also export to other states technologies and knowledge for using ICT to oppress rather than to empower people. Meanwhile, governments of many (or maybe even most) democratic states also spy on their citizens and sometimes their political opponents. Many of their widespread online surveillance practices have been ruled illegal by their own independent courts (Casciani 2018, BBC News 2020) meaning that also these democracies do not respect what this book argues is people's human right to access and use the internet freely. If the internet is to be an empowering technology and one that helps promote human rights and progress, what is therefore needed is a global vision for an internet that is beneficial for humankind. The argument proposed by this book, that public authorities should recognise a human right to free internet access and respect the obligations that come with it, would be an important step in creating such a progressive global vision for the internet.

The internet has been the subject of much research – technological and otherwise. What this book adds to the literature is a comprehensive analysis of the normative significance of the internet. The book is a work in moral philosophy. Moral philosophers investigate not so much what the world is like, but what (we have reasons to believe) it ought to be like. What the world is like is certainly essential for determining what it ought to be like (e.g. we cannot demand changes to human behaviour or institutions that are impossible). But

---

[1] One might argue that asking whether we are better off with the internet than we would have been without it is like asking whether we are better off with roads than without them. Both roads and the internet have beneficial and harmful effects. They are both essential infrastructures that connect people within and across countries. Both are used to move information, knowledge, ideas, and products, and their features and limitations shape the things they are used to transport. Finally, both have become indispensable to people and their lives because of the advantages they bring. That does not mean, of course, that both roads and the internet cannot be improved further to increase the benefits and to decrease the harms they deliver. I thank Stephen Barrell for this point.

the normative ideals and rules that moral philosophers research are essential for human beings as well. Without them, we often do not know what to do or what to aim at. Normative rules and ideals therefore have a guiding function. This book accordingly wants to provide what the epochal political philosopher John Rawls refers to as normative 'orientation' concerning the internet and what we have reasons to want it to be.[2] It does so in two ways. In the first part, the book considers many ways in which the internet has changed people's lives and in particular their opportunities for using and protecting their human rights. In this way, it explains why the internet's effects matter (not only economically or socially, but also morally). In its second part, the book develops a set of standards, rules, and demands for how public authorities ought to treat and protect the internet, which together spell out the concept or idea of the human right to free internet access.

Of course, one might want to object against the formulation of this new right that it seems very unlikely that, for example, governments will not spy on their citizens, that capitalist firms will not thwart attempts to establish legislation to protect consumers' interests that would prevent them from maximising their profits, or that individuals will not try to use the internet to threaten, verbally attack, and harass other people online. This scepticism, though, is not a good reason against calling for the recognition of a human right to free internet access. For one thing, we simply do not know what the future holds and how realistic or not the demands that this new right makes really are. But, more importantly, the plausibility of moral rules and standards does not depend on whether people are likely to adhere to them. 'Do not kill the innocent' and 'do not wantonly lie' are valid moral rules even though they are violated thousands of times each day. Correspondingly, even though governments, private firms, and some individuals will disregard a universal right to free internet access and use, the rules and demands that this right entails can nonetheless be justified. And also for those who fight for free internet access and use, spelling out the idea of this novel right can have an important function. This is

---

[2] For Rawls, 'orientation' is one of the four functions or purposes of political philosophy. As he holds, 'political philosophy may contribute to how a people think of their political and social institutions as a whole, and their basic aims and purposes as a society with a history […]. Moreover, the members of any civilized society need a conception that enables them to understand themselves as members having a certain political status […] and how this status affects their relation to their social world. This need political philosophy may try to answer, and this role I call that of orientation. The idea is that it belongs to reason and reflection (both theoretical and practical) to orient us in the (conceptual) space, say, of all possible ends, individual and associational, political and social. Political philosophy, as a work of reason, does this by specifying principles to identify reasonable and rational ends of those various kinds' (Rawls 2001: 2–3).

because, once we have a grasp of why there should be a human right to free internet access and what such a right plausibly encompasses, this idea can serve as a normative goal and argumentative support for their cause.

The project of formulating a new human right is inevitably an interdisciplinary one. Moral philosophy can provide knowledge of relevant values, theories, and principles, and it can establish normative arguments. But it does not itself offer the required information about the subject matter itself, that is, about the internet as a technology and the effects it has on people and society. The facts about these empirical realities instead are supplied by other experts, and the book's normative analysis of the internet is squarely dependent on the empirical knowledge that they can provide. For this reason, this book heavily relies on facts and insights about the internet from other academic disciplines such as computer science, law, medical science, educational science, economics, psychology, communication and media studies, development studies, but also from non-academic experts such as public institutions (e.g. the UN Human Rights Council, the UN's International Telecommunication Union, the UN's Broadband Commission, UNICEF, the World Health Organization, the European Commission), NGOs (e.g. the Alliance for Affordable Internet, Freedom House, Access Now, the Good Things Foundation), and reputable press sources such as the *BBC*, the *New York Times*, or *The Guardian*. Some empirical data that non-philosophical experts provide are simply facts or best available statistics (e.g. the number of existing internet users worldwide). However, other data is more contentious (e.g. the percentage of populations stuck in echo chambers or the number of people who accept online conspiracy narratives), and where this is the case, contrary claims and studies are considered as well. Even though the work of this book would be impossible without the knowledge provided by empirical research, it primarily establishes a moral argument based on this best available and critically considered evidence, namely that these facts point towards the conclusion that people should have a universally recognised freedom to be able to freely access and use the internet to enjoy their human rights. Of course, much of what people do online does not have anything to do with their human rights. These other uses are morally not important enough to be able to establish a demand for something as serious as a human right. But the practical indispensability that the internet has assumed for our existing human rights can, or so I shall argue.

What is important to note from the start when approaching this book's argument for a new human right is that what is (philosophically and morally) needed is not 'invention' or 'making up an idea', but rather a process of discovery. What rights people should have is not simply up to what the majority thinks or what the law currently happens to say. Rather, as the philosopher Henry Shue (whose work on rights will be crucial for the work of this book) explains, which rights people have and should be recognised ultimately depends on the 'weight of reasons' (Shue 2020: 73). That is, if we want to know what rights people possess or should be granted, it is not enough to look at an existing list of legally codified rights. In many places around the world, people are denied essential entitlements such as human rights even though morally they clearly possess them and should have them respected. Moreover, new technologies (e.g. the development of mRNA vaccines) can change what existing rights (e.g. the human right to healthcare) entail or what rights people have in the first place (e.g. the common availability of mobile phones with cameras has necessitated a new right against 'upskirting' to deter some men from committing the obviously wrong act of taking a photograph up women's skirts). We therefore have to consider, case by case, in light of the best available evidence, what morally relevant interests people have that are strong enough to warrant attributing to them a right that protects these interests. Along these lines, this book argues that there are weighty reasons for lawmakers to recognise that everyone today should have a human right to free internet access because we no longer have adequate opportunities to exercise our existing rights without it.

There is of course a question about the normative grounds of such an argument. What exactly is the basis that such a process of discovering a novel right can start from? How can we be sure that the argument that this book makes rests on a reasonable and respectable normative foundation? The question of the grounds of moral reasoning and first principles in moral philosophy is always a difficult and controversial one because few things are universally accepted to matter decisively so that entire complex arguments and principles can be based on them. However, this book employs a morally, politically, and legally well-established normative framework, namely that of accepted international human rights. It considers how the internet has affected our existing human rights. Based on this, it uses the consequences that the introduction of this digital technology has had to argue that we now need an additional human right to free internet access because such digital freedom has become too essential to leave it up to the good will of governments or private companies and the differing financial fortunes and misfortunes of individuals. Human rights are certainly not all that matters morally. There are, for instance, fundamental questions about what a just distribution of the socioeconomic surplus that societies produce has to look like that exceed what human rights demand. But there is a lot of (even though by no means universal) agreement that human rights do matter if anything does. And because of this, today free internet access matters fundamentally as well because the practical value that our human rights have for us can now depend on whether we can freely exercise and advocate for them online. Existing human rights are therefore the normative foundation of this book's argument.

The fundamental moral importance of human rights, though, also makes the project of justifying a new human right to free internet access a particularly challenging one. After all, human rights are in a sense the most important rights we have because they are the most basic ones. For this reason, only the most essential things should be recognised as human rights. As the legal philosopher James Nickel (whose work is also of fundamental importance for this book) explains, candidates for human rights must fulfil several strict criteria:

1. They must be relevant for people's most fundamental and morally most urgent interests.
2. More specifically, they must provide social guarantees against substantive and recurring threats to the urgent interests in question.
3. The urgent interests protected must be of universal rather than local or national importance because human rights matter to all humans.
4. They must be essential in the sense that no weaker norm (e.g. helping people to help themselves or voluntary aid of others) could provide the required protections.
5. Their fulfilment must not cause unjustifiable financial or moral burdens on others (e.g. require for its implementation unreasonable funds, that we deprive others of their rights, or that we negatively impact on their health).
6. They must be feasible in a majority of countries right now lest most states become liable to criticism that they have not realised something that they lack the means for. (Nickel 2007: 70–79)

However, despite these challenging requirements, we will see throughout the book that internet access indeed has become such a thing that can meet all six of these demanding criteria. To establish the argument that free internet access is a human right, the book is divided into two parts. Part I presents the normative case for the idea. Part II spells out the details of what accepting the idea entails in terms of obligations for public authorities. Each part consists of four chapters. To conclude this introduction, what follows is a short overview of the chapters of the book.

Chapter 1 discusses the very idea of human rights. Without knowing what human rights are, we also cannot understand whether internet access should be one of them. The chapter will outline the philosophical view that human rights have the function to protect the conditions of minimally decent lives. In doing so, it also explains (1) why it makes sense to talk of a moral human right that does not yet exist but that should become recognised by public authorities as a legal entitlement, (2) why there is no problem as such with the demand that something should be a human right that is a modern technology, and (3) why internet access is not sufficiently protected for people if it is made part of, or subsumed under, already existing human rights such as free speech.

Chapter 2 provides us with the other technical tools that we need to make the argument that free internet access should be a human right. These are the ideas of linkage arguments and derivative rights, with the former establishing the latter based on their usefulness for other rights. In this chapter, we will also take a look at how rights generally function, that is, the way that they create duties for others (most prominently public institutions) to respect and protect their object for the right-holder, and obligations to aid the right-holder in case their rights are not fulfilled or violated. Moreover, the chapter explains that rights generally have the point of ensuring that people have adequate (rather than merely formal or implausibly maximal) opportunities to make use of their rights. The reasoning that underpins linkage arguments is essential because this book does not claim that internet access is a good in itself. Rather, the demand it makes for a new right is entirely grounded in the usefulness of internet access for the realisation of other human rights.

Chapter 3 presents evidence for the book's core claim that internet access today is practically indispensable if we are to have adequate opportunities to enjoy and use our human rights – specifically our civil and political human rights such as our rights to free speech, free assembly, free information, political participation, security of person, liberty, and equality before the law. The chapter outlines numerous ways in which the internet has made all of these rights more effective by giving people either new ways to exercise them or to protect them from abuse. These unprecedented opportunities, though, have also created a situation where those who do not have internet access are disadvantaged to the extent that they have to be considered politically excluded. Because such exclusion is incompatible with our human rights, internet access must be seen as a universal entitlement.

Chapter 4 makes a parallel case for the importance of internet access with respect to socio-economic human rights such as the ones to education, health, work, social security, and cultural participation. Also with respect to these, people who cannot access the internet are relatively disadvantaged to others who can use online opportunities to enjoy these rights. That is, for them digital exclusion translates into social exclusion. In conjunction with Chapter 3, Chapter 4 presents the normative core and the justificatory argument of the book. At its end (which is also the end of Part I), we will have a good grasp of the fact that internet access today is no longer a matter of convenience or a luxury for those who can afford it. Rather, we have to acknowledge that around the world internet access has become a basic utility that is practically indispensable for the enjoyment of our most essential rights.

Part II details what follows from accepting the human right to free internet access. It is doing this by considering which serious standard threats people are confronted with when they want to access the internet. By identifying these standard threats, we can also determine what public authorities have to do to prevent them. Moreover, as Nickel's test makes clear, understanding the standard threats to free internet access also in part explains why we need this novel right. Not only has it become essential in many ways for us. Additionally, our enjoyment of internet access cannot be presumed but rather has to be ensured and protected in certain ways.

Chapter 5 identifies poverty as the first standard threat to internet access. As mentioned earlier, large parts of humanity remain offline – mostly because they currently lack and cannot afford the necessary conditions for it. The chapter therefore identifies what public authorities would have to do to ensure that everyone can go online. It addresses four dimensions of internet access: data services, digital devices, broadband infrastructure, and basic digital skills. If people lack one of these, they cannot go online. Chapter 5 identifies a global standard of duties with respect to all four dimensions that is currently feasible for most states to guarantee for their citizens and everyone who cannot themselves afford the necessary tools. It thereby explains that one meaning of 'free' internet access is that the latter should be provided free of charge for those unable to afford it. Moreover, the chapter specifies certain minimal obligations that even those countries that currently cannot afford to realise internet access for all their citizens can and have to fulfil.

Chapter 6 investigates states as standard threats to free internet access. As public authorities, states have the primary obligation to protect and respect human rights. However, unfortunately, they are also major abusers of internet access for their own purposes. Autocratic regimes make internet access unfree by using it to spy on their citizens to identify and eliminate possible opponents, and to manipulate their subjects by feeding them certain information and by withholding other information from them. Democratic states make internet access unfree by monitoring their citizens and potential opponents for the sake of national security. The way they do this is highly extensive and problematic. The chapter therefore introduces the second meaning of 'free' internet access as that kind of online access that is free from arbitrary inferences, for example, by states, and which they instead have a duty to ensure.

Chapter 7 turns to private companies as standard threats to free internet access. Most of the internet's network infrastructure and applications/content for users was developed by businesses, and today is owned and operated by them. Private corporations have used the fact that we can no longer avoid the internet if we want to be socially and politically included to arbitrarily interfere with our human rights in various ways. For instance, they have subjected many routine uses of the internet to extensive surveillance for the purpose of harvesting and monetising our personal information. Some of the major internet-based companies also operate social media platforms whose rules and membership they decide. Their decisions therefore have major effects on our opportunities to use our human rights online, and this chapter will look at which sorts of influences are compatible and incompatible with keeping internet access and use free for their users. Moreover, it considers the matter of the neutral transfer or treatment of data on the internet, known as 'net neutrality'. This standard has increasingly come under attacks by private companies as they hope to generate more profits by treating data unequally. Chapter 6 (like Chapters 4 and 5) considers all these issues with a view to what obligations public authorities would have by accepting the right to free internet access to guarantee the object of that right.

Chapter 8 finally considers internet users themselves as standard threats. This is because individuals can also use the internet to violate or threaten the rights of others when they engage in, for example, the spread of child pornography, revenge pornography, or when they defame or threaten others online. However, cyberspace must be a place where rights are enforced and respected. The chapter therefore outlines what states should do to ensure that people respect each other's rights on the internet. However, this cannot be achieved by threatening punishments for offences alone. Rather, public education should come to encompass not only training of basic abilities to use the internet, but also digital media literacy as well as training in non-vicious online behaviour by teaching people the negative effects of abusing each other online. The chapter also argues that to make the internet a safe place it also has to be part of a larger healthy information environment that must include, for example, independent public broadcast services to provide people with reliable and impartial sources of information. Without these, the internet is likely to confront people with a deluge of information that is difficult to manage, which might lead them to abuse the rights of others in response to their lack of orientation or out of malice.

At its end, this book has made the case for a novel human right. But in doing so, it also contributes to a philosophical understanding of the moral importance of the internet. In this way, it hopes to outline part of a global vision for an internet that is empowering rather than an instrument of oppression. If public authorities were to adopt this new human right, respect the obligations it entails, and work towards a situation in which others also accept these duties, the internet could really contribute to the 'progress of humankind as a whole' (UN 2011a: 19), as the UN hopes. No doubt there are and will be other challenges that exceed the scope of this book. However, the chapters outlined here cover some of the most pressing problems that we are currently faced with concerning this medium. Bar some catastrophic events or developments, we will not get rid of the internet. Because we will not, we had better get it right, which would require that all of humanity can freely go online and use the internet without the morally unjustifiable interferences of others. It is therefore time to accept free internet access as a human right.

PART I
JUSTIFICATIONS

1

Human Rights as Protections of a Minimally Decent Human Life

In this book, I argue that public institutions should recognise a human right to free internet access because in our digital world internet access has become necessary for leading minimally decent lives. More specifically, my argument will be that internet access has become indispensable for the realisation of other human rights that are necessary for a minimally good life, and should therefore be considered a universal entitlement.

Right from the start, this core claim of the book might strike some readers as exaggerated. They might agree that the internet has become central to human life in modern society as it allows us to do most things more easily. But it is quite something else to claim that therefore we should all have something as fundamentally important as a human right to access this technology. After all, the language of human rights is generally reserved for things that are most essential for human beings, such as food, water, shelter, clothing, education, and basic political rights. Cars are useful things too, but this does not mean that everyone has a human right to a car. This is a concern that must be taken seriously. To call something a human right means to attribute to it exceptional moral importance and to declare it a claimable entitlement. It has become a popular strategy to claim many things that are important to be human rights. The aim of this is to have the object that one cares about to be declared a protected, high-priority entitlement. But many rights claims that have been presented in this way seem questionable. Some of the things that have been claimed to be human rights include land (de Schutter 2010), friendship (Wittrock 2022), a happy life (Liu and Yan 2020), and even sexual pleasure (Coleman et al. 2021). Considering this list, one immediate worry we might have is whether such rights are fulfillable at all or who would be required to fulfil them for everyone (Tasioulas 2021). Moreover, we might be concerned that declaring everything that is desirable a human right leads to a counterproductive expansion or inflation of the term 'human rights' (Nickel 2007: 97, Clément 2018). Such an inflation would be unhelpful because it threatens to take away the special moral force that most people attach to human rights when these are extended to desirable things that simply are not as morally urgent and fundamental as traditionally recognised human rights.[1] And in fact internet access, or high-quality internet access, is often mentioned as precisely one of those things that is handy, but that ought not be considered a human right because it is not essential enough to deserve the status of a universally claimable entitlement (de Hert and Kloza 2012, Tasioulas 2021, Theilen 2021).

For this reason, to determine whether internet access can be a human right at all, we first need certain theoretical tools that help us evaluate human rights claims. We need to understand, for example, what human rights are in the first place. Otherwise, we will not be able to tell if internet access qualifies as a human right – even if we know how it is useful. We also have to know how rights operate in general and what it means to assign a right to someone. Otherwise, we do not know when we can say that we have a right to something, and what follows from accepting that someone has a right to something, such as internet access. Accepting a human right to internet access would mean accepting a universal entitlement to a useful technology. It is for that reason also important to see how human rights to technological means are possible. This first chapter will therefore introduce the concepts of rights and human rights. In Section 1.1, we will see that human rights are moral rights of a particular kind that fulfil a specific role in international politics and law. In Section 1.2, I will argue that, from a philosophical standpoint, human rights have the particular function of protecting what everyone needs to live a minimally decent life. Section 1.3 will then explain the implications and obligations that follow from accepting that people have human rights. In Section 1.4, I will clarify two possible misunderstandings about human rights that pertain specifically to the idea of a human right to free internet access. At the end of the chapter, we will have a good grasp of what human rights are, what their function is, what justifies them, and what follows from accepting something as a human right.

---

[1] On the other hand, being too inflexible about what can be called a human right also has its dangers. This is because denying any extension of human rights beyond the classic list enshrined in, for example, the Universal Declaration of Human Rights tends to protect the status quo by denying that new developments or problems can be as morally urgent as the basic entitlements specified in the original human rights documents (Theilen 2021). Important human rights theorists therefore agree that we have to be generally open-minded about what things can reasonably be claimed to be human rights (Nickel 2007: 97).

1.1 WHAT ARE HUMAN RIGHTS?

One might think that, to understand what human rights are, we can simply consult legal human rights treaties such as the Universal Declaration of Human Rights (UN 1948). After all, these documents specify which human rights are accepted and enshrined into international law.

One problem with this approach is that these documents merely give us a snapshot of currently recognised human rights. However, what they do not tell us in detail is what function human rights fulfil or why we should accept them. Another problem with this method is that these treaties might lack certain entries that we think they should include. This book, for instance, argues that one such item that is currently absent from international human rights documents, but should be included, is the human right to free internet access. If this is correct, the concept of human rights is broader than the list of legally recognised human rights. That human rights are not determined by international treaties alone makes sense when we consider that, if this were so, human rights would only come into existence with the ratification of international treaties. In this case, no one has human rights unless some legal document recognises these rights. Consequently, in a world in which there would be no human rights treaties, no one would have human rights that could be violated. But that would mean, for instance, that the Nazis did not violate the human rights of those millions they murdered in concentration camps because the Universal Declaration of Human Rights was only adopted after the end of the Second World War. This seems very implausible because it is clear that the Nazis violated the most basic entitlements of their victims – entitlements that every human being has to have if we have any. No legal document was required to establish the moral fact that this fascist regime violated essential rights of its victims that were so fundamental and universally recognisable that these acts were legally captured by the expression 'crimes against humanity'. This suggests that we all possess certain rights independently of what is recognised by states in international rights treaties. And that, in turn, opens the possibility that there are human rights that have not yet been (but should become) recognised in international law.

To approach the question 'what is a human right?' we therefore cannot simply rely on international legal treaties. Instead, we have to turn to philosophical human rights theory. Philosophers do not think about human rights only in terms of legally accepted human rights. Rather, they study human rights with a view to what characterises them, what justifies them, and what functions they fulfil. Taking a philosophical approach to human rights allows us to do some things that a look at international human rights treaties does not.

For instance, once we know what human rights are, what function they fulfil, and what justifies them, we can understand why human rights are particularly urgent rights that everyone should respect – even if they are often violated in international politics. A philosophical understanding of human rights also enables us to engage critically with internationally accepted human rights and to test whether all of them really ought to have the status of human rights.[2] Finally (and of particular importance for the purposes of this book), knowing what human rights are in the philosophical sense puts us in a position to think about potential human rights that are currently missing from the accepted list of human rights.

It is not surprising that there can be human rights that are not recognised legal human rights. This is because there are many other rights than legal rights that people have irrespective of what public law acknowledges. These non-legal rights are moral rights, and they help us understand how this book can argue for a human right that does not yet exist. Moral rights are claims that we have towards others. Such claims normally have greater normative force than other moral considerations or non-moral reasons for action. For example, it might be a morally good thing for me voluntarily to give money to the person sitting at the side of the street asking for help. But since this person does not have a moral right to my money, I am not under a strict moral obligation to help them. I might deserve some moral criticism if giving help to that person would not have come at a great cost to me because we generally have moral reasons to help others in need. However, if the person is not in distress, they have a general claim to support towards everyone rather than a strong entitlement to my help in particular. Things are different, though, if I promised someone money. My promise gives them a moral right to the promised money and creates a strong obligation for me towards them. This is because promises precisely have the function of enabling us to bind ourselves morally to other people in order to create special relationships or trust. I am under an even more binding (i.e. legally binding) obligation to give someone money if I signed a legal contract to do so because legal contracts are social institutions that are particularly designed to create mutual assurance through enforceable claims. These examples show that between general moral reasons for action and legally binding obligations, there are moral rights that have morally binding force even though they are not backed up by legal sanctions and coercive enforcement.

---

[2] One example of a 'problematic' human right that is legally enshrined in international human rights law, but is often doubted to deserve the status of a human right, is the right to paid leave from work.

There are many moral rights that we can be said to have that are not legal rights. For example, my friends have a moral right to my loyalty and support if they are in urgent need. My partner has a moral right to my faithfulness (unless we have agreed on a different arrangement), and my family members generally have moral rights to my help if our familial relations are intact (and maybe even if they are not). None of these rights are such that we would want them to be legally enforced. Because they are part of people's private lives and personal morality, there are good reasons not to create laws that attach fines or prison sentences to spousal infidelity or breaking promises to a friend. However, violating the moral rights that my family, my partner, and friends have towards me carries with it severe moral and social sanctions because I failed to fulfil important obligations that I have by virtue of others having moral rights towards me. According to the philosopher Joseph Raz (1986: 180), we have a moral right to something if this something is an interest of ours that is important enough to place others under an obligation to respect or fulfil that interest for us. For example, being truthful to my partner, being loyal to my friends, and being helpful to my family members is not merely something that it would be optional or nice for me to do. Rather, because my partner's interest in my fidelity or my friend's interest in my loyalty are morally very important, these interests place me under an obligation to respect them. The same cannot be said of anyone's interest in owning the newest iPhone. This interest is not morally important enough for that person's life to place anyone under an obligation to provide them with such an iPhone. No one therefore has a moral right to the newest iPhone. The connection between rights and corresponding duties also partly explains what is difficult with the claims that we have human rights to, for example, land, friendship, a happy life, or sexual pleasure. These claims are problematic because, for each of them, it is either unclear whether they could be fulfilled (e.g. a happy life) or whether there is anyone who would owe us the object of that claim (e.g. land, friendship, or sexual pleasure). Because my rights have to correspond with others' obligations to fulfil or respect my right, it is not enough that some things are desirable for me to have a right to them. After all, no one might have an obligation to provide these things for me. The claim this book defends is that, in contrast to the newest iPhone, friendship, or sexual pleasure, internet access is morally important enough for us to recognise that we all have a moral claim to it.

Moreover, in contrast to spousal fidelity or promises among friends, some moral rights are important enough to warrant enforcement by legal means and coercive force. All our basic civil rights are of this sort. Our interests in life, bodily integrity, free speech, political participation, and the means of subsistence are sufficiently important to justify legal rights that public authorities enforce. Given the importance these interests have for all of us, we cannot leave it up to the good will of people to respect the moral rights that these interests give rise to. Instead, public authorities are justified in forcing us to respect each other's vital basic rights by punishing their violation. But to make matters even more complex, not all legal rights are moral rights. Some of them only come into existence when a community adopts them. For example, speed limits vary from country to country, and no one has a moral right to a particular speed limit. We all have a moral right to a safe traffic environment, which explains why the state is authorised to impose traffic laws. However, the particular details of these traffic laws are a matter of legal definition, relevant evidence, and public agreement.[3]

What this shows is that there are different kinds of obligations and rights. Not all moral obligations (e.g. the general obligation to be helpful) give rise to moral rights. Not all moral rights (e.g. the moral right to be faithful to my partner) should be legally codified and coercively enforced. This importantly means that there are moral rights that are not legal rights. Very important moral rights, though, are often backed up by the sanctions of the law (e.g. the moral rights to life, freedom from torture, or bodily integrity). Finally, there can be legal rights that are not moral rights because they are not based on

---

[3] How rights operate technically is explained by Wesley Hohfeld's (1919) characterisation of rights. According to Hohfeld, there are different kinds of rights characterised by what they do. He calls these 'rights-incidents'. They bestow certain advantages on their possessor as well as correlative disadvantages on those who are bound by them. Hohfeld identifies four such rights incidents. First, *claim-rights* give their possessor a claim on someone who is placed under a duty by the right to respect or fulfil that claim. For example, if I have a claim-right towards my government to have internet access provided for me, my government has a duty to provide internet access for me. If I have a claim-right against my government to access and use the internet without unjustifiable obstructions, my government must not block, monitor, or censor my access and use of the internet without good reason. Second, rights that are *privileges* (or *liberties*) ensure that others have no right to block the right-holder from exercising their right. For example, if I have the privilege (or liberty) to exercise my human right to free speech online, no one (importantly, my government) has a right to prevent me from, or punish me for, voicing my opinion online. The third kind of rights are *power-rights*. These make those bound by them liable to have their own normative situation changed by the holder's exercise of their right. For example, if I operate an internet server or website and offer it for use to others, I have the power to change the terms of service of my offer. If I do so, I change what others who want to use my service are able to use my server or website for. The users of my services are free to walk away from what I offer. But if they want to use my services, they are liable to having to accept the changes I make to my terms of service. Finally, there are rights that give immunities to their holders. For example, as an internet user, my human right to privacy gives me protection from another's (e.g. my government's) attempts to spy on my internet activities. According to Hohfeld's scheme, all our moral and legal rights consist of at least one of these four rights-incidents. Often, though (as in the case of property rights), our rights entail multiple incidents and advantages (see also Wenar 2023).

particular moral rights (e.g. there is no moral right to a speed limit of exactly 130 kmh).

This distinction between moral and legal rights is important because it enables us to see that there are moral rights that are significant enough that they *should* be recognised and protected by the law – even if they are currently not. For instance, slavery is always a violation of basic moral rights of the enslaved, namely (among other things) their rights to their own body and equality before the law. The enslaved have these moral rights even when they are not legally recognised. Equally, women always had moral rights to vote and to determine their own lives even though those rights were denied to them throughout most of human history (and in many cases are still denied to women today). Historical and current struggles for emancipation and legal equality are particularly salient examples of the idea that people possess important moral rights that ought to receive legal protection irrespectively whether these rights are recognised in the law of their society. The legal denial of the moral rights of slaves and women were the injustices that abolitionists and suffragettes struggled against. The social change they fought for was at its heart a struggle for the legal protection of their basic moral rights. Equally, today there can be moral human rights that are not yet recognised as legal human rights.

According to the philosophical view that I employ in this book, all human rights are moral rights. That is, all rights that deserve the status of human rights – irrespectively of whether they are already recognised as such or not – are moral rights that are based on particularly urgent moral interests. For the argument advanced in this book this means that internet access (for reasons we will encounter in Chapters 3 and 4) is a human right because it is justified by the need to have urgent interests respected and fulfilled. However, human rights are a special subgroup of moral rights. They are particular in that all persons have these rights simply by virtue of being human and irrespectively of what else applies to them. To understand this point it is useful to contrast human rights with some of the moral rights we encountered earlier that only particular people have. Everyone has human rights to life, freedom from torture, to free speech, and free assembly. But not everyone has a moral right to the fidelity of their partner because not everyone has a partner. Equally, everyone has human rights to health care, free information, and the means of subsistence, but not everyone has a moral right to the help of their family members because some people have no living family members. And everyone has a human right to a free conscience and religious worship but only those to whom I made a promise have a moral right to the content of that promise. In their universal nature, human rights also differ from legal rights. Everyone has human rights to a nationality, to an education, and to equal treatment before the law. But only citizens of the US state of Alaska have a legal right to a modest basic income paid by the state of Alaska because of the legal entitlement given to them by the laws of that state. And only US citizens, but not German or British citizens, have a constitutional right to bear arms.

This means, first, that human rights are not conditional on anything but being human. Being a member of the human family is sufficient for having them. Secondly, because these rights are unconditional, unlike certain legal rights (such as a US Green Card that allows a non-citizen to legally stay in the US that can be lost if the holder leaves the country for a certain period of time) we can never lose our human rights. Our human rights might be violated, unfulfilled, misappropriated, or temporarily suspended (e.g. when people's freedoms of movement and worship were limited during the lockdowns to curb the spread of the COVID-19 pandemic), but we normally do not lose them because we never cease to be human beings who have urgent moral rights. Importantly, the interests that ground human rights are so universal and urgent that they demand legal recognition and enforcement around the world. This means that every state ought to recognise in law, to protect and enforce, the human rights of all its citizens and everyone else in their territory.

However, human rights are special in another sense. They are particular in that they fulfil a unique role in international politics and law. If a state is unwilling or unable to guarantee the human rights of its citizens, this makes that state liable to criticism from (or entitles it to the help of) the international community (Beitz 2009: 102–117). In the worst cases of human rights violations, a state may even jeopardise its general right of national self-determination and immunity to outside interference if humanitarian intervention is required to protect the human rights of its citizens. This feature of human rights is explained by the organisation of our social world into nation states and human rights' historical origin as instruments of international law that are rules for this kind of world. In 1948, the United Nations (UN) ratified as its normative basis the Universal Declaration of Human Rights in response to the crimes that Nazi Germany and Japan committed against parts of their own population and the inhabitants of the territories they had occupied. Normally, states are taken to have sovereignty, which means that they have a right to non-interference in their internal affairs. But no state is justified in violating the most urgent moral interests of people, and human rights protect these interests. If human rights are disrespected or cannot be guaranteed because a state is too poor to do so, other states can be authorised or even be under a duty to intervene to protect and guarantee these rights.

Human rights in this respect differ from other legal rights. If a political community decides, for example, to cut the medical services its members are legally entitled to, this remains a matter of domestic politics as long as the state still guarantees decent basic medical care. Only if the political community denies some of its citizens such basic medical care and so is in violation of these people's human rights (particularly their human right to health) does the matter become one of international concern. Similarly, a state might adopt more restrictive speed limits without committing human rights violations. It is only if the state (without proper justification) bans citizens from travelling at all that it would infringe its citizens' human rights and become liable to external criticism. To take another example, if the US democratically decided to abolish the constitutional right to bear arms, this would not be a human rights violation because this right grew out of the US's particular historical context but is not recognised as a moral or legal human right. Human rights are therefore special in that they are never exclusively domestic matters of any state. Rather, they are always matters that concern the entire international community. No state is morally permitted to idly stand by while human rights are violated elsewhere if it can protect these rights at a proportionally reasonable cost. A crucial feature of human rights is thus that politically they are matters of international concern because they function as conditions of the legitimacy (the morally justified exercise of political authority) of all states. States must respect the human rights of their citizens and everyone else to be justified in exercising power. As mentioned in the Introduction, according to the UN, respecting existing human rights online is such a matter of international concern, as shown by the UN's General Assembly's adoption of the non-binding resolution calling upon states to respect the offline human rights of their citizens online in 2016.

To summarise: human rights are moral rights that all persons have by virtue of being human and without having to fulfil any other conditions. They are moral rights that protect universal morally urgent interests, and which should be recognised by law everywhere around the world. Additionally, human rights are moral rights that should be recognised in international law because they are matters of international concern. Every state must respect the human rights of their own citizens and all other persons or risk jeopardising its political legitimacy and with it its right to non-interference. The exercise of political power is only justifiable if it respects the human rights of everyone. Genocide, the systematic oppression of domestic minorities, and aggressive wars of extermination are examples of human rights violations that call for a response by the international community of states.[4] Moreover, human rights

---

[4] It is important to note, though, that the moral obligation to intervene to stop human rights violations is not limitless. Such a duty can be outweighed by the costs of intervention because

are matters of international concern in the sense that, if states are unable to guarantee them for their populations, the international community is called upon to aid, and to help realise and protect these rights. Famines, poverty, and natural disasters are examples of occurrences that trigger obligations for other states in a position to help those whose human rights cannot be guaranteed by their own government. Human rights are therefore universal moral rights that are based on urgent moral interests, and which are matters of international concern. This clarifies several important characteristics of human rights (e.g. their universality and urgency). However, what has been said so far does not explain which urgent interests exactly give normative force to, and allow the identification of, human rights. The question of what justifies human rights is the topic of Section 1.2.

1.2 HUMAN RIGHTS AS PROTECTIONS OF THE CONDITIONS OF MINIMALLY DECENT LIVES

We all have interests that are important to us, but only the most urgent and universal ones are sufficiently important to ground human rights that are matters of international concern. Philosophers have suggested several criteria for identifying these urgent interests that justify rights that every person possesses unconditionally. In this book, the view that I adopt understands human rights as protecting the conditions of minimally decent lives. That is to say, what justifies our human rights is that they have the particular function to protect what all human beings require to live minimally good lives. It is ultimately our interest in these things we all minimally need that provides the reasons that vindicate our human rights. This understanding significantly limits the range of things that can become the objects of human rights claims. Philosophers who hold this view, such as James Nickel, argue that 'human rights are not ideals of the good life for humans; they are rather concerned with ensuring the conditions, negative and positive, of a minimally good life' (Nickel 2007: 138). Accordingly, human rights protect things that are of utmost urgency for us, rather than things that it would be desirable but not essential to have. What

---

these must be proportionate to the good that the intervention has to achieve. For instance, if a humanitarian intervention to stop human rights violations in another state would create more harm that it could prevent, it can be argued that there is no moral duty to intervene in these circumstances (McMahan 2010). This does not mean that no human rights violations occur in this situation. But it means that, regrettably, these rights cannot be protected, and no one fails their duty to protect these rights. It also implies that states that possess large arsenals of nuclear weapons are unfortunately in practice often immune to external interventions when they violate human rights.

is necessary for a minimally good or decent life to a significant extent depends on empirical and contextual considerations. The importance of internet access, as we will see in the upcoming chapters, is a prime example of such an element of a minimally good life that requires knowledge about facts, and not only reliance on theoretical reflection.

We might, of course, wonder why it should be so morally important that all human beings live minimally decent lives. Most people naturally care about the well-being of those near and dear to them. And many also think it matters that their compatriots can live decent lives. But why should we have to care that everyone everywhere lives minimally good lives? The Universal Declaration of Human Rights provides an answer that has philosophical roots going back at least to Immanuel Kant. According to the Declaration's Article 1, 'All human beings are born free and equal in dignity and rights. They are endowed with reason and conscience and should act towards one another in a spirit of brotherhood' (UN 1948). That is, the reason why we cannot ignore the interest of all human beings in living minimally decent lives is that all of them possess equal moral dignity. Different philosophers have given different answers to the question why human beings have dignity, which grounds their moral equality and equal moral status. According to Kant, human beings have dignity because they have the capacity to reason and to determine what is right and wrong, rather than simply following instincts (Kant 1785: 84). For John Rawls, people are owed respect and possess inherent worth and dignity (Rawls 1999: 513) because they are free and equal persons. For him, they are equal moral persons because they possess two crucial moral powers: their capacity for a sense of justice and their capacity for a conception of the good (Rawls 2001: 18–19). However, we do not have to limit ourselves to one or two features of human beings to explain why they possess the dignity that requires us to ensure that their interest in a minimally decent life is fulfilled. Instead, there are a plurality of typical features that human beings possess to various degrees that all help to explain why they possess dignity. Among these features are, for example, 'their ability to suffer, their lives, their agency, their consciousness and reflective capacities, their individuality, their social awareness' (Nickel 2007: 66), their empathy, and creativity (Gilabert 2024: 31).[5] If these capacities

---

[5] This raises, of course, the question whether non-human beings can also have human rights or rights that are of equivalent strengths to human rights because we share some of these capacities (e.g. sentience) with them. What is important for this book, though, is that we can justify human rights as protections of the conditions of minimally decent lives based on the idea that human beings possess particular moral worth and status because they have dignity. For an argument that dignity-based views of human rights do not have to lead to claims of human supremacy over non-human animals, see, for example, Gilabert (2024).

are harmed, this constitutes an attack on a person's dignity. And if any of them is frustrated, people cannot live decent lives. The things that give us dignity as humans therefore justify our claims to have human rights, and they help shed light on what we have human rights to.

Some requirements of a minimally decent life that we must have human rights to are quite straightforward. For example, all our subsistence and security rights are obvious conditions of a minimally good life. No one who is starving, lacks access to clean water or air, is homeless, is tortured, or lives in an environment that makes them sick can lead decent lives. Neither can those living in war zones and whose lives are constantly under threat. Beyond that, socio-economic human rights are also essential for minimally good lives: basic medical care, education, and times for rest and leisure are indispensable for everyone. Human rights will not always guarantee that we can achieve the things they protect for us. Even though we have a human right to health care, we might suffer from an incurable illness. Even though I might have access to food, I might suffer from allergies that make almost all foods inedible for me. And even though we receive basic education, we might fail to acquire elementary knowledge. Neither is it necessary for minimally decent lives that we exercise all our rights (Liao 2015a: 82). We might, for instance, participate in cultural activities and practise a religion but not be politically active. It might also be true that, to lead a fulfilled life and to thrive, human beings need to be culturally, spiritually, and politically active. However, it is not the purpose of human rights to ensure that people engage in all activities that are necessary for flourishing lives. Instead, what human rights do is to ensure that people have the opportunity to do and engage with all those things required for living minimally decent lives. If we consider the list of human rights recognised in international documents, understanding them as protections of the conditions of minimally decent lives explains why we have these entitlements.

One important class of rights, though, seems to be difficult to account for when we take human rights to protect minimally decent lives. These are our political human rights. After all, today and throughout most of human history, many people are and were not able to freely express their views in public, to participate in the political processes of their community, to access information freely, or to choose to associate with whom they want. And yet we might think that people who do not have these freedoms are nonetheless able to lead minimally decent lives even if they are politically disenfranchised. If this were correct, human rights would have to be explained in some other way because the most important international human rights documents, such as the Universal Declaration of Human Rights, put political human rights front and centre. However, it would not be correct to say that we can lead minimally good lives without political freedoms. One observation that points towards this conclusion is the fact that throughout human history countless people have sacrificed their lives in struggles against oppression and servitude or in fights for political self-determination.

There are in fact several reasons why we cannot live decent lives without political freedoms. First, quite directly, if we are not able to express our opinions, to follow our convictions, or to associate with those we want to be with, fundamental universal moral interests are suppressed. In such conditions, people live in fear and are unable to express their views or to learn from those of others. They might be afraid to resist those who silence and threaten them, and their lives in this situation would not be decent because they are not able to act on many of their most deeply held beliefs if these are contrary to the interests of their rulers. Second, our political human rights are the most powerful instruments we have to protect our non-political interests, such as our interests in security and having our basic physical needs met. Theoretically, a benevolent dictator would seem to be able to guarantee these fundamental interests for us as well. However, empirically informed research shows that democratic regimes that respect the political human rights of their citizens are most likely to respect all their other human rights as well (Christiano 2011). This is unsurprising given that having an equal say in democratic elections, being able to access information freely, and unimpededly voicing one's views makes it possible to hold those who govern us accountable, and to appoint new leaders should we disagree with the services our current leaders perform for us. When we lack such political power, our basic needs are threatened. For example, in his work on famines, Nobel Prize for Economics laureate Amartya Sen has shown that starvation events are rarely ever the result of actual food shortages. Rather, it is bad governance and the inability to hold those in power accountable that prevents those who suffer from making their voices heard and from demanding that their situation is improved (Sen 1981: 154–166). Political human rights such as those to free speech, free association, and political participation are essential for holding those who rule us to account, and therefore necessary for the protection of our most basic interests (Shue 2020: 75, 83–87).

Third, as Sen also points out, political freedoms are not simply necessary for holding to account our rulers. Rather, they are also important for formulating our own personal preferences and goals (Sen 2001: 154). Many personal goals and preferences are dependent on the societal contexts people live in. What is popular or deemed desirable changes over time and in the light of personal experiences. But without the possibility to discuss freely and publicly what is desirable, what is popular or dominant will be determined by some (the ones in power) for all others. Only if people can discuss openly what is important, share their own experiences, and learn from those of others, can they form reflected and informed personal preferences rather than adopting the ones others think they should have. Political freedoms (in particular free speech and free access to information) are therefore essential for the exercise of our essential human capacity to make our own choices. Those who do not have political freedoms either have their own preferences frustrated or have to live according to the goals and values set for them by others, none of which is compatible with the idea of leading a minimally decent life as a person capable of self-determination.

Fourth, people who are unable to obtain information freely and to learn from others might be content merely because their preferences are shaped by, and adjusted to fit, their circumstances. But in this case, even if people are satisfied with their lot, their views are not expressions of their own volition. Rather, their preferences are unnecessarily and unjustifiably confined by their circumstances. Philosophers talk about this issue both in terms of the example of the contented slave and the problem of adaptive preferences (Burns 2016). Slaves do not lead a minimally decent life because they are not masters of their own body, choices, or actions. However, a slave might nonetheless be content with her lot if she is taught to accept her position. If she is made, for instance, to believe that being a slave is her natural state, or that she could not exist as a self-determined being, she might not be unhappy with being unfree. Similarly, it is conceivable that citizens in a non-democratic society are indoctrinated to accept their lack of political freedoms as necessary or that political empowerment is simply out of reach. Even if there are some dissenters, most might be content with living an apolitical life. However, this does not mean that these are decent lives because, just like the contented slave, these apolitical citizens are unable to exercise their ability to determine important aspects of their lives (e.g. taking part in making the rules of their society). This deficiency remains even if they do not feel discontent with their position because they have been taught to accept their lack of political freedom.

Moreover, philosophers such as Martha Nussbaum (2000) point out that when people adjust their preferences and expectations to their social circumstances, they are easily deprived of things they are entitled to and accept lives that are unnecessarily impoverished. This is particularly the case with women in patriarchal societies. Here social etiquette demands of women to adapt their preferences to the prevailing social norms, and to limit their ambitions and demands accordingly. A woman who accepts that her natural place is at home taking care of the children and serving her husband might be content with forgoing the exercise of her human rights to development, education, work, or free speech. But without using these rights and making their own decisions, any individual's life lacks essential elements that human rights protect and that make a human life good. Education, developing and pursuing personal ambitions, speaking one's mind freely, associating with others freely are not optional but essential for decent human lives. This is true even if the person in question has adjusted their preferences to fit with social expectations. People who do not have the option of making use of their human rights, and are taught not to want to, do not lead minimally good lives in line with their capacities as human beings.

For these reasons, whether a person's life is minimally decent not only depends on their satisfaction with their available options. Rather, it also depends on whether they can do things they might want to do and should be allowed to do (see van Parijs 1995: 19). To be able to discover justifiable alternatives to their current ambitions, and to pursue these ambitions, people require basic political freedoms such as free speech and free access to information. Of course, what counts as a set of legitimate range of alternative preferences and goals that every person should be entitled to pursue is contentious. However, political human rights are necessary for developing any conception whatsoever of what one wants to do in life. A state that does not respect political human rights might allow its citizens most economic freedoms and the realisation of their non-political ambitions while denying them political freedoms. Many citizens might even be content with their lives. But their satisfaction is entirely dependent on the government permitting these personal pursuits. If the government changes course, or if individual citizens disagree with the way that society is organised, they have no way to hold their government accountable, no recourse for affecting change. Therefore, political human rights (more precisely the opportunity to exercise these rights) are indispensable elements of minimally decent lives. Many of us do not need to vote, take part in demonstrations, or engage in political debates in order to be actually happy in our everyday life. However, all of us must have the opportunities to exercise these freedoms as conditions of minimally decent lives of persons who are generally capable of self-determination and collective political decision-making. Without political freedoms, the satisfaction of our most urgent interests is dependent on the whim of others who have power over us. The fact that people can be content without having political freedoms does not undermine this point. As I will argue in Chapter 3, having sufficient opportunities for exercising our political human rights today requires that people can access the internet.

The view that human rights are justified because they protect what we all need to live minimally decent lives is not without alternatives.[6] However, this account of human rights has the advantage that it aligns well with the common understanding that human rights really are about the things that are of the most basic importance to all persons. It therefore ensures that nothing that it would be 'nice to have' for people, but that is not of fundamental importance, can make it on the list of human rights. This is particularly important with respect to the topic of internet access. As we saw at the outset of this chapter, internet access is often seen as something that cannot be a human right because it is not sufficiently important enough. However, if it can be shown that internet access is necessary for minimally decent lives, denying the claim that it should be recognised as a human right becomes quite difficult.

Another advantage of the 'minimally decent lives' view is that by restricting human rights to what is of basic importance, it limits the demands they make on states. As we have seen, human rights are matters of international concern. This means that when states are unable to fulfil their citizens' human rights (e.g. because they lack the necessary resources), the international community is called upon to make up the resulting deficit. However, the more expansive human rights are, the more likely it is that the number of states unable to fulfil them will grow, and by extension so does the amount of international help that is required of other states that are in a position to help. The more demanding mandatory help becomes for those who deliver support, the more restricted their own resources for pursuing their own national goals become. And the more limiting the demands of international human rights aid are for the national self-determination of states, the more controversial these human rights claims become. For example, it is one thing to help other states to prevent their citizens from starving and to ensure their children receive a basic education. But it would be much more controversial if human rights were to demand of states, for example, that the health care they make available to their

---

[6] According to one alternative view defended by James Griffin (2008), what justifies human rights and explains their function is that they protect the elements of our normative agency and autonomy as human beings. On another view advanced by Martha Nussbaum (1997), human rights have the task of protection fundamental human capabilities that we all need to have the opportunity to lead good or flourishing human lives. A different group of views represented, for example, by Charles Beitz (2009), holds that philosophers should not try to come up with theories of what human rights are. Instead, we have to look at international practice to understand what human right really are and how they are used by states and other participants in international relations (e.g. international governance institutions, non-governmental organisations, political activists) to promote urgent human interests in our modern world of states. For important criticisms of these views, see, for example, Sen (2005), Liao and Etinson (2012), Crisp (2014), Liao (2015a).

own citizens does not exceed what they help less affluent states to provide for their citizens (Nickel 2007: 36–37).

A related advantage of the 'minimally decent lives' view is that it reduces the risk of international disagreements about what can count as human rights. This question might be controversial because, as we have just seen, a more expansive list of human rights entails more expansive international duties of economic and financial support. But beyond this, different cultures have diverging views on what rights people have. By limiting human rights to those things that are most essential for all human beings, it becomes extremely difficult for any government to deny that their people have entitlements to these basic things because the moral weight of people's claims to what they need to lead minimally decent lives is particularly salient.

For all these reasons, the conception of human rights employed in this book understands them as what we need to live minimally good lives. This view is not only theoretically more coherent than rival accounts. It also has pragmatic advantages that will be important for defending the claim that internet access today should be a human right because it has become practically necessary for the enjoyment of most of our existing human rights. In Section 1.3, we will consider what follows from accepting that something is a human right because we cannot live decent lives without it.

1.3 THE IMPLICATIONS OF HUMAN RIGHTS

Human rights, like all moral rights, are claimable entitlements to something. They give us reasons to do or to abstain from something. Standardly, theorists distinguish between negative rights of non-interference (freedoms from something) and positive rights of provision (freedoms to something). The human rights to life, freedom from arbitrary arrest, and free speech give us obligations to abstain from preventing others from living, being free, and speaking freely. Conversely, human rights to health, means of subsistence, and education impose obligations on others to ensure that basic health care, food and water, and education are accessible to everyone. According to some theorists (O'Neill 2005), negative rights are more stringent than positive rights because they are more urgent and have clearly identifiable duty-bearers: everyone simply has a duty not to interfere with other's negative freedoms, whereas it often seems unclear who has a duty to provide the content of positive rights. This is shown by the earlier example of the person in the street asking for money. This person only has a general claim to help towards everyone, which means that their claim to help is weakened by a lack of a distinct addressee or duty-bearer.

However, Henry Shue points out that on closer inspection this simple distinction between negative rights and correlative duties to abstain, and positive rights and correlative obligations to provide, is untenable. Shue argues that if we assume the societal perspective and consider how our rights operate in the social contexts that we live in, even the least controversial negative rights also entail positive duties and all positive rights also encompass negative obligations (Shue 2020: 52). Shue also points towards the central role of public institutions as duty-bearers in modern societies. If as a society we want to ensure that people's rights to life and bodily integrity are respected, we have to commit to establishing and paying for a police force and an army. If we want to ensure that people are presumed innocent until proven guilty and not arbitrarily deprived of their liberty, we have to commit to creating and maintaining legal and penal systems. In the same vein, our most fundamental positive rights entail obligations to abstain from certain things. Our human right to health does not simply require a public health-care system, but also that our health is not negatively affected, for example, by unaffordable prices for healthy food or pollution from industrial production and traffic.[7] And while our human right to education certainly requires a public education system, it also requires avoiding treating students differently on the basis of gender, faith, or social background. What Shue's explanation of rights clarifies is that all human rights justify duties of forbearance as well as duties of provision. This point is essential for understanding that no human right can be fulfilled by simply abstaining from doing certain things or by giving people certain things. Rather, even the most basic negative rights require spending some resources for providing various forms of support, and the least controversial positive rights require protection from various harms.[8]

---

[7] To be precise, Shue's claim about correlative positive and negative rights primarily concerns what he calls 'basic rights', but he points out that the claim holds for 'many other rights as well' (Shue 2020: 52). 'Basic rights' for Shue are those few rights that must be fulfilled before a person can enjoy any other rights (Shue 2020: 19). For Shue, subsistence, security, and liberty count as basic rights. However, many human rights are not basic rights in Shue's sense. For example, for him, publicly supported education (a recognised human right) is not basic because – even though he sees it as intrinsically valuable – it is not a precondition for the enjoyment of all other rights (Shue 2020: 20). The human right to free internet access defended in this book is also not a basic right in Shue's sense. Even though many human rights (unlike basic rights) are not 'inherent [i.e. conceptual or logical] necessities' (Shue 2020: 26) for the enjoyment of all other rights, they are still practically necessary for the meaningful fulfilment of other rights. They are therefore of fundamental importance and urgency because they protect the conditions of minimally decent lives for morally equal people. As such, Shue's insight that fundamental rights all have positive as well as negative correlative obligations also applies to human rights.

[8] Allen Buchanan has argued that the idea that human rights entail claims to certain provision invalidates the idea that human rights are moral rights possessed by individuals. According

Therefore, rather than separating rights into some that create only negative obligations of non-interferences and some that merely give rise to duties of provision, Shue's theory shows that all human rights entail both negative and positive obligations. More precisely, Shue argues that all human rights give rise to three types of duties that public institutions must fulfil (Shue 2020: 52):

i. duties to *avoid* depriving and to *respect* rights;
ii. duties to *protect* from deprivation;
iii. duties to *aid* the deprived.

According to this understanding of rights, for instance, the human right to bodily integrity requires that (1) states do not physically harm their citizens, (2) that they provide services to prevent individuals, private companies, and other states from physically harming their citizens (e.g. by maintaining a police force, food quality standards and controls, and an army and intelligence services for national defence), and (3) to remedy occurrences of physical harm (e.g. by maintaining legal, penal, and public health care systems). As this example shows, the services required to fulfil these obligations are properly tasks for public institutions. The costs that arise for providing the necessary public services are ultimately justified by our universal interest in being able to lead minimally good lives. Therefore, positive rights of provision also have identifiable duty-bearers, which in terms of human rights are primarily the right-holder's state and (if the state is unable or unwilling to guarantee these rights) the international community. Shue's point that all basic rights give rise to three different negative and positive obligations has been extremely influential and has shaped the UN's understanding of human rights as set out, for example, in its *Guiding Principles on Business and Human Rights* (UN 2011b: 1), which we will consider in Chapter 7.

---

to him, this would mean that the moral interests of one person, for example, to health would have to give them a justified claim to the establishment of an entire health care system that can provide the basic health care they are entitled to (Buchanan 2013: 58–64). However, as John Tasioulas has argued, this claim does not follow from accepting the idea that human rights are moral rights of individuals. Rather, everyone's moral interest in health justifies 'the [individual] right-holder's *proportionate share of the costs* of securing his right as one among many other right-holders who also benefit in the same way from the system' (Tasioulas 2017a: 84). Moreover, as James Nickel points out, complex social institutions required for fulfilling human rights such as health care and education are also justifiable as alternatives to the otherwise burdensome fulfilment of the moral duties of families and other (local, national, and international) communities to support those who have a moral claim to their help (e.g. the sick, elderly, unemployed, or disabled). It is therefore not only the moral claim of those in need of support, but also the duties of those who have to help that justify costly and complex social institutions that fulfil human rights (Nickel 2007: 148).

Shue's important work on rights contains another insight that is important for understanding what rights entail in general, and what it means to have a human right to free internet access in particular. As Shue explains, the negative and positive obligations that all rights give rise to are directed towards the protection of these rights from severe, predictable dangers. As Shue puts this point, rights are social guarantees and protections of the objects of rights against 'standard threats' (Shue 2020: 29). The magnitude and ubiquity of standard threats to our essential interests partly explains the important role that social institutions play for the guarantee of our rights. We know from experience that the actions of other individuals or a lack of means often present expectable threats to the conditions of a minimally decent life. Without any protections whatsoever, other people might want to kill or rob us, we might die for want of means to keep us alive, or owing to forces of nature. To address such standardly expectable threats to people, we have established a police force, justice and penal systems, public health care systems, welfare provisions, and public housing. But in our world, it is not merely other individuals or nature that threatens fundamental interests. Rather, among the principal threats to essential individual interests also are a person's own government and other states. Today, we are organised into national communities in the form of states that are the primary addressees for our human rights claims. This organisation into states is so universal and efficient that everyone has a human right to a nationality in order not to be excluded from the international system that we have created. Considering how powerful states are in our world, it is unsurprising that their power is a major danger to essential individual interests. In recognition of this point, Charles Beitz (2009: 109) argues that the particular political role of human rights in international law and politics is to protect 'urgent individual interests against certain predictable dangers (standard threats) to which they are vulnerable under typical circumstances of life in a modern world order composed of states'.

Importantly, though, rights cannot be protections against all kinds of threats to vital human interests. That is the reason why rights are protections against 'standard' threats, rather than all threats. By 'standard', Shue means that these dangers to our rights are 'ordinary' (rather than exceptional), 'serious' (rather than mere nuisances), and 'remedial' (instead of unavoidable) (Shue 2020: 32). This is because it is either not possible, or affordable, to prevent all setbacks to our rights. The human right to health illustrates this point. Standard threats to human health are preventable diseases, a lack of any health care whatsoever that would provide treatment for unavoidable illnesses, and environmental pollution produced by modern civilisation. Against these normally occurring dangers, the human right to health entitles everyone to basic health care provisions, environmental protections, public controls of good food quality, and affordable or free medicinal drugs to treat standard illnesses. However, no health care system can be resourced to prevent or treat all illnesses and suffering. This is partly because for some illnesses there are no cures and partly because some available treatment would require an unjustifiable amount of resources. Moreover, preventing all dangers to human health would be unreasonably restrictive and greatly limit individuals' liberties and economic activity, as the general quarantine measures taken by states in response to the COVID-19 pandemic strikingly illustrate. Rights therefore have to guarantee protections against standard threats to vital human interests rather than guarantees against 'all possible threats' (Shue 2020: 29).

This means that not all harms to the interests that ground human rights count as human rights violations. Rather, human rights violations occur when those with the obligations to uphold human rights (the duty-bearers) fail to provide a 'context-sensitive degree of risk mitigation' (Reeves 2015: 404). States must, for example, provide adequate basic education and health for their citizens as a matter of respecting human rights. This provision ensures that those without sufficient means still receive adequate education and health care. However, states do not have to (and cannot) make sure that no one fails school or dies of illness. If states have done a reasonably good job to provide these services to all citizens, the fact that some (or even many) have the interests that their human rights protect unfulfilled does not count as a human rights violation.

1.4 TWO ADDITIONAL CLARIFICATIONS ABOUT HUMAN RIGHTS

Now that we have seen what human rights are, what justifies them, and what having human rights means and entitles their holders to, we need to dispense with some misunderstandings of human rights. These misconceptions otherwise threaten to get in the way of discussing the idea that something as modern and technological as internet access can actually be a human right.

Human rights often meet with scepticism, some of which is rather cynical. For some critics, human rights are merely handy tools used by some to achieve their political goals (Perugini and Gordon 2015). One version of this criticism sees international political human rights practice as a form of neo-imperialism and neo-colonialism. According to this perspective, human rights are Western values that are enforced on other cultures in pursuit of the interests of affluent Western countries abroad. Humanitarian and other external interventions in developing countries are justified with the ostensible goal of protecting human rights in these nations, even though what is really being pursued are the imposition of Western values and the political and economic interests of the interfering powers (Ingiyimbere 2017). However, even if it is accurate that human rights have been abused for reprehensible, non-moral aims, this does not undermine the entire idea of, or struggle for, human rights. If human rights are feasible and justified, the fact that they are misused does not undermine their validity and usefulness any more than the everyday breaking of moral rules undermines their correctness and importance. This book relies on the normative force of the idea of human rights. The assumption here is that human rights can constitute genuine universal values and rules that are acceptable to, and in the interest of, all human beings.[9] In practice, human rights are also frequently invoked as important international standards and powerful argumentative resources. Moreover, normatively speaking, even if human rights are misused, this does not undermine the claim that they *should* be protected and that they *could* be respected.

Related but different critiques take issue with the limited requirements that human rights entail in our highly unequal world. The historian Samuel Moyn, for example, argues that human rights have been unable to prevent or significantly limit the rise of global socio-economic inequality beginning in the last quarter of the twentieth century. This increase in inequality to a significant extent was caused by the expansion of global free market policies, which increased the mobility of financial capital, forced the opening of economies of developing nations to international markets, and weakened the capacity of developed states to fund redistributive welfare schemes for their citizens. In Moyn's view, even though human rights had some success in protecting individuals and their moral status against attacks by states, they did not address rising material unfairness (Moyn 2018: 173–211). Others, such as the international relations scholar Stephen Hopgood, even see human rights as being partly responsible for the rise of global inequality. To him, human rights have allowed those benefiting from inequality to avoid feeling guilty about the negative effects of the global system. By providing humanitarian aid to the worst off, the 'winners' of global inequality could tell themselves that they did their part for the 'losers' suffering from poverty (Hopgood 2013). However, the philosopher Jiewuh Song (2019) has explained that these 'inequality critiques' of human rights are problematic. Importantly, human rights are not all that justice requires. As we have seen, human rights are sufficiency requirements

---

[9] For defences of the possibility of universal moral values and globally valid normative human rights against claims of cultural relativists that there are no universally acceptable but only locally and contextually accepted values, see Nickel (2007: 168–184), and Caney (2005: 25–62).

that ensure that people can live minimally decent lives while also allowing states to choose their own socio-economic policies beyond these universal minimal entitlements. A full account of domestic and global justice will have to say something about what distribution of socio-economic benefits and burdens of international cooperation is fair beyond the guarantee of human rights. Human rights therefore do not have the aim of addressing all injustices. Moreover, there is no clear-cut case for the causal role of human rights in the rise of global inequality – especially when considering other major factors such as the rise of global corporations, international tax havens, or the politics of the Washington Consensus (see e.g. Rodrik 2011).

In this book, I will therefore accept that human rights can be universal values and effective political instruments that do not represent all that is required by justice, but instead have the task of protecting people's most essential interests. Bypassing the aforementioned critiques, this section instead addresses two different theoretical misunderstandings that are particularly relevant to the idea of a human right to free internet access. One of these misconceptions holds that the idea that everyone has human rights to aspects of modern civilisation by virtue of being human alone is nonsensical. The problem with this idea supposedly is that such rights would have had to be claimable by every person throughout history because they were also human beings. However, it does not make sense to argue that Stone Age people had human rights, for example, to a fair trial or to health care. If this charge were correct, the idea of a human right to free internet access would be a non-starter (Tomalty 2017). According to a second objection, we cannot have human rights to technological artefacts because these are merely means to other important things we actually care about. For instance, we all have the human right to free movement. However, this does not give us a right to a car even though owning a car in modern societies is extremely useful for exercising our right to free movement. This argument has been made, for instance, by Vinton Cerf (2012), one of the so-called fathers of the internet. If this point about what can qualify as a human right were accurate, it would be difficult to see how we could have a right to internet access. After all, online access is not an end in itself but a technological means that is useful for other things. I will explain why these complaints are based on misunderstandings about what human rights are.

First, let us consider the claim that everyone throughout time has been entitled to the full list of rights set out by modern human rights treaties based on their humanity alone. This would seem to commit us to the idea that the ancient Greeks and Romans were entitled to modern health care, equality before the law, public education, or – considering the argument of this book – to free internet access, which is clearly absurd.[10] However, there are several ways to respond to this claim. One would be to deny the plausibility of some rights recognised in international human rights law. This might mean that every person throughout time based on their humanity alone indeed had human rights to life, liberty, the means of subsistence, shelter, and free movement because these were realisable at all times. But according to this view, no one really has or ever had human rights to things that presuppose modern institutions or technology, such as the right to a fair trial, to health care, to education, or to free internet access. The problem with such a perspective is clearly that many of the most fundamental and accepted human rights would be lost. One might then rightly fear that modern achievements such as equality before the law, public education, and health care lose their status as universal entitlements and instead are conditional on the prevailing political opinion in states because nothing about us as persons would entitle us to these rights. This would be a very high price to pay for making human rights fit with the idea that everyone has these rights by virtue of being human.

Fortunately, another response is available. This one relies on separating the purpose or aim of a human right (such as access to available means and knowledge to treat preventable diseases and suffering) from the concrete content or object of that right (e.g. modern health care). If we distinguish purpose from content, we can see that the purpose and aims of human rights are indeed timeless and apply to everyone as conditions of living minimally decent lives (see Liao 2015b: 66). The particular content of these rights, on the other hand, depends on the circumstances that people live in. Accordingly, we can say that every person who ever lived had an entitlement to access the available means and knowledge to treat preventable diseases, for example, which should have been fulfilled. The ancient Greeks and Romans already possessed a degree of medical knowledge that allowed them to treat certain ailments. However, access to such help was often limited to those with the necessary means and status. It does not seem absurd, though, to say that all inhabitants living in the Roman Empire had an equal moral claim to access the medical treatments available at that time. Being of noble birth did not give anyone a weightier claim to the available resources. Of course, this thought was not accepted in ancient Rome, where people's equal moral status was not

---

[10] In fact, Charles Beitz (2009: chapter 3) and Joseph Raz (2010: 40) both take this criticism to be fatal to philosophical conceptions of human rights that see these as based on individual moral rights. Their own solution is to argue that we should instead understand human rights as arising from international political practice as instruments that have the function to constrain what states can legitimately do to their citizens. As pointed out in footnote 8, such political conceptions have weaknesses of their own.

recognised. However, the ancient Hippocratic Oath already recognises a duty of physicians to treat the sick equally to some degree, and not to deny anyone help owing to their background. The claim to equal access to medicinal resources in ancient Rome is therefore not absurd as such, even though it was not respected.

Human rights claim to be universally valid, irrespective of prevailing conventions. It is therefore not absurd to argue that the ancient Romans were wrong to enslave people, to kill people cruelly in amphitheatres for the entertainment of spectators, and to brutally execute prisoners by crucifying them. The interests to life, liberty, and freedom from torture of those enslaved and executed were as salient to people back then as our same interests are to us today. It is therefore not plausible to argue either that slaves or the poor of ancient Roman society had no strong morally relevant interests in life, health, and liberty, or that, despite not having these interests fulfilled, they led minimally decent lives. It makes more sense to acknowledge that slaves and poor citizens did have such morally relevant interests and were not able to lead decent lives. And because human rights are protections of the conditions of minimally decent lives, it makes sense to say that the human rights of slaves in ancient Rome were not respected or fulfilled. Equally, people in ancient societies had a strong moral interest and corresponding human right to the basic medical care that might have been available for everyone at that time, and their lives were worse than they needed to be for not having this important interest met. On the other hand, if we accept that the aims of human rights are timeless, this does not mean that we must also accept that their contemporary content was the same throughout all times. Modern medicine simply was not available in ancient Rome as a means for fulfilling people's interest in avoiding treatable illnesses and preventable suffering. This particular care only became claimable for people in modern times once this level of care had been developed. For this reason, everyone today has a human right to access basic modern health care just as every inhabitant of ancient Rome was entitled to the basic health care that could have been provided for all back then.

This leaves open the possibility that in ancient times no general health care was affordable for everyone or that it might not have been possible for people to respect everyone's moral equality. However, rather than concluding from this that people in the distant past had no human rights, it seems rather reasonable to conclude that they were missing elements of minimally decent lives, which human rights protect. The lives of many human beings before the invention of modern medicine and the rule of law simply were not minimally decent and regrettably could not have been decent as humanity lacked the required social and technological knowledge. This is also consistent with the claim that basic health care became a claimable human right once its delivery became generally possible. We can therefore say the same of other human rights that require modern institutions such as those to a nationality, elementary public education, a free press, or freedom of conscience and religion. These rights have always existed for all human beings, and those who did not have them respected or could not have them fulfilled lacked elements of minimally good lives. Once human development allowed for the general protection of vital human interests, the human rights protecting these interests became entitlements for everyone, even if most were denied these rights.

Accepting the distinction between the universally valid aims of human rights and their context-specific content also makes it possible to accept the claim that today something like internet access has become a human right because the internet exists and since it has become possible universally to provide such access. What needs to be shown, though, for the claim that we have such a human right to make sense is that internet access has indeed become important enough to warrant the status of a human right. This is the task of Chapters 3 and 4. For now, we can assert that the aims and purposes of human rights are timeless but that the particular objects that they entitle people to depend on (1) universal and strong morally relevant interests and (2) the existence and general availability of the means to realise these interests. There is nothing absurd about understanding human rights as rights that people always had by virtue of being humans alone. Accepting this idea does not mean that we must also endorse the idea that all persons at all times had rights to the same things that we have human rights to today.

The second concern about human rights that is particularly relevant to the idea of a human right to free internet access is that we cannot have rights to technologies or artefacts that are only useful for realising other, primary, rights. The worry about accepting rights to technological means, as Vinton Cerf argues, is that their usefulness is often temporary compared with the permanent importance of water, food, health care, or security, to which we have uncontroversial human rights. One might therefore say that, even though internet access is useful for, for example, free speech and free information, we should protect the human rights to these interests rather than elevating internet access, which is merely a means to all of these things, to the status of a human right. The UN seem to have gone in this direction by demanding that the same 'rights that people have offline must also be protected online' (UN 2016: 2), rather than recognising a new right to internet access.

In response to this concern, it is helpful to note that we can become entitled to technological means or artefacts when these are developed because they are essential for realising primary rights. That is in part because we have a human right to enjoy the benefits of scientific progress and its applications (UN 1966a: §25.1b). Moreover, though, as we have just seen, the content of human rights can change over time owing to the discovery of new social and technological innovations, and such new content can comprise technologies or artefacts. We can consider the example of vaccinations. According to the human right to health (UN 1966a: §12), everyone is entitled to basic health care. After the spread of the SARS-COV-2 virus and the development and industrialised production of vaccines to protect against this virus, it is plausible to argue that the human right to health care came to encompass a universal right to these vaccines. Suffering from the effects of COVID-19 threatens people's lives and health. Once an effective, and generally affordable,[11] preventative treatment became available in the form of COVID-19 vaccines, everyone can be said to have a right to this treatment as part of their human right to health. The right to the SARS-COV-2 vaccines is thus encompassed by, and part of respecting, the primary human right to health – even if this vaccine is an artefact. Similar things can be said about the human right to social security (UN 1966a: §9), which is a modern social innovation aimed to protect more basic rights and interests such as health care, support in cases of accidents or unemployment, and the means of subsistence when people become too old or ill to work.

Rights based on technological means can also become rights in themselves if these rights are essential for the realisation of other crucial interests. For example, the human right to a free press (UN 1966b: §19.2) is justified based on the human right to free information. Every person throughout time can be said to have had a vital interest and human right to free information. However, before the invention of modern institutions and the printing press, people did not have a human right to a free press because the required technology had not been invented. Once the institution of a free press became possible, everyone acquired a human right to the institutions of a free press because of the paramount importance of a free press for realising the human right to free information.[12] Having a professional press that can operate freely remains important today. However, as Kay Mathiesen (2012) has argued, what

---

[11] Meaning affordable on a global scale, not affordable for all nations.
[12] To be precise, in many human rights documents, the right to press freedom is subsumed under the right to freedom of expression. According to the International Covenant on Civil and Political Rights §19.2, for instance, 'everyone shall have the right to freedom of expression; this right shall include freedom to seek, receive and impart information and ideas of all kinds, regardless of frontiers, either orally, in writing or in print, in the form of art, or through any other media of his choice' (UN 1966b). However, institutions such as the European Court of Human Rights have explicitly recognised the special status of the press and the freedom of the press. That is because of the central role of the free press in enabling free political participation and because members of the press (e.g. journalists, editors, publishers) face particularly

is required for having a free press has changed over time. In past decades, mass media such as printing presses, radios, and televisions were key technologies for a free press. Today, much information sharing and obtaining has moved online so that internet access has become a key technology for realising the human right to a free press and the human right to free information that it is based on (we will consider this point in detail in Chapter 3).

Neither is the point that the internet is a technology that is useful for our human rights today but that might be superseded by another technology in the future fatal to the idea of a human right to internet access. On the one hand, considering the way that the internet has changed almost all aspects of our lives, it is unlikely that it will become an outdated means anytime soon in the way that horses became outdated as an important means of transportation. On the other hand, though, there are other human rights that are based on contingent inventions that might well become replaced in the future. Two examples here are the human rights to a nationality (UN 1948: §15) and a rights-respecting international order (UN 1948: §28). As discussed earlier, these rights are crucial in our contemporary world that is politically organised into states. But nation states are a relatively recent human invention and people could not have had such human rights before peoples organised themselves into nation states. Moreover, supranational institutions such as the European Union suggest that the institution of nation states might at some point be superseded by other, more international forms of political organisation. In addition, international conflicts have led thinkers as far back as at least Immanuel Kant (1795) to argue that we should not simply accept the existence of nation states but develop global forms of political organisation that can help solve problems among nation states.[13] Modern global coordination problems such as climate change and nuclear deterrence are also seen as evidence that humanity needs to think beyond the power of nation states to secure the survival of humanity (Vergerio 2021). These considerations show that it is by no means certain that the particular invention of nation states will persist throughout time. Yet it is plausible that currently and while nation states exist, people

---

strong and frequent threats to their free expression. These predictable attacks in turn give states special, positive obligations to protect the rights of members of the free press (e.g. by providing protection for journalists who receive threats, see Bychawska-Siniarska 2017: 87–93).

[13] Kant did not argue that humanity should eliminate nation states in favour of a world government, to be precise. Because of a lack of popular support and practical means for realising such an idea, he rather argued for a voluntary association of states. However, commentators have argued that obstacles that existed in Kant's time to establishing a non-optional world republic that has coercive authority over member states no longer apply (Pogge 2009) or that Kant's own theory coherently applied requires the creation of such a global institution once it becomes possible (Reglitz 2019, Wyrębska-Đermanović 2019).

have human rights to a nationality and a rights-respecting international order. If some other form of political organisation were to become dominant in the future and therefore crucial for the fulfilment of human rights, membership in such alternative communities could conceivably become a human right.

The human right to form trade unions (UN 1966a: §9a) can be seen as another example of a temporarily contingent right because it presupposes the existence of capitalist economies that pit the interests of employers and capital owners against those of workers and employees. Capitalist economies, though, are a modern human invention, and there is no guarantee that they will not be superseded one day by other forms of economic organisation, at which point trade unions might become obsolete. A world without nation states and capitalism seems very difficult to imagine, but then so seems a world without the internet. However, even if a new technology should take the place and the functions of the internet, the argument that would justify a human right to free internet access could be applied and transferred to this new means of communication. There is therefore nothing problematic as such about assigning human rights to that which might only be of temporary relevance. If we have a human right to them depends on whether these particular technologies, artefacts, or institutions are of sufficient moral importance for securing minimally decent lives. The idea of how something can acquire the status of a distinct (human) right based on its usefulness (i.e. instrumental value) for other essential interests or rights is a complex one, and will therefore be in the focus of Chapter 2.

1.5 CONCLUSION

This chapter has equipped us with important theoretical tools to make the case for the human right to free internet access. To begin with, there can be human rights other than those codified in international human rights documents because besides legal rights there are moral rights. Some moral rights are important enough to demand legal codification and coercive enforcement. The idea of moral rights therefore allows us to think about the human right to free internet access even though no legal human right of this kind currently exists. The decisive question is whether we can identify a regarding moral right that should be recognised as a human right. We then saw that human rights are protections of the conditions of minimally good or decent human rights. Living a minimally good life is surely of utmost moral importance to all of us, no matter what other things we value. Human rights are also matters of international concern. This means that if a state as the primary duty-bearer of the human rights of its citizens is unwilling or unable to respect or fulfil these rights, the international community of states is called upon to help. This aid can take various forms such as development aid or, in the most serious cases, humanitarian intervention. Importantly, all – and in particular states as the most powerful agents in our world – have obligations to respect everyone's human rights. By virtue of being human alone we are entitled to living minimally good lives free from avoidable suffering, extreme want, or oppression and violence. We thus have entitlements to those conditions that secure such lives for us.

What it means to have human rights becomes particularly clear when we consider Henry Shue's theory of basic rights. According to Shue, all our basic rights justify obligations for duty-bearers to respect and protect our rights, and to aid us if our rights have been violated. Every right, both negative rights to non-interference and positive rights to provision, give rise to all three types of duties. This means in particular that duty-bearers (which in the case of human rights are primarily states) have obligations to protect rights from standard threats that they can be expected to be threatened by. As Beitz (2009) points out, in our world that is organised into states, the standard threats often (but not always) are posed by states. States thus have dual relevance as primary duty-bearers for protecting human rights as well as the primary sources of threats to rights. This means that to explain the human right to free internet access, it is not enough to show that such a human right exists. It must also be clear what standard threats internet access faces and what duties arise from these dangers. This part of the analysis will be the content of Part II of this book.

Finally, we have seen that accepting human rights to anything that presupposes modern technology or social institutions does not commit us to the view that all human beings at all times had the same human rights. Rather, by distinguishing the aims from the content of human rights, we can see that some of these rights that are accepted today (such as the right to a free press or to free public elementary education) were not held before the creation of modern civilisation. However, rather than taking this as proof that the idea of human rights as entitlements that we have merely because we are human is absurd, it is more reasonable to conclude that it was impossible for people in previous times to live entirely minimally decent lives. Moreover, we have also found that people can have rights to artefacts or technology as long as these are necessary for leading minimally decent lives – even if only temporarily. Nothing about the internet as a modern technology as such therefore prevents us from assigning it meaningfully the status of a human right. The crucial question is if internet access has become important enough to deserve the status of a human right.

Chapter 2 explains the remaining theoretical tools that we need to make sense of the claim that free internet access is a human right. The first one is the idea (touched upon earlier) that we can sometimes obtain rights to things on the basis that these are extremely useful for the effective operation or protection of other, primary, interests or rights. The second theoretical idea we will encounter is that having a right to something entitles us to certain opportunities to make use of this right. If this were not the case, many of our rights would merely be formal. Or rights to something would then only consist in the demand that no one hinders us in the exercise of our rights, but not in a claim to be guaranteed the means that are necessary to make use of our freedoms – which would make many rights practically useless for those who do not have the means to exercise them.

2

Derivative Rights and Linkage Arguments for Rights

In Chapter 1, we saw what moral rights are generally and what human rights are in particular. Moral rights are claims that are particularly important and entitle their holders to the protection or provision of something by others. Many (but not all) of our legal rights possess such a moral core. Human rights are special in several ways: they are particularly urgent because they ensure the conditions of a minimally decent life for everyone. That is also why they are matters of international concern and not simply questions that states can claim fall entirely within the scope of their self-determination. If human rights are not respected or fulfilled somewhere, that is a concern for people everywhere, because everyone deserves the chance to live a minimally decent life.

The purpose of this book is to explain and defend the idea that we have a human right to free internet access. But in spite of everything that we considered about rights and human rights in Chapter 1, we might be sceptical about this very idea. We might wonder: how exactly is the internet a necessary part of minimally decent lives? The internet certainly has added a lot of convenience and new ways of doing everyday things to our lives. But do we really need it for leading decent lives? A recent statistic might be taken to confirm this scepticism: according to the 'Top Websites Ranking' list, as of October 2023 the five most popular websites outside China are Google Search, YouTube, Facebook, Instagram, and X (formerly Twitter) (Similarweb 2023). Online searches and social media have certainly made new things possible and familiar things easier. But these activities are as such not part and parcel of minimally decent lives.

The mostly trivial uses of the internet provide important context for the idea of a human right to internet access. This is because being online as such is not a good in itself. Rather, the case for this idea depends on how and for what we use the internet. Still, the mostly trivial uses of the internet should not blind us to the important things people do with and on the internet. Not just any use of it is morally relevant. What *is* relevant for thinking about a human right to internet access, though, is the fact that the internet has generally become very important for the exercise of our human rights (e.g. freedom of speech and freedom of information). This is to say, the reason we should recognise internet access as a human right is that it can be extremely beneficial for making use of our already established human rights. For example, if I Google the opening hours of my favourite restaurant, this is a matter of convenience, not of living a decent life. However, if I search online to learn about my rights as a citizen, to join a public cause or protest, or to find the best lawyer I can afford to represent me legally, my internet use helps me to exercise my human rights to free information, free association, and legal equality. The mere act of being online is not as such a matter of living decently. Instead, only if we access the internet to make use of our human rights is such online access important enough to deserve consideration as a right itself.

Yet this argument based on the usefulness (or the instrumental value) of the internet straight away meets with important questions. One obvious question is how we can have rights to something only because it is useful for something else. For instance, clean water, adequate food and shelter, and bodily integrity are surely all necessary elements of a minimally decent life. It is therefore not puzzling that we have human rights to these things. But how can it be possible that we should have a right to internet access simply because it is useful for our other human rights? How can we have a right to something that is merely a good tool for something else? This question is one of the reasons why, as we saw in Chapter 1, Vinton Cerf has rejected the claim that internet access is a human right. In a 2012 op ed for the *New York Times*, Cerf argues that 'improving the Internet is just one means, albeit an important one, by which to improve the human condition. It must be done with an appreciation for the civil and human rights that deserve protection — without pretending that access itself is such a right' (Cerf 2012). So before we can talk about the usefulness of internet access for human rights, a first puzzle that we need to address is how we can in general have a right to something because it is handy for something else that we ultimately care about.

A second question that arises straightforwardly about the claim that internet access should be a human right because it is useful for important recognised human rights is: how do we know what these rights entitle us to and why is internet access one of these things? For example, lots of things are useful for freedom of expression, such as a good education, good informational sources, good speaking skills, or popularity. But which of these can we have a right to as a matter of having the human right to free speech? And why we should we have a human right to internet access specifically if there are so many other things that are very useful for our right to free speech? This question is made more difficult by the fact that rights permit fuller or lesser realisations, which in turn require different things. To see this problem, consider the human right to health. The health care that we are entitled to as a matter of this human right can take many forms: minimal emergency room treatment, free basic health care, comprehensive free public health care, and expensive specialised health care. How do we know to what level of care the human right to health entitles us to? Expensive specialised medical care is certainly most conducive to our health, but does this right therefore give us an entitlement to this kind of care? Many things are useful for the enjoyment of our rights. Even internet access can be beneficial for our health because we can find medically relevant information online. But to know that something is important enough to justify the claim that we have a right to it, we have to understand how the rights that are based on their usefulness for other things operate.

These are two complex general questions about rights that we need to clarify before it makes sense to consider how the internet has become invaluable for the enjoyment of our human rights. We need to know how usefulness and instrumental value alone can justify rights. We also have to understand how we can determine what things exactly our rights give us entitlements to. Without this knowledge, we cannot understand how we could have something as important as a human right to something that is merely useful (such as internet access) for other things that we really care about, such as the conditions of minimally decent lives. This chapter will therefore address these two questions. Section 2.1 explains the idea of deriving rights from other rights. Section 2.2 looks specifically at so-called linkage arguments as a particular way of deriving rights from other rights. Section 2.3 subsequently considers how we should understand what sort of protections and provisions human rights entail. Finally, Section 2.4 explains the crucial idea of adequate opportunities as that to which rights normally entitle us. Clarifying these points will give us the remaining theoretical tools that we need to make the argument that internet access today should be considered a human right.

What is important to keep in mind is that this chapter primarily explores questions regarding moral rights. Often, but not always, these have legal rights that correspond to them. The focus on moral rights is important because (as explained in Chapter 1) there can be situations in which we can identify a moral right that should have a legal right that corresponds to it, but that legal right has not been recognised yet. This book argues that this is exactly the case with internet access: it makes the case that there is a moral human right to access the internet that should be recognised as a legal human right. Identifying a moral right and understanding what it requires is the first step in arguing for the creation of a corresponding legal right.

2.1 DERIVATIVE RIGHTS

If internet access is to be justifiable as a human right because it is useful for other human rights, this presumes that rights can be grounded solely in their value as tools for something else. As it turns out, such instrumental justifications of rights are nothing unusual. Philosophically, rights so justified are called 'derivative rights' because their ultimate justification lies in the importance of something else for which they are extremely useful. Normally this justificatory link is to other rights because rights protect morally important and urgent interests that are sufficiently strong to serve as grounds for derivative rights.

A good example of a derived right is the human right to a free press. People do not have an interest in press freedom for the sake of press freedom. Rather, the right to a free press is based on (and justified by) its usefulness for another human right that we have a direct interest in, namely the right to free information. We all have an urgent interest in free information that is essential for learning, formulating our life plan, forming our personal beliefs, and for holding those who rule us accountable. However, in our modern societies characterised by the social division of labour, most of us do not have the time, expertise, and opportunities to research the information that is relevant for forming our own views and holding government accountable. Professional journalists and the press business have become established specialists in providing people with important information. Having a free press is therefore extremely useful in making use of our human right to free information.

To understand why we need a special right to a free press, we have to recall Henry Shue's idea discussed in Chapter 1 that rights are social guarantees against standard threats. Realistically, in any given setting, professional journalists will as a matter of course face certain threats if they operate without special protections. Free information distribution via the public press is threatened, for instance, in cases where the information provided is to the detriment of the government or powerful private corporations or individuals. Without special protection, governments, corporations, and powerful individuals are likely to try to prevent or influence the impartial reporting of information that could be to their detriment. To counter these threats, freedom of the press is best protected by a special human right to press freedom. For this reason, the human right to press freedom does not derive from some independent interests of citizens or personal interest of press journalists. Rather, the right derives from everyone's primary interest in free information, which is essential for our living decent lives as people who think for themselves. Rights derivation in the case of press freedom does not stop here, though, because the derived right to a free press can itself give rise to further derived rights such as occupational rights of journalists to protect their anonymous sources. These professional rights are justified because without them, journalists would not be able to do their job effectively (Raz 1986: 179). Moreover, the human right to free information, which the human right to press freedom derives from, is itself derived from the human right to free expression. This example of press freedom therefore demonstrates a whole series of rights derivations and justifications that all start with the human right to free expression. This right gives rise to the human right to free information, which justifies the right to a free press to protect public journalists in doing their job effectively. To ensure their effective work, journalists also have specific professional rights – for example to the status as civilians when they accompany armed forces as war correspondents. Importantly, even though the rights to free information and a free press derive from the right to free expression, none of them is of lesser importance than the other, and only together can they realise the objectives of the right to free expression. That some rights are justified only because they are useful for something else that we aim to protect or promote is therefore nothing unusual or problematic.[1]

2.2 LINKAGE ARGUMENT FOR DERIVED RIGHTS

When exactly is something useful enough for another right so that we can be considered to have a right to it? When is this justificatory link strong enough? This is explained by so-called linkage arguments of rights that derive their justification from other rights.

The structure of all rights derivations is the same: first, there is an uncontroversial right, for example, the right to vote, which serves as an anchor for the derived right. Second, there are certain conditions that are in practice

---

[1] Following Shue, we should also note that the human right to press freedom should not be understood merely as a negative right that bans the government from arbitrarily interfering with the work of journalists. Instead, because all fundamental rights entail negative and positive duties, (as mentioned in Chapter 1, Section 1.4) the right to a free press also gives states obligations to provide special protection for journalists who are threatened by others for doing their work (Bychawska-Siniarska 2017). Moreover, the right to press freedom justifies positive duties for public authorities to ensure that everyone can access the products of the free press, and in this way has opportunities to make use of their human right to free information. Traditionally, this justifies an obligation for governments to maintain public libraries. Today, this book argues, it justifies recognising a human right to internet access.

necessary for the right to be useful. To take an example given by James Nickel (2022: 48), due process rights (such as guarantees to legal counsel, public trials, the right to appeal convictions, or the habeas corpus requirement) derive from the human right to a fair trial. This is because experience tells us that without due process rights, criminal law systems (that include the police, courts, and prisons) can be misused by governments to neutralise their opponents and critics. Justice systems are made less dangerous, and fair trials more likely, by having effective due process rights. It would therefore be irrational to accept the right to a fair trial, but not due process rights that facilitate such trials. Due process rights are essential for the success of the human rights to a fair trial and equality before the law. Following this reasoning, the formal argument with respect to the human right to internet access that this book establishes therefore looks like this:

> Premise 1: Everyone has human rights.
> Premise 2: Internet access is in practice necessary to exercise or enjoy many of these human rights.
> Premise 3: Following a 'principle of rationality' (Nickel 2022: 31), if we endorse an end (i.e. primary or anchor rights), we have very strong or good reasons also to endorse those things and means that are necessary to achieve or realise that end (i.e. a supporting right).
> Conclusion: Insofar as and because internet access is in practice necessary for the exercise or enjoyment of many of our human rights, we have very strong reasons to accept a human right to internet access.

Linkage arguments of this kind are well established and reflected in ideas such as Immanuel Kant's principle of hypothetical imperatives. According to this rule, Kant asserts that 'whoever wills the end also wills (insofar as reason has decisive influence on his actions) the indispensably necessary means to it that are within his power' (Kant 1785: 70). However, Kant's principle is not very specific (see also O'Neill 2009: 96) and more therefore needs to be stated to justify rights based on means–end relationships.

There are generally two ways in which the usefulness (or instrumental value) of something for something else important (normally another right) can be significant enough to justify ascribing to it the status of a derived right. First, something can be sufficiently useful to deserve the status of a right if it is *in practice necessary* or *indispensable (i.e. 'practically indispensable')* for the realisation or enjoyment of an uncontroversial primary or anchor right. As James Nickel explains,

> Indispensable support can be explained positively as assistance that is both greatly needed and irreplaceable in the sense that there are no practical

alternative measures that will adequately provide the support in question. Negatively, indispensable support can be explained as assistance that it would be logically or practically inconsistent to advocate doing without. (2022: 35)

Drawing on empirical information is essential for discovering connections between rights and their practical preconditions. Take, for instance, the human right to literacy (UNESCO 1997). Learning is certainly possible without being literate. However, in the modern world, knowledge is mostly recorded and available in written form. Literacy has therefore become a requirement for receiving a decent education. Literacy is also essential for life in modern societies that operate based on written rules, written contracts, and written texts in general. As a practical precondition of modern education, literacy is therefore recognised as a human right.

Second, certain things can be granted the status of a right if they are not practically indispensable for any single right but are highly useful for a range of other rights. In such cases, the thing in question is not practically necessary for any particular right but *systemically indispensable* for several different rights (Nickel 2022: 35). The notion of systemic indispensability is helpfully explained by using the analogy of a Swiss army knife. If we are embarking on a camping trip, we could take with us a knife, scissors, a corkscrew, a nail file, a bottle opener, a small saw, a screwdriver, and a ruler. Or, considering our limited ability to carry objects with us, we can take a Swiss army knife, which contains all these tools. This analogy demonstrates that when we have the option to choose one polyvalent instrument or all the other tools, it would be irrational not to choose the single polyvalent option.

The justification of the human right to a free press is again a case in point. This right contributes to the protection and enjoyment of several other human rights. The information provided by professional journalists contributes to people's rights to free information, to the right to free expression that the right to free information derives from, to the respect for due process rights, and generally to hold governments accountable for their human rights violations. Crucially, a free press is not absolutely necessary for the enjoyment of any of these rights. Citizens are free to obtain their information in other ways than consuming journalistic media. They can attend public trials in person, they can buy books or loan them from public libraries, and they can try personally to keep tabs on political developments via word of mouth. However, having a specialised journalistic press that provides citizens with objective and reliable information is the most effective way for citizens to be informed. For this reason, even though having a free press is not conceptually necessary for the enjoyment of any other rights, the human right to press freedom crucially supports an entire array of other uncontroversial rights in a highly effective way. This justifies recognising a free press as a right in itself. To take another example, health and adequate health care are practically indispensable for the enjoyment of most other rights. A seriously ill person will not be able to use many of their human rights, such as their rights to education, free speech, freedom of assembly, or participation in culture. They will often be unable to live a minimally decent life or even survive. As a practical precondition of the enjoyment of other human rights, basic health care for treatable illnesses is thus recognised as a human right. As we will see in Chapters 3 and 4, internet access today plays an analogous systemically supportive role for many of our human rights.

Systemic indispensability is a weaker and more complex way of linking the justification of an auxiliary right to its usefulness for other rights. It is weaker because each supporting relationship with other rights has practical alternatives. It is more complex because justification along the lines of systemic indispensability requires weighing up the costs and benefits of different alternatives for protecting or realising an anchor right, one of which is realisation via the derived, auxiliary right under consideration (see Nickel 2010: 437). Such a cost-benefit analysis must show that the auxiliary right is in fact the most effective way to secure the enjoyment of the other uncontroversial anchor rights. This does not mean, though, that this route of systemic indispensability is a less valid or less important pathway for establishing rights derivation between anchor rights and auxiliary rights. The complexity and availability of alternative ways of realising anchor rights does mean, though, that there are few rights that can be justified because they are systemically indispensable to several other rights. This is because there are few things that are powerful and useful enough for sufficiently many other rights that these uncontroversial rights could not be realised equally well in alternative ways. I will argue in this book that internet access is one of these few sufficiently powerful multipurpose tools that warrants recognition as a right in itself.

The idea of systemic indispensability becomes more plausible when we consider that many of the human rights that we are familiar with from the international human rights documents provide support for each other (Nickel 2007: 104). For example, in a positive sense, if my human right to education is realised and guaranteed, I can better make use of my human rights to free expression and free information (because I know more and am better at identifying and transmitting information relevant to me), I can better protect my health (because I am more aware of risks to my health), I can better exercise my freedom of conscience (because I am aware of more things that might deserve my allegiance), and I am more likely to be aware of my human rights in the first place. Fulfilment of one element of a minimally decent life therefore promotes other elements of such a life as well. And in a negative sense, if my human right to freedom from torture is not respected, many of my other human rights will suffer as well, such as my rights to bodily integrity, health, and freedom from cruel or degrading treatment. Violating one human right here undermines multiple other necessary elements of a minimally decent life. In turn, this means that support for one human right (education, freedom from torture) also provides support for other human rights (free speech, health, freedom of conscience or bodily integrity, health, humane treatment). In this way, our human rights are interdependent.

The notions of practical indispensability and systemic indispensability explain in an abstract sense when something can be useful enough for other rights to warrant assigning to it the status of a right. But it would be good to have some more concrete tests at hand to determine whether something is sufficiently important to become a right. Fortunately, Nickel suggests several ways in which we can test the utility of things (such as internet access) for rights. According to him:

> one right can support another by helping:
> 1. Perform or reinforce some of the second right's work.
> 2. Reduce the costs of realizing the second right.
> 3. Make the realization of the second right more secure, stable, or sustainable.
> 4. Block conditions or threats that undermine or retard the realization of the second right.
> 5. Improve the knowledge and capacities of the second right's rightholders.
> 6. Maintain or broaden equitable coverage (that is, a closer approximation of universal provision) of the second right.
> 7. Promote acceptance, knowledge, and use of the second right.
> 8. Promote the willingness and ability of dutybearers to meet their responsibilities under the second right. (2016: 298)

Even though these tests remain abstract without examples, we will explore concrete examples of how internet access supports our human rights in Chapters 3 and 4. My argument will be that internet access is in fact both practically indispensable for the use of many individual human rights *and* systemically indispensable for many of our interdependent human rights because it meets all these eight tests. Crucially, which rights are derivable from uncontroversial primary rights can change over time as the conditions that affect these anchor rights change as well. Even if our primary rights stay the same, as circumstances change, our rights can change. In this sense, rights are 'dynamic' (Raz 1986: 171, 185). As we saw in Chapter 1, this also regards what human rights we can be said to have. These might change as humanity's social and technological development evolves.

What this chapter has explained so far is that it is possible to justify a right on the basis that it is useful for other rights. This is the case when something is 'important enough' for the realisation and enjoyment of other rights. Something is 'important enough' if it is either practically or systemically indispensable for other rights. At the end of this section, we also encountered several specific ways that we can use to test whether something such as internet access is indeed practically or systemically indispensable for other rights. However, before we can begin to study how exactly internet access supports our human rights, we have to consider one final point that is essential for understanding the idea of rights and how they can derive from one another. This point explains how we should think about what rights entail.

2.3 WHAT DO RIGHTS ENTAIL?

Since the aim of this book is to justify a human right to free internet access, the notion of derivative rights is essential. It would seem difficult to explain that being online is a good thing in itself or that the internet as such has moral value. But it is certainly uncontroversial to say that the internet can be good for other important things, such as human rights. And because things that can be extremely useful or indispensable for the enjoyment of our rights can themselves become objects of rights, it is conceivable that we have a human right to internet access if that is important enough for guaranteeing or exercising our other human rights. Chapters 3 and 4 will explore precisely the empirical and instrumental links between internet access and our human rights. However, before we can explore these connections, we need to know how to understand what rights entitle us to as rights-holders. This is because if we are unaware of what rights entail, we also cannot know if we have a (derived or primary) right to something. That is because if a right would require too much of those who have to guarantee it for us, this excessive burdensomeness would count against us having such an entitlement.

To understand this problem, consider the human right to education, which we are all entitled to according to international treaties such as the International Covenant on Economic, Social, and Cultural Rights (ICESCR) (UN 1966a: §13). Someone might claim that, on the basis of this right, we also have a (derivative) right to the provision of free individual tutoring in support of free higher education because such support is indispensable for maximal educational achievement. But is this claim plausible? This depends on what the human right to education entails. If this right guarantees higher education and the chance to achieve maximal educational success, a right to the provision of free individual tutoring for higher education might be derivable from the human right to education. If this right does not include guaranteed higher education and maximal educational achievement, no such right to individual tutoring can be derived. Equally, even though we know for sure that internet access is very useful for many educational activities and for all kinds of learning, this alone does not tell us whether the internet's usefulness justifies ascribing to it the status of a right. Instead, we need to know if the educational opportunities for which the internet is extremely useful are also part of what the human right to education guarantees.

When we attempt to answer the question of what a right entails, one crucial consideration that we have to keep in mind is that, as explained in Chapter 1, rights create obligations for others. More concretely, the object or end of a candidate right must protect an interest of the right-holder that is morally important enough to create an obligation for others to respect, protect, and guarantee that interest (Raz 1986: 180–186). Some desirable things are too burdensome to create duties for others to provide them for us. To return to an example mentioned at the beginning of Chapter 1, it would seem difficult to justify a human right to sexual pleasure (Coleman et al. 2021) because there is no one who can be said to have a duty to provide us with sexual pleasure. That is because sexual activities have to be based on mutual consent and are not something that is owed. Many other desirable things, though, are important enough. For instance, the interest not to be killed is certainly important enough to create obligations for others to respect my bodily integrity. As we also saw in Chapter 1, the first addressee of human rights claims is the government of one's state and in a secondary capacity the international community. The precise interpretation of any right therefore must consider the burdens on the ones who would have obligations imposed on them by a candidate right. These burdens can be moral, economic, or political:

- *Morally*, the more extensive the right to bodily integrity is claimed to be, the more others must limit their own choices and activities to avoid injuring me. An extensive right to bodily integrity would therefore come with high moral costs for others.
- *Economically*, the more extensive the right to bodily integrity is claimed to be, the more costly the services the government as the primary addressee of our human rights would have to provide. In this sense, right claims also impose an economic burden on others that must be taken into account when assessing what a right entails.

- *Politically*, the more extensively we interpret the human right to bodily integrity and the more public resources must be expended on it, the fewer resources remain for the realisation of other rights. The political burdens of a candidate rights therefore concern what economists call the 'opportunity costs' of the right in question.

This explains that not just any interpretation of a right is plausible. Some interpretations demand too little in terms of the respect for, and protection, of a right. Others might be too demanding in that they impose unreasonable moral, economic, or political costs on others or the public as a whole. Certainly not everything that would be useful for the fulfilment of some important interest can therefore give rise to rights claims. For instance, even though it would be expedient for my bodily integrity if everyone around me focuses their attention on not causing me injury, or if I would be provided with personal body armour, the human right to bodily integrity does not give me a right to either. The first one is out of the question because it would impose excessive moral costs on others. The second measure is problematic because it would impose unjustifiable financial burdens on the public, which in turn would divert an unreasonable amount of resources from the realisation of other rights. For these reasons, when considering what a right entails (in order to see whether it can justify other rights that derive from it) we have to keep an eye on the various types of costs that recognising such a right would impose on others. If these burdens would be unreasonable, the candidate right in question (or the particular interpretation of it under consideration) would not be justifiable either.

When considering what a right reasonably entails, we can very roughly distinguish between three different interpretations of that right: a minimal, a medium, and a maximal one. These interpretations indicate what sort of guarantees a right secures for its holders.

- On its *minimal* interpretation, a right – for example, the human right to education – only protects its holder from arbitrary discrimination and secures the formal freedom to do something. In this case, it would entitle its holder to pursue the educational opportunities available to them (if they can afford to pay for tuition) and protect them from being denied these opportunities because of irrelevant factors (e.g. their nationality, gender, or race). What this right in its weak interpretation does not entail is some form of free or guaranteed provision of education for the right-holder.
- According to its *medium* interpretation, the right to education would guarantee for its holder everything that the weak version does. Additionally, though, the right would also secure a certain amount of educational

opportunities to everyone, for instance through the public and free provision of some form of education.
- Finally, on the *maximal* interpretation, the right to education would entitle its holder not just to some, but the free provision of the best and fullest educational opportunities possible. Only if this maximal interpretation of the human right to education were correct could one hope to derive from the right another right to free individual tutoring.

Each different interpretation would entail different services that the government as the primary duty-holder would have to provide. On the weak interpretation, the services required would be those institutions that enforce the formal freedom to seek educational opportunities and that punish those who violate that freedom. On the medium interpretation, some form of free public education must be provided by the state, and on the maximal interpretation the provision of these public education services would have to be as extensive as is reasonably feasible for public authorities. All interpretations therefore come with different burdens that ultimately fall on citizens as taxpayers who fund the required services.

2.3.1 Examples: The Human Rights to Education and Health

To understand how to interpret the scope of rights, we can revisit the example of the human right to education. Education can take many different forms such as primary, secondary, and higher education, vocational training, or lifelong learning. This means that this human right (according to a maximal interpretation) could theoretically guarantee all these forms for everyone. The ICESCR, though, is quite specific in its determination of what the human right to education demands. The object or end of this right is that 'education shall be directed to the full development of the human personality and the sense of its dignity, and shall strengthen the respect for human rights and fundamental freedoms' (UN 1966a: §13.1). To this end,

a) Primary education must be free and compulsory (§13.2a). Everyone is therefore guaranteed a primary education. Any state signing up to this Covenant that does not already offer free primary education to its citizens has to do so within two years of ratifying the Covenant (§14).
b) Secondary and vocational education should be made available to all. Free provision of this education is not currently required but should be the ultimate aim of governments (§13.2b). At the moment, where secondary education is not free, only those with the means to pay for it can access it but no one who can afford tuition must be arbitrarily discriminated against when seeking secondary or vocational education.

c) Higher education should be made accessible to all. Free provision of this education is also not currently required but should be the ultimate aim of governments (§13.2c). At the moment, where higher education is not free, only those with the means to pay for it can access it but no one who can afford tuition must be arbitrarily discriminated against when seeking higher education.

This specification of the human right to education therefore accords with a medium interpretation of the right. It requires more than a possible minimal interpretation because (besides freedom from discrimination in the pursuit of education) the right guarantees some primary education to everyone through the provision of a free public service. This makes sense because otherwise education that is necessary for minimally decent lives would be the privilege of those able to afford its provision. But the right stops short of a maximal interpretation because the calls for guaranteed, free education beyond the primary level are aspirational. This also means that no right to free individual tutoring in support of free higher education is derivable from the human right to education because free higher education is not encompassed by this right.

The ICESCR's specification of the guarantees and obligations that are entailed by the human right to education make sense given the right's object and the purpose of human rights. To recall, human rights have the function of securing the conditions of minimally decent lives. And while free secondary and higher education are plausibly required for the 'full development of the human personality', they are arguably not required for the development of a sense of ourselves as a person and our dignity, which are necessary elements of minimally decent lives. A fully developed human personality is a hallmark of a flourishing life, a feature of a person who has a secure idea of who they are, what they want to do with their lives, and how to go about achieving their goals. This is a demanding ideal that not everyone will achieve. But all of us at least must be able to develop a sense of who we are and of the world around us. A primary education is therefore needed to enable us to learn basic facts about the world (so we do not depend for our understanding of it mostly on opinions), reading and writing (to be able to function in modern societies), and about society (so that we are aware of our options and worth as persons). Everybody therefore must have access to a primary education to lead minimally decent lives, and the human right to education guarantees exactly that for everyone. That is, considering the object or end of this human right, a medium interpretation is the most reasonable one.

The ICESCR's medium interpretation of the human right to education also makes sense when we consider the costs and obligations that the right imposes on others. From an economic perspective, considering the existing poverty and inequality in our world, a maximal interpretation of the right (which would demand that states guarantee free secondary and higher education to all citizens right away) would simply be unfeasible for many countries. It is also unlikely that there would be sufficient political will among affluent states (that often themselves do not meet this maximal interpretation of the right to education) to provide poorer nations with the resources required to guarantee free secondary and higher education to all citizens. Nor does the interest in free maximal education of those who would need the help of others to obtain it morally trump the interests of those whose help is required to realise their own goals. This means that if the human right to education is understood in a maximal, demanding sense, it is likely that all states would fail their regarding human rights obligations one way or another. From a political point of view, the maximal realisation of the human right to education would divert scarce resources from the guarantee of other rights and other important tasks of states. The more is spent on education, the less is available for health care and infrastructure provision, for example. If states were to guarantee maximal educational opportunities, they would only seem to be able to prevent falling short of their duties concerning other rights and services if they were to raise more taxes from their citizens. But this might, from a moral perspective, unduly limit citizens' means and options to realise their own goals and to exercise their own freedoms. Therefore, also considering the various kinds of burdens that different interpretations of the human right to education would impose on states and citizens, the medium interpretation of the human right to education appears to be the most reasonable one.[2]

---

[2] One might of course want to object that the demands and ambitions of human rights should not be limited by existing global inequalities, poverty, and a lack of political will. If the human right to education as a matter of justice demands the full realisation of the human personality, states should strive to realise a maximal interpretation of this right. In this case, we might wonder whether the purpose of human rights is really limited to guaranteeing minimally decent lives. Since the full realisation of the human personality is not part of such lives, but demanded by the ICESCR, maybe the function of human rights is accordingly more expansive as well. However, it is important to note that the maximal realisation of education according to the ICESCR is only an aspirational goal and not an immediate duty of states. There are therefore three possible conclusions that we might draw from this clash between the idea that human rights protect the conditions of minimally decent lives and the ICESCR's statement that the human right to education ultimately entails education that leads to the full realisation of the human personality, which is an aspect of flourishing (rather than minimally decent) lives. As a start, the view that human rights protect minimally decent lives might be mistaken. However, considering the explanations in Chapter 1, I will exclude this possibility for the sake of the argument in this book because (as we saw) we have good reasons to adopt this particular interpretation of human rights. This leaves us with two other possible conclusions. First, we might

In support of these reasons for the medium interpretation of the human right to education, we can also consider the parallel case of the human right to health care. According to the ICESCR, this entails 'the right of everyone to the enjoyment of the highest attainable standard of physical and mental health' (UN 1966a §12). This suggests a maximal reading of the human right to health with the according moral, political, and economic burdens that come with providing the best possible health care free for all. However, in its 2000 General Comment 14, the UN's Committee on Economic, Social and Cultural Rights recognises the problems with such a maximal interpretation of the human right to health (Wolff 2015: 492). In its comment, the Committee clarifies that states too poor to afford expensive medical care for their populations only have duties to fulfil certain 'core obligations' and must work (where feasible) towards the 'progressive realisation' of health care that goes beyond these core obligations.[3] These core obligations include a duty to prevent arbitrary discrimination in the provision of health care (which corresponds with a minimal interpretation of the right), the provision of basic health-care services, the physical preconditions of health (such as food and shelter), and essential drugs, as well as the adoption of a national public health strategy (Wolff 2015: 494). This is to say that the aspirational goal of the human right to health aims for a maximal interpretation of the right, while the actual obligations and guarantees entailed by the right exceed its minimal interpretation and rather aligns with a medium interpretation of this human right. Because maximal health is not necessary for decent lives, this is fully in line with the purpose of human rights to secure the conditions of minimally decent lives as well as with the observation that a maximal interpretation of the human right to health would generate moral, economic, and political costs that would currently be unreasonable (and thus unjustifiable) for many countries.

    think that, once global inequality is reduced and poverty eliminated, the purpose of human rights should become more ambitious. In this case, since decent lives would be guaranteed for everyone thanks to the raising of global minimal living standards, the aim of human rights should shift to securing highly valuable or fulfilling lives for everyone. Alternatively, we might want to stick with the view that the point of human rights is to secure minimally decent lives for everyone. After all, human rights are not all that justice requires, and states can decide to provide more comprehensive educational opportunities than free primary education for all their citizens. In this case, we would have to think that the ICESCR is simply mistaken to declare that the full realisation of the human personality is entailed by the human right to education. For the argument in this book, nothing hangs on which view we take, and so I will not pursue this question further here.

[3] The distinction between the core obligations entailed by socio-economic human rights and their remaining content that states that are not affluent enough are unable to provide immediately are allowed to realise progressively will be of central importance for the arguments in Chapter 5.

Returning to our initial question about rights derivation, we can now appreciate the point that derivative rights are only justifiable if they support the primary right in its proper interpretation. With respect to the human rights to education and health care, anything that we might want to derive from them (for instance, internet access) therefore must conform to their medium interpretation.

2.4 ADEQUATE OPPORTUNITIES TO ENJOY AND REALISE HUMAN RIGHTS

So what do rights generally entail? If we are particularly concerned about the burdens that rights impose on others, we might of course wonder why the ICESCR does not adopt a minimal interpretation of human rights. If public authorities only have to guarantee formal freedom – the freedom to pursue our rights without arbitrary discrimination if we have the means to do so – citizens only have to fund relatively limited public services. The various kinds of 'costs' that rights interpreted in such a minimal way impose on others would then also be relatively small.

Ultimately, the question about what rights entail is a question about which opportunities for the enjoyment of the right's object we think a right has to guarantee. To use the language of John Rawls, what we are interested in is what 'worth' a right must have for the right-holder (Rawls 1999: 179). As Rawls points out, the worth of a right for its holder is strongly affected by the means (in terms either of money or knowledge) that the holder has to enjoy the right. Without any guarantees or provisions, a lack of means lowers the worth of that right. For example, if primary education or basic health care are not freely provided, they can only be accessed by those who have the money to afford them. That is, these elements of a minimally decent life (and therefore a minimally decent life as such) would then be dependent on having certain financial means. But this goes against the very idea of human rights that have the end to guarantee such lives for everyone. Because the objects of all rights are usually important, we normally want to make sure that they have a certain worth to everyone.

The point of having rights is usually that we want to ensure that people's enjoyment of the objects of their rights is not a matter of happenstance but guaranteed. This explains why minimal interpretations of rights, which only secure formal freedom from arbitrary discrimination, are inadequate for determining the worth of rights – especially the worth of very important rights such as human rights. It simply should not matter if you are rich or poor, or if you happen to know someone willing to pay for the fulfilment of your rights – everyone should be able to enjoy the objects of their rights. To put this point differently, we want to make sure that our rights do not simply secure the abstract, formal freedom for us to do something if we have the resources necessary for it. Rather, we want our rights to secure 'real freedom' (van Parijs 1995) for us, which means that public authorities must make sure that we have guaranteed opportunities to enjoy important freedoms, such as our human rights. Without public guarantees, formal freedom is mostly useless to those who do not have their own means to afford opportunities to realise their rights. Usually, these public guarantees take the form of the public provision of some service, such as free primary education or basic health care. On the other hand, as we saw earlier, resources are normally scarce, and therefore a maximal interpretation of rights exceeds what is politically, morally, and economically feasible. Guaranteeing maximal opportunities to enjoy the objects of rights for everyone (e.g. the free provision of all forms of education and health care, generous social security payments, or legal representation by the best available lawyers) for this reason is only feasible if societies are affluent and there is a public consensus that private wealth should be highly taxed to collect the revenues required for providing the regarding extensive public services. As this situation mostly does not apply (and because minimal realisations of rights are insufficient since they make the enjoyment of rights dependent on irrelevant factors such as personal wealth), what we are left with as reasonable contents of most rights are something that we can call *adequate* opportunities (Tomalty 2017).

Adequate opportunities are neither limited to formal freedom from arbitrary discrimination, nor do they entail maximal opportunities to enjoy the objects of rights. Rather, they ensure that everyone has at least some reasonable degree of opportunities to make use of their rights. What counts as adequate opportunities differs for each right. The adequate worth of rights cannot be determined theoretically and abstractly, but rather involves normative argument, political judgement, and empirical information to take into account the burdens generated by the right. Normative argument is required to determine which interests are morally important enough to place others under a duty to provide certain services or protections as part of a right. Political judgement is indispensable because the burdens placed on the political community by rights claims need to be justifiable to the members. For instance, if extraordinarily expensive drugs developed to treat rare illnesses are included in free public health care, this creates costs for the taxpayers who fund the public provision. These costs must be weighed against the costs of other public services the community has to provide. Deciding how public funds are spent is thus a matter of public debate and decisions. Finally, opportunities to make use of rights are affected by various empirical factors (e.g. social norms, technology, and even geography). New technological advances, for instance, can lead to new rights when this technology becomes essential for the realisation of other rights. For instance, before the development of mass media, the human right to a free press was inconceivable. Knowledge of empirical factors is thus essential for understanding what rights people can claim to have and the worth that these liberties have for them.

Even though the notion of adequate opportunities might seem abstract and nondescript, there are many concrete real-life examples that help us make sense of this idea. For example, democratic states should provide mail-in ballots upon request to people who cannot vote in person, and entitle workers to take time off work to cast their vote. This ensures that those with limited mobility or those who work during elections have adequate opportunities to make use of their right to vote. However, having adequate opportunities to exercise the right to vote does not entail a free public chauffeur service to the polling station. Similarly, states should provide a public attorney free of charge to those unable to afford the services of a lawyer. This public provision of legal expertise ensures that people's enjoyment of their right to equality before the law does not depend on their private means. However, having adequate opportunities to enjoy legal equality does not require free public provision of the best legal counsel available. And the ICESCR entitles people to 'an adequate standard of living [...] including adequate food, clothing and housing, and to the continuous improvement of living conditions' (UN 1966a: §11). Again, this human right indicates that its medium interpretation (which guarantees adequate opportunities) is the correct one, while a more maximal interpretation and realisation of the right should be the aspiration of states.

Most of the time, the fact that people have different financial resources means that their rights are of different worth for them. Money usually allows us to purchase specialised services that help us make the most of our freedoms. Money can buy, for instance, private tutoring and access to the highest available quality of education, the best available medical care and legal representation, or the healthiest foods and best housing. Within limits, such inequalities in the worth that our rights have for us is not problematic if we assume that the financial inequalities that give rise to these inequalities are unproblematic. As Rawls points out, 'some citizens have [legitimately] greater income and wealth and therefore greater means for achieving their ends' (Rawls 2005: 350). This makes good sense, too, because we have many rights of which it is unreasonable to think that they can or must have comparable value to all of us. For example, we all are entitled freely to practise a religion. But this right will be of little use to those without a faith. We also all have the right to a family, but not all of us want to start a family. Furthermore, we all have equal rights to an education and to pursue a profession. However, this does not mean that everyone must end up with equal knowledge and equally wealthy. This is because it is either impossible to guarantee equal outcomes or (even if these would be achievable) it would require unjustifiable interference with the lives of people to ensure they end up the same. However, the notion of adequate opportunities and the regarding public provisions guarantees that rights have a certain absolute worth for everyone in the sense that everyone can enjoy at least a decent level of access to the object of their rights. Adequate opportunities are therefore the baseline of guaranteed options that rights normally must ensure for us.

One final aspect is worth noting about adequate opportunities specifically with respect to derivative rights. A derivative right normally offers specific ways of realising the object or end of the rights that they derive from. This means that there are normally other ways to realise these anchor rights. But the existence of alternatives does not as such undermine an argument for a derivative right. For example, the human right to freedom of expression entails the right to demonstrate in public. Of course, there are other ways to express our views than to demonstrate in public. But this alone does not show that we do not have the right to organise or join public demonstrations. Equally, the human right to free information gives rise to the right to a free press. There are other ways to acquire information than to use the services of the free press. But this alone is not sufficient to deny that we have a right to a free press. Moreover, we have the right to a decent standard of living, which justifies our having a right to work, which has the object of ensuring that everyone has 'the opportunity to gain [their] living' (UN 1966a, §6.1). There are other ways to gain a living than work (e.g. some people live off the land they own, others off their inheritance). However, these alternatives do not show that the right to work is unnecessary and therefore unjustified.[4] In general, the existence of alternative ways of enjoying an original right do not as such undermine the claim that we have a particular derivative right. Whether a derivative right is justifiable always depends on the balance of reasons as to whether having it is necessary for having adequate opportunities to enjoy or realise the anchor right from which it derives. With respect to these examples, this is to say that the right to demonstrate in public is necessary for having adequate opportunities to

---

[4] I thank Jeremy Williams for this point.

express our opinions freely; press freedom is necessary for having adequate opportunities to exercise our right to free information; and the right to work is required to ensure that we can make use of our right to an adequate standard of living. This point about adequate opportunities and derived rights will become important when considering the ways in which the internet is now useful for our other human rights. This is because normally we also have offline ways to exercise these rights. However, as we will see, the mere fact that there are offline alternatives to exercise our rights does not show that we cannot have a human right to internet access. That depends on whether internet access is required for having adequate opportunities to exercising other human rights. The argument presented in this book is that internet access has indeed become necessary in this way, as we will see in Chapters 3 and 4.

2.5 DERIVATIVE RIGHTS AND HUMAN RIGHTS INFLATION

Now that we are equipped with an understanding of how rights derivations work and what rights normally entitle us to, we can return and respond to an important potential objection against the idea of a human right to free internet access that we encountered at the beginning of Chapter 1. That objection says that recognising a human right to something (such as internet access) that is merely valuable as a tool for other important things (i.e. human rights) threatens to lead to dangerous human rights inflation. Lots of things are useful for other things, but few things are important enough to deserve the status of human rights. If we are too permissible with the label of human rights, we might therefore ultimately lessen the normative force and special nature of this entire important category. However, the logic of rights derivation clarifies why recognising a human right to internet access does not open the floodgates of human rights inflation. As explained earlier, the requirements for something to become a right based on its practical or systemic indispensability for other rights are exceptionally high. Few things will pass this instrumental test of being sufficiently useful for grounding obligations to it in others. But, additionally, human rights only protect those things that are necessary for leading minimally decent lives. For something to become a derivative human right, it must therefore be of exceptional practical value *and* necessary for minimally good lives. It is unlikely that there will be many things that pass this dual test. Press freedom is one of these things. A nationality and social insurance are others. As this book argues, free internet access is another one of the select few things that are important enough to warrant assigning to it the status of a general entitlement because it is practically indispensable for other things that are themselves necessary for leading minimally decent lives.

2.6 CONCLUSION

With the notion of adequate opportunities as being those which most rights aim to guarantee for their holders at hand, we are now able to more precisely state the formal argument for the derivative human right to internet access that this book defends, and which we provisionally established in Section 2.2 of this chapter. Specifically, we can see that this formal argument contains one additional, important premise (i.e. Premise 2):

Premise 1: Everyone has human rights.
Premise 2: Everyone must have adequate opportunities to enjoy their human rights.
Premise 3: Internet access is in practice necessary for having adequate opportunities to exercise or enjoy many of these human rights.
Premise 4: Following 'a principle of rationality' (Nickel 2022: 31), if we endorse an end (i.e. primary or anchor rights), we have very strong or good reasons also to endorse those things and means that are necessary to achieve or realise that end (i.e. a supporting right).
Conclusion: Insofar as and because internet access is in practice necessary for having adequate opportunities to exercise or enjoy many of our human rights, we have very strong reasons to accept a human right to internet access.

In Chapters 3 and 4, we will consider in what ways internet access concretely supports many different rights. We will see that internet access in our digital age has indeed become practically indispensable for having adequate opportunities to enjoy human rights. Moreover, this practical indispensability applies to so many rights that it is also justified to say that internet access has become systemically indispensable for much of the list of our interdependent human rights. These two chapters therefore establish Premise 3. Doing so is no mean feat. We have to keep in mind that something cannot simply be useful for other rights to deserve the status of a right itself. It has to be extraordinarily useful and important to justify imposing various kinds of burdens on those who then have a duty to guarantee the derived right for us.

The discussion in this chapter has been crucial for understanding the argument for the human right to free internet access because, first, we now understand that we can indeed be justified in ascribing the status of a right to something based on its usefulness for other rights. That is the idea of rights derivation. Second, we also saw that we have to know exactly what a right requires in order to derive other rights from it. It is no good to say, for example, that we have a right to a lot of money because a lot of money is necessary for obtaining the best education, medical care, or legal representation. This is (in part) because the human rights to education, health, and legal equality do not guarantee the best possible education, medical care or legal representation for us.[5] What rights normally guarantee for us is that we have adequate opportunities for the enjoyment of the object or end of these rights to ensure that our rights are of a certain worth to all of us. This worth exceeds merely formal freedom and protection from discrimination, but stops short of maximal or very extensive guarantees. Chapters 3 and 4 will show why internet access today is required for such adequate opportunities to exercise our rights, not just as a matter of convenience or the best possible option. It is to these many examples that illustrate the exceptional value that internet access can have for other rights that we now turn, starting with the importance of internet access for the enjoyment of civil and political human rights.

---

[5] Another reason this claim does not work is that rights often do not entitle their holders to cash grants but rather to resources in the form of public services.

3

Internet Access and Civil and Political Human Rights

This book defends the claim that public authorities should recognise a human right to free internet access. In Chapter 1, we saw that human rights protect the conditions of minimally decent lives. Consequently, for internet access to be a human right, it has to be a condition of minimally decent lives. As pointed out at the beginning of Chapter 2, though, it would be wrong to think that internet access is as such an element of a minimally decent life. Being online is not valuable as such but only because we can do certain things when we are online. Having the opportunity to shop online, stream videos, or socialise with friends on social media is certainly convenient and enjoyable. However, none of these uses is essential for a minimally good life. None of these activities are therefore morally urgent enough to ascribe to internet access the status of a human right. For something to be a right, as we saw in Chapter 2, it needs to be morally important enough to justify obligations for others to secure, respect, and provide my enjoyment of the object of that right. And for something to be a human right, it needs to help secure the conditions of a minimally decent life for everyone. But the fact that streaming videos or shopping online is convenient or enjoyable cannot justify a duty for others such as the state to guarantee online access for everyone. No one has a duty to provide us with luxury goods. To be a human right, then, internet access must be useful for something much more essential. It must be an essential utility securing what is vital for living a decent life today.

So, what is internet access good for that is of extreme importance? As we saw in Chapter 2, rights can be grounded in their usefulness for other things. Such derived rights are normally grounded in other rights because rights often protect morally important objects. For internet access to be a human right, it makes sense to think that it must be extremely useful for other human rights. This is because it seems unlikely that a right that derives from something else can be more important than that which it derives from. To put this differently, it does not seem plausible to think that something (such as internet access) can be a condition of minimally decent lives if it supports something that is not itself a part of minimally decent lives. In this chapter and Chapter 4, we will therefore consider the internet's unique ability to enable the enjoyment of many of our other human rights. The 2016 United Nations (UN) report mentioned in the Introduction, which demands that offline rights are to be protected online, supports the idea of basing the claim for internet access as a human right on its usefulness for other human rights. In another report, the UN Special Rapporteur on the Promotion and Protection of the Right to Freedom of Opinion and Expression asserts that internet access has become 'indispensable' (UN 2011a: 22) for realising key human rights, in particular freedom of expression (see UN 2011a: 7). In this chapter, we will see how internet access has become vital for those key human rights that are categorised as so-called first-generation human rights, namely civil and political human rights, which protect basic security, equal treatment, and political freedoms and participation. In Chapter 4, we will do the same with respect to socio-economic human rights. To understand the role that these two chapters play in the overall argument of this book, it is helpful to recall that argument in its formal form:

> Premise 1: Everyone has human rights.
> Premise 2: Everyone must have adequate opportunities to enjoy their human rights.
> Premise 3: Internet access is in practice necessary for having adequate opportunities to exercise or enjoy many of these human rights.
> Premise 4: Following a 'principle of rationality' (Nickel 2022: 31), if we endorse an end (i.e. primary or anchor rights), we have very strong or good reasons also to endorse those things and means that are necessary to achieve or realise that end (i.e. a supporting right).
> Conclusion: Insofar as and because internet access is in practice necessary for having adequate opportunities to exercise or enjoy many of our human rights, we have very strong reasons to accept a human right to internet access.

This chapter and Chapter 4 defend Premise 3. To provide the normative and empirical support required for this premise, we will consider examples that illustrate concretely how the internet helps secure the conditions of living minimally good lives. As we will see, we can establish a linkage argument for a human right to internet access because such access is now both (1) practically indispensable for individual civil and political human rights as well as

Internet Access and Civil and Political Human Rights 73

(2) systemically indispensable for the enjoyment of a whole range of interdependent human rights.

Section 3.1 outlines some of the most important ways in which internet access enhances the enjoyment of human rights that protect basic security and equal treatment. Section 3.2 discusses how internet access has become essential for ensuring political freedoms and participation. Section 3.3 responds to the important objection that a special right to internet access is unnecessary because such access is already sufficiently protected by other human rights (e.g. free expression). Section 3.4 summarises the argument for the human right to free internet access. At the end of this chapter, we will have established that internet access has become indispensable for adequate opportunities to protect and enjoy our civil and political human rights. This will provide crucial support for the claim that public authorities should recognise a (derived) human right to free internet access.

3.1 INTERNET ACCESS AND HUMAN RIGHTS TO SECURITY AND EQUAL TREATMENT

Among the most fundamental and least controversial human rights are those that guarantee our basic security and equal treatment. It is difficult to think of anything more essential than the universal human interests in life, liberty, and security of person (UN 1948: §3), freedom from torture and cruel treatment (UN 1948: §5), equality before the law (UN 1948: §7), and freedom from arbitrary arrest (UN 1948: §9). All of these are quite obviously necessary elements of a minimally good human life. Human rights are meant to justify social guarantees against standard threats to these vital interests. Correspondingly, states (in the first instance) and the international community (as secondary guarantors) have obligations to respect, protect, and remedy violations of these human rights. There are many examples that show how the internet provides new, unique, and often extremely effective possibilities for protecting and promoting these core human rights to security and basic treatment.

At a structural level, the reason that the internet can support the protection of these human rights effectively lies in this medium's very architecture and nature. The internet does not simply permit us to access information; it also makes it searchable. But more importantly, the internet has changed the opportunities of people to access and report information widely, cheaply, and quickly. By contrast, traditional mass media such as newspapers, television, and radio separate people into (relatively few) senders/producers and (many) recipients of information. They create what the philosopher Vilem Flusser (2022) calls 'amphitheatre discourses' in which the authors of mass media communications use technological means to impart information into many recipients. Few of these recipients have themselves the opportunity to react to, or influence, the senders. However, the internet enables for the first time what Flusser calls large scale 'net discourses' among billions of communicators. It allows everyone with online access, without requiring much technical expertise, to become a sender of information and to communicate with others – rather than to remain a mere recipient of what others have said. In this way, the internet has democratised mass communication, a development that brings with it many opportunities as well as new dangers.[1]

That online access can help protect life, liberty, security of person, freedom from torture, freedom from arbitrary arrest, and equality before the law is precisely due to the internet's purpose of disseminating various forms of information widely and quickly. Especially photos, videos, and written documents about criminal activities and misuses of power can be shared globally and instantaneously by anyone with internet access and little technical knowledge. The fact that crimes and abuses of power can be documented and revealed can disincentivise governments and individuals from violating human rights and help to prosecute perpetrators. Moreover, documentation of human rights abuses can lead to action that prevents further crimes. Of course, the possibilities for manipulating photos and videos are becoming increasingly sophisticated too, but so are the methods for distinguishing 'fake' from real evidence. One successful example of using the internet for the prevention of human rights violations is mentioned by Amartya Sen (2010). In 2009, the Taliban established their rule in the Swat valley of Pakistan without generating much public concern in the rest of the country. As Sen points out, it was footage of the whipping of a young girl by the Taliban shared online that changed this situation (Walsh 2009). The video caused public outrage in a previously rather uninterested population, turning public opinion against the Taliban. This led to government action to move against the terrorist group, thereby preventing them from committing other human rights violations (albeit at the cost of military conflict that led to displacement of local residents, see Walsh and Tran 2009).

Other examples of using the internet to confront oppression and to report human rights violations and murders by governments include the revolutions of the Arab Spring 2010–2012 and the 2013 case of the Syrian military defector with the code name 'Caesar'. When fleeing the country, he took images of 53,275 torture victims of Bashar al-Assad's regime with him. This information was made public online globally by non-governmental organisations (NGOs)

---

[1] We will consider these dangers and drawbacks of the internet in Part II (Chapters 6–8).

such as Human Rights Watch and serves as an internationally accessible indictment of the criminal Syrian dictatorship. Another example of the power of the internet to report on violations of human rights is the work of the online investigators belonging to the international open source intelligence group Bellingcat (2023). Bellingcat's method is to research and compile information that is publicly available online (such as photos and videos) to investigate crimes committed by powerful agents such as states. In this way, Bellingcat provided documentation that strongly suggests that Russian military forces were involved in the shooting down of passenger flight MH17 over eastern Ukraine in July 2014. The network's findings were crucial for establishing the guilt of three men who were legally held responsible in 2022 for the murder of the 298 people on board the plane (Rankin 2022). Investigative work of this kind would be impossible without data that is available on the internet. Moreover, reporting on violations of human rights by public authorities is much less effective if it has to take the route of established offline mass media that are much more easily influenced by governments and often owned by powerful individuals who use them as megaphones for their own agendas.

There is of course a straightforward objection to the claim that the internet is a uniquely expedient means of protecting fundamental rights such as those to life, liberty, and freedom from torture. After all, most of those responsible for crimes such as the mass murder and torture perpetrated by the al-Assad regime have not been held to account. The men found guilty by a Dutch court of the murder of the people on board flight MH17 are still walking free. And most of the revolutions of the Arab Spring of 2011 were unsuccessful and have not led to the emergence of stable democratic regimes. These revolutions were dubbed 'Twitter revolutions' because of the use of social media platforms such as Facebook and Twitter by insurgents and protesters for the coordination of their revolt. Even worse, though, in the case of the Arab Spring, social media platforms were also used by authoritarian regimes to identify and persecute individual insurgents. This shows that the internet can also be an effective way for committing, rather than preventing, human rights violations – a problem we will consider in detail in Chapter 6.

However, the lack of success of these attempts to use online resources to overthrow authoritarian regimes and to punish human rights violations does not undermine the value of the internet as a tool for the protection of crucial civil liberties. The failures to topple dictatorial regimes, to hold accountable those who commit mass torture and murder, and to deliver to justice those responsible of shooting down flight MH17 are not due to the ineffectiveness of the internet. They are rather the consequence of the unwillingness of those who have obligations to respect human rights (such as authoritarian governments) or who are able to help and to punish the perpetrators (such as the international community of states) to comply with their duties. Other political agents who violate human rights are too powerful to punish in the sense that trying to bring them to account would require disproportionate costs such as international wars. But this only shows that no single institution, social arrangement, or technology can on its own guarantee the protection of human rights and the prosecution and punishment of crimes. Democratic institutions are important for protecting basic human rights (Christiano 2011). But these institutions depend on internal support and the absence of undermining efforts to provide reliable protection of fundamental human rights. If there are forces at work within or outside a democracy that are determined to destabilise it, democratic institutions will be incapable of safeguarding fundamental rights. Historical instances of such failures include the end of the German Weimar Republic in 1933, the overthrow of Salvador Allende's democratic government in Chile by Augusto Pinochet in 1973, the overturn of the democratically elected Iranian government and the installation of the Persian shah in 1953, and the return of Egypt to autocratic rule in 2013. In all these cases the democratic institutions either collapsed owing to a lack of popular support or because of interference from domestic or external adversaries. Any social arrangement (be it a democracy, a functioning legal system, a free press, or the internet) can only function as a reliable protection if it is not actively undermined, and if it has the support or respect of internal and external forces. It is therefore not surprising, nor a decisive argument against the claim that internet access is a uniquely powerful tool, that it cannot on its own reliably guarantee civil human rights. Rather, going back to Shue's account of rights (Shue 2020), it is unsurprising that human rights are violated when there is no one to provide effective social guarantees for their protection. Internet access can only ever be one crucial instrument that supports the processes and social institutions that enforce human rights and punish their violations.

That said, though, the internet is indeed a highly effective instrument for safeguarding crucial human rights whenever there are willing and capable political agents who take seriously their responsibilities to protect human rights. Normally needed for human rights protection are a functioning democracy, effective police forces, and an international community willing to counteract violations of human rights. To see this, we need to consider situations where accountability mechanisms and agents that take seriously their human rights responsibilities exist. We need to ask how valuable the internet can be when these conducive social arrangements obtain. That is, what we need to ask is: can the internet make a crucial contribution to the protection of human rights when there are agents and institutions that take seriously their obligations to guarantee human rights? When that is the case, there are indeed instances that clearly show that the internet does have that effect. One example of the internet's usefulness for the protection of human rights in a democratic state is its use in documenting unjustified police violence against African Americans in the US that gave rise to the Black Lives Matter movement. The ability to publicise excessive police force via the internet allows for injustices to be reported and for public debates about abuses of power and the basic liberties of marginalised groups to be initiated. The ability for individuals to record and share evidence with everyone only arose when access to the internet became widespread. This way of documenting crimes and abuses of power makes it much more difficult for anyone to prevent the spread of incriminating material. Irrefutable evidence of police brutality against African Americans did not routinely become available before the internet. Of course, digital devices such as mobile phones with cameras are also needed to record such evidence. But without the internet, individual citizens would have no way to share critical information at little cost and instantaneously with the world. The crucial importance of the digital documentation of rights violations by individual citizens is highlighted by the Pulitzer Prize special citation awarded to Darnella Frazer. Passing by the scene of the crime, Frazer filmed the murder of George Floyd by members of the Minneapolis police with her mobile phone and posted her video on Facebook. Her recording was crucial in the conviction of Floyd's murderer, and it is highly unlikely that it could have been prosecuted without the video Frazer disseminated via social media, which was the prosecution's centrepiece of evidence (Sheehey 2021).

Another example of the new possibilities that the internet offers for protecting basic civil human rights in democracies is the #MeToo campaign that makes public sexual harassment of women by powerful men. In October 2017, actress Alyssa Milano spoke out against the sexual harassment of women by men on Twitter and encouraged others to share their own experiences of abuse. Her message was retweeted half a million times within a day. The internet enabled mass-scale public engagement with the issue of sexual harassment in several ways. First, social media forums provided effective ways of reporting cases of harassment. Especially in the time after discourse about this topic came into the public spotlight following Milano's post, reports about harassment by influential men attracted widespread attention. None of these individuals was powerful enough to prevent online reports of their offences. However, they might well have been able to prevent reporting of these accusations in traditional mass media outlets, which might have feared lawsuits brought against them by powerful perpetrators. Second, the publicising of instances of harassment encouraged more women to share their own experiences. This created a storm of testimonial evidence that forestalled the claim that the problem was only one of individual and rare incidents rather than a systemic issue. It cannot be estimated how many such violations of women's freedom from degrading treatment and of their bodily integrity would have been publicised offline, but it seems safe to say that it would have been far fewer. Third, the online discourse created unprecedented public awareness of the issue of sexual harassment. The months after Milano's tweet saw the greatest ever number of online searches for the topics of sexual harassment and for information on how to report sexual assault in the US (Caputi et al. 2019).

We must of course be realistic about the role of the internet in the development of the online #MeToo movement. Other things than internet access are required to raise public awareness and combat sexual violence. Researchers have, for instance, found that public engagement with the concerns of the #MeToo movement correlates with how well countries protect civil and political human rights. The better these protections, the more intense the public engagement (Lee and Murdie 2020). But this simply supports the point discussed earlier that the effective protection of human rights depends on more than one thing. Internet access can only effectively contribute to the protection of our rights if other social arrangements also exist, such as public institutions that provide guarantees of protection. Nonetheless, the importance of the internet for the development and success of movements such as #MeToo cannot be underestimated. In addition to the reasons mentioned here, the public discussion online of an issue such as sexual assault can also have the important function of deterring potential perpetrators. Once potential abusers know that there is public awareness of the problem and that their potential victims have ways to share their experience with the public, committing rape and sexual harassment becomes much riskier for them. Other victims have used the internet to document past attacks and thereby created public awareness and concern about sexual attacks on women. The internet in these ways provides unprecedented opportunities to promote the protection of women's physical and psychological well-being. No alternative means of communication offers anywhere near the same options for documenting, reporting on, and thus disincentivising murder, rape, torture, or arbitrary arrests than the internet.

It is important to recognise, though, that the increased protection that the internet offers is mostly a cooperative benefit created by large numbers of individuals. This means that my use of the internet to document and report offences might not directly protect my own life, bodily integrity, or save me from degrading treatment. It is certainly possible that the use of online resources by a potential victim saves that particular person from suffering harm and injury as well. However, it is more likely that the use of the internet by many people to protect civil liberties creates a situation that makes the occurrence of human rights violations generally less likely. This in turn increases the protection of everyone's vital security and equal treatment rights. For instance, if those who can abuse state power or those who hope to abuse their follow citizens know that most citizens have internet-capable mobile phones that can record videos, they know that their misbehaviour is much more likely to become public knowledge than before the internet became widespread. An example of such 'crowdsourcing' information about threats to basic rights is the Egyptian civil initiative HarassMap that enables citizens to fight sexual harassment in Egyptian cities (HarassMap 2023). Here, individuals can anonymously report incidents of sexual harassment to a website. These reports are then displayed on a digital map that highlights areas where such incidents frequently occur. Those reporting incidents are directly supplied with information about legal and counselling help, and volunteers of the non-profit organisation visit particularly affected areas to raise awareness of the problem among public officials such as police officers as well as locals (Not An Atlas 2023). In this way, a civil society initiative uses the internet to promote the protection, and to help remedy the violation of, crucial security interests that ground human rights to the security of person and to freedom from degrading treatment.[2]

As these examples show, the internet can be crucial for establishing an environment that disincentivises human rights abuses if access to this medium is widespread and if there are political agents that take seriously their responsibilities to protect people's freedoms. In turn, this means that the more people can use the internet freely, the more robust the protection of civil liberties based on the use of this medium can be. If internet access is recognised as a human right and universally available, if this access is generally not curtailed by censorship or surveillance, and if there are strong political (domestic and international) institutions willing to defend basic security and equal treatment rights, then the internet can fulfil a uniquely effective role in the protecting these freedoms. Using the internet, every individual citizen can play a powerful and vital role in this endeavour. This shows the individually empowering

---

[2] One might wonder whether this counts as a protection of human rights as the reported offences are committed by individual citizens rather than public officials because human rights are first and foremost obligations limiting the power of states (see Chapter 1). It is important to note, though, that we as individuals, not just public institutions and officials, also can violate each other's human rights and have responsibilities to respect and protect each other's rights wherever we can.

potential of this medium and its power to help collectively to protect some of the most fundamental interest of every person. In other words, internet access is practically indispensable for our collective ability to protect each other's human rights to security and equal treatment because the internet alone enables each of us individually to report rights violations. Not accepting a human right to free internet access would mean to ignore this medium's unique power. It would therefore be grossly negligent and irresponsible for political institutions not to recognise such a right. After all, the protection of the rights to life, liberty, and equal treatment is one of their most essential duties.

3.2 INTERNET ACCESS AND HUMAN RIGHTS TO POLITICAL FREEDOMS AND PARTICIPATION

As we saw in Chapter 1, minimally decent lives also require political freedoms and opportunities for political participation. Without the rights to free speech, free association, and free information, we are unable to develop as autonomous persons and depend on the good will of those in power for living our lives the way we want to.

Having just considered the fundamental human rights to security and equal treatment, we can turn to an argument by Henry Shue to understand how political freedoms are also essential for these basic security and equal treatment rights. As Shue points out, without political freedoms and rights to political participation, citizens have no guaranteed influence on the policies and institutions that are to protect their fundamental human rights. In an authoritarian state, citizens have to hope that their rulers will protect them from attacks on their most basic rights and abstain from violating these rights themselves. However, if non-democratic regimes do nothing to prevent assaults on the fundamental freedoms of their citizens, or decide to attack their citizens themselves, there are few if any institutional paths of influence and accountability that citizens can use to change the situation. And because having rights means having social guarantees against standard threats, citizens of regimes that disallow political freedoms and participation do not have effective rights to security and equal treatment either (see Shue 2020: 70–78). They are at the mercy of those who have power over them, which prevents them from living minimally decent lives as vulnerable, autonomous human beings. This instrumental link between political rights and human rights to security and equal treatment therefore provides additional reasons for the claim that political human rights are necessary elements of decent lives to those discussed in Chapter 2.

When considering the internet's impact on political freedoms, what is important to keep in mind is that what matters are people's opportunities to exercise these rights, not necessarily the actual frequency or likelihood of using them. Freedoms, after all, provide opportunities, not obligations, to do certain things. A person might well have a minimally good life while never exercising their rights to speak publicly on political matters, to run for a public office, or to demonstrate for a political cause as long as they have the freedom to do so. But if they do not have the possibility to exercise these rights, to influence how political power is exerted in their community, and to hold those in power to account, their lives lack some vital conditions of a decent human life. Internet access, if it is free from arbitrary interference such as censorship and online surveillance, offers crucial new opportunities and resources for citizens to make use of their political freedoms. Considering that the internet is all about communication and sharing information, it is unsurprising that its effects are particularly pronounced with respect to our human rights to free speech, free assembly, and free access to information. To appreciate this, we have to go into more detail about the internet's effects on the key human rights of free speech, free assembly, and free information. These examples illustrate that to have adequate opportunities to exercise our political freedoms today, we need guaranteed access to the internet that is free from arbitrary interference.

3.2.1 *Internet Access and Freedom of Expression*

Commentators have so far mostly thought about the practical value of internet access for human rights with respect to its usefulness for political freedoms, in particular the right to free expression. For instance, in his landmark 2011 report, the UN Special Rapporteur on the Promotion and Protection of the Human Right to Freedom of Opinion and Expression 'underscores the unique and transformative nature of the Internet [for people] to exercise their freedom of opinion and expression' (UN 2011a: 1). As far back as 1996, the internet was identified as 'the most participatory form of mass speech yet developed' (Schwartz 1996). Since then, we have become accustomed to an ever-growing number of applications and forums that we can use to express ourselves online.

It is obvious that a person who can access the internet has many times the opportunities to make their voice heard than someone who has no such access, even though it might be impossible to quantify this difference precisely. Online we can set up a blog, post videos, have conversations via Skype or Zoom, post on social media platforms such as Facebook, Reddit, or X (formerly Twitter). Political use of these opportunities has become commonplace.³ Social groups use online petitions to create public pressure on governments. In the UK, the online platform CrowdJustice allows individuals to join and donate to political causes that take legal actions (CrowdJustice 2023). In 2017, the platform was used to collect money for launching an ultimately successful challenge at the UK Supreme Court against Prime Minister Theresa May that prevented her from triggering the Brexit process without parliamentary approval. Online petitions are another example how individuals can use the internet to express their views collectively. In the UK, for instance, anyone can start an online parliamentary petition that will receive a guaranteed government response if it attracts 10,000 signatures and will be considered for debate in Parliament at 100,000 signatures (UK Parliament 2023). Even though physical petitions are possible as well, online initiatives reduce access costs and increase the reach of petitions. The European Union (EU) Commission and the European Parliament, too, both have online-based public consultation systems (the 'Your Voice in Europe' platform and the 'European Parliament Petitions Portal') allowing citizens from across the EU to express their views (Nielsen et al. 2020: 340)

In general, sharing (political and other) content online has become easy for individuals since smartphones became widespread. According to the Oxford Internet Survey (a representative study of the internet access and use by the population of the UK), in 2019, 86 per cent of the British public sent videos or photos online to others and 77 per cent posted their own videos and photos online (Dutton 2023: 87). In contrast, someone without internet access is limited in their exercise of free speech to speaking in public to those who are present in any given situation – in private venues, at town hall meetings, or at places such as Hyde Park's Speakers' Corner.⁴ They might also try to send their written opinions to a newspaper in the hope that these are printed. Alternatively, they can create a citizens' radio broadcast in the hope that those within broadcasting range will listen to their contribution.⁵ But all these offline options remain much more limited in their reach and involve more costs than the options that the internet provides. The costs to be considered for the

---

3   Donald Trump, for instance, before he was banned from the service, used Twitter as his main way of communicating with his voters. But government institutions at all levels are now regularly using social media to communicate with their citizens, especially if information is time-sensitive (e.g. real-time information about ongoing public security or health dangers).
4   Unless, of course, their speech is reported by other mass media such as newspapers or television. However, this is rarely the case for people who do not fulfil official roles or functions.
5   The reach of radio stations has become greatly extended as their programmes are streamed online. However, a person's opportunities to have their voice heard via radio broadcasts streamed online itself depends on others having internet access.

comparison between offline and online ways of exercising the right to free speech are not limited to monetary costs. Instead, there are also opportunity costs attached to speaking offline, such as time and effort. For instance, it is not only more expensive to print physical pamphlets, but it also takes more time and effort to distribute them in person in a busy public street than to post messages in local public online forums. Comparatively limited offline opportunities to express our political views are acceptable if they apply to everyone. More generally, opportunities to exercise free speech are always unequally distributed because politicians have more opportunities to make their views heard (indeed, that is part of their job). This is acceptable, though, when everyone has equal opportunities to run for public office. It is therefore not the comparatively limited nature of offline opportunities to exercise free speech as such that is problematic.

A problem occurs when some or many suddenly have many more opportunities to speak freely and publicly than others. The introduction of the internet creates such a situation between those who can access this global medium and those who cannot. This is not a side effect of the internet but a necessary result of its nature and purpose, which is to provide additional and more effective ways of communicating. Once the internet becomes widespread, given our socio-economic order that allows for poverty, there are some who would like to use it but who are unable to afford access. From their perspective, the internet has devalued their right to free speech because they have relatively fewer opportunities to make use of it than those who can afford to buy internet access. From a human rights perspective, this is a serious problem because, if political freedoms are to be effective in empowering everyone, all individual members of a community must have adequate opportunities to exercise them. Adequate opportunities to speak freely publicly exist in offline societies in which everyone can effectively exercise their fundamental political freedoms. But opportunities become inadequate for those who do not have internet access once this medium becomes widely available in society.

A controlled and randomised experiment that tested to what extent internet access contributes to free speech found that those without online access are considerably limited in the expression of their views (Shandler et al. 2020). For this experiment, which took place in a university library, researchers assigned several tasks that simulated various political activities to two groups of participants. The goal with respect to the exercise of free speech was to 'express your opinion on a social or political issue such that it reaches a wide audience' (Shandler et al. 2020: 623). Crucially, only members of one group were allowed to use the internet for the completion of this task. The researchers found that 'in the Internet access (control) condition, 61% of participants were able to successfully engage in expression, compared to only 29% in the no Internet access (treatment) condition' (Shandler et al. 2020: 624). Participants with internet access were therefore more than twice as likely to make effective use of their freedom of expression than their counterparts. Even though it would seem difficult to generalise these results to all social contexts, this experiment's outcomes are plausible considering the reduction in various kinds of costs for voicing our opinion publicly that the internet offers. The worth of this freedom for those who do not have internet access is accordingly much reduced because they lack comparable means for exercising the right. This significant reduction in the effectiveness of offline free speech compared with online free speech therefore demonstrates that having internet access today is practically indispensable for having adequate opportunities to exercise our freedom of opinion and expression. Offline opportunities alone are inadequate because they are significantly less efficient than using online means to express our views. Those who have no internet access are excluded from the most common and most effective way in which most people who have internet access express their political opinions today.

Of course, having adequate opportunities to speak publicly does not mean that our attempts to voice our opinion must be hugely impactful. Such impact of the exercise of this right could never be guaranteed owing to the many uncontrollable factors that cause some individual views to garner public attention. Guaranteed impact of free speech would also not be desirable given the vast number of voices that everyone would have to listen to and considering the differential merit of individual opinions. Freedom of speech does not guarantee freedom of reach. Guaranteed effectiveness is desirable and achievable with respect of the exercise of the right to an equal vote, but not concerning the rights to run for public office or free speech. What is important with respect to free speech, though, is that everyone has adequate opportunities to try to generate attention for their views. In our virtual societies, some form of guaranteed and unimpeded internet access arguably is now part of what it takes to secure adequate opportunities for everyone to exercise their right to free speech.

We might think that it is good that some people are less able to express their views because we find these problematic or offensive. However, in a society that secures decent lives for all members, we have to accept that others express views we do not agree with, and we have to ensure everyone (even those whose views we strongly oppose) is given adequate opportunities to voice their opinion. This does not mean, though, that the right to free speech is unlimited. No right is absolute and free speech is no exception. I cannot, for example, run into a cinema and scream 'fire' just for fun because this endangers the safety of others. Similarly, speech that incites violence against people can justifiably be curtailed. Article 19.3 of the International Covenant on Civil and Political Human Rights, for instance, sets out specific reasons for which the exercise of free speech can be legitimately curtailed (UN 1966b). In Chapter 7, we will see that such questions about the justified limits of free expressions online are particularly pressing when it comes to the question of how to limit social media platforms where much political expression takes place today. And in Chapter 8, we will consider how people can be protected from other's abuse of their right to free speech online. However, these thorny questions about the limits of free speech do not undermine the claim that this freedom requires that everyone is given comparatively equivalent opportunities to express their political views. In a society in which the internet is widespread, this includes ensuring some form of online access for everyone.

Crucially, though, internet access is not simply a matter of being able to use our right to free speech more effectively. As ever-more public and political debates are taking place online, having access to the internet is also a matter of having access to the public venues in which public conversations happen. Lack of internet access therefore amounts to exclusion from the essential, virtual parts of the public sphere. This might seem to overstate the importance of the internet because many people do not actively contribute to public debates online or even use the internet. And yet the claim that the online sphere is an essential part of the public sphere has been made by important political institutions such as the US Supreme Court in its 2017 ruling Packingham vs North Carolina. This case assessed a North Carolina law that banned individuals previously accused of sexual offences from accessing social media websites with the intention of protecting children from sexual offences. However, the US Supreme Court ruled that this was unconstitutional because this law 'with one broad stroke bars access to what for many are the principal sources for knowing current events, checking ads for employment, speaking and listening in *the modern public square*, and otherwise exploring the vast realms of human thought and knowledge' (SCOTUS 2017: 8, emphasis added). The court therefore acknowledges that internet access today is required for having adequate opportunities to access the public sphere where we can exercise our right to free speech (see also Jasmontatie and de Hert 2019: 172). Being online is to take part in public life in the digital age. Lack of online access therefore excludes people from being full members of the political community, and such political exclusion is incompatible with leading minimally decent lives.[6]

---

[6] This claim might seem controversial considering that many of the crucial virtual forums that make up the online public sphere today, such as social media platforms, are privately owned

Because the internet provides unparalleled opportunities for free speech, if people can use it without undue restrictions, it can help bring about political change. Speaking out against those in power is a necessary first step to challenge them, and the internet provides unlimited, global, and accessible platforms and spaces for free speech. A global study of the role that internet access played for resistance against political oppression between 1993 and 2013 concludes that the internet was a very effective tool in several ways for enabling political mobilisation in authoritarian states despite attempts of these regimes to control the virtual space:

> First, the internet has lowered the costs and risks for oppositional movements facilitating the organisation of collective oppositional action. Second, the internet can instigate attitudinal change by exposing citizens to alternative information. Third, the internet can push potential protesters into action by removing informational uncertainty; and, fourth, the internet mobilizes by confronting citizens with videos and pictures. (Ruijgrok 2017: 514)

Of course, as discussed earlier, the effectiveness of the internet alone is insufficient to guarantee that democratising efforts are successful. Those who bear responsibilities to protect human rights must play their part as well for this to be the case. Moreover, the internet can only unfold its empowering potential where people can access it largely without undue interference. As we will see in Chapter 6, autocratic regimes have unfortunately found ways to block the exercise of free speech online and, even worse, to use people's online speech against them. However, this does not detract from the fact that internet access structurally provides – if free from arbitrary interference – unparalleled platforms for exercising speech, and in this way can politically empower people.

3.2.2 Internet Access and Freedom of Information

According to the Universal Declaration of Human Rights (UN 1948), the right to free speech entails the freedom 'to seek, receive and impart information and ideas through any media and regardless of frontiers' (§19). Even though this right is normally justified as deriving from the freedom of speech, it is also seen as an important distinctive right, for instance, as a right to access information held by public authorities.

> companies. However, as we will see in Chapter 7, such private ownership does not present a problem as such for the claim that the internet has established a public forum for the formation of a public sphere and public opinions. Rather, private ownership of these platforms calls for appropriate regulation of these businesses to ensure that our virtual public sphere can function in a healthy, empowering way.

The internet enables the exchange of information in an unprecedented way. Before the internet was widespread, the most common sources of information for citizens in democracies were public authorities, the free press, and public libraries. But the internet has made more information accessible easily and cheaply to more people than ever. Those who have access to it have opportunities to 'seek, receive and impart information and ideas' (UN 1948: §19), with a speed, on a scale, and with a range unimaginable some mere decades ago. According to the Oxford Internet Survey, the internet has become the first place for most people to look for information, even though few use the internet exclusively for this purpose. As early as 2013, a majority of British people (including non-users of the internet who asked a relative or friend to search online for them) used the internet to search for information on all topics included in the survey (that included political, educational, work-related, and private matters). Over time, the number of people who predominantly use online resources to obtain information has grown as smartphone use has become more widespread (Dutton 2023: 64–65). Those who remain offline are excluded from these opportunities or are dependent on the help of others. Moreover, public authorities are increasingly moving public information (in particular time-sensitive information) and services online, which disadvantages all those who do not have internet access. In countries such as the US or the UK that no longer have a comprehensive system of physical air raid sirens, government agencies have set up emergency messaging systems via smartphone alerts warning citizens about dangers such as extreme weather or attacks (BBC News 2023, FEMA 2023). Emergency messages are also sent via other media, but the more urgent a warning is, the more likely it is to reach people in time on their switched-on mobile phone rather than a television they might not be watching or a radio they might not be listening to. After the illegal 2022 Russian invasion of Ukraine, for example, the Ukrainian government coordinated the development of a smartphone app used for warning the population about impending Russian attacks. According to one study, alerts via this messaging system reduced civilian casualties by up to 45 per cent during the early stages of the invasion (Van Dijcke et al. 2023). A different study of 3,950 natural disasters in 120 countries between 1980 and 2013 estimates that the use of mobile phones for disseminating public alerts and coordinating recovery efforts has reduced disaster-induced fatalities by nearly 50 per cent, and by up to 69 per cent in cases of geological disasters (Toya and Skidmore 2018).

Democratic institutions have also begun to offer critical political information to voters to make political processes such as elections more inclusive and transparent. In Germany, for instance, the interactive election tool

Wahl-o-Mat (roughly translating to 'vote-o-meter') provided by the Federal Agency of Civic Education enables citizens to test which political party best represents their own opinions and priorities without having to read extensive election campaign programmes (Martin and Chase 2017, BPB 2023). Such tools allow citizens to be better informed and to make better informed political choices. Those without internet access, on the other hand, have to revert to offline options, which minimally involves greater costs in terms of time and effort. Considering the ease with which information is available online, this difference involved in acquiring information offline has become unreasonable and exclusively offline ways to access information inadequate.

In their experiment testing the effects of internet access on political freedoms mentioned earlier, researchers also considered the internet's effects on realising the right to free information. The task set for the two groups here was to 'identify the names of the Members of Parliament who initiated the [Israeli] Anti-Terrorism Law 2016' (Shandler et al. 2020: 623). A total of 71 per cent of those participants allowed to use the internet successfully completed this task but only 44 per cent of those without internet access were able to do so (Shandler et al. 2020: 624). Again, one must be careful not to generalise these findings from a controlled experiment to all conventional contexts. As long as there are printed books and newspapers, public libraries, TV and radio stations, people have other ways of obtaining much of the same information offline as online. However, various kinds of opportunity costs also matter with respect to accessing information offline compared with online: a trip to the library takes longer than opening an internet browser, and reading through party manifestos to identify the part that best represents one's political convictions and goals takes much longer than using an online political information tool such as the Wahl-o-Mat. This is because the internet makes vast amounts of information not only accessible, but also searchable. The increased costs of accessing information offline become less and less a matter of inconvenience but rather a genuine disadvantage the more often important information is made available online. The more opportunity costs are avoided by accessing information online, the more internet access becomes a matter of having adequate opportunities to exercise our right to free information. Where the internet is widespread, it has become an essential medium for public authorities to communicate with their citizens and to provide public information and services. These societies have now arguably reached the point where internet access is required for adequate access to information relevant for the exercise of many of our human rights.

However, the internet does not only increase effective opportunities to receive and send information. Rather, as in the case of free speech, it has also created unique venues in which such information is distributed. Much of today's politically relevant information is shared online and many important political discussions take place online. People with internet access can, for instance, access journalistic reports of political information on demand (e.g. on the websites of public news broadcasters such as the BBC, ZDF, ARD) while those without online access are limited to watching or recording live news. Moreover, a significant amount of in-depth information supplementing broadcasted news is only available via the websites of these broadcasters. Even if we might worry about the quality of online political discourse, those who do not have online access do not even have the opportunity to access the information generated and shared on online platforms and to evaluate it for themselves. The problem, again, is not that everyone wants to make use of their freedom of information online. The point rather is that those without online access have much fewer opportunities to do so should they want to. They are also excluded from information that is only available online. We would not tolerate a society in which the main analogue channels of sharing information (such as radio, TV, telephone, or newspapers) were available only to some parts of the population.[7] Thus, we should not tolerate a society in which some have internet access and others do not. The worth of the right to receive and share information freely is therefore problematically diminished for those who cannot go online. This divides democratic citizens into those who can invest little time, effort, and resources into acquiring and sharing politically relevant information online, and those for whom these costs (in particular the opportunity costs involved in accessing and sharing information offline) are much higher because they do not have internet access. But if we take seriously the idea that to live minimally decent lives people must have adequate opportunities to exercise their political freedoms (such as their right to access information freely), a situation in which some can access and search the internet and some cannot is unjustifiable. Instead, if we want to guarantee adequate access to information to everyone, it must be guaranteed that all citizens have online access.

[7] Some countries provide money to people so they can afford a basic TV service as part of the social minimum welfare payment. In most countries, access to print mass media is available in public libraries. There are more than 320,000 libraries worldwide – most of them in developing and transitioning countries in which internet access is least widespread (Bill & Melinda Gates Foundation 2023). It is plausible to think that one major reason for the decline of public libraries in developed countries is that information traditionally accessible only in public libraries is now available online and internet access is already very widespread in these countries. However, the decrease of public libraries in developing countries puts those who remain offline in these societies in a particularly difficult situation as they also have fewer opportunities to access information via libraries.

3.2.3 Internet Access and Freedom of Assembly

A parallel case for the human right to free internet access can be made considering its effects on the human right to free assembly. The internet has created unprecedented possibilities for joining others for common purposes. Social media platforms, for instance, allow people to create common interest groups and to associate with other people around the world in a way unimaginable before the creation of the World Wide Web. But joining a Facebook group dedicated to the cuteness of kittens is, morally speaking, the equivalent of online shopping: it is fun and interesting for many but not part of minimally decent human lives. The moral importance of the internet rather lies in the way it enables political association and mobilisation.

Politically, it is undoubtedly of vital importance that people can join others to promote a common political cause. Joining others for common causes is normally the most effective way to influence the fundamental rules of society, and common action is the best way of promoting our interests and protecting our rights. Effective free collective political action is only possible in democratic regimes because only these have the accountability structures required for public political action to have guaranteed political consequences. Today, the possibilities for engaging in these political liberties are heavily mediated by whether people have online access. This is also shown by the experiment that has already been mentioned, in which two groups of participants were asked to complete tasks that simulated the exercise of political freedoms but where only one group was allowed to use the internet to complete these tasks. The objective given to the participants that simulated the exercise of free assembly was to 'ascertain the topic and content of the viral political campaign organized by the non-governmental Israeli Democracy Institute that is running under the tagline: "There is No Such Thing as That"' (Shandler et al. 2020: 623). The result of this experiment was that 93 per cent of the group with internet access were successful in reaching their goal while only 47 per cent of those unable to use the internet succeeded at the same task (Shandler et al. 2020: 624). In the controlled environment of this experiment, people's opportunities to exercise their right to free assembly was therefore significantly influenced by whether they had access to the internet.

The importance of internet access for our freedom of association might be less obvious in domestic politics where people regularly come together at party meetings and conferences, where political information is still often received via analogue mass media, and where in-person demonstrations to promote political causes are normal. However, this is different with respect to international political matters. The problem in the international sphere is that there are few political institutions that allow for direct political representation and accountability. Those whose democratic government is involved in the steering of global governance institutions such as the World Trade Organization (WTO), the UN, the International Monetary Fund (IMF), or the World Bank might be said to have a certain indirect influence on these institutions. But this is really only the case for citizens of the most powerful democratic nations, and even their governments can only influence the operations of these institutions together with other governments. The undemocratic nature of these institutions, though, is problematic from the perspective of justice and political human rights. To see this issue, we have to consider the importance of being able to influence fundamental political rules.

We have essential political freedoms because, as healthy human adults, we can form our own views about what is right and good in life, and we are capable of pursuing these interests in a way that respects the equal autonomy of others. As we saw in Chapter 1, respect for our normative agency is one necessary element of living minimally good lives. What is important is that we can only really exercise our autonomy and pursue our aims within our social environment. This social environment is fundamentally shaped by coercively enforced laws. If we do not have a meaningful way to influence the making and shaping of the basic rules that we have to live by, we are unjustly dominated by those who impose these rules on us without our say. This domination is based on unevenly distributed social power in which one party can arbitrarily and for no good reason force another to do what they want. Characteristically, the dominant party imposes their will on the dominated one without considering, or showing respect for, the interests of the coerced party (Pettit 2010). This arbitrary exercise of power violates our very normative agency. Countless revolutions, wars of independence, and social conflicts have been fought against various forms of political domination. Democratic institutions, on the other hand, are designed to give members of a political community the chance to influence the fundamental rules they live by, to hold those who enforce rules of them to account, and to exchange their leaders peacefully.

The problem in the international sphere is that such democratic representation and accountability is lacking even though many of the most fundamental decisions that affect all of us are made at this level. Global governance institutions such as the World Bank and the IMF can practically enforce economic policy on countries dependent on the financial support of these institutions. The UN Security Council can declare the national sovereignty of a country void and legitimise external interventions. And WTO rules dictate how states can trade with one another. Membership in these institutions is formally voluntary, but effectively states have no alternative to membership if they are to survive in our world of states. Moreover, democratic states are not always transparent with respect to the aims they pursue in international negotiations, nor are they always responsive to the political preferences of their populations. Instead, the influence of corporate lobbyism and global power dynamics often shape their decisions in the international sphere. Finally, globally operating corporations are themselves major global players which have enormous political clout. They can use the threat of withholding financial investments and relocating jobs to pressure states into adopting laws and policies favourable to their pursuit of profit. In this way corporations can influence the laws of states they operate in while they are only directly accountable to their owners. This explains why the lack of global structures of popular representation and accountability is a problem of justice. The current lack of effective official international political structures to hold key global players to account is difficult to reconcile with the idea that we are autonomous beings who should have a meaningful influence on the fundamental rules that determine how we can live our lives.

There is a lively philosophical debate as to whether this problem demands a resolution in the form of adopting global democratic institutions (Pettit 2010, Valentini 2014, Lu 2021). But whether or not we think that it does, it is extremely unlikely that such structures and processes will come about any time soon, or that even if they would be created these would not be hijacked or unduly dominated by undemocratic global forces, such as vast global economic interests. In the present international context, though, internet access is indispensable for political association and mobilisation in the global political sphere. The internet is indispensable here because it is only in the virtual space that people can internationally collectively organise and inform themselves to try to influence those global players that determine the fundamental global political laws and politics. An early example of the crucial role of the internet in organising international political movements were the 1999 protests against the World Trade Organization summit in Seattle. Those opposing the power and decisions on global trade of this global governance institution used the internet to share information, discuss their aims, and to coordinate their protests internationally (Eagleton-Pierce 2001).

Another example of the indispensability of the internet for joint international political action is the EU-wide protests against the European and American negotiation of the Transatlantic Trade and Investment Partnership (TTIP) between 2013 and 2016. The treaty was opposed by many European citizens, unions, NGOs, and civil society groups, who objected to the secrecy of the negotiations, the intended use of investor–state dispute settlement courts, and proposed changes to workers' rights, environmental protection, and food safety standards. Protest took the form of rallies of hundreds of thousands of individuals, but information about TTIP was shared via the internet. The 'STOP TTIP' campaign (an alliance of 500 European organisations), for instance, consisted of an online European Citizens' Initiative that collected over 3 million signatures. The protest put enormous pressure on the EU and national governments to uphold EU standards in these negotiations, which were extended and then halted by President Trump. Protest against TTIP could have been possible offline, but it is reasonable to suggest that the costs of informing individual citizens offline (i.e. via leaflets, radio and television messages) would have significantly restricted the campaign. Information sharing, protest coordination, and direct forms of protest online on this scale, at this speed, and with this force was only possible because many EU citizens had access to the internet.

A different case that shows that the internet is essential for international political action in the absence of international democratic structures is online campaigns against global corporations. To recall, these companies are directly accountable mostly to their owners and they can shape the legal environment of the states in which they operate owing to their enormous economic power. But these corporations can be influenced indirectly by affecting the thing they care about the most: making a profit. The internet provides unprecedented ways for customers, employees, and others affected by the operations of these global corporations effectively to hold accountable these global players. An example of such online coordinated action is the case of Nestlé versus the Ethiopian government in 2002. The multinational demanded USD $6 million in compensation for the nationalisation of a company by a previous Ethiopian military government in 1986. After being inundated with thousands of emails in response to an Oxfam report on Nestlé's claim, the multinational withdrew its demands, and in 2003 accepted the USD $1.5 million that Ethiopia offered, which Nestlé subsequently invested in three charitable projects in Ethiopia. Similarly effective was the international protest organised by Greenpeace in 2010 against Nestlé/KitKat's use of palm oil and the destruction of rainforest. The campaign video was watched over 1.5 million times and more than 200,000 emails were sent. Nestlé/KitKat ultimately agreed to use rainforest-sustainable palm oil. A final example is the 2014 case of Greenpeace lobbying LEGO to stop distributing its products at Shell petrol stations. Key were a Twitter campaign, a YouTube video (viewed over 6 million times) and over 1 million protest emails, resulting in LEGO not renewing its contract with Shell. Campaigns like this are becoming standard and more effective. As researchers of online campaigns assert, 'online protests do hurt. Firms can expect to suffer financial, reputational, and sales damages when an online protest campaign mobilizes consumers successfully' (Van den Broek et al. 2017: 279).

Not all online movements and campaigns to influence global governance institutions, states, and global corporations are successful. Neither do online campaigns eliminate the need to develop more direct mechanisms of international political participation and accountability that can exert effective control over powerful international agents that set the fundamental rules we all must live by. However, considering the current state of the world, internet access is the only meaningful way for individual citizens to join others to try to exert some control and force some accountability on many international agents and processes. In the international political arena, internet access is therefore practically indispensable for having any sort of meaningful opportunities to exercise our freedom of assembly. Moreover, if new international democratic institutions were to come about, it is unlikely they could have meaningful democratic participation without the possibilities that the internet provides. This is shown by the example of the EU.

The EU to date is the only effective international democratic institution ever created. It has elements of direct democratic authorisation, such as the elections of its law-making body, the European Parliament, as well as pathways of indirect democratic control, such as the influence that governments of democratic member states exert on the EU's agenda-setting body, the European Commission. However, the EU lacks an effective pan-European 'demos' because political publics largely exist only within each member state's own democratic sphere. The EU also lacks ways for political participation comparable to those in member states because there are no pan-European parties to join and no pan-European platforms that would allow all EU citizens to discuss political matters. One obvious obstacle to a pan-European public and political participation is the twenty-four official languages spoken within the union, which impede communication among those who do not speak the same language. Another issue is the complex system of European multi-level governance in which some laws operate at the EU-level while others can only be influenced at the domestic level (Nielsen et al. 2020: 334–336). To enable European political participation and input from citizens, the EU has created an online-based civic agenda-setting mechanism, the use of which obviously presupposes internet access. The European Citizens' Initiative is an attempt to promote participatory democracy. Using this mechanism, citizens can jointly try to influence the agenda of the European Commission by calling upon the Commission to start legal initiatives. If proposals attract the online signatures of 1 million citizens, a binding vote on the suggested proposals is required.

The problem with this international, online-based collective action platform is that it has so far not greatly promoted political engagement and mobilisation within the EU. Relatively few proposals have been made and even fewer accepted. A good deal of knowledge about EU structures and processes is required for campaigns to be successful, as is the ability to coordinate large-scale civic initiatives via this specialised participation mechanism. This is why this online participation tool 'favours organized interests over individual citizens' (Nielsen et al. 2020: 338) and has not led to greater involvement of citizens in EU political processes. In fact, there are worries that the failure of online processes such as the European Citizens Initiative could have detrimental effects for democracy in the EU as citizens see their concerns about a lack of effective participation in EU politics confirmed (Nielsen et al. 2020: 240). However, the problems of this particular mechanism and other forms of 'e-democracy' should not be taken to show that online association and political engagement are necessarily ineffective. Rather, it has been pointed out that the basic failure of many attempts of democratic institutions to use online tools to promote political participation and engagement is that they do not make use of the genuinely novel possibilities of this medium. As researchers such as Hennen (2020) and Bastick (2017) have pointed out, the main problem with current uses of the internet to promote joint political action is that these initiatives mostly attempt to use online processes to replicate existing offline processes or to make these more efficient. Online petition portals, social media presences of political parties, and digital communication and consultation tools for public administrations do not change how political processes work (Bastick 2017: 10).

More generally, there are several hurdles that can prevent political group engagement online from effecting change and supporting democratisation. Collective online action might, for example, only be short-lived or unable to engage with political institutions in a sustained and competent way. Moreover, political online campaigns might not really permit people to play an active role but only use internet platforms to gather data about supporters (Benkler et al. 2018: 341–346). However, these pitfalls are not unavoidable for collective political online initiatives. This is demonstrated by the example of new, online-based forms of political engagement such as the Australian online movement platform GetUp!, which was founded in 2005. GetUp! promotes political initiatives by providing ways for citizens to contact their representatives to enable ongoing political engagement, rather than one-off participation in political protests in 2018, the GetUp! movement had more than 1 million members (more than all Australian political parties combined). It has influenced the outcome of national elections, has won a landmark ruling in

Australia's highest court promoting voting rights, and has helped to pass legislation protecting refugees and the environment (Timms and Heimans 2018: 55–58). The key idea behind GetUp! is to provide a forum through which individuals can engage with political initiatives and movements spontaneously and interactively.

But online movements and coalitions can also form around specific issues and on a temporary basis without requiring a long-standing commitment or agreement on a wide range of issues. That such temporary and flexible political online associations can be highly effective is shown by the example of Beatriz Ehlers, a student of the municipal Friedenreich School in Rio de Janeiro, who successfully organised a protest against the city's government. The school, which serves underprivileged and disabled students, was selected for demolition by the city government to make space for sporting venues for the Rio Summer Olympics 2016. To protect her school, Ehlers used an online tool called Panela de Pressão (pressure cooker) that enables citizens to identify and lobby political decision-makers. Thousands signed up, and the local government reversed its plans to demolish the building within seventy-two hours of the website's launch (Timms and Heimans 2018: 74–75). These examples also demonstrate that the internet is relevant for political association within the domestic political sphere, and not just with respect to international political matters.

In fact, the examples that we have previously discussed to illustrate how internet access can protect human rights to basic security are also examples of the effective political use of the internet to exercise our human right to associate with others. Black Lives Matter and #MeToo are social movements that have been highly effective in achieving many of their goals. They are predominantly one-issue movements joined by people from a great variety of backgrounds who might not easily fit under the roof of a particular political party that requires a commitment to a broader suite of values and objectives. These movements are all promoted and coordinated online. They show that those without internet access are excluded from new ways to engage effectively in joint political action. Because of the importance and impact that such movements can have, digital exclusion today means that those excluded do not have adequate opportunities to make use of their human right to free assembly compared with those who have internet access. Those who are digitally excluded often also face other disadvantages (such as poverty, unequal social and economic opportunities, or social isolation). The fact that they are deprived of effective virtual platforms that they could use to highlight their plight and to promote their interests is therefore a case of compounded disadvantage (Wolff and de-Shalit 2007): the disadvantage of a lack of access to the internet leads to a lack of opportunities to make others aware of, and to try to change, other disadvantages they suffer from. In other words, internet access today is practically indispensable for adequate opportunities to freely associate with others for political purposes.[8]

3.2.4 Summary: Internet Access and Political Human Rights

To summarise this section, there are two steps that lead from the importance of political liberties to the idea of a human right to free internet access.

First, the internet has created new opportunities to exercise our political human rights effectively. Internet access matters because it generally affects the worth and the opportunities individuals have for making use of their political freedoms. Those with online access enjoy many more and more effective ways to speak freely, associate with others, and to access information. Those without such access are importantly excluded from these virtual options and essential parts of the (virtual) public forums where information is shared and political influence created.

Second, if we take seriously the importance of political freedoms, it would be inconsistent to be indifferent about the kind of opportunities that we have to use these liberties. If some have many more or better opportunities than others this undermines the very idea that everyone should have adequate guaranteed options to enjoy and use their human rights. Not having internet access excludes people from important and powerful opportunities and from political venues. Not having internet access is therefore an unjust form of political exclusion. For this reason, internet access should be recognised as a human right. Without it, people do not have adequate options for exercising and protecting their political human rights, which are crucial elements of living minimally good lives.

---

[8] A lot could be said about the importance that the internet acquired for the exercise of political human rights during the lockdowns to curb the COVID-19 pandemic. During these times of emergency, when essential human rights were temporarily restricted with the overriding goal of saving vast numbers of lives, the internet provided a virtual back-up infrastructure. It was only because of this that locked-down citizens could publicly exercise their human rights to free speech, free assembly, free information, freedom of worship, and others. Our reliance on the internet during this pandemic has also accelerated its use for everyday activities. However, because the COVID-19 pandemic was an exceptional situation, the argument for a human right to internet access does not rely on the usefulness of the internet during these times. Rather, the argument builds on the practical indispensability the internet has acquired for everyone during normal times. For similar reasons, we will also not discuss the undoubted usefulness that the internet has for the exercise of human rights for particular groups, such as people with disabilities (for more on this see, e.g. Jaeger 2022; de Vries 2022).

A critic might object that it is rather unlikely that our individual online exercises of free speech attract a sizable audience, that we find the information we want online (or are not misled or confused by the vast information that can be found online), or that we can identify others with whom effectively to associate online. It might therefore seem that the effectiveness of internet access is overstated. However, this ignores that the individual exercise of most political freedoms often does not have an enormous effect on the world. Individual votes, for instance, are normally unlikely to have significant weight in large-scale elections, offline expressions of free speech do not often attract massive audiences, and collective political action does not always succeed in the offline world either. What matters from the perspective of justice, though, is that everyone has the freedom to try to use their human rights to good effect and is given a fair chance of success – no matter how small that may be. It is therefore the importance of having opportunities to gain political influence and for advancing our interests, and not the actual effectiveness of the exercise of political freedoms, that justifies these rights. And such adequate opportunities are no longer to be had in the offline world alone.

Based on the examples of the internet's usefulness for many civil and political human rights that we studied in this chapter, we can now spell out in detail the formal argument for the human right to free internet access:

Premise 1: Everyone has civil and political human rights (such as the rights to free speech, free information, free assembly, to security of person, and to equality before the law).

Premise 2: Everyone must have adequate opportunities to enjoy their civil and political human rights.

Premise 3: Internet access is in practice necessary (i.e. practically and systemically indispensable) for having adequate opportunities to exercise or enjoy many of our civil and political human rights.

Premise 4: Following a 'principle of rationality' (Nickel 2022: 31), if we endorse an end (i.e. civil and political human rights), we have very strong or good reasons also to endorse those things and means that are necessary to achieve or realise that end (i.e. a human right to free internet access).

Conclusion: Insofar as and because internet access is practically and systemically indispensable for having adequate opportunities to exercise or enjoy many of our civil and political human rights, we have very strong reasons to accept a human right to internet access.

To put this into the terms of the explanations of human rights that we considered in Chapter 1, internet access is properly a human right because it is practically and systemically indispensable for many conditions of minimally decent lives, namely for our civil and political human rights. That is true for people wherever the internet has become widespread enough that not having access to it puts a person at a morally problematic disadvantage to exercise their civil and political human rights. This also means that internet access has become morally urgent enough for people everywhere to be considered a proper matter of international concern. As such, public institutions should accept certain negative and positive obligations to ensure and protect internet access, which Part II of this book will spell out.[9] The basic argument, though, is that because civil and political human rights are necessary conditions of minimally good lives today, and because internet access is indispensable for having adequate opportunities to enjoy these human rights, it should itself be recognised as a human right.

If we accept this line of reasoning, this is sufficient for justifying the claim that public authorities should recognise a human right of everyone to access the internet freely. However, the unique practical value of the internet is not limited to our civil and political human rights. Rather, online access has also become crucial for another set of rights, our socio-economic human rights. In Chapter 4, we will therefore consider the internet's effects on these important rights. This will be relevant for getting a more complete picture of the positive power of the internet. Doing so also provides crucial additional support for the claim that internet access should be a human right.

3.3 WHY DO WE NEED A NEW AND DISTINCT RIGHT AT ALL?

Before we consider the internet's indispensable value for socio-economic human rights, though, it is important to address a significant objection against the claim that public authorities should recognise a novel human right to internet access. According to this criticism, we might think that such a new and distinct right is unnecessary because internet access can be guaranteed simply by properly protecting existing rights, such as free speech. The point here is that a guarantee to internet access can be subsumed under, or included in, the right to free speech because free speech today requires internet access – as the right to a free press is subsumed under the right to free expression. Such inclusion of guaranteed internet access in existing human rights might be desirable

---

[9] These two related reasons follow the reasoning of both moral/naturalistic and political philosophical conceptions of human rights. Morally, internet access is a vital universal moral interest of all persons and, politically, this urgent interest is properly conceived of as a matter of international concern that implies obligations for states and the international community of states (Liao and Etinson 2012).

because it would prevent concerns about an inflation or broadening of the list of human rights from occurring in the first place. Inclusion in existing rights, rather than the creation of a new one, might therefore be seen as the proper way to deal with the importance of internet access. However, there are several reasons against subsuming internet access under existing human rights and in favour of creating a new right. One of them is theoretical, one strategic, and some are practical.

First, theoretically, subsuming internet access under existing human rights might not be as straightforward as it may appear. What is fact is that Article 19(2) of the International Covenant on Civil and Political Human Rights (ICCPR) states that 'Everyone shall have the right to freedom of expression; this right shall include freedom to seek, receive and impart information and ideas of all kinds, regardless of frontiers, either orally, in writing or in print, in the form of art, or through any other media of his choice' (UN 1966b). The reference to 'any media' clearly indicates the forward-thinking nature of this right that is meant to apply to new media, such as the internet, as well. Free speech should be guaranteed on the internet in the sense that people should not be prevented from expressing their views online as well as offline. However, it is not clear that Article 19(2) also implies that people must be guaranteed internet access to express their views online. Put differently, Article 19(2) does not clarify whether it obligates public authorities merely not to interfere with people expressing themselves on the internet or whether they also have to provide internet access for those who do not have it so they can then use it to speak freely online. The UN Human Right Council's interpretation of this article, though, shows a clear inclination to interpret the right to free speech with respect to the internet primarily negatively, that is to say, to demand that states abstain from interfering with the online speech of those who have internet access. In its much-discussed non-binding resolution from 2016, the Council demands that 'rights that people have offline must also be protected online' (UN 2016: 2). However, limiting free speech on the internet to non-interference significantly limits the value that this right has for those who do not currently have internet access. To be sure, the UN Special Rapporteur on the Promotion and Protection of the Right to Freedom of Opinion and Expression already in 2011 reminded states 'of their positive obligation to promote or to facilitate the enjoyment of the right to freedom of expression and the means necessary to exercise this right, including the Internet' (UN 2011a: 19). However, these duties are not framed as corresponding to a claimable entitlement of people that states should provide as a matter of priority but rather as a matter of 'good policy to realise freedom of expression' (Çalı 2020: 280). This means the UN have not recognised a clear positive duty to provide internet access as a definite necessity for all people as part of the human right to freedom of expression (see also Shandler and Canetti 2019: 92). Considering that the UN has acknowledged the importance of internet access for free speech, it is reasonable to assume that it would also have endorsed a clear entitlement to internet access for all persons if this would be recognisable as a straightforward aspect entailed by that right. The recognition of an independent, stand-alone human right to internet access would sidestep debates about whether online access is implied by or entailed by existing human rights such as free speech.

Second, though, even if a universal entitlement to internet access would be clearly included in the human right to free speech, we have reasons not to make a right to internet access dependent on this right alone (or to any other single right, e.g. the human right to free assembly, see Skepys 2012) for strategic reasons. This is because hardly any right, also not the right to free speech, is absolute so that it cannot be restricted for some important reason. Article 19(3) of the ICCPR allows that free expression can be justly limited if such limitations are provided by law and necessary for achieving some important goal such as the protections of the rights of others or of national security, public health, or public order.[10] Even though restrictions on free speech are rarely permitted in the US as almost all speech is protected by the First Amendment to the US Constitution, other political authorities such as the European Court of Human Rights take a different view. For the European Court, the internet has not simply enhanced opportunities for free speech but with these also produced more opportunities to violate the fundamental rights of others by using the internet – for example, by causing harm through defamation or extreme speech, or disseminating false information that threatens public health (e.g. false information about COVID-19) or public order (e.g. false information about election processes). It therefore has argued that the internet makes it necessary to think more often about restrictions of free speech to account for the increased harmful potential effects of online communications (Pollicino 2020: 272–273). But if internet access is entailed by, and depends on, any single right, such as freedom of speech, and this right can be legitimately restricted in an increasing number of cases, this consequently weakens the protections and guarantees of internet access that this single right can offer. In fact, as the non-profit organisation Access Now shows in its annual 'Keep It On' reports, governments around the world regularly and increasingly shut down internet

---

[10] We will return to these limitations permitted by Article 19(3) of the ICCPR in Chapter 7 when considering for what reasons social media companies can legitimately block or take down content or speech of users of social media platforms.

access regionally or even nationally with the justification that such steps are needed to curb the spread of 'fake news' or other online misinformation (Access Now 2023). If public authorities were to recognise an independent, stand-alone human right to internet access based on its practical and systemic indispensability for many other human rights, this would make it harder for governments to justify such restrictions of online access. This is because the supposed benefits of restricting or preventing internet access would have to outweigh the costs of limiting not simply one human right (e.g. free speech) but the costs of curtailing many human rights for which internet access has become indispensable (e.g. as shown in this chapter, civil and political human rights). This therefore increases the argumentative burden of proof that public authorities would have to meet to be able to claim that restrictions on internet access are justified because they are necessary and proportionate to the costs they impose on people.

Third, practically, including the right to internet access in (or subsuming it under) any particular human right would be inappropriate because, as we have seen in this chapter, internet access is always practically indispensable for the enjoyment of a multitude of human activities and rights. Here we have considered its practical value for civil and political human rights. Chapter 4 will do the same with respect to socio-economic human rights. What both chapters point to is the fact that the internet has become a crucial gateway technology that profoundly affects all aspects of human life. By 'gateway technology' I mean a technology (e.g. the written word, electricity, printing press, computers) that is a necessary requirement for a multitude of new activities and opportunities based on that technology. Those who can access this gateway have significant and morally problematic advantages over those who cannot. At a basic structural level, it is not surprising that the internet impacts most human rights and aspects of life. After all, human beings require information for everything we do. To think, to make choices, to have beliefs, to act beyond instinct, to learn – we need information. The entire point of the internet is to make it easier to access and send information. The internet therefore affects how we can use our human rights and live as individuals and groups in digitalised societies. Digital technologies have made possible the creation and use of innumerable innovations that have enhanced our opportunities and activities. Just in this chapter we have seen that the internet makes it possible to share information instantaneously and widely, and so can, for example, contribute to better holding those to account who violate rights, to avoiding places of danger, to communicating and coordinating actions internationally, and to obtaining an unprecedented amount of information. Looking to the future, technologies that are currently under development (such as large language modules-based artificial intelligence including OpenAI's ChatGPT or Microsoft's Bing) are expected to fundamentally change essential aspects of human life such as work and creative activities. However, only those who have internet access even have a chance to engage with and to keep up with these developments. The importance of internet access can therefore not appropriately be reduced to its usefulness for any individual human right. Rather, the internet has become the currently essential gateway for the receiving and sending of information that underpins most aspects of human existence and all human rights. As Jeroen van den Hoven (2009) has argued, opportunities to access information are a matter of basic distributive justice.[11] By extension, internet access is a matter of global basic distributive justice and adequate opportunities to access information. Internet access is therefore properly conceived of as a stand-alone human right and an essential element of any theory of justice that does not ignore the essential importance of information for human beings.

Another way to make this point that the internet is a gateway technology is to draw an analogy with the human right to literacy. As mentioned in Chapter 2, literacy is an indispensable tool for education and therefore justifiably based on its instrumental value for other human rights (UNESCO 1997). However, we can also understand literacy in another way, namely, as providing entry for those who are literate to an important plane of social reality. In this way, internet access is valuable in itself, rather than for other things such as other human rights. Those who can read have access to what people have put for millennia in writing. People who are illiterate therefore not only have problematically limited opportunities to exercise human rights such as education and freedom of information. Rather, they are dependent on others to help them access all the knowledge, ideas, thoughts, and imagination that people have written down. Excluding people from all this information is deeply problematic because their dependency on others is avoidable and unjustifiable. Analogously, excluding those who remain offline from communicating, acting, and accessing information online means unjustly denying them entry into the part of social reality that exists in cyberspace, which is growing in importance every day. Moreover, as the US Supreme Court ruling referred to earlier shows, being online means being in the modern (online) public square. This is to say that being able to go online has become

---

[11] To be precise, van den Hoven argues that the freedom of information is a basic liberty, and access to information should be considered a social primary good whose distribution should be subject to requirements of equality of opportunity, within the framework of John Rawls's theory of justice. I thank Philip Brey for this reference.

a condition of being able to participate in an essential area of public life. Such participation in public life, though, is politically essential for respecting people's equal moral status and, for that matter, the ability to participate online is a demand of fundamental justice. If we accept these analogies between literacy and internet access and between cyberspace and the public square, we do not even have to employ a linkage argument to justify internet access as a human right. That is because internet access is not only instrumentally valuable for the exercise of other human rights. Rather, it is directly indispensable for, and a part of, gaining access so something of great moral importance, namely the sphere of human life and existence that happens online.

Fourth and finally, also from a practical perspective, accepting a standalone human right to free internet access also allows for the straightforward recognition of distinctive, derivative rights related to the provision and protection of internet access. To draw an analogy, as we saw in Chapter 2, one of the reasons for having a distinctive human right to a free press is that this right in turn justifies derivative professional rights of its own, such as the rights of journalists to protect their sources. The human right to free internet access can operate in the same fashion. There are many institutions involved in providing us with internet access. Among them are internet backbone cable operators, internet service providers, and internet applications and service providers such as Apple, Facebook, and Google. As we will see in Chapter 6, many of those involved in providing internet access have come under pressure to yield personal information about their users to governments. Many of these application and service providers currently themselves do not respect their customers' rights appropriately (e.g. to privacy, see Chapter 7). However, if they were to respect, and to be given fiduciary obligations and privileges concerning, their users' rights, these internet companies could play an important role in protecting their clients from undue incursions by powerful agents such as governments. Recognising a human right to free internet access can provide a clear way of justifying rights on the part of digital service providers to protect the online activities of their users from unjustifiable state control. Assigning professional rights to those involved in the provision of internet access and applications would therefore add an additional layer of protection for internet users. Such special, derivative professional rights of those involved in our internet access, though, are most easily tied to an independent right to internet access. This is because the threats that these professional right-holders are to protect their clients from are specifically related to interferences with internet access that affect a multitude of human rights rather than to interference with any single human right alone (e.g. free speech or privacy).

There are therefore many reasons why public authorities should accept a stand-alone human right to internet access rather than to subsume internet access as an entitlement to any single human right – even if such inclusion in another right would be possible. An independent human right to internet access makes it harder to justify restrictions of online access or internet shutdowns. Practically, it would be inappropriate and therefore implausible to make internet access dependent on any particular human right because online access has become relevant or indispensable for most aspects of life and most human rights. Chapter 4 will demonstrate this polyvalent practical indispensability of internet access with respect to socio-economic human rights.

4

Internet Access and Socio-economic Human Rights

In Chapter 3, we saw that a human right to internet access is justifiable because of the internet's crucial role in ensuring adequate opportunities for everyone to exercise and protect their civil and political freedoms. We found that internet access is practically indispensable for the fair worth of particular rights such as free speech, free assembly, free information, and the security of person. Additionally, we saw that online access is systemically indispensable for civil and political human rights: it is not simply a tool for promoting one or a few of these rights, but rather the means for realising many interdependent human rights simultaneously. This chapter will strengthen the case for the argument for a human right to free internet access by providing additional empirical support for

> Premise 3: Internet access is in practice necessary for having adequate opportunities to exercise or enjoy many human rights.

It does so by establishing a parallel case to the one we encountered in Chapter 3, but with respect to another group of human rights. As we will see, internet access today has also become pragmatically necessary for our socio-economic human rights. More precisely, universal online access is a practically necessary condition of adequate opportunities to enjoy and make use of these human rights. Demonstrating the indispensability of the internet for socio-economic human rights provides more reasons for the argument of this book that public institutions should accept and implement a human right to free internet access. Ultimately, we will see that lack of online access not only causes political exclusion (as seen in Chapter 3), but also leads to unjust social and economic disadvantages. This means that in our increasingly digitalised societies, social and economic inclusion requires internet access.

This chapter proceeds in a similar fashion to Chapter 3. The goal, again, is to provide examples that show that a human right to internet access is justifiable through linkage arguments owing to its practical value for supporting other well-established (socio-economic) human rights. After a brief explanation of socio-economic human rights and their importance, we will first consider how internet access has affected opportunities to enjoy and promote these rights in developed societies where many people can go online. Subsequently, we will see that the internet also offers novel opportunities to promote socio-economic human rights in developing countries. This distinction is relevant because both levels of internet penetration and public service provision differ between developed and developing societies. Internet access therefore has different effects on socio-economic human rights in these two types of society. One important conclusion of this chapter will be that, if we are serious about remedying human rights deprivations and poverty in developing affluent societies, we cannot ignore the practical importance that internet access has for promoting human development in developing countries. As with civil and political freedoms, internet access is no cure-all or guarantee that socio-economic deprivation will be overcome. Other factors, such as duty-bearers of human rights willing to fulfil their obligations, also must apply. However, implementing universal internet access presents the most promising way of working to eliminate simultaneously the deprivation of several key human rights.

The chapter therefore provides two additional reasons for accepting a human right to internet access. First, because not doing so would mean wilfully accepting that those who do not have online access suffer social and economic disadvantage and exclusion. And, second, because denying such a human right would be pragmatically inconsistent with the internationally accepted goal of eliminating world poverty. In conjunction with its importance for the enjoyment and protection of civil and political rights, this explanation of the internet's crucial role in the promotion of socio-economic human rights forms the foundation of the moral argument for the human right to free internet access.

4.1 SOCIO-ECONOMIC HUMAN RIGHTS

Socio-economic human rights are so-called second-generation human rights codified in the United Nations (UN) International Covenant on Economic, Social and Cultural Rights (ICESCR, UN 1966a). The reason why they are called second-generation rights is primarily that this set of rights was ratified later than the civil and political first-generation rights of the Universal Declaration of Human Rights (UN 1948). Among the socio-economic rights in the ICESCR that are of particular importance for our argument are:

- the right to work (§6),
- the right to social security and insurance (§9),

- the right to an adequate standard of living, 'including adequate food, clothing and housing, and to the continuous improvement of living conditions' (§11.1),
- the right to 'the enjoyment of the highest attainable standard of physical and mental health' (§12.1),
- the right to education (§13), and
- the right to take part in cultural life (§15.1).

Even though they are called second-generation rights, socio-economic rights are no less important than first-generation civil and political freedoms. What justifies the universal entitlement to the fulfilment of these socio-economic rights and the costs involved in their fulfilment is that they are (in some cases probably even more straightforwardly than political freedoms) essential conditions of minimally decent human lives. If a person has no food and water, they die. If that person does not have access to adequate food and water, their thirst and hunger can lead to malnutrition. This can impede the development of children and generally makes difficult or even impossible the enjoyment of other freedoms. According to Henry Shue (2020: 19), subsistence rights to adequate sustenance, clothing, and shelter are thus 'basic rights'. They are basic in the sense that we need to secure their fulfilment before we can reliably (or at all) enjoy other rights. Subsistence rights share this feature with our right to physical security. Other socio-economic human rights might not be 'basic' in this extreme sense, but are no less essential for leading decent lives. Without social security systems, for instance, people often have to begin contributing to the subsistence of their families as children and work until they are physically or mentally unable to, both of which threaten their personal development and can prevent decent lives. And without basic health care, people are prone to illnesses and short lives as was the case before the discovery of the tools of modern medicine. Back then, if people did not die young, they were at constant risk of becoming ill and suffering the life-long effects of diseases, both of which undermine quality of life. Moreover, without a basic education, people are often unable to make informed life choices, to use existing knowledge for having some control over their lives, and to effectively improve their own situation. Furthermore, if people's ability to participate in the economy is limited, they will have difficulties finding employment or operating a business. This can severely limit how many resources they have available for the enjoyment of many of their other rights. Finally, without being able to take part in cultural life, people are socially excluded from their social community. This kind of exclusion is detrimental for people's quality of life and (as many who are otherwise socially active had to experience during the COVID-19 pandemic lockdowns) mental health.

For these reasons, socio-economic human rights are quite clearly conditions of minimally decent lives. Just as with political human rights, people might well choose not to exercise some of these rights. However, they must have the opportunity to do so to function well in society and as individuals. Socio-economic rights also demonstrate again that many human rights are interdependent: we cannot reliably enjoy some of them (e.g. participation in cultural life) without the fulfilment of others (e.g. an adequate standard of living). This interdependence applies across different generations of human rights as well. For example, it is unlikely that we can use our political rights in an informed way to promote what we think is right and good if we lack the basic education that informs us about our options and rights. The interdependence of rights is of practical importance even though not every right is crucial for the realisation of all other rights. This is because the non-fulfilment of some human rights can have direct and indirect knock-on effects on many other rights that are essential for minimally good lives. For instance, without adequate social insurance and basic health care, a person might struggle to achieve even modest financial freedom because having to pay expensive medical bills does not leave much room for any other goals in life. Other freedoms, such as participating in politics, having a family, or opening one's own business can therefore become quite useless and the possibilities for participation in cultural life extremely limited. The guarantee of socio-economic human rights is thus central for our ability to lead minimally decent lives.

In Section 4.2, we begin our inquiry into how internet access has become practically indispensable for the enjoyment of socio-economic human rights by considering the situation of these rights in the context of developing societies. The point here again is to show that online access has become practically necessary for having *adequate* opportunities to exercise these rights. There is no claim that people must have equal opportunities to make use of socio-economic rights, that people's exercise of them must have equal outcomes, or that there are no offline alternatives to enjoy these rights. Rather, the point to be demonstrated is that those without internet access are unjustly disadvantaged in their enjoyment of socio-economic rights. That is in part because we have fewer options to use our socio-economic rights offline. Moreover, the additional costs in terms of time, effort, and money involved in making use of socio-economic freedoms offline mean that the practical value that these rights have is problematically reduced for us. That is why internet access now is practically and systemically indispensable for us to have adequate options to enjoy socio-economic human rights.

4.2 THE IMPORTANCE OF INTERNET ACCESS FOR SOCIO-ECONOMIC HUMAN RIGHTS IN DEVELOPED COUNTRIES

The reason this chapter distinguishes between the effects of internet access on socio-economic rights in developed versus developing societies is that these effects differ with the levels of internet penetration, economic development, and the provision of public services. In developed countries where there is often a substantial level of universal public services available to people and where the internet is widespread, not having internet access primarily reduces the practical value that socio-economic freedoms have relative to the worth that these rights have for people with internet access. For instance, not having reliable access to the internet makes it more difficult to access public services. In contrast, in developing societies where internet access and public service provision often are much less comprehensive and patchy, having online access can make the difference between enjoying *some* level of public service provision that guarantees socio-economic rights and none at all. This will become clear in Section 4.3.

We begin, though, in the context of developed countries. Even though internet access is rather widely available here, it is by far not ubiquitous or guaranteed for everyone. In the UK, for instance, about 7 per cent of citizens aged sixteen or older had no internet access in their homes in 2023 (Ofcom 2023a: 14). In the US, data from the 2021 census shows that at least 15 per cent of households did not have a broadband internet subscription in 2018 (US Census Bureau 2021: 3). As the following examples show, those without online access no longer have the same guarantees and opportunities to live decent lives as those who can access the World Wide Web.

4.2.1 *Education and Internet Access*

A first example regards the human right to education. Here, having internet access generally has become necessary for students to have adequate opportunities. In other words, students without internet access are unfairly disadvantaged in achieving a good education. The situation here is parallel to people's opportunity to exercise their political rights. Before the internet was widespread and there was little educational content online, students did not require online access to have adequate opportunities to achieve good learning outcomes. However, now that the internet offers many educational resources, those who cannot access them are objectionably disadvantaged compared with those who have internet access.

Online access has become essential for primary and secondary school education. A 2018 survey in the UK by the price comparison website Uswitch finds that 69 per cent of parents think the internet has become essential to their child's education, and that half of their child's homework is reliant on online access (Uswitch 2018). This is because students now find essential learning aid and study materials online, for example, via BBC Bitesize and YouTube channels such as the Crash Course Channel or The Brain Scoop. But it is not only students who rely on the internet. Another survey from 2020 conducted by the broadband provider TalkTalk finds that three in four parents rely on the internet to help their children with their homework (TalkTalk 2020). Of course, Uswitch and TalkTalk are private businesses that have a stake in highlighting the importance of high-quality internet access. However, there is also academic research that confirms the importance of internet access for educational success. For example, according to a 2020 study by the Quello Center at Michigan State University, 'students who do not have access to the Internet from home or are dependent on a cell phone for access perform lower on a range of metrics, including digital skills, homework completion, and grade point average. They are also less likely to intend on attending college or university' (Hampton et al. 2020: 5). In some settings, schools provide students with digital devices for learning (e.g. laptops or tablets) and expect students to use them. However, if students have no internet access at home, they are seriously disadvantaged in their attempts to learn and keep up with their peers (Fox 2016). The need for internet access for fair opportunities to achieve educational success was also exacerbated and highlighted by the lockdowns of 2020 and 2021 to combat the spread of COVID-19. Schools were among the first institutions to close and the school education that was possible for most pupils at this point took place via the internet. In recognition of this fact, the UK's government promised to loan laptops and provide free Wi-Fi via mobile phone hotspots to those children who suffered from digital poverty to prevent them falling behind their peers who had online access at home (UK Government 2020a).

None of the value of online resources supporting learning in schools means that digital learning can replace in-person teaching, classroom interactions, or assessment and feedback by human teachers. In September 2023, a UNESCO report on the effects of remote learning forced by school closures during the COVID-19 pandemic highlighted the negative impacts that this switch to online teaching had on the learning outcomes and mental health of students. Some problems caused by moving all teaching online affected most students. Confined to their home, pupils did not get to socialise and interact in-person with their peers and lost out on the essential non-academic benefits of education (UNESCO 2023: 166). Varied and individual learning was replaced by 'a daily routine less of discovery and exploration than traversing file-sharing systems, moving through automated learning content, checking for updates on corporate platforms and enduring long video calls' (UNESCO 2023: 165). In particular, though, the move to digital learning was particularly detrimental for already disadvantaged students as the reliance on digital technologies worsened the effects of existing inequalities on their development and attainment. Affluent families had more means to supplement and support the online instruction of their children. Pupils from poorer backgrounds were impacted by the limitations of their families' homes (UNESCO 2023: 101, 113). And crucially, even though in May 2020, 60 per cent of national distance learning schemes around the world exclusively relied on online platforms to replace in-person teaching, almost half a billion pupils (or about 50 per cent of all primary and secondary pupils globally who had attended in-person schools before the outbreak of the pandemic) had no internet access at home and were thus excluded from schooling (UNESCO 2023: 87). Pandemic experiences therefore show that entirely replacing in-person teaching with digital learning is not beneficial for pupils. This, however, does not detract from the benefits that online resources have for supporting regular in-person school learning.

Also for education beyond secondary school, the internet is indispensable for many. Universities' distance learning programmes, for example, are inaccessible or at least not accessible without great practical difficulties (such as having to use Wi-Fi in libraries for all learning activities) for those who do not have internet access at home (Kalid and Pedersen 2016). Even though, as we saw in Chapter 2, the human right to education only includes the free provision of higher education as an aspirational goal (see UN 1966a: §13.2), it also demands that 'higher education shall be made equally accessible to all, on the basis of capacity, by every appropriate means, and in particular by the progressive introduction of free education' (UN 1966a: §13.c).Public student loans can be seen as one such practical precondition of fair opportunities, and internet access as another. Especially for many mature students, distant learning programmes are the only feasible option to complete university programmes. Child-rearing duties or work often prevents them from undertaking in-person studies. However, if a person in these circumstances has no easily accessible internet access, their opportunities to study distant learning programmes at university are extremely limited. Consequently, a lack of online access runs counter to the demand entailed in the human right to education to make higher education equally accessible to all.

These examples demonstrate the importance that online access has acquired for the opportunities students have relative to each other to obtain an education in most developed countries. They show that internet access is indeed essential for having adequate educational chances today. This claim is supported by an important ruling of the High Court in the Indian state of Kerala. In this case, an undergraduate student living in university accommodation filed a legal complaint against their education provider. The hostel in which the student stayed had banned all laptop use and all mobile phone use on its premises between 10 pm and 6 am. The student argued that their educational opportunities were unduly restricted by this rule. The court agreed with the student and ruled that 'the right to have access to Internet [is] part of [the] right to education' (Kerala High Court 2019: 20). Despite Kerala being among the poorest states in the country, its High Court ruled that internet access is a human right precisely *because* it has become necessary for students to have adequate opportunities to achieve a good education. Not having internet access in our digital age thus amounts to exclusion from educational opportunities that are protected by the human right to education.

The example of reduced educational opportunities without internet access also explains why having limited internet access (for example, only in public places) is insufficient where internet access is widespread. Rather, adequate opportunities can require that people have a reliable online connection at home or via their own portable device when most others have easy internet access in these ways. School and university students might have internet access in public libraries and the Wi-Fi services of supermarkets or other shops. But public places normally have limited opening hours and might be difficult to reach for a person – especially if they have care duties at home – so that the lack of reliable internet access creates unfair obstacles to their educational opportunities. People should not have to choose between raising or supervising their children and their own educational opportunities. Having a decent chance to obtain a good education today generally requires internet access. Where such online access has become the norm, people must have more than limited internet access in public places to not be relatively disadvantaged in comparison with the majority of their fellow citizens who already enjoy easily available online access.

4.2.2 Social Security and Internet Access

A second case that highlights the indispensability of internet access for enjoying our socio-economic human rights is online-based social security programmes. Offering online ways to access public programmes (so-called e-government) for many governments at first was a matter of improving services for their citizens. But especially after the global financial crisis of 2008, online services increasingly became a method of cutting costs for governments of developed countries (Hardill and O'Sullivan 2018: 3; see also the UK Government's Digital Efficiency Report (UK Government 2012)). For those who have reliable internet, e-governance is often much more convenient than visiting government services in person. However, for those without internet access, e-government creates significant barriers that make it more difficult to make use of some of the most crucial socio-economic human rights. Several examples illustrate this problem. In the UK, the social minimum scheme Universal Credit is an online-based system. Applicants are expected to communicate with the Department for Work and Pensions through email to apply for this most basic subsistence benefit. Even though internet access is not, strictly speaking, a necessity for receiving this payment, in practice the scheme is online-based and difficult to use offline. To make a claim, for instance, an applicant requires an email address. Receiving Universal Credit payments is conditional upon setting up a Claimant Commitment with a work coach, which specifies the duties of the benefit recipient. The Claimant Commitment can be accessed via the claimant's online account. Standard elements of a full-time work search requirement oblige the claimant to 'job search and set up job alarms online', to 'make it easy to be found online', and to 'network with friends, family and on social media' (UK Department for Work & Pensions 2020). All these commitments can only be complied with online.

In the US, internet access is often assumed for accessing social security services. The states of Connecticut (State of Connecticut 2021) and Iowa (State of Iowa 2021) only permit applications for unemployment insurance payments through their online systems or in-person at their job centres. Most other US states do not offer paper forms for applications for unemployment insurance claims but require applicants to file these online or via the phone. However, phone lines for public services are often busy so that much more time is spent in phone queues than is required for making claims to public support online. In the state of New York, those claiming unemployment insurance must re-certify that they are unemployed and willing to look for work on a weekly basis. They can do so either by phone (but are discouraged to use this option) or via an online process (New York State 2021). Reminders to recertify by state's labour department are only sent to applicants via email. Thus, if public services are moved online, having adequate opportunities to access these services requires that all have easy access to the internet. Even though internet access is not absolutely necessary, it has become practically indispensable for the enjoyment of adequate opportunities to utilise the right to social security and insurance. For the reasons mentioned here, easily available internet access (rather than limited access in public places) is also essential for having adequate opportunities to use online-based public services where such access is already widespread. Here, those who remain offline are objectionably disadvantaged compared with their fellow citizens who already enjoy internet access at home or via their own mobile devices.

Governments have a duty to care equally for all their citizens. This also includes the obligation to make public services equally accessible to all citizens. Not having internet access in effect constitutes unequal treatment and discrimination against those suffering from digital deprivation by their own government. Moreover, those suffering from digital poverty who are in this way treated unequally by their government are often precisely those people who rely the most on public services. E-government is therefore another example of how internet access mediates access to what our rights entitle us to. To be sure, internet access alone is often insufficient for accessing public services – especially where digital provision is complicated and prone to errors. Sufficient human contact and support for automated public services is necessary to make them work effectively (Booth 2023; see also the UN Special Rapporteur on Extreme Poverty and Human Rights Philip Alston's 2018 critique of the British welfare state as disappearing 'behind a webpage and an algorithm' (OHCHR 2018)). But without internet access, people can often no longer even try to access public services. Lack of internet access generates new and serious ways of socially excluding the poorest and weakest members of society. For this reason, universal internet access in developing countries has become a major question of social justice. It has become a condition of giving people adequate means to claim the public support they are entitled to.[1]

4.2.3 Housing and Internet Access

A third example of the relevance of internet access for socio-economic human rights in developed countries is the right to an adequate standard of living, which includes adequate housing. In many developed countries, significant parts of the

---

[1] Increased reliance on the internet to access public services has also created barriers for those who remain offline and for those who lack basic digital skills. This especially regards older adults. However, this age-based digital inequality has been found to be related to socio-economic status: those less well-off are also the ones most likely to lack digital skills. That is, the disadvantages of socio-economic inequality are compounded by a lack of digital skills (Hargittai et al. 2019). Besides its relevance for a great number of human rights, the internet is also important in other ways for older people. Various studies have found, for instance, that internet use reduces their loneliness and social isolation (Stockwell et al. 2021, Yu et al. 2021, Silva et al. 2022). The right response to the problem of lacking digital skills among older adults is therefore not to reject the idea of a human right to internet access. Rather, acknowledging such a human right plausibly entails accepting a duty of public authorities to provide digital skills training for older adults. This is also a central demand of digital inclusion charities such as Citizens Online (2023) and an aspect of free internet access that we will discuss in Chapter 5.

rental housing market have moved online. Craigslist, the dominant online rental platform in the US, for instance, is the country's fifteenth most frequented website overall (Boeing 2020: 250). Online rental platforms have various advantages for home-seekers: they reduce search costs enormously and provide information on available housing in real time. Of course, to access these advantages, one needs online access. Those without reliable internet access face considerable disadvantages in a housing market that is operating online to a significant extent. This unfortunately means that people who have difficulties affording decent housing also encounter difficulties finding better accommodation because of a lack of internet access. They have to use offline resources that contain less information, which are also more difficult to access than a website. Thus, digital poverty reinforces existing socio-economic disadvantages by preventing people from voting with their feet by leaving neglected or dangerous areas:

> Disadvantaged communities miss out on the reduced search costs and expanded choice sets provided by online platforms—benefits that instead primarily accrue to already-advantaged communities. A two-tiered system emerges in which privileged communities exchange housing information through one channel, while all others resort to separate channels. These forces perpetuate the self-reinforcing cycles of durable inequality: information segregation limits homeseekers' discovery of housing in neighborhoods different from their own—in turn limiting the ability to integrate neighborhoods for more diversity of incomes, education levels, ages, and ethnicities. (Boeing 2020: 462)

Living in poor neighbourhoods with high crime rates and low-quality education can make adequate living standards impossible. Of course, public authorities have an obligation towards their citizens in these areas to improve the local situation. However, in the absence of such efforts, residents should have the opportunity to better their situation by moving elsewhere, and internet access has become one practical necessity for having this option. From the perspective of human rights, internet access affects people's opportunities to obtain an adequate standard of living and housing. Those with online access generally have more opportunities to access vital housing markets because online platforms reduce their informational costs. In other words, adequate opportunities to obtain a decent standard of living and housing today require internet access.

4.2.4 *Work and Internet Access*

A crucial human right is the right to work, as specified in Article 23 of the Universal Declaration of Human Rights. In developed countries today, having access to the internet has become indispensable for finding and applying for jobs. In these digitalised societies, open positions are increasingly advertised in real time online, and people have to be able to access jobs and professional networking websites to make effective use of their right to work. It is estimated, for example, that more than 90 per cent of jobs in the UK are now advertised online only (House of Lords 2023: 15). But internet access is not just useful for jobseekers who are finding information about available jobs. Employers also expect job applicants to use online application and communication processes. This poses a significant problem for those without internet access. One study finds that

> Resumes must be stored online, applications must be completed online, and the recommendations, research, and scheduling necessary to land a job all typically involve access to computers, Internet, and cellphones. In other words, to be employed in the United States today, one is presumed to have reliable access to a range of digital technologies that enable digital storage as part of the employment process. (Gershon and Gonzales, 2021: 854)

The effects of digital poverty on employment are therefore parallel to the ones on housing. Those without online access are comparatively and objectionably disadvantaged because they are limited in their access to real-time information concerning open posts and channels of communication with potential employers. Digital poverty for this reason significantly limits people's ability to make use of their human right to work. Adequate opportunities to enjoy this right therefore include the reliable availability of internet access.

4.2.5 *Health and Internet Access*

Health is a human right (UN 1966a: §12.1). Before the COVID-19 pandemic, in developed countries the importance of internet access for health care provision was especially salient in rural areas. According to Public Health England, for example, 'digital exclusion in rural areas is a particular problem [because] in a number of areas, digital technology is being used creatively to link people living in areas that are geographically remote with both health and care services' (Local Government Association 2017: 22). States must use their public resources effectively and providing in-person care in remote areas can be challenging. In-person medical facilities in remote regions involve high per capita costs. They also require medical professionals to staff them, which can be problematic in rural areas. This is particularly the case in territorially large countries such as Canada and the US where it is especially indigenous communities that live remotely and that are underserved in terms of medical services. Thus, insofar as adequate digital alternatives to in-person health care exist, the usefulness of internet access for the realisation of the human right to health care offers grounds for recognising a right to internet access (see Reglitz and Rudnick 2020).

More generally, though, digital access, skills, and confidence are now part of the social determinants of health. People use the internet to find information about medical services, conditions, and treatments. For example, 'Patients Like Me' is an integrated community and health management online platform that as of 2023 had over 830,000 members and covered more than 2,900 medical conditions. On this platform, members can find information about their condition, learn new ways to manage it, and exchange experiences and advice with others afflicted by the same illness (PatientsLikeMe 2023). But also, more indirectly, internet access contributes to health by preventing problems that have a negative impact on health. Social exclusion, unemployment, and poverty are all social phenomena that negatively impact on a person's health. They are therefore called social determinants of health. Because, as we have already seen, internet access is important for educational opportunities, finding employment, and associating with others, it is also relevant for our health: 'being able to afford internet access and having the digital skills to use the internet safely are now essential for education, employment, income, social participation, and access to information and services. All are wider determinants of health' (Good Things Foundation 2020: 7). This also demonstrates the systemic indispensability of internet access because having such access is crucial for the enjoyment of a whole range of rights, all of which in turn are conducive to a person's health. Directly relevant for promoting health is the fact that the internet gives people access to medically relevant information, allows them to manage their health using digital services, and to have medical consultations online. Conversely, lack of internet access widens the gap with respect to health outcomes between the most disadvantaged members of society and the better off. This means that internet access itself has become a 'super-determinant of health' (Bauerly et al. 2019). Inequalities in digital access are thus now considered 'a public health issue' (Benda et al. 2020: 1123). The COVID-19 pandemic increased the importance of accessing medical services and information online (Thakur et al. 2020: 945). In the UK, for example, in March 2020 alone, online medical consultations doubled from 900,000 to 1.8 million appointments (Bibby and Leavey 2020: 10). Thus, the pandemic, remote locations, and existing social disadvantages all show that internet access has permanently become nearly indispensable to ensure all have adequate opportunities to access and use their human right to health.[2]

---

[2] It has to be noted that the internet can also be detrimental to public health as it enables the distribution of false health-related information, as, for example, during the COVID-19 pandemic

4.2.6 Cultural Participation and Internet Access

Online access has also become crucial for the enjoyment of the human right to take part in cultural life and to enjoy one's cultural heritage (UN 1966a: §15). Just as other mass media before it, the internet offers new ways of taking part in and accessing culture. Before the introduction of television, for instance, the only way for people to see famous paintings was to go to museums or to look at photographs of these works of art. Television generated new ways for people to view objects of art. The internet has added further options of making cultural objects virtually accessible to large numbers of people. But the online sphere is not simply a platform for observing cultural objects or events. It is also a unique forum for everyone for creating and sharing culture. With a little bit of technical knowledge, everyone can set up their own YouTube channel and virtually share practical advice, poetry, or other cultural products with the world. Users can also help others to contribute to culture by teaching them how to write, paint, and be creative in other ways. The app TikTok alone has been credited with having had a significant influence on culture in many countries since the start of the COVID-19 pandemic. It is said, for instance, to have changed comedy, music, and activism by offering venues and tools for individuals to easily create and share content (Smith Galer 2020). A study commissioned by the Council of Europe in 2018 finds that around 71 per cent of the citizens of the member states of the European Union engaged online in the discussion, creation, or enjoyment of cultural activities, events, or artists that year (Council of Europe 2018). And the UK 2018 government report *Culture is Digital* (UK Department for Digital, Culture, Media & Sport 2018) explicitly aspires to promote online cultural activities to make them accessible to a wider audience.

However, online use of the human right to participate in culture cannot equalise access to culture. Virtual tours of the Louvre in Paris, the museums on Berlin's Museum Island, the British Museum in London, the Colosseum in Rome, or the Acropolis in Athens cannot entirely replace the experience of visiting these places in person. But for many people, virtual access is the only option feasible for them. That is to say, for them internet access has arguably

---

(Parmet and Paul, 2020, Shelton, 2020). However, this should not lead to a paternalistic refusal to guarantee internet access for all in order to protect those who remain offline from coming into contact with misinformation. Instead, a human right to internet access plausibly requires that public authorities combat the spread of false information, for example by requiring social media platforms (that are often main conduits for misinformation) to remove false claims that can jeopardise public health, public security, or public order. This issue will be discussed in Chapter 7.

become a necessary element of adequate opportunities to exercise their right to enjoy and participate in culture and cultural heritage. Trips to major places of culture are expensive, especially if they involve international travel, and are not affordable for everyone. People with disabilities or who are ill might lack the mobility necessary to access places of culture or cultural events in person. And many cultural activities (such as the activities of people on social media referred to earlier) only take place online. If a person has no internet access, they are excluded from accessing most of the cultural activities that take place online, which objectionably limits their options for making use of their right to cultural participation. In fact, recent research finds that, in part because of the digital poverty of those worst off in society, making culture available online often reproduces and compounds existing socio-economic inequalities and disadvantage (Mihelj et al. 2019). Virtual access to cultural objects and activities adds opportunities for those who can already enjoy culture in traditional, non-digital fashion. But for those who are unable to afford a visit to a concert or a museum, the inability to access the internet only widens the gap between them and the more privileged. Digital deprivation thus exacerbates existing social disadvantages.

4.2.7 The Links between Internet Access and Socio-economic Human Rights in Developed Nations

As all these examples demonstrate, the same reasoning that justifies a human right to internet access via its role in realising civil and political human rights also applies to socio-economic rights in developed countries. Having internet access today is necessarily part of having adequate opportunities to make use of our socio-economic rights. On the one hand, online access is practically indispensable for people to be able to make effective use of these rights vis-à-vis other people. In developed countries, those without internet access are objectionably disadvantaged and indeed sometimes socially excluded. On the other hand, though, internet access is even more crucial than that because it has become systemically indispensable as many of our human rights are interdependent. Without an education comparable to that of their peers, for instance, a person is significantly hindered in their enjoyment of their economic freedoms, their right to cultural participation, or the exercise of their political rights. One instrument that helps promote people's enjoyment of a great number of their most vital human rights today is internet access. This view is shared by the UN, which asserts that internet access 'has become an indispensable tool for realizing a range of human rights, combating inequality, and accelerating development and human progress'

(UN 2011a: 22). There might be alternative ways to prevent social exclusion. Private tutors and smaller school classes are likely to lead to better educational opportunities for those currently struggling the most with their education. Additional in-person government services would make public services more accessible to a greater number of people – in particular the worst-off members of society who rely on these services the most. And financial subsidies (e.g. discounts or vouchers) for many people might promote greater access to cultural venues and activities. However, especially considering that public resources are always scarce, ensuring universal internet access presents an effective alternative that promotes the enjoyment of all these human rights simultaneously.

It is important to stress again that not having internet access reproduces and exacerbates the socio-economic exclusion of people who are already disadvantaged in developed countries. As we saw, those who suffer from digital poverty have fewer opportunities to find decent housing; their educational opportunities are diminished as they can access fewer resources that help them study and help parents support their learning; they have worse prospects for finding and applying for jobs; and they are unable to participate online in cultural activities. The reason that lack of online access compounds existing inequalities and disadvantages is that the internet creates new venues for exercising human rights and new ways of making use of these rights. Internet access conditions our access to the objects of many of our crucial socio-economic human rights. Those who cannot avail themselves of online options and forums are often those who already suffer from poverty, are educationally disadvantaged, or limited by illness or disability. Especially for them, online access offers valuable new options. If they have no access to these online options, they instead fall further behind better-off members of society. The fact that a lack of online access increases the gap and relative inequality between the digitally excluded and those who have internet access stresses the point that today internet access is an essential element of adequate opportunities to enjoy our human rights.

Online opportunities cannot and should not entirely replace offline activities and in-person support. Educational online resources, for example, cannot make up for an engaging teacher in the classroom. And internet access also, on its own, cannot realise human rights fully. If there is, for instance, insufficient decent housing available, accessing rental market information online does not guarantee adequate accommodation. However, for some, online opportunities can be the only feasible way to enjoy socio-economic human rights (e.g. when it enables disabled people to access cultural venues and activities). Most commonly, though, not having online access disadvantages many people vis-à-vis others (e.g. when others can search and apply for jobs online and they cannot). Those with internet access have more, faster, and better opportunities to enjoy their human rights, while those without remain restricted to the options they have offline, which continue to decrease as services and businesses move online. Because online access is practically indispensable for fair opportunities to enjoy our socio-economic rights in the wealthiest societies, it has become a basic utility to which people must have easy access.

4.3 THE IMPORTANCE OF INTERNET ACCESS FOR SOCIO-ECONOMIC HUMAN RIGHTS IN DEVELOPING COUNTRIES

Internet access is a lot less widespread in developing societies than it is in developed countries. Of the 2.9 billion people that were digitally excluded in 2021, 96 per cent lived in developing countries (ITU 2021a: 1). This is relevant for our argument because for internet access to be a truly global human right, it has to be of relevance around the globe. This does not mean, though, that internet access has to be relevant in the same way for everyone everywhere. If it is necessary for the enjoyment of some human rights everywhere, internet access is a truly global human right. As this section will show, internet access is also relevant in developing countries albeit in often different ways than in developed countries.

There are several reasons for this difference in practical relevance of the internet in developing countries. One is the lower internet penetration rate. If internet access is not widely available, businesses and public authorities have less reason to move their operations online because they will in this way not reach many people. Second, because of their lower levels of national affluence, developing nations often have a lower degree of public service provision than developed nations. They have, for instance, fewer resources to provide public education or public health care. As we will see, in developing countries, internet access can sometimes make the difference between people receiving *some* form of public services that their socio-economic human rights entitle them to and *no* realisation of these rights at all. The UN has therefore recognised the internet and other information communication technologies as 'a catalyst' for achieving its Sustainable Development Goals (UN 2022). This is different in developed countries where, as we saw earlier, online access is often a more efficient option for accessing existing public services. There are therefore different reasons for recognising a human right to internet access in developed and developing countries. In this section, we will therefore specifically look at various examples of the ways in which the internet enables the realisation of currently unfulfilled socio-economic human rights in developing countries, and how it offers options for better fulfilling these rights.

4.3.1 Education and Internet Access

Education is a key human right on which the value of many other human rights depends (e.g. economic freedoms and political freedoms). In developing societies too, internet access has become important for educational opportunities, albeit in different ways than in developed countries. Developing countries around the world encounter similar problems in ensuring primary and secondary school education for their citizens. But children in Sub-Saharan Africa face some of the most significant obstacles to their education. We will therefore focus here on their situation.

According to UNESCO, Sub-Saharan Africa experiences the highest rate of educational exclusion worldwide, with every fifth child between the ages of six and eleven being out of school. The rate of those out of school increases to a third between the ages of twelve and fourteen. In the cohort of young people between fourteen and seventeen, up to 60 per cent are not in school. The problem of educational exclusion affects girls more than boys, with 23 per cent of girls not attending primary schools compared with 19 per cent of boys (UNESCO 2020a). But various problems undermine the quality of education even for those who are able to attend primary and secondary school in Sub-Saharan Africa. Many children face long walks to their schools. Distance to school consequently constitutes one of the main reasons why children drop out of school (World Bank 2018a: 175–179). Class sizes are routinely very large and often exceed fifty pupils, so individual needs of pupils cannot be addressed. School building infrastructure is often poor, and many schools lack sufficient sanitary installations. In 2018, only 44 per cent of Sub-Saharan African primary schools had access to drinking water. And only 34 per cent of these schools had access to electricity, therefore a lack of adequate light and ventilation hinders children's learning (UNESCO 2016a: 17). Extremely problematic for children's education is the lack of textbooks, which often have to be shared between a number of pupils. Another serious issue is the quality of school education in Sub-Saharan Africa: in 2018, only 64 per cent of primary school teachers and 50 per cent of secondary school teachers had received formal training (UNESCO 2019: 1). Besides the lack of trained teachers, there is also a general shortage of them: according to UNESCO estimates from 2016, Sub-Saharan African countries will require an additional 17 million primary and secondary school teachers by 2030 (UNESCO 2016b). Additionally, UNESCO identifies teacher absenteeism as another serious concern. According to one of its studies of six low and middle-income countries, teacher absenteeism averaged 19 per cent in 2017 (UNESCO 2017a: 64). Even though the reasons why teachers are absent are often beyond their control (e.g. closed schools, bad access to school, or inoperative school buildings), their absence still negatively affects pupils' educational opportunities. Consequently, in 2017, 88 per cent of children and adolescents in Sub-Saharan Africa were unable to read proficiently and 84 per cent lacked minimal mathematical skills when leaving primary or lower secondary education (UNESCO 2017b: 7). This lack of educational attainment presents a rather problematic basis for the political and economic development of the children so disadvantaged.

Moving primary and secondary education online cannot address all of the worst problems for school children in Sub-Saharan Africa and, as the 2023 UNESCO report on digital education during the COVID-19 pandemic shows, can create issues of its own. Sufficient teachers need to be trained (also in digital education), school buildings have to be built and maintained, and unequal gender norms addressed to achieve a minimally adequate education for all children. However, online education tools can address some of the fundamental problems of Sub-Saharan African primary and secondary education and therefore make a significant difference. For example, education becomes less dependent on presence in the classroom if it can be delivered online. This can allow children living remotely from schools to complete their education. More students can be taught more effectively if teaching materials are available digitally and pupils do not have to share books. And gender disparities in education can diminish if girls do not have to undertake unsafe walks to school but can study at home where they are also not forced to use unisex toilets. Moreover, education is less dependent on functional school buildings and teacher presence if studying is based on online teaching resources.

The non-profit organisation Worldreader has demonstrated through its work the positive potential of digital learning (Worldreader 2023). Since 2010, more than 13 million students from sixty-two countries have been freely and equitably able to access the many thousands of e-books that Worldreader has in its digital library. By December 2019, the organisation had distributed digital books to 552 schools and 154 libraries as well as thousands of e-reader devices in seventeen Sub-Saharan African countries. This has led to measurable educational success. In an evaluation of pupils who participated in Worldreader's iREAD2 programme, '41 percent of grade 3 iREAD 2 students could read above the minimum proficiency level of 45 correct words per minute in English, compared with 13.4 percent of students in the control group' (Kwauk and Perlman Robinson 2016: 12). Pupils' interest in learning was also increased by having access to more textbooks (in 2012, in Ghana, pupils supported by Worldreader had access to 140 books compared with regular pupils who on average only had access to 1.2 books; see Kwauk and Perlman Robinson 2016: 11–12). The work of Worldreader has also provided teachers with educational materials that they previously did not have access to for improving the planning and content of their lessons (Kwauk and Perlman Robinson 2016: 11).

Another example that demonstrates the important potential of digital education for reaching large number of children is the iMlango (meaning 'doorway' in Swahili) programme that ran in Kenya from 2015 to 2016. During this time, this educational technology initiative that was delivered by a public–private sector partnership used high-speed satellite broadband to provide individualised math tutoring, literacy training (also via online debating contests among students), life skills training, digital attendance monitoring, as well as teacher training to 205 primary schools in underprivileged and poor rural and semi-urban settings that serve 180,000 pupils, including 70,000 marginalised girls. The programme also provided schools with the necessary digital technology and e-learning platforms. It had a positive effect especially on girls, 'with 60.5% saying that they were now more interested in attending school while 67.8%, compared to 47.9% at baseline, reported that they found school more exciting' (iMlango 2022). The digital attendance monitoring also for the first time allowed a realistic estimate of school absences.

A final example to be mentioned here is the Global Education Coalition organised by UNESCO in May 2020 in response to widespread school closures caused by the global COVID-19 pandemic. Members of this coalition such as the digital services providers Orange and Vodafone enabled free access to distance learning platforms for millions of learners around the world who otherwise would have had limited or no access to education during the lockdowns implemented to contain the spread of SARS-COV-2 (UNESCO 2020b).

None of these examples imply that developing countries should not improve their in-person education or that they should strive to replace classroom education with digital learning. But considering the benefits that online learning can offer those who are disadvantaged in, or excluded from, education, it is unsurprising that UNESCO finds that in developing countries in particular 'a great deal is riding on the use of information communication technologies in education' (UNESCO 2015: 48). Among the benefits of digital education highlighted by UNESCO are new possibilities for the personalised evaluation of pupils' performance, test preparation, distance tutoring, learning tools based on play, improved teacher training, and better national educational policymaking based on data on student learning (UNESCO 2015: 50–53). Considering the investments that developing states would have to make in physical learning resources, teacher training, and school infrastructure, the costs of digital education appear comparatively reasonable. Online-based education can therefore improve or make possible the enjoyment of the human right to education of large numbers of children in the poorest regions of the world. It can enable many pupils in the poorest countries to receive a decent minimal school education.

4.3.2 Health Care and Internet Access

For people in developing countries, internet access can also make the difference between receiving some adequate level of health care or receiving little to none. Internet access in these situations is at present a necessary condition for some minimal level of realisation of people's human right to health. Internet access can improve health care in non-affluent societies because it is essential for digital health care, or eHealth, which refers to 'the use of information and communication technologies (ICTs) for health purposes' (Broadband Commission 2017: 4).

Sub-Saharan African countries in particular face several obstacles to guaranteeing adequate health care. They have relatively few health care professionals to begin with and medical service provision is particularly problematic in remote and rural regions. People in these areas often also lack knowledge and awareness relevant for preventing and treating illness. Digital health offers numerous benefits that can help overcome these obstacles to a significant degree. According to the UN's Broadband Commission, the use of digital technology via the internet can increase access to, and improve the quality of, health care. Digital health tools also diminish the costs of providing health care and enable patients to take more responsibility for the management of their own health. Concretely, digital health care enables these advantages by

- Connecting remote, rural and underserved communities with referral centers and expert care,
- training healthcare providers (e.g. by eLearning and mLearning),
- improving quality of care through digital solutions for diagnosis, clinical decision support systems, supportive supervision or monitoring patient compliance with treatment,
- optimizing resource allocation and lowering healthcare costs through more efficient care coordination (e.g. with electronic medical records),
- improving data management for surveillance, reporting, accountability and monitoring, and
- facilitating communications between health workers, specialists and patients. (Broadband Commission 2017: 4)

In light of these options enabled by digital health care, the World Health Organization (WHO) stresses the crucial relevance of the internet for realising the human right to health, especially in developing countries. In its 2016 report *Global Diffusion of eHealth: Making Universal Health Coverage Achievable*, the WHO explicitly acknowledges that 'it has become increasingly clear that universal health coverage cannot be achieved without the support of eHealth' (WHO 2016: 5). In other words, internet access is practically necessary for guaranteeing everyone's enjoyment of a minimal degree of their human right to health. Several examples illustrate how internet access helps facilitate medical care for people in developing countries that they would otherwise not receive.

For instance, digital health tools can help diagnose illnesses, which is a precondition of treatment. In Kenya, a smartphone-based Portable Eye Examination Kit (known as Peek) has been used to test people's eyesight by using cell-phone cameras and a retina adaptor. This cost- and time-saving procedure allows the identification of people who need treatment, especially in remote areas that are underserved by medical practitioners. These people would otherwise not receive a diagnosis because they would have to travel to urban centres and be assessed in medical facilities that have limited capacities. The WHO estimates that 'if all people with eye or vision problems had immediate access to diagnosis and prompt care [as enabled by Peek], 80% of the world's blindness could be eliminated' (WHO 2016: 72). Furthermore, in rural Kenya, a mobile phone-based electrocardiogram application was successfully used to detect atrial fibrillation, which helped prevent strokes in patients (Bervell and Al-Sammaraie 2019: 12). Tele-pathology was also used in South Africa in the form of a medical hearing impairment device (Bervell and Al-Sammaraie 2019: 4). In rural Uganda, the local scarcity of pathologists was overcome with the help of web-based media for the analysis of samples and specimens (e.g. cells) to diagnose health issues (Bervell and Al-Sammaraie 2019: 8). In Ethiopia, telemedicine was used to enable radiological and dermatological consultations for diagnosing and treating skin diseases (Bervell and Al-Sammaraie 2019: 6). During the Ebola outbreak in West Africa in 2014, health care workers in Sierra Leone used remote sensor technology to monitor changes in the vital signs of Ebola patients. This use of internet-enabled monitoring saved critical time and reduced the exposure to and transmission of the virus (Steinhubl et al. 2015).

A common problem preventing the delivery of health care in developing countries is unreliable or limited health data, which hinders medical decision-making and treatment. Thus, many African countries utilise electronic management record systems 'for keeping of laboratory test results, prescription, monitoring, x-rays, pathological specimens and preparations, patient indexes and registers, pharmacy and drug records, nursing and ward records' (Bervell and Al-Sammaraie 2019: 6). Electronic health records have also been used to monitor and improve treatment, for example, of HIV/AIDS patients in Mozambique (Bervell and Al-Sammaraie 2019: 5).

Moreover, internet-enabled digital health solutions are crucial for educational and information-sharing purposes. In Uganda, internet-based sex education programmes are used to teach young people how to prevent infection with HIV (Bervell and Al-Sammaraie 2019: 6). During the Ebola outbreak in West Africa in 2014, internet-based social media platforms were used to spread misinformation about the disease. However, social media use is also credited with correcting false information and with providing people with vital information that limited the spread of the disease, for example, in Nigeria (Carter 2014, Fayoyin 2016: 3). In Ethiopia, where most births occur outside health care facilities, the use of a free smartphone app developed by the Danish Maternity Foundation in collaboration with the Universities of Copenhagen and Southern Denmark improved the skills and knowledge of birth attendants. Randomised controlled trials show that the use of the app reduced perinatal mortality from 23 per 1,000 births to 14 per 1,000 births (Lund et al. 2016). Another example of the use of the internet in the delivery of health care and health-related knowledge is the 'Save Heart Kashmir' initiative (Bhat et al. 2020). Here, local volunteers and cardiologists in distant urban centres use the messenger service WhatsApp to enable basic cardio emergency diagnosis and treatment instructions in remote mountainous regions where people are days away from the nearest hospital (Ellis-Peterson 2020). By way of this digitally enabled service, cardiologists and volunteers have been able to save the lives of patients who otherwise would have had no access to diagnosis or treatment. The internet shutdowns imposed in the region by the Indian government in 2019–2020 therefore led to the death of people suffering cardio emergencies as the initiative was not able to operate.

One might object that for some of these ICT-enabled medical services, all that is needed is a mobile phone rather than internet access. So-called mHealth services that only require access to a phone network are indeed frequently used in developing countries – for example, to remind people to adhere to their treatment plan or to disseminate medically relevant information. However, many mobile phone-based services also require internet access. This is because of the data density involved in many forms of mHealth. Because of the limited data transmission involved, reminders to adhere to treatment plans can in fact be sent via SMS without using the internet. However, sending retina scans taken with a mobile phone camera or images of bodies for diagnosis involves larger amounts of data the transmission of which requires 4G or 5G networks, and thus internet access. Consequently, many mobile phone-based digital health solutions also presuppose internet access.

As these examples show, in developing countries, internet access is indispensable for realising some degree of medical care for many people. This is especially the case for those who live in rural and remote areas that are underserved by medical professionals and are unlikely to see the installation of new health care delivery facilities any time soon. Internet access for these people has enabled, and therefore become a necessary condition of, the provision of the medical care entailed by their human right to health. None of this means that people in developing countries are merely owed second-best online solutions for guaranteeing their human rights if online options cannot make up for in-person services. Instead, they deserve the full realisation of their human rights (as well as everything else that they are entitled to as a matter of justice). However, if (in our non-ideal world) the internet can make the difference between some degree of human rights enjoyment or none at all, ensuring that everyone has internet access is of particularly moral urgency. Moreover, as examples from affluent societies show, once human rights, for example, to health and education are fulfilled, the internet remains important for people's relative opportunities to enjoy these rights.

4.3.3 *Economic Freedoms and Internet Access*

Another crucial area of life for which the internet has great positive potential in developing countries is work and participation in the economy. More specifically, internet access can help create jobs and enable financial inclusion. Some people might find better and higher paid employment when internet access is available. More fundamentally, though, empirical studies show that for many people having online access can make the difference between having a job and being unemployed, or between having access to financial services and being excluded from them.

When it comes to the relation between internet access and employment, it is generally difficult to determine the directionality of impact between these two factors. This is because, while a reduction in unemployment might be caused by a wider spread of internet access, correlation is not causation. It might equally well be the case that improvements in the job market make people more affluent so that they subsequently can afford digital technology and other costs of internet access. However, recent empirical evidence demonstrates a clearer direction by studying the development of job markets in African countries following the introduction of fast internet access infrastructure (Hjort and Poulsen 2019). In the late 2000s and early 2010s, Africa saw the arrival of fast internet infrastructure in the form of the installation of submarine internet cables from Europe. These were brought to shore at major cities that were connected to the existing national telecommunication backbone infrastructures (Hjort and Poulsen 2019: 1039). The resulting better connection and faster data speeds led to a reduction of the price of internet access and an increase in internet use. In the following years, employment increased in the newly connected countries, and in particular in the regions that had the best digital access.

Employment in various newly connected African countries rose up to 13 per cent after the arrival of fast internet. Importantly, though, this employment growth was not accompanied by a loss of jobs in less connected areas, suggesting that online access created new jobs rather than merely displacing existing ones (Hjort and Poulsen 2019: 1034). This is partly explainable by the creation of new businesses that followed the introduction of fast internet, which often occurred in sectors that heavily rely on internet use, such as finance and services (Hjort and Poulsen 2019: 1062). However, the arrival of fast internet access was also found to increase hiring by already existing firms, for example, in Ethiopia. This shows that online access does not just benefit segments of the economy that largely work digitally (Hjort and Poulsen 2019: 1063). Moreover, this positive employment trend equally affected people at all skill levels so that it was not only better educated people who gained employment (Hjort and Poulsen 2019: 1034). Beyond that, the arrival of fast internet access also significantly increased the likelihood that people would become employed in higher skilled occupations. This, though, did not lead to an increase in unemployment of less educated people because more companies offered skill-improvement training to their existing workers (Hjort and Poulsen 2019: 1034). All sectors of the job market therefore benefited from the introduction of fast internet access. Finally, as a consequence of these developments, average wages in the newly connected areas increased in the first couple of years after the arrival of better digital infrastructure (Hjort and Poulsen 2019: 1068).

The internet also offers opportunities for jobseekers in developing countries by connecting them with employers more efficiently. In South Africa, for example, UNESCO supports the automated job matching platform Giraffe (UNESCO 2020c). Jobseekers can create their CVs and store them on this platform. The platform's algorithm then matches them with businesses looking for employees. This process also helps companies to identify suitable candidates by enabling jobseekers to submit voice notes in support of their applications. By 2020, the platform had attracted more than 1 million jobseekers and thousands of employers. This example also shows that internet access has important potential for realising people's human right to work in developing nations. Because these countries currently have the lowest internet penetration, their job markets also stand to benefit the most from online access. The example of African countries accordingly shows that internet access can improve people's opportunities to make use of their right to work and to participate in the economy.

Internet access alone can certainly promote business activity, but it cannot on its own transform economies. Other factors are relevant in this respect as well, such as education, digital skills, and sometimes even the ability to speak a foreign language. For instance, a study of the effects of internet access on the Thai silk industry finds that even though there were definite benefits to adopting online trading practices, these gains were mostly not captured by silk producers themselves, who are often the ones most in need of an improvement of their situation. Rather, the increases in revenue generated by trading silk online mostly benefited silk industry intermediaries. Even though the internet reduced distances and enabled producers to sell Thai silk products in more places than before, certain micro-level barriers prevented them from receiving a significant part of the new profits. Concretely, many silk producers 'are functionally illiterate, monolingual, and inexperienced in basic mathematics [and so] necessarily rely on intermediaries' (Graham 2019: 277). Communication barriers are therefore not the only problem that prevents the weakest participants in the economy from improving their situation. Economic, cultural, and educational barriers also matter. However, these problems do not undermine the positive potential of internet access on economic development. After all, trading online reduces informational costs, helps cross global distances, and connects market participants. Similar to the case of the internet's effects on human rights to basic security (discussed in Chapter 3), the example of the Thai silk industry rather shows that the internet alone cannot guarantee human development or the successful exercise of our human rights. As we saw, human rights are interdependent. Therefore, if duty-bearers take seriously their responsibility to respect, protect, and guarantee the enjoyment of human rights (in this case the right to education), internet access can play an important role also for economic development of people in developing countries. This is shown by other examples too.

One of these examples is the way that internet access promotes the enjoyment and realisation of economic human rights by enabling financial inclusion. Financial inclusion means that people have access to financial services such as a bank account, payments, transactions, savings, credit, and insurance (Evans 2018: 568). Financial inclusion is currently not recognised as a human right.[3] However, access to financial services is crucial for everyday life (e.g. for paying bills or receiving a salary) and for running a business. In modern societies it is difficult to make use of economic freedoms without access to such services. It is therefore highly problematic that in 2017, 1.7 billion people (of whom 65 per cent were women) were 'unbanked', that is, without a bank account (World Bank 2017: 4). Besides a lack of money, the most common reasons for this financial exclusion are the costs and distance involved in accessing financial institutions (World Bank 2017: 5). It is precisely these issues that internet access can help solve.

In developing countries, people are often confronted with a lack of bricks-and-mortar banks. Before the invention of digital services, if there was no bank, or none sufficiently close, people could not make use of financial services. However, in these societies internet access now makes possible financial inclusion in two ways. First, online access enables 'mobile money' (e.g. internet banking) and makes financial services and products available without the need to visit a bank in person. It is therefore unsurprising that in 2016 there were already 100 million active users of mobile money in Sub-Saharan Africa (Makina 2019: 309). There is also empirical evidence that internet access has increased financial inclusion in forty-four African countries (Evans 2018). Moreover, financial inclusion via the internet has sometimes become the only reliable way for many people in developing countries to purchase essential services. In Sudan, for example, the military junta shut down the internet in 2021. The regime thereby made it impossible for many citizens to purchase the electricity needed to run air-conditioning when temperatures reached 40°C outside. For them, payment for this basic utility was dependent on the use of a mobile phone app (Bergin et al. 2022).

Online access alone is insufficient for financial inclusion. States also need to guarantee an effective regulatory environment to ensure that economic activities can safely and reliably take place. Moreover, financial inclusion requires lenders to be willing to lend to poor customers (Evans 2018: 577). Problematically, many small and medium-sized enterprises in developing countries have difficulties obtaining financial credit from banks because they do not have sufficient guarantees to become attractive customers. There is a second way, though, in which internet access can help precisely such small and medium businesses that would be excluded from credit even if they had access to physical banks. Online access allows these businesses to raise funds via internet-based crowdfunding platforms. In this way, they can attract credit directly (and without involvement of intermediaries such as banks) in the form of small contributions from groups or individuals that are willing to lend

---

[3] A philosophical case for such a right has been made by Queralt (2016).

to them. The World Bank expects the sums raised in Africa via crowdfunding to rise from USD $32 million in 2015 to USD $2.5 billion in 2025 (Makina 2019: 313). However, a major obstacle to the use of crowdfunding is the low internet penetration in African countries (Makina 2019: 315).

The examples of mobile money and crowdfunding show how internet access can promote financial inclusion. Given the lack of physical financial institutions in many places, and the fact that many small businesses are unattractive as customers for these banks, financial technology (FinTech), enabled by the internet, is the only way for many people to escape financial exclusion. And because financial inclusion is essential for participating in the economy and for exercising economic freedoms, internet access in many developing countries is a practical necessity for at least some level of realisation of important economic human rights, such as employment and participation in the economy. For people who depend on FinTech, internet access is not a luxury. For them it is rather a necessity if they are to have the opportunity to be active economic agents and to be able to manage effectively their everyday lives in modern societies.

4.3.4 *Subsistence Farming and Internet Access*

The important role that the internet plays in enabling participation in the economy positively affects the realisation of other human rights. For instance, internet access can help boost agricultural production, and thereby contribute to the protection of the human right to food and an adequate standard of living (UN 1966a: §11). As part of this right, the UN explicitly calls upon states to 'improve methods of production, conservation and distribution of food by making full use of technical and scientific knowledge, by disseminating knowledge of the principles of nutrition and by developing or reforming agrarian systems in such a way as to achieve the most efficient development and utilization of natural resources' (UN 1966a: §11a). Today, making full use of technical knowledge requires internet access.

Studies from developing nations show the impact that the introduction of internet access can have on the production of food. For example, when internet access first became widespread in Vietnam between 2008 and 2012, the agricultural output increased by almost 7 per cent (Kalia and Tarp 2019: 675). This occurred especially in the least developed northern provinces of the country. This increase in production is to an important extent attributed to farmers being able to access new information provided on governmental and private web platforms about, for example, how to use fertilisers more efficiently (Kalia and Tarp 2019: 676). The case for internet access as a human right can therefore be supported by the relative increase in agricultural output that can be achieved by farmers' knowledge gains because increased food production reduces the risk of famines and malnourishment. The same positive trend of increased agricultural production owing to informational gains via the internet has also been shown to occur in developed countries such as Australia (Salim et al. 2016). Those who have online access can benefit from new insights, while those who do not have online access remain ignorant or dependent on others for receiving knowledge crucial for their work.

But internet access protects the human right to adequate food in other ways than increasing technical knowledge relevant to the production of food. Online access has also been found to reduce the abandonment of farmland by agricultural workers. Cropland abandonment is a major threat to food security as farmers quit agriculture and move to cities because farming is unprofitable. In twenty-two rural Chinese provinces, internet access has significantly reduced the abandonment of cropland by more than 40 per cent (Deng et al. 2019). The reasons for this positive influence of online access on the continuous use of farmland are complex. Importantly, internet access helps farmers participate in the wider economy by providing market information and thereby lowering transaction costs. With the help of the internet, farmers can find new customers and identify the best prices they can obtain for their products, and in this way make farming more financially viable. Availability of the internet also creates opportunities for farmers by making it easier to develop family businesses, which makes them less dependent on migrant labour (Deng et al. 2019: 3). Similarly, in Kenya, the use of the mobile phone app AgriManagr helps small farmers to increase their efficiency and income (Virtualcity 2023). The app allows food producers to transmit data on their electronically weighed produce, to connect with buyers, and to trace their product through the supply chains. The system decreased the delay in payments to farmers from 120 to 31 days and reduced purchasing times from three minutes to two seconds (Braumüller 2018: 146). Internet access therefore contributes significantly to food security and thereby to people's enjoyment of the human right to food and an adequate standard of living, by making farming more financially viable. Those who study the effects of the internet on agricultural production thus call for public investment in internet access and training in online skills so farmers can harness the opportunities that internet access offers (Deng et al. 2019: 10).

Moreover, financial inclusion via FinTech, in particular, makes farming financially viable in developing countries. The internet allows farmers to use mobile money to, for example, send and receive remittances, pay taxes, pay bills, and receive payments from governments, non-governmental organisations, or businesses. Further important online services for farmers in developing countries include digital crop insurance (e.g. against weather shocks).

Satellite-based remote sensing and image-based monitoring of crop health enables farmers to document damage to their insured crops in cost-effective ways and helps them claim insurance pay-outs in a timely (digitalised) fashion. Another way in which FinTech makes agriculture in developing nations more viable is by enabling investments in green technology to overcome the shortage of electricity that is prevalent in many rural areas. Using mobile money allows farmers to set up payment plans to afford green technology such as solar panels. The power thus generated makes possible the use of new agricultural technology such as monitoring (e.g. ground sensors) and mechanisation (e.g. irrigation) devices that improve production (Hinson et al. 2019: 3).

The possibilities that internet access opens up for financial inclusion and, consequently, for rural agriculture in developing countries are good examples of the cascading benefits that internet use can have in many areas of life and of the systemic indispensability of internet access. They demonstrate the fittingness of the analogy between the internet and a Swiss Army knife that explains the systemic indispensability of internet access for many different human rights. All these rights could be promoted individually in different ways. For instance, local banks and libraries could be set up everywhere in rural areas of developing nations to overcome information deficits and to enable financial inclusion. However, owing to the costs involved, this has not happened and remains a theoretical option only. Providing universal internet access, in contrast, requires fewer resources and positively affects many human rights at the same time. Additionally, the internet makes possible a number of new and unique opportunities for rural farmers (e.g. crowdfunding). Internet access should therefore be a human right because it is practically necessary and systemically relevant for the realisation of many socio-economic rights, such as the human right to an adequate standard of living.

4.3.5 *The Links between Internet Access and Socio-economic Human Rights in Developing Nations*

To summarise this section of the chapter, internet access is of crucial practical relevance for the human rights of people in developing countries too. We have seen that for many people in the poorest countries, internet access is currently practically indispensable for enjoying some of their socio-economic human rights. Online education is for many the only way to receive a primary education; eHealth for many offers the only chance to receive minimal medical care; and FinTech for the first time allows for the financial inclusion of those who live far away from physical financial institutions or who would not receive financial credit from them. These examples demonstrate that internet access is relevant to the realisation and promotion of socio-economic human rights everywhere, and not only in developed societies where it is already widespread.

Despite all the benefits it has for the promotion and protection of human rights in developing countries, internet access as such cannot solve on its own the overarching problems of global inequality and world poverty. The advantages it brings contribute to incremental improvements of lives in a non-ideal and unjust world. We therefore have to be clear about what internet access can and cannot achieve. It is no cure-all for human rights deprivations or violations in developing countries. Giving people universal access to the internet is as such not going to end starvation, political oppression, and global inequalities in economic power. Nonetheless, internet access can help better the situation of many people and open up possibilities to further improvements for them. For instance, as people have access to more information, they can join others to promote common causes. When they get access to financial services, they can participate in the economy and grow their businesses. And, as we have seen, against the backdrop of existing global inequality, internet access is practically and systemically indispensable for helping many people to realise some of their human rights even to a minimal degree (e.g. education, health care). For these reasons (and even though universal online access alone will not solve global inequality, world poverty, and gender injustices), it provides new opportunities for many people in developing countries to improve their own situation and to escape poverty. If we are serious about their human development and about ending world poverty, it would be pragmatically inconsistent not to care about their digital inclusion as well. Internet access in many instances is currently the only that way many people in developing countries can enjoy some of their human rights. This justifies their entitlement to guaranteed access to this powerful medium.

4.4 SOCIO-ECONOMIC HUMAN RIGHTS AND THE HUMAN RIGHT TO INTERNET ACCESS

Rights are important claims that entitle right-holders to certain freedoms and provisions. Because violating rights is met with (social or legal) sanctions, they are no trivial matter. Because of this, and since rights impose certain obligations on others, they require thorough justification. Human rights are those universal rights that secure the conditions of minimally decent lives. That makes them particularly urgent entitlements, which is the reason why they are also matters of international concern. This is to say that the international community of states is called upon to guarantee the universal fulfilment of human rights and to protect them from standard threats. Because of the urgency of human rights and the sanction-backed obligations that they impose on others, a novel human right to free internet access requires a strong justification. In this chapter, we have seen that such a justification can be found in the many ways that internet access helps to realise socio-economic human rights. We can therefore derive a human right to free internet access from the internet's unique practical and systemic indispensability for our socio-economic rights in the following way.

> Premise 1: Everyone has socio-economic human rights (such as the rights to education, health care, work, social security, a decent standard of living) because these are necessary protections of minimally decent lives and as such matters of international concern.
> Premise 2: Everyone must have adequate opportunities to enjoy their socio-economic human rights.
> Premise 3: Internet access is in practice necessary (i.e. practically and systemically indispensable) for having adequate opportunities to exercise or enjoy many of our socio-economic human rights.
> Premise 4: Following a 'principle of rationality' (Nickel 2022: 31), if we endorse an end (i.e. socio-economic human rights), we have very strong or good reasons also to endorse those things and means that are necessary to achieve or realise that end (i.e. a human right to free internet access).
> Conclusion: Insofar as and because internet access is practically and systemically indispensable for having adequate opportunities to exercise or enjoy many of our socio-economic human rights, we have very strong reasons to accept a human right to internet access.

Of course, much depends, again, on how we understand what 'adequate' opportunities to enjoy socio-economic rights entails. Just as in the case of political and civil rights, the argument here is that these opportunities cannot be too unequal lest people are unfairly disadvantaged. The strongest examples of people having *inadequate* opportunities without online access are those cases where having internet access makes the difference between some level of enjoyment of human rights and none at all. For example, it is clear that people's need for the internet is particularly great in the mountainous regions of Kashmir where their only hope for treatment in cases of cardiac emergencies depends on specialist advice given to local first responders via WhatsApp. The importance of internet access is also particularly salient for children in Sub-Saharan Africa who are unlikely to receive a decent primary school education without access to digital learning tools. No opportunities to enjoy the human rights to health and education are clearly inadequate opportunities. If the internet makes possible *some* realisation of these rights, this lends strong support to the claim that internet access itself is an entitlement for those who depend on it.

However, this does not mean that if people have *some* opportunities to use their human rights, they thereby have adequate opportunities. Strongly unequal options to, for example, receive a decent education, find adequate housing, or take part in cultural events and activities are also problematic. It would be deeply unfair to tell some children that as long as they receive some formal education they have nothing to complain about, even if their opportunities for learning were much more limited than those of some of their peers simply because they had no access to the internet. After all, their interest in receiving a decent education that allows them to compete with others later in life is just as valid and morally important than the interests of any of their peers. Similarly, it would be unjust for some to have fewer opportunities to find new employment because they have no secure access to the internet while the best jobs and easiest ways to apply for these are online. And it is also unjustifiable if for some (often those who already face significant disadvantages and hurdles) it is a lot more difficult to apply for minimum social security support than for others simply because they have no (or no reliable) access to the internet. After all, no one's fundamental interests are morally more important than those of anyone else from the perspective of the public authorities that have to guarantee our rights. Our governments are the primary duty-holders that must provide social guarantees against standard threats to our human rights. They therefore must guarantee that we have adequate opportunities to exercise our socio-economic (and other) human rights. Today, worldwide, this requires ensuring that everyone has access to the internet. Once we understand that everyone's chances to enjoy their socio-economic freedoms depend in one important way or another on internet access, we see that everyone has a strong, legitimate interest in a guarantee to be able to go online. Ultimately, that is why internet access has become a moral human right that ought to become legally recognised around the globe. The internet's role in realising socio-economic human rights is therefore the second pillar of justification upon which the case for a human right to free internet access rests.

This concludes Part I of the book, which provides normative justifications for the human right to internet access based on empirical examples of the internet's indispensable usefulness for other human rights. We will now turn to Part II that will look closer into the obligations that arise specifically for duty-holders from acknowledging this novel human right. What we have seen so far, though, is that public authorities have very strong reasons to acknowledge that internet access today is a basic utility to which everyone must have guaranteed access. The human right to free internet access is the logical conclusion of accepting this reality.

PART II

OBLIGATIONS

INTRODUCTION TO PART II

In Part I, we have seen that all people have a weighty and urgent interest in being able to access the internet without arbitrary interference. This is because online access is practically necessary for them to be able to make adequate and effective use of many of their fundamental human rights in today's increasingly digitalised societies. Internet access has become more than a matter of convenience. It has become a morally important matter and a basic necessity for people everywhere. That is why public authorities should recognise a human right to free internet access. Because having access to the internet to avoid political and social exclusion is a universal morally urgent interest, it also engenders duties for the international community of states to help those beyond their own borders who lack internet access.

What Part I has not done, though, is to explain what content such a human right to free internet access must have. It has not spelled out what people would be entitled to and what obligations public authorities would have to accept as a matter of this right. Explaining this content is the task of the remainder of this book. Crucial for this task is another idea that we encountered in Part I – Henry Shue's insight that rights are social guarantees against standard threats (Shue 2020: 29). Rights cannot protect their holders against just any danger. This would not be realistic, and attempts to provide complete protection would be too draining on public resources and require unacceptable restrictions of people's freedoms. The human right to health and basic health care, for example, cannot protect us from ever becoming ill just as the human right to life cannot guarantee that no one dies through accidents or criminal offences by others. What rights do, instead, is to create obligations for public authorities to provide reasonable protections for those they govern against serious threats that are standardly predictable and can be remedied. What exactly constitutes standardly expectable and remediable threats to a right, and what protections against these can reasonably be provided and expected, are 'largely empirical questions' (Shue 2020: 33). Answers to these questions are also affected by the fact that standard threats are not static but often develop over time, for example, as new technological developments are made or as new threats to rights emerge.

In Part II, we will therefore consider what the standard threats to free internet access are today. Doing so will enable us to fill the idea of a regarding human right with content, and to specify concrete obligations for states and other public authorities. As we will see, without offering social guarantees against these threats, having access to the internet can actually be harmful for people. As a mass medium, the internet is a two-edged sword like other mass media such as the radio, print, or television. The information it transports can be used to inform or misinform. Access to the internet therefore requires certain protections to be a benefit to people. The dangerous potential of the internet, though, is even greater than that of other mass media. That is because when people are online they do not simply receive information; they leave informational traces behind. This offers opportunities for others to obtain information about internet users in ways that are impossible through other mass media. The potential harms of using the internet therefore exceed being misinformed and are greater than those of other mass media. The potential benefits of internet access are enormous, but so are the dangers if accessing the internet becomes unfree. As will become clear, many of these risks and dangers are not merely unfortunate and unavoidable side-effects of using the internet. Rather, they are foreseeable problems from which public authorities should protect us. A lack of such protections consequently constitutes violations of the human right to internet access. This new right therefore provides a forceful argumentative resource to demand that states do something about these risks. After all, they present standardly expectable and remediable threats to something that has become extremely morally and practically important to all of us: that we can exercise our human rights online. Focusing on standard threats to internet access therefore does three things.

It reveals the potential downsides that are inevitable if internet access is not safeguarded in certain ways. It shows the specific content of the novel human right by identifying obligations for public institutions to protect internet users against these predictable dangers. And it explains why we need a human right to free internet access because the latter would give people claimable entitlements to protection from these standard threats.

5

Poverty as a Standard Threat

This chapter addresses the problem of digital poverty, that is to say, the issue of digital exclusion caused by a lack of means to access the internet. Billions of people still have never used the internet. Some of them have been unable to because they live in areas where the required broadband internet infrastructure does not yet exist. But many of them remain offline even where this infrastructure does exist because they are unable to afford what is required to access the internet, such as end user devices or data services. Others lack the basic digital skills to use the internet even though they might be able to afford data and devices. Digital poverty is therefore a predictable threat to free internet access in our world of rich and poor societies. But even in affluent countries, as long as our socio-economic order allows for people to be poor, digital poverty will remain a threat to some.

This chapter will outline what obligations the human right to internet access imposes on public authorities in terms of reasonable social guarantees against digital poverty. This is a first step in determining what content this novel human right has to entail. To offer effective protection of internet access, the right has to secure a level of digital sufficiency in terms of access and usability of the internet for all who want to use it. It has to contain certain duties of provision that public authorities must fulfil for those threatened by digital poverty. Because internet access is now a basic necessity, just as with other essential needs (e.g. food, water, clothing, and shelter), this human right has to include requirements for public institutions to provide the means of online access – at least for those who cannot afford them. This, then, is a first meaning of the term 'free' internet access. Being able to use the internet must be guaranteed for all, and therefore free for those unable to afford such access for themselves.[1] Because human rights are global standards that

---

[1] A second meaning of 'free' internet access regards access that is not constrained by arbitrary interferences. This is the topic of the following chapters.

create international obligations, and because the number of people worldwide remaining offline is so enormous, this might at first seem like a thoroughly unrealistic obligation to impose on states, the international community, and other duty-holders. It might seem simply too expensive for anyone to guarantee, or to have to work towards, universal internet connectivity. There are of course also many possible technologies for accessing the internet and it is, without further considerations, not yet clear what sort of technological support a human right to internet access would entitle people to. The chapter will therefore explain what global standards of provision this right should plausibly contain. Such standards have so far not been clearly specified. Moreover, their particular details will require adjustment as technology becomes more advanced, widespread, and affordable. That is why this chapter makes specific suggestions for what is required of public institutions to protect everyone against digital poverty right now. Throughout, we will encounter numerous examples of steps that states and other agents are taking to allow people to go online. These examples also have the purpose of showing that the demands in terms of provision that this human right necessarily entails are realistic ones, and that this right therefore has a concrete practical reality.

In Section 5.1, we will take stock of the challenge of achieving universal internet access by considering facts about who remains offline and what is required to make the internet available to all of humanity. Section 5.2 will then set out an important distinction that is essential for understanding the content of the right in terms of provisions against digital poverty. That is the distinction between its general content and certain minimum core obligations it includes. The problem that this distinction addresses is the fact that there are some countries, the least developed countries (LDCs), that (as with other human rights, e.g. to education or health care) are currently not affluent enough to fulfil the human right to internet access for their citizens. Even though these countries are not at fault for the non-fulfilment of human rights they cannot afford to guarantee, there are still certain minimum core obligations of human rights that they are able to fulfil and that they are obliged to realise for their citizens.

Equipped with this distinction, Section 5.3 subsequently spells out the general content of the human right to internet access in terms of provisions against digital poverty. It explains what standards all states have to guarantee for their citizens. Internet access has several preconditions all of which must be met for people to go online. These include (1) broadband infrastructure, (2) digital end devices, (3) data services, and (4) basic digital skills. Section 5.3 details what public authorities have to provide for their citizens with respect to all these dimensions of access. Section 5.4 concludes by detailing those minimum core obligations that must be (and can be) met immediately by all states – including those unable to afford to meet the general requirements of the human right to internet access. At the end of this chapter, we will understand an important part of what it would mean for public institutions to accept a human right to free internet access. Doing so generates obligations for public authorities not only towards their own citizens, but also globally towards all of humanity. If the guarantees and provisions detailed here were to be realised, a crucial step towards universal and free internet access would have been taken in that no person would be forced to remain offline. Digital poverty would be eradicated and everyone who wants to use the internet would be able to do so. On its own, the obligations set out in this chapter would not ensure that internet access is free from arbitrary interferences. This goal requires further steps that the next chapters will discuss. But by providing social guarantees against the standard threat of digital poverty, public institutions would make internet access for everyone a global reality.

5.1 FACTS ABOUT DIGITAL POVERTY WORLDWIDE AND WHAT IT WOULD TAKE TO OVERCOME IT

The figures concerning digital poverty provided by the United Nations' International Telecommunication Union (ITU) and its Broadband Commission show the size of the challenge of making universal internet access a reality. But these facts also in part explain why the world needs a human right to internet access because connectivity cannot be relied upon to come about naturally everywhere. Moreover, considering how many people in the world remain offline is also necessary for understanding whether universal internet access is something achievable rather than a pipedream. This matters since, simply because something is extremely important for our lives, this does not mean we have a right to it. It is possible for something to be necessary for a minimally decent life but at the same time to be too expensive for a person to have a right to it. There are, for instance, certain life-saving drugs that are considered too expensive (at least at a certain point in time) for public health care systems to provide, even though some are likely to die without them. Therefore, feasibility in a technical and economic sense is a crucial consideration for determining whether we can be thought to have a right or claimable entitlement to something. In this regard, the challenge posed by digital poverty and the numbers of people who cannot currently access the internet is – without doubt – enormous.

According to estimates by the ITU, 3.7 billion people (or 46 per cent of the world's population) had no access to the internet in 2019. In the subsequent years, the COVID-19 pandemic forced people to move large parts of their lives online as lockdowns and other restrictions on social life were imposed to curb the spread of the novel virus. This also led to an increase in those accessing the internet in some form. As a result, 2.9 billion (or 37 per cent of humanity) remained offline in 2021. Of these 2.9 billion digitally excluded people, 96 per cent lived in developing countries (ITU 2021a: 1). By 2023, the number of people remaining offline globally had slightly sunk to 2.6 billion (or 33 per cent of humanity, ITU 2023a: 1). However, there are questions about the quality of access of those who can use the internet. Many who count as internet users 'only get the chance to go online infrequently, via shared devices, or using connectivity speeds that markedly limit the usefulness of their connection' (ITU 2021b). The ITU, for instance, considers everyone who has gone online at least once in the last three months an internet user. This is problematic from the perspective of human rights because it is not only internet access as such, but also the quality of it, that matters. Without online access of a certain kind, it is not possible to exercise human rights online effectively. For example, to search and apply for jobs, to access and stay up to date with political information and developments, to associate with others online for political or social reasons, to search for housing, or to search for important medical information cannot be done effectively if a person can only access the internet a couple of times per month. Either the information involved is time-sensitive or activities require more frequent engagement than is possible with sporadic internet access. This means that the real figure of people in the world who can make effective use of the internet to enjoy their human rights is far lower than the number of internet users counted by the ITU.

Besides this 'usage gap' between those who access the internet and those who do not, there is also a 'coverage gap' between those who are already covered by broadband infrastructure, particularly mobile broadband, and those who are not. Broadband internet can be generally defined as 'high speed telecommunications systems, i.e. those capable of simultaneously supporting multiple information formats such as voice, high-speed data services and video services on demand' (European Commission 2022a). According to figures from the ITU, the coverage gap worldwide is considerably smaller than the usage gap, meaning that many more people are already within reach of broadband internet than can actually access it. 'Ninety-five per cent of the world population [in 2021] has access to a mobile broadband network. Between 2015 and 2021, 4G network coverage doubled to reach 88 per cent of the world's population' (ITU 2021a: 10). To understand the magnitude of the difference between the coverage gap and the usage gap, one has to consider that in 2020, 85 per cent of those who remain offline already lived within areas covered by mobile broadband networks. However, in Sub-Saharan Africa, 80 per cent of people covered by G4 broadband networks at that time were unable to use them because they were unable to afford to or because they lacked the skills needed to do so (ITU 2020: 9).[2]

The residual digital exclusion occurs along several dimensions, as the ITU explains. First, there is age. In 2020, 71 per cent of the people aged fifteen to twenty-four worldwide were using the internet but only 57 per cent of the rest of humanity. In developed countries, 99 per cent of young people in the fifteen to twenty-four age group used the internet but only 87 per cent of those older than twenty-four did, while in developing nations 67 per cent of young people used the internet but only 51 per cent of people aged twenty-five and older (ITU 2021a: 5). Another factor that determines internet use is geography. In 2020, globally 76 per cent of the urban population accessed the internet but only 39 per cent of the rural population. In the developed world that difference was 89 per cent of the urban population and 85 per cent of the rural population, while in developing countries it was 72 per cent of city dwellers but only 34 per cent of the rural population. Specifically in Africa, the continent with the lowest internet penetration, only half of the people living in cities used the internet but rurally that number fell to only 15 per cent (ITU 2021a: 6). There is also a gender gap with respect to internet use, even though it has shrunk significantly in recent years. In 2020, 62 per cent of men used the internet but only 57 per cent of all women. The digital gender gap remains an issue especially in the LDCs, where 31 per cent of men used the internet but only 19 per cent of women. In Africa specifically, 35 per cent of men versus 24 per cent of women were internet users and in the Arab states 68 per cent of men but only 56 per cent of women (ITU 2021a: 3). As already mentioned, lack of affordability of available broadband internet services (and therefore socio-economic poverty that translates into digital poverty) is one major reason why people do not use the internet. According to figures from the World Bank from 2018, 10 per cent of the world's population (736 million) lived in extreme poverty, which is to say on less than USD $1.90 a day. About 85 per cent of these poorest of the poor lived either in Sub-Saharan Africa (56 per cent) or South Asia (29 per cent) (World Bank 2018b). Africa is also the continent with the countries that have the highest rate of digitally disconnected people among their citizens (World Economic Forum 2020).

---

[2] The ITU mentions as another reason why some people remain offline: a lack of digital content relevant to them. As this factor is not caused by digital poverty (and likely affects fewer people than are affected by the lack of broadband infrastructure and the affordability of online access), it is beyond the scope of this chapter.

All these details about the digitally excluded show that the lack of internet access is most widespread in the LDCs. However, available data also shows that internet access is by no means enjoyed by everyone in developed nations either. In the UK, for instance, 7 per cent of citizens above the age of sixteen did not have internet access at home in 2023 (Ofcom 2023a: 14). Moreover, the UK government regulator for broadcasting and telecommunications industries, Ofcom, 'estimates that in October 2023 about 2.4 million (+/− 500,000) UK households with fixed broadband found it difficult to afford their fixed broadband service and 2.4 million (+/− 500,000) UK households with a mobile phone had difficulty affording their mobile phone service', which is to say that millions of UK households 'which currently have access to the internet [were] at risk of having to modify or even cancel their service, or reduce household spending elsewhere to be able to afford it' (Ofcom 2023a: 15). In the US, data from the 2021 census shows that at least 15 per cent of households did not have a broadband internet subscription in 2018 (US Census Bureau 2021: 3). Moreover, 9 per cent of the population did not use the internet in 2020 (ITU 2023b). And in Germany, 9 per cent of the population did not use the internet and 8 per cent of households had no internet access at home in 2020 (ITU 2023b). Each figure represents millions of people who are offline in countries that belong to the most affluent on the planet. Of course, of those not using the internet some will voluntarily remain offline even though they could afford online access.[3] However, other statistics reveal that lack of affordability is in fact the reason why large numbers of people in developed nations remain offline. According to the European Union's (EU's) Eurostat agency, '2.4% of people in the EU were unable to afford an internet connection for personal use at home' (Eurostat 2023: 26). That amounts to roughly 11 million people in one of the most affluent areas of the world who cannot afford to access the internet in their homes. In the US, according to the non-profit organisation EducationSuperHighway, 18.1 million households comprising 46.9 million Americans who were covered by broadband networks were unable to pay to connect to them in 2021 (EducationSuperHighway 2021: 5). As these figures show, even though digital exclusion today is mostly concentrated in the LDCs, dozens of millions of citizens in the richest societies of the world still remain unable to afford internet access as

---

[3] It remains unclear, though, how many of these people do not use the internet because they lack the basic digital skills required to do so. If lack of such digital skills is the reason why they remain unconnected, they are therefore affected by another dimension of digital poverty, as will be discussed in Section 5.3.4.

well. Digital poverty therefore remains a standard threat to internet access worldwide.

Having established who did not use the internet in 2023, we now have to consider what would be required to establish universal online access by 2030, the delivery date of the UN's Sustainable Development Goals (SDGs). The basic precondition for this goal is to extend broadband networks to cover all of humanity. The ITU also has data on the size of that particular challenge. According to its estimates, nearly USD $428 billion would be required to realise universal broadband coverage until 2030. For this, 'around 2.6 million 4G BTS [base transceiver stations] and 700,000 km of backbone fibre transmission infrastructure would have to be rolled out on top of the existing broadband network capabilities' (ITU 2020: 4). About 90 per cent of these investments would be required to build and maintain broadband networks and 40 per cent of the sum for the construction of 'last mile' broadband and transmission networks.[4] Twenty-five countries specifically would account for 75 per cent (or USD $312 billion) of all required investments, with the largest sums needed in India, China, Indonesia, Bangladesh, Pakistan, Nigeria, and Mexico (ITU 2020: 7). The ITU further estimates that of the USD $428 billion required overall, USD $288 billion would have to be funded through private investments that would go towards the construction of broadband infrastructure. A further USD $140 billion would have to be paid through public funds that primarily are used to fill infrastructure gaps where private investments are deemed unprofitable (e.g. in remote areas), for digital skills training, and for the design and implementation of policy frameworks (ITU 2020: 16).

There are generally several dimensions (or factors) to internet access that must all be considered for the internet to offer people crucial opportunities for the enjoyment of their human rights. Each of these dimensions is a prerequisite for accessing the internet. All of them can be affected by people's lack of (often financial) means and therefore be a cause of digital poverty. First, there is broadband internet infrastructure, which can be too expensive for governments to construct and insufficiently economically attractive for private companies to invest in. Second, there are digital end devices such as mobile phones, laptops, desktop PCs, or tablets that are too expensive for individuals or households to afford. Third, there are data services that are too costly for people to buy. Finally, there are the basic digital skills without which people are unable to make use of the internet even if they have access to all the other requirements. The governments of the LDCs, though, might be unable to

---

[4] That is, the infrastructure and services connecting local households and institutions to the global internet.

afford to educate their entire populations in these skills. If a human right to free internet access is to be effective, it must speak to these four dimensions of online access. However, before this chapter addresses these factors in detail, Section 5.2 sets out a distinction that is crucial for understanding the obligations entailed by the human right to internet access. This is the distinction between the general content of the right and a set of more limited, minimum core obligations.

5.2 HUMAN RIGHTS AND THEIR MINIMUM CORE OBLIGATIONS

The facts about global inequality are staggering. According to the World Inequality Report 2022, the richest 10 per cent of humanity earn 52 per cent of global income and own 76 per cent of all wealth (World Inequality Database 2022). And according to Oxfam's 2022 'Inequality Kills' report, socio-economic inequality contributes to the death of about 21,300 people each day, 5.6 million people die from lack of health care in non-affluent countries annually, and hunger kills more than 2.1 million people each year (Oxfam 2022). As explained in Chapter 1, human rights are best understood as protections of the conditions of minimally decent lives. As these facts show, there are several countries, especially those least developed, that lack the resources to guarantee even these minimal entitlements for their citizens. However, human rights are supposed to be universal standards that governments, private companies, and the international community respect and protect. That is why human rights are matters of international concern and those capable of providing help to guarantee them in states whose governments are unable to do so have obligations to provide such aid. But global inequality and poverty pose two important questions for our understanding of human rights. First, do human rights lose their effectiveness and practical reality if some states are not able to guarantee them? That is, what good are human rights if they are not universally realisable for all states so that these have to rely on the willingness of others to fulfil their obligations to offer help for securing what everyone needs to lead minimally decent lives? And, second, are those states that are unable to realise all human rights of all their citizens therefore free from human rights-related obligations? This second question is addressed by the idea of minimum core obligations, which we will discuss further later.

The first question, though, requires us directly to consider the issue of what level of support for human rights fulfilment can reasonably be demanded of states and the international community. It forces us to confront a question: how do we determine what a human right can require? Global inequality and poverty mean that, when we think about what human rights entail, the question of what is required for a minimally decent life is not the only aspect that matters. Instead, we must also ask what can feasibly be demanded globally as guarantees from those who have to fulfil human rights, such as states and the international community. The higher these standards are set, the more states are unable to fulfil them because they lack the necessary resources. This would then require more support from the international community whose members would have to devote more of their resources towards the fulfilment of human rights of people in other countries. This might ultimately become counterproductive if delivering support for human rights elsewhere reduces aid-providing states' own ability to help or even overstretch their capacity to provide aid. On the other hand, the lower human rights standards are set, the more countries could fulfil them on their own. At the same time, though, fewer things are guaranteed for everyone. At some point, if human rights are interpreted too restrictively, they no longer guarantee minimally decent lives. Because of the dire realities of global inequality and poverty, the demands of human rights therefore must be determined in consideration of (1) what is required for minimally decent lives and (2) what can be guaranteed by a substantial majority of countries in the world (Nickel 2007: 149–150).

Human rights so understood are realistic global demands but not standards that are entirely dependent on global levels of affluence. Even if all countries were to become affluent, what is required of public authorities by human rights is limited to what is needed for leading minimally good lives. As technology develops, those requirements can change. For instance, the provision of new and better medicines might fall under what is demanded by the human right to health care. The use of technological means might become necessary for adequate basic education covered by the human right to education. As this book argues, internet access has become a requirement for leading minimally decent lives in our digitalised societies. But human rights never guarantee what is required for excellent or flourishing lives. This would go beyond their function and exceed the burdens that can be justified to those who have to fulfil human rights. But also considering the opposite case, what is required for minimally decent lives (e.g. the means of subsistence, shelter, legal equality, free speech, freedom of conscience) does not depend entirely on how affluent societies are. We can, for instance, imagine a situation in which many societies fall into poverty or are struck by natural disaster so that they can no longer guarantee for their citizens what is needed for living minimally decent lives. This would resemble earlier times in human history when many human rights were unfulfillable. Public authorities here would be excused from failing to fulfil human rights owing to their genuine inability to do so. But even then, human rights still retain their normative force because obligations for public authorities to realise them would set in as soon as they are in a position again to provide what is needed for decent lives.

In situations in between these extremes, though, such as the state our world is currently in, the determination of the content of human rights must consider what is feasible for a majority of countries right now to avoid making unrealistic claims. Human rights that are so demanding that they cannot be guaranteed by most countries would to a significant extent be inoperable and thereby ineffective standards (Nickel 2007: 79–82). For these reasons, neither what is required by minimally decent lives, nor what is currently realisable for most countries, can alone determine what human rights require. Both aspects must be considered when specifying what a human right generally entails. Importantly, the formulation and widespread acceptance of the United Nations' SDGs (UN 2023a) indicate that political leaders at the highest level are convinced that it is feasible to guarantee minimally decent lives for all people on the planet because the realisation of these goals would eradicate indecent living conditions. This means that the considerations of feasibility and what minimally good lives require do not practically diverge. That is, there are good reasons to believe that limiting human rights to what is feasible for most states in the world right now does in fact mean that the fulfilment of human rights secures decent lives for people. Even though human rights so understood are fulfillable for a majority of countries right now, this does not mean that they are superfluous demands. That is because, while human rights are realisable for most states, this does not mean that countries that could fulfil them indeed do so. Human rights therefore provide important critical standards and normative claims for people everywhere whose governments fail to provide them with the conditions of minimally good lives.

This leaves the second question posed earlier regarding the duties of those states that are excused for failing to fulfil all human rights for their citizens because they are unable to do so. If human rights would make no claims on these states whatsoever, their fulfilment would entirely depend on outside support. The governments of non-affluent states would then have no duties concerning those human rights that they cannot guarantee. However, the United Nations' Committee on Economic, Social, and Cultural Rights (CESCR) has made clear that even the governments of the least affluent nations are not free from obligations that derive from human rights – even if they are genuinely unable to realise these rights completely. In its 'General Comment 3: The Nature of States Parties' Obligations', the Committee notes that 'a minimum core obligation to ensure the satisfaction of, at the very least, minimum essential levels of each of the rights is incumbent upon every State party' (CESCR 1990: §10). Minimum core obligations are therefore a way to acknowledge the unfortunate reality of poverty, inequality, and 'the constraints due to the limits of available resources' (CESCR 1990: §1) that exists in our world, while at the same time preserving the universal force of human rights (Tasioulas 2017b). These still make demands on states that are too poor to fulfil them in their entirety. As the Committee states, even the poorest states must make 'every effort' to use 'all resources' at their disposal to meet as 'a matter of priority' these minimum core obligations of human rights (CESCR 1990: §10).

Core obligations therefore constitute duties for all states that they have to fulfil 'with immediate effect' (CESCR 1990, §1; see Tasioulas 2017b: 12). Minimum core obligations in this way contrast with other aspects of human rights that are subject to 'progressive realisation' (CESCR 1990, §1) through the continuous efforts of states. This distinction between minimum core obligations and those aspects of the general content of human rights that states are permitted to realise progressively if they cannot be guaranteed right away is limited to socio-economic human rights and does not apply to civil and political human rights.[5] With respect to socio-economic rights, though, the idea of core obligations is universally authoritative and specific. For example, concerning the human right to health, the CESCR states in its 'General Comment 14: The Right to the Highest Attainable Standard to Health' that this right entails the following minimum core obligations:

- non-discriminatory access to health care facilities, goods, and services;
- the provision of a minimum of essential food, basic shelter, and sanitation;
- access to essential drugs as specified by the World Health Organization's Action Programme on Essential Drugs;
- the equitable distribution of health care facilities, goods, and services; and
- the adoption and implementation of a national public health strategy and plan for action. (CESCR 2000: §43)

---

[5] One reason for not allowing for a progressive realisation of any aspects of civil and political human rights can be seen in the thought that these rights primarily require abstaining from hindering others to exercise these rights, for example, to freely voice their opinions and to freely associate with others. Another reason might be that these first-generation rights are deemed especially important so that states cannot be permitted not to respect them even for a short period of time. However, the restriction of the idea of minimum core obligations to socio-economic human rights is itself contentious because (as we saw in Chapter 2) the effective protection of civil and political human rights requires a lot of resources as well and not merely abstaining from preventing the exercise of these rights. Moreover, socio-economic rights are no less urgent than civil or political human rights.

In our determination of what the human right to free internet access must entail as reasonable social guarantees against digital poverty, we must therefore apply an important distinction. Considering the facts about digital poverty outlined earlier, it is clear that realising the human right to free internet access will require enormous resources. Because it is unlikely that all states can immediately guarantee free internet access to all citizens, we have to distinguish between the right's general content and those minimum core obligations that are to be fulfilled immediately even by those states unable to afford to realise the entire human right. The aspects of the human right to free internet access that are not its core obligations, on the other hand, are a matter of progressive realisation for these states. Therefore, in a first step we have to ask what is the general content of the human right to free internet access that presents the global standard that all states have to aim to meet? This general content has to address all four elements or dimensions of internet access whose non-fulfilment causes digital poverty. These are (1) broadband infrastructure, (2) digital end devices, (3) data services, and (4) basic digital skills. In a second step, we then have to identify the minimum core obligations that are currently universally feasible and must be fulfilled immediately by all states. These two steps are taken respectively in Sections 5.3 and 5.4.

5.3 THE GENERAL CONTENT OF THE HUMAN RIGHT TO FREE INTERNET ACCESS REGARDING DIGITAL POVERTY

The novel human right has to guarantee that nobody who wants to access the internet is unable to do so. Having access to the internet has become too important to leave it up to chance and how well-off people are individually. Everyone has to have sufficient data, access to a digital device, be covered by internet broadband networks, and possess the skills minimally required to use the internet. Whatever is to become part of the content (and therefore a demand) of this human right must fulfil two requirements. First, it must secure adequate opportunities for the exercise of human rights online for everyone. That, after all, is the point of having this right in the first place. Second, for the reasons discussed in Section 5.2, what the right demands must be feasible for a substantial majority of states in the world right now. In this section, we will consider plausible demands or standards that the human right to free internet can make on public authorities around the globe. For this purpose, we will consider numerous examples of actual internet-related policies and projects that indicate the feasibility of the suggested standards. Since there are more people who are already covered by broadband networks but cannot access the internet because they lack digital devices and/or affordable data than there are people who are beyond the range of broadband networks (i.e. the point that the usage gap is larger than the coverage gap), we will first consider the requirements the right has to make in terms of data and digital devices. Subsequently, we will look at standards for broadband infrastructure and digital skills.

5.3.1 Social Guarantees for Data

Without affordable data,[6] even owning the most recent digital end device does not allow a person to access the internet. Limited access to data also does not allow someone to exercise human rights on the internet effectively. So what universal social guarantee does the human right to internet access plausibly require concerning data?

A plausible standard in this respect is the Broadband Commission's affordability target that it considers achievable globally by 2025 (Broadband Commission 2022). According to this goal, entry-level broadband services should cost people no more than 2 per cent of their country's monthly gross national income (GNI) per capita. For the Broadband Commission, entry-level broadband services include data-only mobile broadband plans with a minimum monthly allowance of 2 GB (gigabyte) and fixed-broadband plans with a minimum monthly allowance of 5 GB. Data affordability varies significantly around the world depending on countries' level of economic development. As the ITU states, in 2021 'the share of income that entry-level fixed and mobile broadband represents for users in low- and middle-income economies is typically five to six times greater than in high-income economies' (ITU 2021c: 1).

To understand whether the 2 (GB) for 2 (percentage of monthly GNI per capita) standard is realistic for a majority of countries, we have to know what digital data services cost around the world, which countries already fulfil this target, and where it is within reach. Data from the ITU supports the view that 2 for 2 is indeed a feasible standard that can be met by a substantial majority of countries. According to the ITU, in 2020, 103 out of 185 countries covered in its study already met the 2 GB data-only mobile broadband data target. In a further forty-seven countries, the cost of entry-level mobile broadband services

---

[6] To clarify, 'data' is technically speaking the information transmitted itself. This section focuses on access to data networks. However, since the use of the term 'data' has been widely accepted (i.e. one pays for a subscription to access data networks that can be used to send and receive information rather than for the actual information itself), I use it here instead of the more cumbersome term 'data network access'.

was between 2 per cent and 5 per cent of GNI. For the fixed-broadband data target that number was lower and only sixty-six out of 174 countries covered met the 5 GB for 2 per cent of monthly GNI per capita target and in a further forty-five countries the price was between 2 per cent to 5 per cent of GNI (ITU 2021c: 2–3). This is in part because fixed broadband networks are much less widely available globally than mobile networks. According to the ITU, though, 'fixed broadband [accounted] for 83 per cent of all [internet] traffic' in 2022 (ITU 2023a: 24). The COVID-19 pandemic lowered GNIs worldwide. Consequently, the number of economies meeting the mobile broadband target in 2021 decreased to ninety-six and the number of economies that met the mixed broadband target fell to sixty-four. Despite data services becoming more expensive during that time, the number of people using the internet increased owing to the pandemic. From this trend, the ITU draws the conclusion that 'the fact that the demand for broadband services increased in [2020 and 2021], even as they became less affordable, shows that Internet access is not a luxury but a necessity' (ITU 2021c: 1). Before the COVID-19 pandemic, there had been a trend of steadily decreasing prices especially for mobile broadband data. But even though recent price increases might be temporary until the effects of the pandemic recede, in the near future the 2 for 2 affordability standard is only feasible for mobile data while 'entry-level fixed broadband Internet remains unaffordable for a majority of the world's population' (ITU 2021c: 7). However, the ITU is clear that 'adjusted for GNI per capita, the world price [for data-only mobile broadband reached] 1.9 per cent in 2021' (ITU 2021c: 4). This indicates that the 2 for 2 for mobile internet data standard is feasible for a majority of countries, and as such a plausible demand that the human right to free internet access can include.

Importantly, data affordability is not simply a matter of what internet service providers are willing and able to offer their customers. States can adopt policies that promote data affordability. This is in part why the 2 for 2 standard creates political obligations for public authorities rather than presenting a purely economic target to be reached by the efforts of private sector agents alone. One policy that states can pursue to help reduce the price of data is the adoption of national broadband plans. These are policy documents that specify targets and aspirations for the development of the information and communications technology (ICT) sector in a country and often include public investment commitments into ICT development (A4AI 2020a: 17). According to the Alliance for Affordable Internet Access, 'national broadband plans correlate positively with greater internet affordability. Countries with a national broadband plan that sets clear, time-bound targets and interventions for reducing broadband cost and increasing penetration tend to have lower internet prices relative to average income' (A4AI 2020a: 19). By setting out public commitments and targets, broadband plans can, for example, provide certainty for private sector investments and thereby contribute to making data services less expensive. Besides national broadband plans, there are other policy options for states to promote the 2 for 2 target. Not all of these might be possible or sensible to adopt for all states, but they give an idea of the policy choices available to states to influence the affordability of data for their citizens. The ITU, for instance, suggests the following steps as 'golden rules for mobile and fixed broadband adoption' that help to bring down the price of internet data (ITU 2020: 13):

- States should eliminate public monopolies on the provision of information and communication technology (ICT) services and ensure that there is full competition among private sector providers of mobile and fixed data services. For the resulting choices to present effective alternatives for citizens, it is important that public authorities legally mandate mobile number portability so customers can easily switch service providers.
- States can also promote competition among service providers by requiring those who privately own broadband infrastructure to share it for a fee with other ICT service providers.
- Ensuring that there is full competition in international gateway services and permitting foreign ownership of, and participation in, national internet services is another way to bring down their price for citizens.
- Finally, as an additional policy option, the Alliance for Affordable Internet points out that in some cases like that of Sweden, the provision of broadband services by public authorities themselves, such as municipalities, has had a positive impact on data affordability as they appear as one competitor in broadband service markets. (A4AI 2021a: 18)[7]

Having established that 2 GB mobile data for 2 per cent of monthly GNI per capita is a realistic goal for a majority of states, we now have to consider whether this standard also meets the second desideratum of enabling the effective use of human rights online. To see whether 2 GB is sufficient for this purpose we need to know what a person can do with that much data. Various private companies offer estimates of what 2 GB data can be used for. According to a 2018 statement from the American internet service provider Verizon, 2 GB data

---

[7] However, a specific issue with the Swedish municipal broadband service provision is that households need to pay for their own connection to the broadband network, which does not help lower data costs for poor households.

a month enables a person each day to send or receive 100 emails, visit 100 websites, stream fifteen minutes of music, and to watch two minutes of videos (Verizon 2018). And a look at the mobile usage calculator of the UK price comparison website Confused.com suggests that with 2 GB of data per month, in terms of individual activities, a person is able to either browse the web for eighty-nine hours, send or receive 68,533 emails or WhatsApp messages, chat for nine hours via Skype, use Google Maps for thirty-four hours, or play 137 YouTube videos (Confused.com 2023). These examples suggest that 2 GB of mobile data is enough to allow a person to use the internet effectively, and to have adequate opportunities to realise their human rights online. This amount of data gives them decent options to communicate and receive information on a daily basis. Of course, 2 GB does not permit the daily streaming of movies or hours of video consumption on social media. However, that is not a problem from the perspective of the human right to free internet access because human rights only secure what is needed for minimally decent lives. Watching movies or streaming dozens of social media videos daily arguably are neither necessary for a decent life nor for adequately enjoying our human rights online.[8] Moreover, it is important to note that the 2 for 2 standard does not limit the data a person can use to 2 GB per month. The point of this target is to ensure that a person can afford at least that much data. If 2 GB of mobile data costs no more than 2 per cent of monthly GNI per capita, it is reasonable to think that most people can afford more than those 2 GB of monthly data.

Fulfilment of the 2 for 2 affordability target set by the human right to free internet access can be expected to ensure that most citizens have sufficient data to make adequate use of their human rights online. This means that, just as is the case with other necessities of minimally decent lives (e.g. means of subsistence, shelter, clothing), most people will not need public support for access to what is required in terms of internet data for decent lives when this standard is met. But what about those who are unable to spend as much as 2 per cent of monthly GNI per capita on internet data services because their income is below that of the average person? One way to support them, and to ensure they have access to adequate internet data, is for public authorities to subsidise their data purchases, as several countries have done. For example, as part of its 2016 Internet Móvil Social para la Gente programme (MINTIC Colombia 2016), the Colombian government provided 3–4 GB data packages

---

[8] This also explains why the Alliance for Affordable Internet's idea that unlimited broadband at home, the workplace, or place of education is required for meaningful internet connectivity (A4AI 2020b: 8–9) would be a too demanding standard for the human right to free internet access – even if this goal was to become globally feasible.

at a discounted social rate of COP $6,000 (c. USD $2) with free data between 11 pm and 5 am as well as a smartphone at a subsidised price to low-income citizens (A4AI 2017: 12, OECD 2019a). Similarly, the Ecuadorian government's 2018 Social Tariffs Project reduced the cost of data for eligible citizens by almost 90 per cent and enabled an estimated 644,000 Ecuadorians to become new data service users (A4AI 2020c). In the US, the Federal Communications Commission (FCC) through its Universal Service Fund operates the Lifeline programme that subsidises phone and broadband services with USD $9.25 per month for low-income citizens (FCC 2023a). Additionally, the FCC's Affordable Connectivity Program provides discounts of up to USD $30 per month for eligible households towards their internet service (FCC 2023b). In May 2022, the US government also secured a commitment from twenty leading internet service providers that serve areas inhabited by 80 per cent of the US population to provide discounted data services at no more than USD $30 to these households, thereby making internet services effectively free for them (The Guardian 2022).[9] And in the UK, people who receive certain social benefits are also eligible to benefit from specific social tariffs on broadband services that decrease their monthly costs to GBP £10–20 (Ofcom 2023b). Publicly funded programmes such as these can further reduce the number of citizens who are priced out of data services. However, even such programmes are unlikely to fully ensure that everyone has access to sufficient internet data because some people have no income of their own. For those people still unable to afford the data they need to use their human rights online, public authorities have to provide funds for the required services as part of sufficiently generous unconditional social welfare benefits.

This point explains one essential meaning of the term a human right to 'free' internet access. Internet access – here the aspect of data needed to access the internet – has to be provided free for those who are unable to afford it. One way such free access can be realised is by including and earmarking a certain amount of money specifically for internet data use in the means-tested social minimum benefits that are available to all who have to rely on them. An example of such a policy is the German social welfare benefit scheme that contains a specific sum for internet data services. The reason for including this specific item of support is the German government's recognition that the use of fixed broadband and mobile data services is now part of 'the socio-cultural minimum level of subsistence' (Deutscher Bundestag 2020: 13). In 2020, the government

---

[9] It is important to note, though, that the Affordable Connectivity Program is a temporary programme dependent on renewed funding by the US Congress, and therefore does not provide lasting security for connectivity for citizens depending on it (FCC 2024).

specified as fundable costs for a flat-rate fixed broadband connection and a mobile phone plan the sum of EUR €33.45 as part of an overall monthly benefit payment of EUR €434.90 (Deutscher Bundestag 2020: 29). Whether allowances such as this suffice to guarantee sufficient data to use the internet to exercise human rights depends on the prices of the internet services available and whether the overall welfare benefit payment is sufficiently generous to cover all other essentials of life as well.

Another way that states can try to ensure that all their citizens have sufficient data is to impose a legal requirement on companies to provide free basic data services for the minority of citizens unable to afford even discounted data services, and who qualify for this support, for example, because they receive basic social welfare benefits. Such mandatory basic support could be funded through surcharges on high-end data services that internet service providers collect from their customers. Such a surcharge could not be imposed on all data plans as this would make it too expensive for some people to afford less than maximal data services, but who could pay for them without the extra fee. Taxing high-end plan data users would not merely be financially viable. It would also be based on a particular moral justification. On the one hand, those who can afford extensive data services have certain advantages in the ways they can exercise their human rights online. On the other hand, taxing these data services that confer the advantages would raise revenues to limit the scale of these unequal opportunities to help fund data services (and therefore also increased opportunities to exercise human rights) for those who can otherwise not afford these services. More affluent people's purchase of high-end data services would thus fund data for less fortunate people, thereby ensuring that everyone has at least a minimum level of data available to use the internet. Alternatively, public authorities could tax the profits of internet service providers and internet-based content/application companies explicitly for the purposes of funding public guarantees for internet data services. Such an approach would have to be balanced against potential disincentives for these companies to invest in improved or new ICT infrastructure or the development of better data services. A policy of this kind could be modelled on the universal service fee that the US government imposes on the revenues of telecommunication providers to fund its universal service fund, which resources programmes such as Lifeline and E-rate (FCC 2023c). However, this pathway is only effective in economies in which a majority of people are already able to afford more-than-minimal broadband plans for themselves as the number of those contributing to the public programmes might otherwise be too small. Finally, governments could also incentivise internet data providers to participate in schemes such as the 'Donate your Data' programme in Australia

(Optus 2023). Initiatives of that kind enable users to donate their unused data that they have paid for to others who cannot afford data for themselves. Such programmes do not generate disadvantages for data service providers as they have been paid for the data that is donated. They also do not lose out on the sale of additional data because those using the donated data are unable to pay for it otherwise.

Finally, instead of providing funds for affording data services directly to citizens, public authorities can ensure universal access to sufficient data by offering low-cost or free internet access via Wi-Fi hotspots in public buildings and spaces. Initiatives of this kind have already been implemented around the world and public access options are also important for women who face barriers to accessing data and devices at home (A4AI 2019: 29). For instance, the European Commission's WiFi4EU initiative awards vouchers of EUR €15,000 to municipalities in EU member states for the installation of free Wi-Fi hotspots in public spaces such as public buildings, libraries, health centres, museums, squares, and parks (European Commission 2023a). By 2022, more than 8,800 municipalities across Europe have benefited from this programme, which has paid out EUR €132 million (HaDEA 2020). In May 2021, as part of its Internet Master Plan for Universal Broadband, New York City announced it would spend USD $157 million to build publicly owned, open-access broadband infrastructure to make the internet accessible for up to 1.6 million residents (NYC 2021). Boston's public libraries on their part provide free, outdoor Wi-Fi twenty-four hours per day in fourteen locations throughout the city (City of Boston 2023). In affluent societies, free internet access in public libraries plays a particularly crucial role for providing internet access to homeless people who often have no other place to go online. Studies in the US have found that public online access for those often worst-off in affluent societies is crucial for passing time and developing social connections with others (Marler 2023), as well as for searching for housing, finding medical care, and accessing social benefits and emails (City Bar Justice Center 2020), or, in other words, for exercising their fundamental human rights (e.g. to health care, a decent standard of living, free information) as best as they can given their situation.

Free public Wi-Fi initiatives have also been implemented by governments in developing countries. For example, in 2016 the Thai government began work on its Village Broadband Internet Project (Net Pracharat). As part of this project, it installed free Wi-Fi hotspots in underserved rural villages. By 2018, these hotspots had served more than 4.5 million registered users (Net Pracharat 2018). In the Philippines, the government has committed to providing free Wi-Fi to all citizens in all public places through its Pipol Konek project (Republic of the Philippines 2023). In 2018, the government partnered with the UN Development Programme to add to the existing 2,677 public Wi-Fi sites (UN Department of Economic and Social Affairs 2022). As a result, the number of free Wi-Fi hotspots had increased to over 8,900 by 2022. As part of its National Telecommunication Development Plan 2015–2021 (PNDT), the Costa Rican government spent USD $8.1 million on creating 510 free public internet access zones that had already been used by more than 1 million users in 2020 (Sutel 2020: 27, 210). To take another example, in 2016, the South African province of Western Cape began offering free Wi-Fi services at 178 public buildings that allowed the use of up to 250MB data per device per month (West Cape Government 2022). In 2022, the province government then partnered with a South African private sector company to expand its network of free public Wi-Fi hotspots at public buildings to 1,600 places, which now allowed the use of up to 3 GB data per device per month.

All these examples that aim to provide citizens with the data they need to exercise their human rights online effectively show that there is a large variety of policies that governments throughout the world can adopt to meet the data-related standard of the human right to free internet access. Once 2 GB of mobile data costs no more than 2 per cent of monthly GNI per capita, it can be expected that most citizens are able to afford the data needed to use the internet to enjoy their human rights. However, because our economic systems and property rights schemes allow for people to become poor, there will be those who will be unable to afford sufficient data even under these circumstances. The examples considered in this section also suggest that meeting the data target of the human right to free internet access is not limited to states of the developed world. Cases from various developing countries indicate that it can reasonably be argued that the target is met by, or within reach for, a sizeable majority of nations around the world. We also saw that the 2 for 2 standard secures sufficient internet data to adequately use one's human rights online. As data from the ITU shows, guaranteeing this data for all citizens would not be overburdening for governments in most states. In Section 5.3.2, we turn to another dimension of internet access that requires public support to ensure everyone can access the internet, namely access to an adequate digital device.

5.3.2 Social Guarantees for Digital End Devices

Those who want to use the internet need a digital end device to do so. Current examples of such devices are desktop personal computers, laptops, smartphones, and tablets. These are still unaffordable for many people in developing countries and also for some in affluent societies. What would the human right to free internet access demand in terms of public guarantees for access to digital devices? Any standard regarding this will have to adapt as information and communication technologies develop and become more widespread, and as the uses of these technologies change. But we can nonetheless specify a plausible standard for the present.

A reasonable demand that the human right to free internet access can include is that everyone should have permanent access to a smartphone. This is one of four dimensions of 'meaningful connectivity' as suggested by the Alliance for Affordable Internet. A smartphone can be specified as 'a device that has a minimum screen size of 3", a touch screen, the ability to install apps (i.e. with no restriction on the number of apps by the app store), and a camera' (A4AI 2020b: 7). There are numerous reasons for adopting this particular device standard. First, a significant number of people already have access to a smartphone. According to the Global System for Mobile Communications Association (GSMA), in 2020, the share of smartphone subscriptions of all mobile phone subscriptions was at least 57 per cent in all parts of the world – apart from Sub-Saharan Africa, where it was 48 per cent (GSMA 2020). In 2021, there were 6.2 billion smartphone subscriptions worldwide that accounted for three-quarters of all mobile phone subscriptions. That year, 4.2 billion people globally used mobile broadband networks, which amounted to 53 per cent of the estimated 7.9 billion people on the planet. The GSMA projects that the number of these subscriptions will rise to 7.4 billion by 2025, when more than four out of five mobile subscriptions globally will be for smartphones. The number of mobile broadband users is expected to reach 5 billion (GSMA 2022: 6–7) and global smartphone penetration to reach 80 per cent that year (GSMA 2020: 5). These figures suggest that the majority of people in the majority of countries will have permanent access to a smartphone by 2025. Accordingly, the number of people who need public support for having permanent access to a smartphone is decreasing steadily, which reduces the burden on states that the human right to free internet access imposes on governments concerning digital devices. And as we will see later in this section, just as with internet data services, there are also policies that public authorities pursue to ensure that people can afford their own smartphone.

Second, the existing infrastructure for mobile broadband is much more widely developed than that for fixed broadband. As explained in Section 5.1, the ITU finds that 'ninety-five per cent of the world population now has access to a mobile broadband network. Between 2015 and 2021, 4G network coverage doubled to reach 88 per cent of the world's population' (ITU 2021a: 10). Moreover, 70 per cent of those who remain offline live within the reach of 4G mobile broadband networks (ITU 2020: 9), which means that the coverage gap is much smaller than the usage gap. The situation is very different for fixed broadband connections. In 2021, there were seventeen fixed broadband connections per 100 people globally. These, though, were mostly concentrated in the wealthiest nations. 'In the LDCs, [...] fixed broadband remains the privilege of a few, with only 1.4 subscriptions per 100 inhabitants' (ITU 2021a: 7). The fact that mobile network infrastructure is much more widely developed than fixed broadband matters because to access mobile broadband networks one usually requires a smartphone. Universal internet access is therefore much more quickly achievable through mobile rather than fixed broadband. However, the availability of broadband infrastructure also affects the price of internet data and therefore how many people require public support to access the internet. As we saw in Section 5.3.1, mobile internet data is more affordable than fixed broadband subscriptions. That is shown by the fact that many more countries already fulfil (or are close to fulfilling) the 2 GB data for 2 per cent of monthly GNI per capita for mobile broadband data standard than fulfil the 5 GB for 2 per cent of monthly GNI per capita for fixed broadband data target. This, too, suggests that universal internet access is most quickly achievable through mobile broadband connectivity.

Third, smartphones have particularly useful features and capabilities that are helpful to users from various backgrounds. Among the key advantages of smartphones are their portability and their multifunctionality that enable people to use video, voice, and apps. Voice recognition specifically can help illiterate people and persons with disabilities to use the devices through voice command and services such as voice notes (A4AI 2020b: 7). Ownership of smartphones has also been shown to be potentially important for the empowerment of women (ITU 2021a: 18). Since women can use these devices to access crucial information online, 'mobile-phone access is associated with lower gender inequality, higher contraceptive uptake, and lower maternal and child mortality' (Rotondi et al. 2020: 13413). Moreover, UNESCO has used mobile phones in various projects to promote the literacy skills of women and girls in Africa and Asia (UNESCO 2015). However, the availability of smartphones alone is unlikely to empower women if existing traditional gender norms and roles are not challenged independently (Summers et al. 2020). After all, if women are oppressed by men, their access to and use of smartphones is also likely controlled by men. Nevertheless, the portability and multifunctionality of smartphones makes them uniquely useful for the exercise and protection of human rights. Because of these features, people can, for example, access and send important information without having to be in a specific place, and record videos and other evidence of human rights violations that they witness.

As in the case with data, the main problem that those still offline face with respect to devices is affordability. According to the Broadband

Commission, as of 2021, 'nearly 2.5 billion people live in countries where the cost of the cheapest available smartphone is a quarter or more of the average monthly income. In Africa, devices remain out of reach for many, where devices cost on average 62.8 per cent of average monthly income' (Broadband Commission 2021a: 6). The issue of unaffordable devices is not limited to the developing world, though. 'Even in higher-income countries such as the US, tens of millions of students were still without digital devices or home Internet prior to the pandemic' (Broadband Commission 2021a: 25). In some instances, new technological developments help to meet the affordability challenge. For instance, a new, inexpensive internet-capable phone, the Jio Phone, became available in India in 2017. This is a smart feature phone that uses its own operating system (KaiOS) as an alternative to more expensive global brand operating systems. As a result, the production costs of a Jio Phone were limited to USD $23, and it was sold by the Jio telecommunications company at a discounted cost of USD $20 to make it affordable for more new customers (Broadband Commission 2019: 88). However, the Jio Phone also has drawbacks. It is not a complete smartphone but only has smartphone features, and those who use it are dependent on the phone's producer for their services. The phone is also not available throughout the developing world. Nonetheless, the example of the Jio Phone shows how new technological developments can make digital devices available to more people.

States, though, are not limited to waiting for technological innovations to promote smartphone accessibility for their citizens. Rather, as in the case of internet data, governments can adopt policies that can help people afford a basic smartphone. For example, governments can reduce import and sales taxes that they apply to digital devices. In this respect, the UN Broadband Commission recommends that countries sign up to the World Trade Organization's Information Technology Agreement (WTO 2023). This would eliminate import duties on ICT equipment and thereby reduce the costs of digital devices for users (Broadband Commission 2019: 70). States can also reduce value added taxes on digital devices, as some states have already done. In 2016, for instance, the Colombian Congress removed taxes on the purchase of low-end mobile devices and computers, and instead increased the tax on digital services marketed predominantly to affluent users, such as Netflix and Uber (A4AI 2020d). This change in taxation was therefore a redistributive measure designed to promote digital uptake and inclusion of the poorest in society. As a result, from 2017 onwards mobile phone sales in Columbia increased. Today the country has a relatively high rate of mobile phone ownership and one of the lowest digital gender gaps in the region. To take another example, in 2009 the Kenyan government eliminated value-added tax for mobile devices. This correlated with an increase in the mobile penetration rate from 50 per cent to 70 per cent (Broadband Commission 2019: 85). Reducing taxation and tariffs on digital devices leads to a loss of revenue for states in the short run. From the perspective of the human right to free internet access, though, it is important to remember that it is a matter of justice to enable people to access the internet so they can use their fundamental rights online. For them, using the internet improves access to health care, education, government services, and political information. But also economically, internet access has benefits for countries. Digital inclusion 'has the potential to create more jobs, encourage entrepreneurship among the youth, increase farmers' productivity, bring more women into the labor force, and create markets' (Broadband Commission 2019: 28). These benefits must be weighed against the cost of losing tax revenue in the short term. As the Broadband Commission notes, 40 per cent of the price of entry-level smartphones in Sub-Saharan African countries can consist of import duties and tax (Broadband Commission 2021a: 41). Therefore, policies that reduce taxes and tariffs have a real potential to make digital devices affordable for many more people in developing countries.

Governments can also directly subsidise digital device ownership. The US's Affordable Connectivity Program (FCC 2023b), for instance, provides eligible households with a one-time USD $100 support for the purchase of a laptop, desktop computer, or tablet. Similar approaches have been pursued in other parts of the world. In 2014, the Malaysian government launched the Government Youth Communications Package that gave a USD $65 rebate on the purchase of a smartphone costing of up to USD $165 for citizens between the ages of 21–30. A total of 440,000 people applied for this rebate (GSMA 2017: 105). In Costa Rica, the government helped fund digital devices as part of its PNDT. Until 2020 it had spent more than USD $100 million to provide subsidies for internet service and devices to more than 155,000 socio-economically vulnerable households. Of these households that comprise more than 510,000 individuals, 68 per cent had a female head of household (Sutel 2020: 206, 207). And in Colombia, the government offered subsidies for smartphone purchases to a number of low-income citizens as part of its 2016 Internet Móvil Social para la Gente programme (MINTIC Colombia 2016). The same year, the Argentinian government implemented the Plan Mobile Internet Access, a national programme that provided funds for 8 million citizens to upgrade from 2G smart feature phones to 4G enabled smartphones that cost up to ARS $2,200 (~USD $138) (GSMA 2017: 57).

Adoption of such policies would still leave offline those who are not affluent enough to afford a smartphone or other digital end devices. As in the case of digital data, governments should provide at least smartphones for this group of people or provide them with a specific grant for the purpose of purchasing one. Those on minimum public social benefits cannot be expected to save up to buy a basic smartphone. It is therefore practically inconsistent if a public social minimum payment includes monthly allowances for fixed and mobile internet data plans but no provision for the purchase of a digital end device. If internet and mobile phone use are now indeed part of the socio-cultural minimum level of subsistence, help must be provided for a digital device for accessing the internet as well. Financial support for a digital device was offered exceptionally by some governments during the COVID-19 pandemic. For example, in 2020 the UK government provided more than 1 million tablets and laptops to schools and councils to distribute to disadvantaged children and young people to enable them to study remotely during the pandemic (UK Government 2020b). This was because education had been forced to take place online owing to the lockdowns to curb the spread of the virus. And in 2021, for the same reason, recipients of the German minimum welfare benefit payment were able to apply once for up to EUR €350 to pay for the costs of a digital end device (e.g. a tablet or laptop) that had become required for taking part in public education (Bundesagentur für Arbeit 2021). These were positive and necessary initiatives of public institutions during the height of the COVID-19 pandemic. But even though the pandemic exacerbated the need for internet access, as we have seen in Part I of this book, being able to go online is also vitally important during non-emergency times and for many other purposes than education. Public authorities therefore have to ensure that everyone has permanent access at least to a smartphone that makes it possible for people to access the internet. Governments of less affluent countries have also provided digital devices to promote internet access for those needing support. For example, in 2016, as part of its Benazir Income Support Programme the Pakistani government gave 30,000 smartphones to low-income women (Haq 2016). In 2021, the government of the Indian province Uttar Pradesh distributed 40,000 tablets and 60,000 smartphones to final year undergraduate and postgraduate students in the state (Indian Express 2021). And in Costa Rica, the Connected Homes programme ('hogares connectados') funded up to 100 per cent of the costs of a laptop for eligible households (Q Costa Rica 2018), which has benefited tens of thousands of families (Sutel 2017: 179, A4AI 2021b: 9).

Importantly, digital devices provided by public institutions do not have to be of unused quality. Instead, public authorities can run, or cooperate with, initiatives such as the DeviceDotNow campaign in the UK that calls for companies to donate used digital devices (Future.Now 2023). These are then given to those who require them via the campaign's Online Centres Network. In Luxembourg, the non-profit organisation Digital Inclusion is supported by the Luxembourgian Ministry of Families and Integration. Digital Inclusion collects donated digital end devices, repairs them, and gives them to people who cannot afford them (Digital Inclusion 2023). The same idea is realised by the National Device Bank operated in the UK by the Good Things Foundation (Good Things Foundation 2021a). Refurbishing and providing used digital devices to those who cannot afford their own is a strategy that can rely on an ample and steady supply of the necessary technological materials. This is because, according to the World Economic Forum, more than 5 million tons of smartphones were discarded in 2019 alone, which accounted for approximately 10 per cent of the overall global e-waste that year (World Economic Forum 2021).

Digital devices are expensive. However, billions of smartphones have been produced and sold since Apple introduced the iPhone in 2007. It has been reported that more than 1.43 billion different smartphones were sold in 2021 alone (Gartner 2022). Smartphone adoption rates are high in many parts of the world and are expected to grow. States can promote smartphone adoption in various ways by enabling people to afford these devices themselves and by providing devices to those unable to pay for them. Smartphones have features (such as photo and video recording capabilities) that are particularly useful for individuals for exercising human rights online and to evidence human rights violations. And considering the current state of broadband network development worldwide, access to a smartphone is the quickest way to achieve universal internet access. Permanent access to a smartphone is therefore the device standard that the human right to internet access reasonably includes. Next, we turn to the factor of broadband infrastructure that is the basic technical precondition of internet access.

5.3.3 *Social Guarantees for Broadband Infrastructure*

Duties of public institutions to ensure that people can use digital devices and data to access the internet are only meaningful where there is broadband internet infrastructure. Realising universal availability of broadband networks is therefore the fundamental requirement for universal internet access. In determining what the human right to free internet access requires in terms of broadband infrastructure to prevent digital poverty and exclusion, the important parameters again are what is feasible for a substantial majority of countries and what is required for adequate opportunities to use human rights online.

A reasonable demand in this regard is a reliable, good quality broadband connection (mobile or fixed) that allows for daily use of the internet. The ITU defines good quality broadband 'as [enabling] an average download speed of at least 10 Mbit/s and [being] technology neutral (meaning that data may be transmitted via cable, fibre, satellite, radio, or other technologies)' (ITU 2020: 3). To meet this speed, broadband networks of the fourth generation (4G) are required (Ofcom 2023c). For our present purposes, what is crucial is that connectivity provided by such 4G networks aligns with the aims of the human right to free internet access. That is because 4G broadband is needed for regularly accessing (other than text-based) online content, such as videos. Receiving and sending such non-textual content can be essential for the exercise of human rights, for instance when people want to document and report human rights violations, watch news and political reports, access tutorials and educational or medical video content, or send data or images for medical or political purposes. Using video material, though, requires more data than text-based activities such as reading websites or sending/receiving emails. These considerations in combination with data on broadband technology that is already in place means that the human right to free internet access in practical terms contains as an infrastructure requirement the availability of at least mobile 4G broadband networks.

As previously mentioned, the number of people who already live within range of mobile 4G broadband networks in the world is considerable. According to the ITU, in 2021 mobile networks reached 95 per cent of humanity. The percentage of the global population within reach of 4G networks specifically was 88 per cent (ITU 2021a: 10). That means that the vast majority of humanity is already covered by 4G mobile broadband infrastructure. Many more, though, remain offline owing to other factors such as unaffordable digital devices and data services or lack of digital skills. However, the specific problem with those still not reached by 4G mobile networks is that these are also the most difficult ones to connect. This is because they often live in remote, sparsely populated rural areas where private sector investments in broadband infrastructure are deemed unattractive.

The human right to free internet access demands that the remaining broadband infrastructure gaps are closed. Such coverage gaps are not limited to developing countries. However, very few areas in developed countries are entirely without broadband coverage. In the EU, for example, 97.4 per cent of households 'had access to at least one of the main fixed broadband access technologies at the end of June 2020' (European Commission 2021a: 4) and 'nearly all EU households (99.6%) were covered by LTE [long-term evolution] mobile networks' by June the same year (European Commission 2021a: 5).[10]

---

[10] LTE is a recent standard for wireless broadband communication for mobile devices and data terminals, based on the GSM/EDGE and UMTS/HSPA standards (Wikipedia 2024a).

The main remaining problem in developed countries is therefore not areas that are entirely without coverage but rather providing citizens with broadband of adequate quality. Minimally adequate broadband speeds are defined differently by countries. For example, according to the US's FCC, at the end of 2019, up to 14.5 million US Americans were 'living in areas without [broadband] access to at least 25/3 Mbps (the Commission's current benchmark)' (FCC 2021: 2). In Canada, 99.5 per cent of the population had access to a mobile LTE network in 2022. However, only 89.5 per cent of Canadians (and 53.4 per cent of the rural population) had access to broadband networks with at speeds of at least 50/10 Mbps, which is considered adequate by the Canadian government (CRTC 2023).

Relative differences in the quality of available broadband network can be an issue from the perspective of the human right to free internet access. This is because these inequalities can affect people's relative opportunities to exercise their human rights online. For example, education, health care, work opportunities, access to government programmes, and access to political information might increasingly require more data, and a growing number of people might use more data via faster broadband connections. In this situation, having access to a mobile 4G internet connection with an average download speed of at least 10 Mbps might become inadequate. That is why all states should adopt universal broadband service guarantees that give citizens a legal claim to the availability of an internet connection with a minimum speed and therefore ensures adequate broadband coverage for everyone. To address market failures where private sector investments in infrastructure are deemed unprofitable, states should also raise funds (e.g. via so-called universal service funds) to be able to afford eliminating infrastructure gaps and to upgrade existing infrastructure where this is necessary.

There are multiple examples of universal service guarantees throughout the world. In July 2010, Finland became the first country to adopt a legal right for all citizens to have access to a 1 Mbps broadband connection. By October 2021, that right had expanded to connections with speeds of 5 Mbps (European Commission 2023b). In the US, in 2021 Congress adopted the Infrastructure Investment and Jobs Act that entailed spending of USD $65 billion to expand broadband networks to ensure that all citizens are covered by high-speed internet infrastructure (US Department of Commerce 2021). In 2022, the Canadian government as part of its 'High-Speed Access for All' strategy committed CAD $2.75 billion to its Universal Broadband Fund that aims to provide all citizens with internet at speeds of at least 50/10 Mbps (Government of Canada 2022). In Australia, the government adopted a Universal Service Guarantee that created a right for Australians to a broadband connection with speeds of at least 25/5 Mbps in 2021 (Australian Government 2021). To pay for the necessary infrastructure investments, the government's Regional Broadband Scheme provides AUD $700 million annually. This money is funded by registered broadband carriers that have to pay AUD $7.10 a month per eligible premise on their communication network with an active fixed line for broadband services (Australian Communications and Media Authority 2022). In 2022, the UK government adopted a Universal Service Obligation regarding broadband services that gives a legal right to all citizens to be covered by a decent internet connection. Such a connection is defined as having speeds of minimally 10/1 Mbps and not costing more than GBP £45 monthly (UK Parliament 2022). As part of this universal service obligation, broadband providers have to pay for new connections the costs of which do not exceed GBP £3,400. And in June 2022, the German government introduced a legal right for all inhabitants to basic broadband services with a connection speed of minimally 10/1.3 Mbps (Bundesnetzagentur 2023).

Universal service guarantees that primarily task the private sector with closing coverage gaps are viable instruments to meet the infrastructure requirement of the human right to free internet access particularly for affluent countries. However, the situation is more challenging for developing countries. Even though 88 per cent of humanity is already covered by 4G mobile broadband networks, the remaining 12 per cent predominantly lives in non-affluent countries whose governments do not have much room for public digital infrastructure investments in areas where its construction is considered unprofitable by the private sector. As stated earlier, according to the ITU, nearly USD $428 billion would be required to realise universal internet access until 2030. 'Around 2.6 million 4G BTS [base transceiver stations] and 700,000 km of backbone fibre transmission infrastructure would have to be rolled out on top of the existing broadband network capabilities' (ITU 2020: 4). About 90 per cent of the investments would have to be dedicated to the roll-out and maintenance of broadband networks and 40 per cent to build-out of last mile broadband infrastructure. '25 countries […] account for nearly 75 per cent of all the investment requirements at USD 312 billion. Further, 20 of these 25 countries are in Sub-Saharan Africa, East Asia/Pacific and South Asia and all are low and lower-middle income countries' (ITU 2020: 7).

Owing to the widespread existence of 4G internet networks, the infrastructure standard of the human right to internet access is nonetheless feasible for the majority of countries. However, it presents a challenging task for states beyond the developed world, and in particular for the LDCs. Still, globally there are also multiple examples of public investments in broadband infrastructure, particularly in developing countries, that show that working towards universal 4G coverage is feasible in most parts of the world. As mentioned in Section 3.1, in the context of states' obligation to ensure that their citizens have sufficient internet data, the Philippine government and the South African province of West Cape have shown how millions of people can be given internet access through the construction of public Wi-Fi infrastructure. But there are also examples of digital infrastructure other than Wi-Fi hotspots that governments have built to extend broadband availability.

In Colombia, for example, by 2018 the government had installed almost 900 internet access centres ('puntos digitales') in underprivileged municipalities of the country that have enabled more than 1.9 million citizens to access the internet (MINTIC Colombia 2018). These centres aim to fulfil multiple aims for people who are otherwise unable to access the internet such as entertainment, accessing services, and acquiring basic digital skills. In Malaysia, the Communications and Multimedia Commission as part of its Universal Service Provision had established more than 870 internet centres by 2019 (MAMPU 2021). These offer free internet access to many users (e.g. students, people with disabilities, pensioners) as well as digital training and education opportunities and are used by up to 1 million Malaysian citizens. In Thailand, between 2016 and 2018, the government implemented its Village Broadband Internet Project (Net Pracharat 2018). This initiative provided free public Wi-Fi to more than 4.5 million users and connected more than 24,700 villages with fibre broadband internet, thereby bringing online more than 1.7 million rural households. In Indonesia, the government is building a national 4G network that aims to leave no one behind with its Base Transceiver Station (BTS) for Rural, Remote and Border Area of Indonesia project (ITU 2019). As part of this, it has allocated IDR 11 trillion (~USD $683 million) for the construction of 4,200 BTSs that are planned to be completed in 2022 (Republic of Indonesia 2022). The BTS system is designed to run on solar energy that is stored in batteries lasting up to 100 hours as this sustainable energy model saves costs in the long run (Antara 2021).

Besides these instances of public projects to promote mobile broadband infrastructure, there are also examples of public–private investment schemes in broadband infrastructure intended to cover significant numbers of citizens in developing countries. In 2020, the Ghanaian government's universal access fund, the Ghana Investment Fund for Electronic Communications (GIFEC 2019), which is resourced by funds from public and private sources, signed a contract with the US-based company Parallel Wireless. As part of that contract, the company is to set up 2,000 mobile infrastructure sites using 4G-capable Open RAN (radio access network) technology. These sites target those communities that remain unconnected to mobile networks with the aim of achieving universal mobile phone service coverage throughout Ghana (Dzopko 2020). And in 2021, the Indian government announced its PM-WANI scheme, which intends to increase broadband connectivity in the country by enabling shopkeepers to offer Wi-Fi services to customers (India Telecom 2022). The scheme relies on small, local private businesses to proliferate mobile broadband by offering them the opportunity to register as 'public data offices' with a 'public data office aggregator'. As public data offices, these businesses resell data services to individual clients who register for using specially developed WANI apps. A central registry stores the details of the public data offices, the public data office aggregators, and of the app providers. By April 2022, almost 57,000 Wi-Fi hotspots had been registered under the PM-WANI scheme. There are concerns about the scheme, which has been criticised for lacking sufficient protection against hacking and for not doing enough to safeguard individual users' private data (Internet Freedom Foundation 2021). These concerns notwithstanding, the initiative presents an example of how a government of a developing country attempts to leverage private businesses to expand mobile broadband infrastructure without investing large funds itself.

All these examples, though, cannot deny the fact that at the lower end of the affluence spectrum among the states of the world the challenges of providing universal broadband infrastructure remain truly enormous. According to the Broadband Commission, the mobile coverage gap is largest in Africa where in 2018 3G networks reached 71 per cent of the population and only 40 per cent were covered by 4G infrastructure (Broadband Commission 2019: 40). By 2020, 47 per cent of the world's population who remain offline lived in Sub-Saharan Africa (GSMA 2021: 14). Here, even supporting infrastructure such as reliable electricity is often missing. For example, in Sub-Saharan Africa, only 44 per cent of households overall, and only 23 per cent of rural households, had access to electricity in 2017 (Broadband Commission 2019: 42). Connecting those who remain offline in these LDCs is particularly difficult because the investments required here are often the least attractive ones to private companies and the governments of these countries are unable to fill the gaps left by this market failure (Bamford et al. 2021: 32). For these least affluent countries, it is particularly important that internet access is recognised as a human right. That is because human rights are matters of international concern. As such, human rights are to be supported by the international community where states are genuinely unable to realise them. States that have signed up to the UN's SDGs have in fact already committed to providing support for the development of broadband infrastructure around the globe. In recognition of the internet's systematic support for the achievement of many other sustainable development targets (UN 2022), SDG 9.c explicitly includes the provision of 'universal and affordable access to the internet in the least developed countries by 2020' (UN 2023b). This goal remains unachieved, and recognising a human right to free internet access could be a crucial step towards its realisation.

If the members of the international community want to make good on their explicit commitments, there are different ways in which they can support countries unable to fund universal internet access themselves. One way that they can do so is through financial support provided by multilateral development banks (MDSs), which are themselves funded by members of the international community. MDSs are, for example, members of the World Bank Group as well as regional banks such as the Asian Development Bank, Inter-American Development Bank, African Development Bank, Development Bank of Latin America, and the European Investment Bank. The main task of these banks is to promote infrastructure and other development in recipient members through grants and loans funded by more affluent donor members. Between 2012 and 2016, MDBs have given approximately USD $525 billion to development projects in low- and middle-income countries globally. However, the Alliance for Affordable Internet estimates that only 1 per cent of this money was targeted at projects in the ICT sector (A4AI 2018: 10). There is therefore a disparity between the widespread recognition that internet access and other information communication technologies are crucial for human development and the actual amount of international funding provided for the development of these technologies in developing nations. The Alliance for Affordable Internet sees one main reason for this discrepancy in the perception common among the governments of borrowing states as well as MDBs that funding for ICT infrastructure development is a matter of private sector investment. Even though the rapid growth of internet and other ICT infrastructure in recent decades was indeed largely funded by private investments, this development path is becoming increasingly narrow as profit prospects are riskier and more limited when it comes to bringing online those living offline in remote and non-affluent areas of the world (A4AI 2018: 19). One way that the international community can therefore promote universal internet access is by challenging the dominant narrative about ICT development as primarily a task of the private sector. This would result in directing more MDB funding towards internet infrastructure projects, which would bring MDB priorities better in line with the World Bank's recognition that 'broadband (or high-speed) internet access is not a luxury, but a basic necessity for economic and human development in both developed and developing countries' (World Bank 2023).

Another way for members of the international community to support states unable to realise the infrastructure requirement of the human right to free internet access would be to support politically and financially the creation and operations of an International Broadband Development Fund (IBDF). This fund would be specifically tasked with achieving universal internet connectivity, as suggested by a Working Group of the UN's Broadband Commission (Broadband Commission 2021b: 57–65). This new agency could be hosted by an existing international financial institution such as the World Bank to benefit from the bank's expertise in terms of funding development projects. The main role of the IBDF would be to attract voluntary donations of donor states and non-state actors (i.e. investors, private companies that would benefit from expanding the digital economy, corporate social responsibility funds, philanthropists, non-governmental organisations, and international development agencies) for the specific purpose of funding at low cost and long-term the development of ICT infrastructure in countries unable to do so themselves. A new institution of this kind would have multiple benefits. Its centralised capacities would reduce the need to duplicate administrative functions across multiple independent ICT funding initiatives directed at the same objectives (Broadband Commission 2021b: 60). As an institution operating at the international level, it could offer risk mitigation for investors by providing a level of protection against the effects of possible political instability, environmental hazards, as well as currency and demand volatility in recipient countries (Broadband Commission 2021b: 59). Finally, the World Bank could also provide technical advisory services to borrowing governments on how to efficiently invest the funds provided (Broadband Commission 2021b: 60). As the Working Group points out, international funds of this kind already exist for other purposes. Examples in this regard are GAVI – the global vaccine alliance aiming to provide 'immunization for all', Power Africa – a global coalition of more than 170 public and private partners aiming to bring electricity to Sub-Saharan Africa, and UNITAID – a international organisation hosted by the World Health Organisation that provides funds to prevent, diagnose, and treat HIV/AIDS, TB, and malaria effectively and affordably (Broadband Commission 2021b: 61–64).

This list of examples of international development support is not meant to be exhaustive. It only shows that international support for developing countries that cannot afford to build the mobile 4G infrastructure necessary for universal internet access clearly appears feasible if there is political will for this kind of aid. However, it is important to note that, from the perspective of the human right to free internet access, such international development aid for broadband infrastructure is not a matter of charity or strategic national self-interest of donor states. Rather, it is an obligation for those members of the international community that are able to help and an issue of international justice because human rights are matters of international concern. 4G broadband infrastructure is a requirement that is feasible to guarantee for a substantial majority of countries right now. With international will and support, global broadband coverage is a realistic possibility in the near future as well.

5.3.4 *Social Guarantees for Basic Digital Skills*

According to the human right to free internet access, sufficient data (and meeting the 2 GB for 2 per cent of monthly GNI target per capita), permanent access to a smartphone, and 4G mobile broadband network coverage for all citizens are demands states must meet. However, fulfilment of these obligations does not guarantee internet access if people lack the necessary digital skills to use the internet. As a final requirement to safeguard people against the standard threat of digital poverty, the human right to free internet access therefore also includes a duty for public authorities to ensure everyone has opportunities to gain the basic digital skills needed to make adequate use of their human rights online. People can choose not to acquire basic digital skills or they can fail to acquire them even though they try, but they must be given the chance to learn them.

There is no universally accepted definition of basic digital skills. However, the ITU describes them as those necessary for people to 'function at a minimum level in society' (ITU 2018: 6). Today, basic digital functioning has become as important as traditional literacy and numeracy. Basic digital skills 'cover hardware (for example using a keyboard and operating touch-screen technology), software (for example word processing, managing files on laptops, managing privacy settings on mobile phones), and basic online operations (such as email, search, [...] completing an online form' (ITU 2018: 6), creating a professional online profile, and effectively managing password and security settings of online applications and processes).

Around the world, the lack of digital skills remains a major obstacle to ensuring universal internet access. Digital skills are measured by the kind of digital activities individuals are able to carry out. A 2021 study of the ITU considered digital skill development in the seventy-seven countries for which respective data was available. In thirty of them, less than 40 per cent of the population reported that they had performed a computer-based activity that required basic digital skills (such as 'copying or moving a file or folder, using copy and paste tools to duplicate or move information within a document, sending emails with attached files, and transferring files between a computer and other devices' (ITU 2021a: 19)) in the past three months. This statistic does not adequately illustrate the global problem of inadequate digital skills, though, because no data on digital skills was available for many of the LDCs, all of Sub-Saharan Africa except South Africa, and India. In these regions, digital illiteracy can be expected to be most widespread because of the still widespread lack of internet access and high levels of general illiteracy. But inadequate digital skills are also an issue in affluent countries. According to the UK Parliament, for example, in 2020:

> 22% [of the British population] did not have 'essential digital skills for life' [such as using word processing software and sending emails, the ability to use search engines, to buy and sell goods and services online, using a live chat or tutorial video, controlling privacy settings on social media, and the ability to recognise suspicious emails], and 16% could not carry out a full set of [foundational] digital tasks [...] (such as the ability to use a web browser). (UK Parliament 2021: 2)

As a consequence of overall digital skills shortages, a UK House of Lords report estimates that the UK economy loses GBP £63 billion each year (House of Lords 2023: 6). With respect to the US, a 2012 Organisation for Economic Co-operation and Development (OECD) study revealed that 16 per cent of the US population were digitally illiterate (NCES 2018: 2–3). And the European Commission states that in 2019, 44 per cent of the EU population did not possess basic digital skills defined as those needed to 'enable individuals to take part in the digital society and consume digital goods and services' (European Commission 2021b: 20).

To offer the chance to acquire basic digital literacy to all their citizens, states have to realise plans that many of them have already announced and embraced. The leaders of the G20 group, for example, vowed in 2019 to 'promote digital literacy and digital skills in all forms of education' (European Commission 2017). Similarly, recognising the crucial importance of basic digital skills, the OECD's 2016 'Cancún Declaration' includes a commitment to 'promote digital literacy as well as inclusive and effective use of ICTs in education and training' (OECD 2016: 4). An essential measure for realising these objectives is therefore to make the teaching of basic digital skills part of the curriculums of public education. Many states have in fact already incorporated digital literacy and skills training as important elements of their school education. Among them are the nations of the UK (UK Parliament 2021: 3–4), Austria (BMBWF 2023), Germany ('Initiative Digitale Bildung' (BMBF 2021), 'DigitalPakt Schule' (BMBF 2023)), Sweden (European Union 2021), Australia, Ireland, Portugal, and Norway (OECD 2019b). For public schools to offer basic digital skills training, though, the schools themselves must be digitally equipped as a matter of priority. Public authorities therefore have a duty to ensure that the necessary ICT is available to schools. In line with this obligation, the European Commission, for example, has launched its 'Digital Education Plan (2021–2027)' (European Commission 2020a). This plan includes the creation of a European Framework for Digital Education Content (Action 3), the provision of funds to help member states to supply their public schools with ICT technology for digital skills training (Action 4), the development of 'common guidelines to help teachers and educators promote digital literacy and to address disinformation through education and training' (European Commission 2020b) (Action 7), and a digital skills certificate (Action 9) that allows people to evidence their level of digital competence. With this Digital Education Plan, the European Commission aims to realise the target that at least 80 per cent of the population of the EU has basic digital skills by 2030.

However, making digital equipment available in schools is not a goal that is realisable only for the most developed countries. As the OECD states, 'around 18% of Latin American 15-year-olds from socio-economically disadvantaged backgrounds lack an internet connection at home and at school, in contrast to less than 2% on average across OECD countries. Some 24% of them do not have access to a computer (desktop, laptop or tablet) neither at home, nor at school' (OECD 2020: 8). This means in turn, though, that a higher rate of students in Latin America have access to the internet and a digital device than the rest of the population in these countries. Moreover, a significant number of Latin American children only have access to the internet at school (OECD 2020: 12). The use of digital technology is comparatively rather advanced in Latin America, as the OECD finds, since 'Latin American teachers seem to use ICT in class with relatively higher frequency than their OECD counterparts' (OECD 2020: 61).

The importance of digitalised schools and basic digital skills training is in fact globally recognised as essential. In 2019, for example, UNICEF and the ITU launched the Giga initiative, which has the aim to connect every school in the world to the internet by 2030. It advises governments, and it partners with the private sector to raise funds to realise its goals. By 2021, Giga had connected 3,200 pilot schools (teaching 1.1 million children) to the internet in Africa, Central Asia, Latin America, and the Eastern Caribbean. It aims to connect up to 8 million schools and more than 25,000 schools globally by the end of 2022 (UNICEF 2022). EQUALS is another international initiative that demonstrates the widespread recognition of the importance of digital skills training (EQUALS 2022). This is a global partnership of governments and private sector organisations started by UN Women and the ITU in 2015 that works towards achieving gender equality in terms of access to and use of digital technologies by 2030. Its various initiatives (such as Her Digital Skills and eSkills4Girls) provide resources for gender-sensitive digital skills training particularly in the Global South.

Teaching digital skills in public schools has to be a priority because all children have to complete mandatory minimum education and a significant part of the population can be given the opportunity to acquire basic digital skills in this way. But this does not mean that governments can ignore the lack of digital skills of those who have completed their school education. There are also examples of initiatives that help adults become digitally literate. In the UK, for instance, the Department for Education has supported the Good Things Foundation to run its Future Digital Inclusion programme (Good Things Foundation 2021b). Since 2014, the charity through this programme has supported over 1 million people in the development of basic digital skills via its Online Centres Network and by offering its free Learn My Way curriculum. The Online Centres Network is furthermore supported and hosted by community partners such as public libraries, community centres, and churches. Other non-profit organisations, such as Citizens Online in the UK (Citizens Online 2023) and Emmaüs Connect in France (Emmaüs Connect 2023), similarly offer digital skills training to the general population in their countries.

Public libraries are crucial for offering digital skill training to everyone – especially in developing countries where home internet access is not as widespread. According to the ITU, there are more than 300,000 public libraries globally, of which 70 per cent are in developing countries (ITU 2018: 34). In Chile, for example, the Ministry of Culture, Arts, and Heritage, with support of the Gates Foundation, has been offering digital skills training in 400 public libraries through its BiblioRedes programme since 2002 (Government of Chile 2023). In Sri Lanka, the eLibrary Nenasala Project provides free internet access and digital skills training in almost 300 religious institutions and public libraries (IFLA 2014). Other states have created special tele- and internet centres that offer online access, promote local entrepreneurship, and train citizens in digital skills. As mentioned earlier, the almost 900 'puntos digitales' established by the Colombian government have as one of their explicit purposes the training of non-affluent citizens in basic digital skills (MINTIC Colombia 2018). In Malaysia, the almost 900 Pusat Internet Centres operated by the Communications and Multimedia Commission offer not only internet access, but also teach basic computer skills to young people and senior citizens (MCMC 2019). Moreover, in Rwanda, in 2017, the Ministry of Youth and ICT started the Digital Ambassador Programme whose purpose is to train 5,000 digital ambassadors who are intended to teach basic digital skills to up to 5 million Rwandan citizens (Government of the People of Rwanda 2023). And in 2020, the non-profit organisation Electronic Information for Libraries (EIFL) together with the National Library of Uganda started a three-year project to teach digital skills specially to women and unemployed young people in twenty-five public libraries in Uganda (EIFL 2023). This programme trains librarians in teaching digital skills and also organises digital literacy camps in remote rural areas.

Just as electricity is a precondition of broadband infrastructure, general literacy is arguably a necessary requirement for achieving basic digital skills. For this reason, the fact that there are still illiterate people is also a problem for the goal of achieving universal digital literacy. This problem is most prevalent in Africa where, according to the Broadband Commission, 36 per cent of the population was illiterate in 2019 (Broadband Commission 2019: 79). The existence of illiteracy, though, does not undermine the demand that everyone should have the opportunity to acquire basic digital skills just as illiteracy does not undermine political rights such as freedom of information and speech, which often require literacy for their effective use. Rather, the duty to offer digital skills training re-emphasises the need for states and the international community to realise the human right to education for everyone.

The requirement to offer everyone the chance to acquire basic digital skills probably presents the most challenging demand of the human right to free internet access in terms of guarantees against digital poverty. That is because even many developed nations are still performing rather poorly along this dimension. However, that is not to say that it presents a practically infeasible obligation for a sizeable majority of states. Formal education is not the only way in which people can acquire digital skills. Countless people have become digitally literate before such formal training existed simply by having access to digital devices and the internet. It therefore seems reasonable to expect that ensuring that people have internet access will allow many who are currently digital illiterates to teach themselves the necessary basic skills they need to participate in digitalised societies. But states have to ensure that those who require formal training have access to it. Public institutions worldwide certainly show awareness of the importance of teaching citizens basic digital skills and digital literacy. The main stated motivation of public authorities concerning digital literacy is to equip citizens for participation in today's digitalised economies. However, from the perspective of the human right to free internet access, having basic digital skills is first and foremost essential for social and political inclusion, and for being able to exercise one's human rights today. All states should therefore work towards realising universal basic digital literacy in their own population as well as in other countries that need assistance in achieving this goal.

5.4 MINIMUM CORE OBLIGATIONS OF THE HUMAN RIGHT TO FREE INTERNET ACCESS

Achieving universal internet access will require enormous resources that are unaffordable for a significant number of countries, especially those least developed. This does not mean, though, that the human right to free internet access cannot specify global standards for social guarantees against digital poverty. That is because 4G mobile broadband coverage, sufficient affordable data, permanent access to a smartphone, and the opportunity to acquire basic digital skills are feasible obligations for a majority of states in the world right now. But, as we saw in Section 5.2, socio-economic human rights also make demands on those countries unable to fulfil the general requirements of these rights. The same is true of the human right to free internet access. First, countries that cannot meet its general demands at present have to work to progressively realise them in the medium and long term. Moreover, though, there are certain minimum core obligations with respect to eliminating digital poverty that are feasible for all states right now, and that they therefore have to fulfil immediately. This section outlines the minimum core obligation that the human right plausibly entails.

The first core obligation mirrors the first of the Broadband Commission's '2025 Broadband Advocacy Targets', namely that all states should adopt a national broadband plan (NBP). A NBP is 'a strategic vision for a country's ICT development [and consists of] policy documents that set out objectives and aspirations for the ICT sector over the medium- to long-term [that are] drafted and published by a government authority, usually the ministry responsible for telecommunications or the relevant regulator' (A4AI 2020a: 17). The vast majority of states already comply with this requirement, with the number of states that have adopted a NBP having risen from 102 in 2010 to 174 in 2020 (Broadband Commission 2020: 13). According to the Broadband Commission, a good NBP meets several desiderata. It is developed in consultation with a wide range of stakeholders from the public and private sector, covers a timeframe of three to five years, aims to take stock of existing infrastructure, includes measurable targets for the expansion of broadband networks that take into account specific local challenges (e.g. geography), assigns clear responsibilities for enacting the plan, and also addresses the legislation needed to achieve its goals (Broadband Commission 2020: 12). NBPs should also include goals that aim to reduce the gender digital divide (A4AI 2020a: 38). Often, an NBP also includes dedicated public investments in the development of broadband infrastructure. In this respect, the Broadband Commission recommends specifically as an immediate policy action the creation of 'Universal Access and Service Funds' to promote internet access in remote areas where service provision is less profitable, for low-income citizens, and for women (see the fifth policy objective of the Broadband Commission's roadmap and action plan for connecting Africa to broadband, Broadband Commission 2019: 100).

Many of the positive examples of initiatives that have increased internet access that we encountered in this chapter were devised as part of NBPs. Among them are Thailand's Net Pracharat programme, which was designed using guidelines from its 2010 National Broadband Policy (APT 2023). The Costa Rican programme subsidising internet services and devices for tens of thousands of economically vulnerable households was part of the country's PNDT (2015–2021). In Malaysia, the establishment of hundreds of community internet centres by the Malaysian Communications and Multimedia Commission was a stated objective of its National Broadband Initiative (MCMC 2023). And the creation of the almost 900 'puntos digitales' by the Colombian Government was an initiative under its Vive Digital (2010–2014) and Vive Digital Para la Gente (2015–2018) national broadband plans (MINTIC Colombia 2015).

NBPs can have positive effects on internet adoption by providing targets backed by public authorities and public funds for broadband development. In this way, they can create confidence and predictability for private sector investments that then contribute to achieving the NBP objectives for their own reasons (A4AI 2020a: 29–30). As noted in Section 3.1, the Alliance for Affordable Internet states that countries that have adopted a NBP have also seen internet access become more affordable for their citizens, and especially for the poorest 20 per cent (A4AI 2020a: 20). Adopting a NBP is particularly important for countries that are unable to fulfil the general requirements of the human right to free internet access. This is because a NBP provides the fundamental planning and coordination that is needed to get countries into a position from which they can work towards the progressive realisation of these general requirements. Just as the human right to health contains as a minimum core obligation the adoption of a national public health strategy and plan, the human right to internet access therefore calls for the immediate development and adoption of a NBP as an initial and essential step towards realising universal internet access.

Second, all governments are under a core obligation to establish broadband connectivity in public buildings and venues (such as town halls, public libraries, schools, and health care facilities) throughout their territory and to develop e-government services and networks (see the Broadband Commission's policy objective 4 of its roadmap and action plan for connecting Africa to broadband, Broadband Commission 2019: 99). Even though governments of the LDCs are unable to fund large-scale broadband infrastructure projects, public spending to connect public buildings to the internet is much more targeted, limited, and therefore feasible for all states. The establishment of broadband networks that can be used by public administrations and citizens fulfils several important functions at once. These public broadband networks create initial connectivity throughout a country that can serve as the basis for further local developments of broadband infrastructure. By using online networks, governments also provide 'anchor tenant assurance to private telecommunications operators' (Broadband Commission 2019: 99). Doing so can incentivise private sector operators to invest in broadband infrastructure and services beyond the needs of public institutions. In addition, public broadband networks offer citizens access points that provide opportunities to engage with the internet and to acquire digital skills. Finally, such public networks can allow for more effective government services that also generate demand for internet access among local populations. Government-based broadband networks can therefore provide starting points for the development of further local connectivity while requiring comparatively limited and targeted public investments.

Third, and finally, should the international community choose to discharge their obligations towards other countries in terms of the human right to free internet access through forming an IBDF, those countries that can benefit from such an institution are under an obligation to cooperate with the Fund. This would require applying for loans for developing broadband infrastructure and potentially for subsidising digital devices. Recipient states should also make use of the technical expertise that an IBDF could offer in terms of managing loans and effectively constructing the necessary infrastructure. Cooperation in an IBDF would therefore be a crucial practical step towards progressively realising the social guarantees against digital poverty for those states that are currently unable to meet the demands of the human right to free internet access in full.

5.5 CONCLUSION

Digital poverty in its various forms is the dominant reason why billions of people in the world remain offline. They are either not covered by mobile broadband networks, do not have access to a digital end device, are unable to afford data services, lack the basic digital skills needed to use the internet, suffer from a combination of some of these factors, or are lacking in all of them. Achieving universal internet access and eliminating digital poverty is a task that will require enormous resources. Unsurprisingly, not all countries are currently able to guarantee internet access for all their citizens.

However, internationally the importance of internet access for the enjoyment of fundamental rights as well as for human and economic development is widely recognised. This chapter has identified several demands that the human right to free internet access places on public institutions in terms of social guarantees against digital poverty. These demands are realistic in the sense that they are feasible for a majority of states in the world right now. According to these demands, states have to ensure that everyone has

(a) access to sufficient digital data (i.e. by meeting the 2 GB for 2 per cent of monthly GNI per capita target), and
(b) permanent access to a smartphone; that all are
(c) covered by at least 4G mobile broadband networks, and that
(d) everybody has the opportunity to acquire basic digital skills.

But also those states unable to meet these demands at present are not free from obligations to fight digital poverty. According to the concept of minimum core obligations, they must

(a) adopt a national broadband plan,
(b) develop broadband networks that connect their public administration offices and public venues to the internet, and
(c) join an IBDF (or similar organisation) should such an institution be set up by the members of the international community. Founding and resourcing such a fund can be a way for more fortunate states to meet their own obligations in terms of the human right to free internet access towards societies that are currently genuinely unable to meet the right's requirements.

Meeting these core obligations, which are feasible globally at present, will put countries in a position to work towards the progressive realisation of the general demands that the human right to free internet access places upon them. Achieving universal internet access is not a pipedream and enormous progress has been made in the past decade to connect most of humanity. The remaining challenges are enormous, though. By fulfilling their obligations, also and especially their international ones, public institutions can ensure that soon no one is left offline. According to the human right to free internet access, the needed efforts are matters of justice, and the goal of universal internet access cannot be left up to private profit interests and the financial fortunes of individuals alone. These might never be enough to make sure that everyone has adequate opportunities to exercise their human rights online.

This chapter has defined a first sense of the idea of 'free' internet access as entailing a positive duty of public institutions to fund online access for those unable to afford it themselves. Chapter 6 will introduce the second sense of 'free' as the negative obligation of states not to interfere with people's internet access without justifiable cause.

6

States as Standard Threats

Chapter 5 has shown that we can meaningfully identify the content of, and the obligations imposed on public institutions by, a new human right to free internet access. We can do this by considering what standard threats free internet access faces and which social guarantees help protect people against these threats. As we saw, the problem of digital poverty leads to a demand to help those unable to afford internet access. Consequently, the first meaning of the idea of a right to 'free' internet access is that such access has to be provided free of charge for those unable to afford it. But there is a second crucial meaning of 'free' internet access that we turn to now, and which also will be the focus of Chapters 7 and 8.

This second meaning is crucial because it is likely the one that attention with respect to a human right to free internet access will increasingly shift towards in the future. In the short and medium run, establishing universal internet access for those billions who remain offline must be a priority for the countries where these people live. If one cannot go online, one has to worry about few other direct standard threats to internet access. In the long run, though, it is likely that digital poverty will increasingly diminish as technology becomes more advanced, cheaper, and because of this, more widespread. However, once people can go online, they face other serious standard threats to accessing and using the internet freely. That is because no mass medium, also not the internet, automatically promotes human rights and well-being. Without certain protections by public institutions, the internet is in fact much more likely to be used to undermine human rights and to turn people's use of their rights against them. Internet shutdowns, online censorship and surveillance, fake news and computational propaganda are but a few of the new and unprecedented ways in which the internet can be used to misinform, manipulate, spy on, silence, and repress citizens (Woolley and Howard 2018). If it is employed in such ways, the internet does not bring progress for mankind or help realise human rights. Instead, it becomes a technology of oppression that allows for unparalleled ways to control individuals and societies.

In the long run, it is therefore to be expected that the biggest priority concerning free internet access will be that people can access and use the internet without being subjected to online attempts to undermine their human rights. This, then, reveals the second meaning of *'free'*. Internet access can only be free when it is not corrupted by arbitrary interference. An interference is *arbitrary* if it causes an obstruction to internet access that cannot be morally justified and unjustly benefits the interferer at the expense of those who access and use the internet. As we will see in this chapter and Chapters 7 and 8, such arbitrary interference unfortunately is already the standard experience of those who can go online. Internet access, though, can only reliably promote human rights and human progress if it is free from arbitrary interferences.

In this respect, states have a dual role to play. First (as we saw in Chapter 1), because free internet is a human right, they are the primary duty-holders and have obligations to keep internet access free. Second, though, they are themselves one of the main (and arguably the most pressing) standard threat to free internet access of people who already have the means to go online. Many states currently try to control the internet and to use it to repress, or at least to spy on, their citizens. Moreover, even though in many countries internet services are provided by private companies, states have the monopoly of coercive and legislative power and can shape how these companies do business. States alone also have the power to force the configuration of the basic digital infrastructure in such a way that the internet can become a tool of repression. Since states are simultaneously the primary duty-holders and the most pressing standard threat to free internet access where the necessary infrastructure already exists, this chapter focuses on them before Chapter 7 turns to those private businesses that dominate much of the internet in democracies today.

Because of the moral importance of internet access for our opportunities to lead minimally decent lives in the digital age, states have certain obligations to guarantee that such access is free. They must provide protections against arbitrary interference with online access and must not themselves use the internet to undermine the rights of individuals within and outside their territory. The importance of these duties has also been identified by major institutions such as the United Nations (UN). For instance, in its 2016 non-binding resolution on the *Promotion, Protection, and Enjoyment of Human Rights on the Internet* that we already encountered in the introduction, the UN General Assembly demands that 'rights that people have offline must also be protected online' (UN 2016: 2). Free speech, for example, that must not arbitrarily be blocked offline (e.g. if people want to demonstrate) must also not be arbitrarily prevented online (e.g. if a person wants to post their views via a website).[1] But, as we will see in this chapter, much more is required for the protection of a free and open internet than guaranteeing existing rights online. One aim here is therefore to spell out the most important obligations that states can be said to have and that they must abide by lest they themselves undermine free internet access. The second aim of this chapter is to explain why the internet becomes the most potent technological means of oppression and controlling populations that humanity has ever created if states do not accept and fulfil their obligations to keep internet access free from arbitrary interference. We will approach these two aims in reverse order.

Section 6.1 will explain how the internet can be (and unfortunately is) used to establish *informational autocracy* (i.e. an authoritarian regime that relies more on the manipulation of information than naked repression to secure its rule, see Alyukov 2022: 763) and *digital authoritarianism* (the 'use of digital information technology by authoritarian regimes to surveil, repress, and manipulate domestic and foreign populations' (Polyakova and Meserole 2019: 1)). It will give an overview of some of the most widespread and egregious methods employed by states to turn internet access and use against internet users and their human rights. We will see how online activities of citizens create opportunities for states to manipulate and control citizens, to alter their behaviour and even their sense of self. Section 6.2 then explains that it is not only authoritarian regimes that interfere without adequate justification with the internet access and use of their citizens. Democratic states, too, have been tempted to exploit the opportunities offered by digital technology to spy on their own citizens and those of other countries – often in the name of protecting national security – as was most prominently revealed by Edward Snowden in 2013. Section 6.3 draws conclusions from the previously canvassed practices and technologies used by states in the form of a list of obligations that all states have and must respect as part of the human right to free internet access.

It is unlikely that humanity will abandon the internet again just as it will not voluntarily give up writing, de-electrify societies, or forgo the advances of modern medicine. All these achievements are too useful and have made possible enormous human progress. To make the internet an instrument of progress, though, special protections from and by public authorities are required. The dangers of misuse of digital technology by states and the need for social guarantees against such abuses explain two things. First, they help us spell out

---

[1] There are, of course, limits on what views are protected by free speech. These will be considered in Chapters 7 and 8.

further what the human right to free internet access entails. And second, these dangers add more reasons to the claim that public authorities need to adopt this novel human right in the first place. Accepting and respecting a human right to free internet access would go a long way towards establishing a positive global vision for the internet and ensuring that it is not used as a technology of oppression, but as one that indeed promotes human progress.

6.1 DIGITAL AUTHORITARIANISM

The internet can only be a tool for the liberation and empowerment of people if it can be used without arbitrary obstruction. For this to happen, states need to resist the political incentives they have to interfere with citizens' online activities. Further, they must protect their citizens from intrusions by other ill-intended agents (such as criminals and hostile states). The internet generates these political incentives for states because of the unprecedented opportunities it provides for gathering information about people, for controlling the flow of information that citizens have access to, and for feeding people specific information that political authorities want their subjects to consume and believe.

The internet is not exceptional in only having good effects if certain conditions obtain. For example, even though democratic rule is morally and politically of important value for empowering citizens and protecting their human rights (Christiano 2011, Landemore 2013), democratic rule can also cause much harm. It can become a method for a majority to oppress a minority. This was one major concern of, for instance, James Madison, one of the authors of the Federalist Papers (see Hamilton et al. 2008: No. 10), of Alexis de Tocqueville (2009), and John Stuart Mill (2012). The tyranny of the majority can only be safely prevented if certain principles and rules are respected, such as the separation of powers and respect for the basic civil rights of everyone. Moreover, other mass media, such as the radio, television, or newspapers, can become tools of misinformation and political control if their operation is not free but serves to arbitrarily promote the interests of only some at the expense of others. For example, when the radio was on the brink of becoming a mass medium, in 1932 the Communist German playwright Bertolt Brecht advocated its use among workers with the aim to educate and to collectively organise them so they could better defend their interests against the owners of capital and the means of production (Brecht 2003). A few years later, though, after assuming power the Nazis instead misused this novel medium for their own purposes. They promoted the mass adoption of the 'people's receiver' (an inexpensive mass-produced radio) to make radio sets widely affordable, and to use this medium to spread their propaganda through radio broadcasts. Television, as well, has been used to misinform and manipulate, rather than to empower, people. In 2022, in Russia, TV broadcasting was entirely controlled by the Putin regime and presented the main source of information for 60 per cent of the population. Through biased reporting and news framing as well as the fabrication of facts, the regime uses this mass medium to control how Russians view their government and its activities, such as its 2022 invasion of Ukraine that broke international law and yet was reportedly supported by most of the Russian population (Alyukov 2022: 763).

Even though the internet is therefore not alone in only being an instrument for good if certain conditions apply and certain protections are in place, as we will see, its harmful potential is especially powerful. The internet's pernicious capacity originates from the same reasons that make it a potent tool for promoting human rights and well-being: it allows information to be conveyed and obtained in unparalleled ways. If it is used as an instrument of oppression, though, the information that people send and seek online is used against them and their interests rather than to realise their human rights. This is possible because when people do things online, they leave traces and personal information that can be collected, analysed, and stored by those who control the ICT infrastructure (i.e. primarily states and private companies) to an extent that was impossible without the internet (Xu 2020: 310). Control of digital information makes the pursuit of certain political goals much easier for powerholders. Crucially, the internet offers much more effective ways to monitor what citizens do and think than traditional methods of surveillance. It is, for example, easier to identify and record individual dissenting voices online than in a protest crowd or on a public street corner. It is also much less difficult to access a person's private correspondence by intercepting and analysing their emails with the help of artificial intelligence than by employing teams that steam open and read citizens' physical letters (as was done, for instance, by the Communist regime of the German Democratic Republic as shown in the Oscar-winning movie *The Lives of Others*). And with the help of the internet, it is now even possible to identify or to infer what a person thinks by accessing their browser, online search, or their shopping histories when before only direct conversations or interrogations could reveal such most private information. Moreover, it is no longer necessary to have police officers or spies physically follow a person to keep track of them. Rather, people can be located with the help of their IP address and their online behaviour recorded to produce a virtual profile of them that is easily accessed, expanded, and combinable with other information to create an almost transparent citizen (Henschke 2017: 29–34). Rights-violating regimes can even use the internet to identify those they oppress based on the most intimate details of their personalities. In Egypt, for instance, the dictatorial regime has used dating apps and social media to identify and imprison homosexual citizens (Shihab-Edlin 2023).

Autocratic governments have no strong motivation to resist using the internet to undermine or violate the human rights of their citizens because they generally do not respect their subjects' rights, such as those to (genuine) political participation, free speech, privacy, or equality before the law. In autocratic states, the introduction of the internet therefore naturally creates incentives (or the internet is even introduced by regimes with the intention) to adopt 'digital authoritarianism' – 'the use of digital technologies to enhance or enable authoritarian governance' (Sherman 2021: 107). As Freedom House notes in its *Freedom of the Net 2018* report, digital authoritarianism in effect inverts the concept of the internet as a liberation technology, turning it into a tool of oppression (Freedom House 2018: 2). The practices of digitally enhanced autocratic rulers therefore demonstrate with terrifying force the internet's harmful potential if it is controlled by a regime that does not respect the rights of its populace, such as citizens' right to access the internet without arbitrary interference.

As their name signifies, the fundamental problem with autocratic regimes is that their exercise of power lacks morally justified authorisation and is largely unchecked. They resist a major step in the social evolution of humanity that is based on the acceptance of the idea that all people are morally equal. As we saw in Chapter 1, this universal moral equality is also the normative foundation and premise of human rights. It implies, as stated in the Universal Declaration of Human Rights (UN 1948), that no one's interests are as such more important than those of others, and that no one's basic moral interests must be frustrated with adequate justification to benefit others or some overarching cause. The political expressions of the idea of moral equality are democratic governance (however imperfect it may be in practice) and respect for fundamental civic and human rights. Through free and fair elections, power is given by all eligible to determine the political direction of their community to those who apply to rule on behalf of the people. Political power in democracies in this way is exercised by those in power not to further their own interests, but the interests of those who gave them their power (Reglitz 2015). As persons with diverse backgrounds, experiences, and beliefs, if we live under institutions that allow us to develop and explore our own convictions, we generally disagree on what is good and worth pursuing in life and as a political community (Rawls 2005: 4). This electoral procedure of giving everyone an equal chance to influence the outcome of elections and the political trajectory of their community is the only procedure available to us that realises in political terms the idea that everyone is morally the same and possesses equal moral worth (Christiano 2008). If a democratic majority wins a decision on which political programme to pursue, those whose own preferences lost out can still support the choices of the government for which they did not vote for at least two reasons: first, because they were given a fair chance to influence the outcome of the elections, and second, because their own fundamental rights and interests must be respected by the winning majority in the pursuit of its political agenda.

Autocratic regimes, in contrast, do not derive their authorisation from the popular will and through free and fair elections. Their trademark is their disrespect for their subjects' fundamental civic and human rights as well as their lack of accountability to their subjects. Instead, such regimes serve the purpose of promoting the interests and political goals of one or a few individuals – either directly (when the state is used to materially enrich and politically protect the position of those in power) or indirectly (when those in power pursue a grand national vision that they determine, and to which citizens must subordinate their own interests). The reasons why democracies essentially have to be concerned with the protection of their citizens' fundamental rights are the same as those why autocratic regimes violate these rights: free speech, free assembly, free information, privacy, and political participation all empower citizens and enable them to control together the political agenda and institutions of their community. Citizens' fundamental civic and human rights are therefore naturally in opposition to the political goals of autocratic leaders and regimes.

What is essential for the purposes of our discussion is that the internet on its part generates opportunities both to protect and to undermine human rights. Moreover, though, the internet offers illegitimate non-democratic regimes novel, effective, and fine-grained options to control their citizens and to keep them from challenging their rule. Because their power does not rest on popular support, autocratic regimes must secure their rule in different, coercive ways. The standard ways they do this are through (1) fear and violence (when they use or threaten brute force to incapacitate those who oppose them), (2) co-optation (when autocratic regimes spend resources on, e.g. jobs, gifts, or public services and investments to gain the support of those who might otherwise resist them), and (3) controlling the flow of information (through censorship and propaganda). However, all three of these methods have drawbacks for autocrats. Co-opting potential opponents can be costly and, in any case, uses up resources that autocratic leaders likely prefer to spend on direct benefits for themselves. Fear and brute force, on the other hand, have serious downsides if they are used indiscriminately and on a large scale, for example to quash demonstrations and uprisings or to incarcerate or kill large numbers of opponents. Such measures are risky for autocrats because they can lead to further mobilisation of the population against the regime, to international sanctions and diplomatic isolation, or to a reduction of economic productivity (Xu 2020: 312). And as the political scientist Margaret Roberts points out, the internet has made fear-based repression more costly for autocratic regimes even when it does not lead to ending their rule. That is because the internet allows individual citizens to share information without the help of traditional news media that are controlled by their regime.[2] To be effective, fear requires credible threats of punishment by the oppressing regime. Once the internet is widespread, though, no regime can credibly threaten to punish millions of internet users who report mass atrocities and regime violence at the same time (Roberts 2018: 54).

What is therefore crucial for autocrats who want to secure their rule without having to credibly threaten violence against large numbers of people and who do not want to spend vast sums on co-opting their potential opponents is the prevention of political opposition before it forms or becomes organised. To achieve this, violating people's human right to free information by controlling the information that is available to citizens through censoring knowledge that could be dangerous to the regime is vital. Roberts defines censorship as 'the *restriction* of the public expression of or public access to information by *authority* when the information is thought to have the capacity to undermine the authority by making it accountable to the public' (Roberts 2018: 37). The sort of information that autocrats generally try to repress pertains to their own actions and to new ideas (e.g. knowledge about human rights or how to covertly organise political opposition) that could endanger their grip on power (Roberts 2018: 21–22, Chang and Lin 2020: 875). Importantly, successful censorship also prevents opponents from knowing about each other's willingness to resist the regime by making it impossible for them to exercise their human right to free expression (Xu 2020: 310).

However, censorship, too, has serious drawbacks for oppressive rulers that get worse the more information they prevent from being expressed or accessed. These disadvantages to the regime have been described as various forms of the so-called dictator's dilemma; that is to say, the trade-offs that exist for autocrats between the costs and benefits of repression and censorship. First, if autocratic regimes visibly block certain information, this can attract public attention

---

[2] As explained in Chapter 3, in democratic societies the fact that the internet enables individuals to bypass traditional media sources helps citizens protect their basic civil rights.

because such censorship is like a signal to citizens that their regime has something to hide. In this way citizens can become interested in something that they otherwise would not even have noticed (Roberts 2018: 23) or they might come to doubt the regime's problem-solving capabilities (Wong and Liang 2021). Second, blocking information that is useful for economic activity and growth can function like an import tariff on the national economy when companies lack access to knowledge or connections to trading partners that would improve their productivity (Roberts 2018: 76). Third, and crucially, though, censoring the expression of citizens keeps an oppressive regime from effectively monitoring its population. Censored citizens are unable to publicly air their grievances about local regime officials that can increase dissatisfaction with the autocratic government as a whole if left unaddressed. Censored citizens also cannot express their views on the government as such so that the regime might miss early warning signs that resistance to its rule might be building. Moreover, the more people are afraid to speak out in public, the less a regime can know whether its subjects genuinely are behind it or only feign support (Roberts 2018: 23–24).

Ideally, an autocratic regime therefore wants to resolve these various kinds of dictator dilemmas in its favour while keeping the costs needed for co-optation as low as possible. It wants to block speech and knowledge that could be dangerous to its rule but allow expressions and information that help it secure its grip on power and that promote its own interests. Most importantly, autocrats want to prevent organised resistance before it becomes a serious problem for them with as little brute force as necessary. In this way, autocrats do not have to exercise indiscriminate violence and mass repression to secure their power. What autocratic regimes aim to use is therefore *preventive* and *targeted* forms of repression rather than *reactive* repressive measures that are the cause of the most violent human rights violations such as mass atrocities (Dragu and Lupu 2021: 3). The internet is a particularly useful means for autocratic rule since it enables exactly this kind of preventive repression in unprecedented ways. It does so because it allows autocrats to collect information on individual citizens in an extremely targeted way and to control the information that citizens have access to without shutting off the flow of information entirely. In other words, the internet allows for the gathering and release of information in fine-grained ways that were previously unthinkable.

The proof of this usefulness of the internet for autocrats is that digital authoritarianism is spreading worldwide because it works for them. What helps in this respect is that digital technologies as tools of repression are not only effective, but also relatively inexpensive and widely available (Rød and Weidmann 2015: 347). According to Freedom House's *Freedom of the*

Net 2022 report, internet freedom and the free use of human rights online has declined steadily worldwide for more than a decade. In a majority of the seventy countries covered by the 2022 report (which were home to 89 per cent of global internet users at that time), the use of the internet was 'not free' or only 'partly free' (Freedom House 2022: 5). Moreover, in fifty-three of these states, online users (accounting for 76 per cent of global internet users according to Freedom House's estimates) were threatened with legal sanctions for voicing their views online (Freedom House 2022: 1). More support for the effectiveness of digital authoritarianism comes from the fact that those autocratic regimes that employ the most sophisticated forms of digital authoritarianism, Russia and China, have to use little reactive and violent repression to secure their rule. There is also agreement among scholars that 'when a regime is able and willing to exercise control, and when news outlets are used to perpetuate regime-friendly messages, the people in power are likely to fend off potential opposition and stay in power' (Rød and Weidmann 2015: 340). With these points about how autocrats secure their rule and why the internet is generally useful for this purpose in mind, we can now turn to the specific ways in which autocrats and their authoritarian regimes use various digital technologies, and specifically the internet, to oppress and control their populations.

The crudest form of state interference with internet access is complete internet shutdowns. Cutting all domestic internet traffic in this way can even have effects on internet access in other countries because of the internet's globally connected digital pathways and protocols that information has to travel to reach users (Bergin and Lim 2022). Internet shutdowns also are a sort of digital canary in the coalmine because, if they occur, bad things are often happening or about to take place (Bergin et al. 2022). Examples of this are the internet shutdown that was imposed during the military coup in Myanmar in February 2021 or Russia's cyber-attacks one hour before its 2022 invasion of Ukraine. But complete internet shutdowns are not only crude instruments. They are also costly in social, political, and economic terms. According to the non-governmental organisation (NGO) Access Now, internet shutdowns that were imposed around the world are estimated to have cost USD $5.5 billion in 2021 alone. In 2022, there were 187 instances of internet shutdowns imposed in a record thirty-five countries (Harter 2023). And even though complete internet shutdowns help governments to prevent the organisation of resistance and the circulation of information that they deem undesirable, such shutdowns also extremely limit the information that regimes can obtain from their populations. Moreover, entirely losing internet access not only affects citizens' opportunities to use their political rights, but also their options to exercise their socio-economic human rights, as explained in Chapter 4. Especially in countries that are not highly developed, losing the ability to access the internet keeps people from conducting basic economic activities, such as paying bills, obtaining financial credit, or selling products. For most autocratic regimes, complete shutdowns are therefore no long-term method for securing their rule because they cause serious social and economic harm, which itself can undermine autocrats' goals.

If autocratic regimes can afford and know how to operate digital technologies that enable them to control their subjects' internet access and use, they have more sophisticated options to secure their power. They have used, for instance, 'voice recognition to scan mobile networks, tracked citizens' movement using GPS, read emails and text messages in order to monitor dissident groups and selectively censor information, and used malware and spyware to secretly turn on webcams built into personal laptops and microphones in cell phones' (Dragu and Lupu 2021: 6).

6.1.1 Online Preventive Repression 1: Digital Surveillance and Identification of Opponents

One effective way for autocrats to prevent the formation of widespread vocal public opposition against them is the digital surveillance and selective suppression of citizens' opinions. They can effectively use the online expression of their citizens' views to turn people's exercise of their human right to free speech against them. Autocratic regimes that can monitor internet activities effectively can therefore (with the help of computer-based analysis tools such as algorithm-based surveillance programmes) easily identify who opposes them and with what intensity. This is because, unlike most offline speech acts, when a citizen voices their dissent online, they normally leave a traceable, preserved record of their views and opposition.

Under the rule of Vladimir Putin, for example, Russia has built one of the most sophisticated state-operated digital surveillance regimes and systematically represses free expression by imposing legal punishments for openly opposing the regime. To monitor compliance with these laws, the Russian government requires all internet service and telecom providers to install a digitally adapted version of the Soviet System for Operative Investigative Activities (SORM) surveillance hardware into their systems. This technology produces copies of all data flows that travel on internet and telecommunication networks. Once created it can send these copies to the Russian security service, the FSB. This government enforcement agency can then analyse the data produced by SORM without legal oversight (Polyakova and Meserole 2019: 7). Russian telecom service providers also have to give the FSB unencrypted access to messages sent via internet or mobile phone networks that use encryption technology. Moreover, Russian law requires telecom providers to store the general details of voice calls and text messages (so-called metadata about who made a call to whom, for how long, to where, etc.) for three years and their content for thirty days (Ermoshina et al. 2022: 72). The use of public laws and the digital monitoring of citizens' compliance with these rules by the Putin regime therefore creates a chilling effect on free speech that forces its critics to censor themselves for fear of being easily identifiable and punished.

Even though the Russian system of monitoring and silencing public expression is highly effective, it is still relatively crude when compared with the methods of the Chinese regime that has developed the world's 'most extensive and sophisticated online censorship system' (Yuan 2019). A vital component of China's all-encompassing domestic surveillance system is the so-called Golden Shield Project. This consists of local population databases that contain information about the addresses, biographical information, photos, and household composition of local residents that are connected to several national databases. The system also uses identity scanning and tracking terminals in public places such as airports, train stations, hotels, and internet cafés. Moreover, part of the surveillance grid is a ubiquitous camera surveillance system that often includes facial recognition technology to follow the movements of citizens. But crucially, the Global Shield Project also comprises internet modules that monitor important websites, social media, and online forums, for instance with the help of keyword search software that alerts authorities to the online use of certain words or search terms. The Project's internet modules also track IP addresses and can combine these with its population databases. The regime can therefore track the identity and location of those citizens who post or search for information that the government deems dangerous to its rule (Xu 2020: 316). In China, public dissent voiced online (e.g. criticism of the government's handling of the COVID-19 pandemic) can lead to extensive punishments such as long prison sentences (Freedom House 2021: 7). To make surveillance more complete, the 2017 Cybersecurity law requires all companies to store the data of their users on servers in China and to make it available to the authorities on demand (Freedom House 2021: 18). To greater repressive effect, the Chinese regime also employs censors who actively remove undesirable expressions and information online (Wu and Fitzgerald 2021). This highly selective, digitally based form of preventive repression makes the use of indiscriminate violence largely unnecessary in China and has additional benefits for the autocratic government. As one study shows, China's digital surveillance and preventive repression allows the government to spend less on co-opting its citizens. Those Chinese administrative counties that have fully implemented the Golden Shield Project were shown to be able to reduce their overall costs on public spending necessary to keep their citizens obedient compared with those counties in which the Project has not (or not fully) been adopted. For these Golden Shield Project compliant counties, the costs of implementing the new digital technology required to identify and silence the most vocal opponents were lower than what they were able to save in local expenditure for public goods such as welfare provisions and agricultural investments (Xu 2020).

However, the full extent of the sophistication of the Chinese regime's digital censorship lies in the fact that it does not suppress all outright expressions of criticism. Instead, the Chinese government permits some public critique for two specific reasons. First, it permits public criticism when this helps the central government to identify weaknesses in its own local administration in the form of governance failures or unpopular policies that could stir up more widespread dissent if left unaddressed. Second, some criticism online is allowed to give the impression that free speech is not significantly obstructed by the government. What is decisive for the censorship of expression on the internet is whether a view has 'collective action potential' (King et al. 2013: 2). Research on online censorship practices in China has found that information that is seen as likely to motivate collective opposition to the government is suppressed, such as, for example, reports about protests in Mongolia that resulted from the death of an ethnic Mongol herder at the hands of a coal truck driver or the arrest of the artist Ai Weiwei. On the other hand, individual expressions of dissent deemed unlikely to cause greater unrest are left uncensored even if they criticise the central government directly, such as, for example, criticisms of China's previous One Child Policy or of specific local government officials (King et al. 2013: 8, 13). In this way, China's Communist Party selectively permits people to express their dissatisfaction online when it serves its own interests and in effect manipulates citizens' exercise of their right to free speech, not to empower the people, but to secure its own rule.

6.1.2 *Online Preventive Repression 2: Strict and Porous Censorship*

However, to preventively repress dissent, the Russian and Chinese autocratic regimes do not just rely on identifying and selectively silencing their opponents. A second effective way for them to use the internet to protect their power is to control more or less tightly the information that their subjects have access to. By controlling the flow of information, autocrats can block some information and promote their own message to control their subjects' knowledge and opinion of their rulers. This undermines people's ability to freely form their own opinions by frustrating their attempts to exercise their human right to access information without obstruction. Establishing this kind of *informational autocracy* is central for these regimes, which do not want their subjects to have their own views or to act on them. In this way, autocrats do not simply want to control the information their citizens can access. Rather, they also aim to shape their subjects' identity and self-understanding. This is because people develop a sense of self by forming beliefs and opinions about themselves and the world that they live in, and it is ideally all information about the world that autocrats want to control through censorship.

In Russia, the media regulator, Roskomnadzor, has the authority to block websites and online content without requiring judicial authorisation. Other Russian authorities also have powers to blacklist and make unavailable online content such as websites that the government deems problematic (Polyakova and Meserole 2019: 7, 9). To appreciate the scale of Russian online censorship it is worth noting that, according to a 2020 study of these practices, in April 2019 there were at least five blocklists that were enforced domestically by Roskomnadzor, which contained 132,798 domains and 324,695 IP addresses (Ramesh et al. 2020). But autocratic regimes such as Russia do not simply rely on taking away certain information to control what their subjects know and think. Part of their censorship practice is also to highlight or spread other information that is intended to sway their subjects in their favour. The Putin regime, for instance, manipulates the country's most popular internet search engine, Yandex, to list government-friendly information and state-controlled sources more prominently, and to demote news that is detrimental to its interests. This is done though automated software applications, so-called internet bots, that send and repeat certain information to make it more visible on online search engines (Alyukov 2022: 2). Beyond this, many autocratic regimes, such as the one in Russia, operate so-called troll farms and employ paid commentators. Their job is to flood online forums with pro-regime messages and to discredit anti-regime views and sources (Woolley and Howard 2017: 6), with the aim of misinforming citizens and distracting them from politically important discussions (Alyukov 2022: 2).

Freedom House estimates that in 2022, 69 per cent of global internet users lived in countries in which 'authorities deployed progovernment commentators to manipulate online discussions' and 64 per cent lived in countries 'where political, social, or religious content was blocked online' (Freedom House 2022: 9). Many of these internet users live in China, where the regime's control of the flow of information online is of unparalleled sophistication. Unlike the Putin regime, the Chinese informational autocracy does not simply rely on blocking websites to manipulate public opinion. Instead, the Chinese government filters all digital information streams and thereby determines which online content is available in the country without interference in the first place. This practice of 'whitelisting' instead of 'blacklisting' online content, though, requires a much greater level of regime control over the domestic internet. A central part of China's informational autocracy is a mechanism known as the 'Great Firewall of China' that has been studied by Roberts (2018). The Great Firewall is a sophisticated system that blocks foreign websites that the Chinese party does not want its subjects to access. Entering the URL of these websites returns an error page rather than the actual website. The system operates by scanning transmission protocol packets (TCPs) for blacklisted keywords and denies access to any TCPs that contain banned keywords. Even though it is relatively easy for Chinese citizens to circumvent this system with the help of a virtual private network (VPN), the use of which is not legally forbidden, this requires awareness of the existence of the Great Firewall and that it can be evaded, as well as some technical knowledge and often some financial resources to purchase the necessary services (Roberts 2018: 61). Because of all these hurdles, only a minority of internet users in China use a VPN to jump the Great Firewall (Roberts 2018: 164–173).

Another censorship practice that the Great Firewall makes possible is the throttling of the speed of certain websites (Roberts 2018: 56–64). Because IP addresses can be tracked, this has the advantage for the regime that it can identify those citizens who are patient enough to wait even a few seconds to access websites for which internet speed is throttled. These individuals can then be identified as those who are most interested in information deemed dangerous by their oppressors. This practice relies on the impatience of internet users and is particularly effective when there are regime-controlled substitutes for many online services and information that people want to access. In China, there are many government-conforming equivalents of popular websites and online platforms. For example, there is Weibo instead of X (formerly Twitter), WeChat instead of WhatsApp, Baidu instead of Google, Alibaba instead of Amazon, and Douyin – a regime-friendly version of the Chinese international export success known abroad as TikTok. Unlike the blocking of websites, the practice of slowing internet speeds for specific online content is unobservable for citizens and therefore less likely to attract attention or raise their suspicions (Roberts 2018: 59–60).

A third kind of censorship practice that the Chinese regime employs (as does the Russian government) is the use of paid commentators, known as the 'Fifty Cent Party' (because they are paid 0.50 Renminbi per post) (Roberts 2018: 85). These agitators flood social media and other online forums with pro-government messages to generate support for the ruling party or to distract the public from topics that could generate dissent or opposition. Technically, the guiding principle behind all sophisticated Chinese censorship practices is to 'tax' (i.e. attach a cost to) the searching of particular information for Chinese citizens (Roberts 2018: 25) through a 'porous' (rather than an absolute) form of censorship (Roberts 2018: 26). This porous censorship mostly does not operate based on the outright use of fear and deterrence. Instead, it relies on imposing friction on the distribution of information. Porous censorship practices nudge rather than coerce citizens into freely adopting certain behaviours desired by their regime (Roberts 2018: 228). An added benefit of this tactic is that it makes government censorship less obvious. For example, of the participants in Roberts's study, only 30 per cent reported awareness of the existence of the Great Firewall and that it could be circumvented (Roberts 2018: 165). Porous censorship therefore serves autocrats by making it impossible or difficult for their subjects to access certain information, but to do so without raising awareness or suspicion on citizens' part of their own manipulation. At the same time, porous censorship contributes to preventive repression by helping to identify and silence the most serious opponents who seek out information that the government disproves of, while at the same time creating the impression among citizens of a free flow of information because information or websites are not entirely blocked (Roberts 2018: 226). Porous censorship practices therefore abuse citizens' pursuit of their human right to free information by manipulating them without their awareness or by revealing them as interested in certain information that their rulers do not want them to have.

6.1.3 Online Preventive Repression 3: Social Credit Scores

China's dominant position in the mastery of digital authoritarianism, however, is marked by yet another way in which it uses the internet and other digital technologies to control its population. This third method goes beyond the censoring of free speech or information online. It targets more than the political human rights of citizens. It not only manipulates their own actions, but also aims to control citizens by affecting their relationships with others and their reputation in society. This third approach to online preventive repression is based on China's growing network of social credit scores. This system is not yet a unified or finished one. It consists of various governmental and commercial credit scores that rate citizens' 'trustworthiness' and 'creditworthiness'. These scores are used to administer reputational and material rewards and punishments as incentives to socially engineer citizens' behaviour and lives. The idea of social credit scores arose in China in the 1990s to tackle widespread fraud and lack of trust issues in the Chinese economy. However, in 2014, China's State Council published a planning outline for a national social credit system with a clear social-maintenance function that was to be implemented by 2020 (Xu et al. 2022: 2231, 2234). This deadline was missed, and a unified national social credit system is still in development. However, the extensive and devastating effects of social credit scores on human rights are already clearly identifiable.

Most operative social credit scores in China still exist as local platforms that are used by government and financial agencies to evaluate citizens within their local jurisdictions (Xu et al. 2022: 2234). These social credit scores in effect form a surveillance system that collects enormous amounts of data on citizens' personal, social, economic, and political activities and assigns to people various scores according to their behaviour (Xu et al. 2022: 2231). Scores are on the one hand based on whether citizens break laws and commit fraud or default on repaying debts. However, scores are also based on the 'morality of citizens' actions, covering economic, social, and political conduct' (Xu et al. 2022: 2234). By bundling this information into scores, the database operators incentivise desired behaviour and outcomes without having to resort to brute force or coercion (Tirole 2021: 2008). The commercial versions of social credit scores, such as Zhima (Sesame) Credit, use numeric scores to evaluate individuals. These commercial scores do not administer punishments but are purely reward-based loyalty schemes that give access to benefits such as qualifications for personal loans, access to sharing economic services, or the fast-tracking of visa applications (Kostka and Antoine 2019: 261–262). Government-operated credit scores, on the other hand, offer benefits such as tax reductions, cheaper public transportation, and easier access to public services as well. However, these kind of social credit scores also impose punishments for unwanted behaviour. That is, people who are assigned bad social credit scores can be blacklisted. This means that they can become, for instance, ineligible 'to receive government welfare or benefits, [are banned] from taking up employment in the public sector, [have] limited access to high-speed trains and financial service' (Kostka and Antoine 2019: 261) and good schools, but also can have their internet speed throttled by the authorities. Beyond this, government agencies have also publicly shamed those with low social credit scores by publishing their names on billboards, government websites, or social media (Xu et al. 2022: 2235).

As mentioned earlier, there is currently no unified Chinese national social credit score for citizens. The use of advanced government algorithms for calculating social credit scores is not yet common practice either, nor is the real-time monitoring of individuals (Xu et al. 2022: 2234–2235). However, the existing use of social credit scores already clearly constitutes a morally highly problematic form of social conditioning and engineering (Xu et al. 2022: 2232) that uses the violation of human rights or the curtailment of other rights to make citizens obedient. If a unified national social credit score were to be fully implemented, Chinese society would fully become a digitally enabled dystopian nightmare in which the population is entirely controlled by an unelected, unaccountable government that determines on a microscopic level which behaviours get rewarded and which ones punished. Such a unified national social credit system would turn China into one giant panopticon (a prison designed to condition prisoners by depriving them of all privacy, Wikipedia 2023b). It would allow the regime to identify and repress its opponents without openly cracking down on or having to arrest them. Importantly, this form of social conditioning is an effective tool of political oppression because people's political views and actions can be factored into establishing their credit scores. There is already significant evidence that the Chinese social credit system is used by the government to repress journalists and stop protests (Xu et al. 2022: 2231). Moreover, the effectiveness of social credit scores as tools for social conditioning has been demonstrated in practice. One study, for example, showed that a significant number of citizens do change their views about friends who obtain low social credit scores and that some have unfriended a friend on social media because of their low scores. Others have reported that they have changed what content they share online to obtain more favourable social credit scores (Kostka and Antoine 2019: 274). Even though it remains unclear whether being friends or in contact with low credit score individuals as such lowers a person's own score, it seems plausible that the social credit score system harnesses the natural human tendency to not to want to be associated with those who are deemed socially undesirable. In China, such social ostracism can be the result of economic as well as of political activities.

A system such as China's social credit scores quite obviously undermines and violates many fundamental rights of those who are so assessed. Specifically, people's opportunities to enjoy their human or other fundamental rights is made dependent on their conformity with authoritarian laws, but also on their obedience to their rulers whom they are unable to choose and who are not accountable to them. Citizens' exercise of their political and civil rights is severely curtailed because they cannot freely speak their mind or associate with others for fear of receiving a lower credit score if the government does not approve of their views or choice of friends. But beyond these, many basic socio-economic human rights are affected too. People's enjoyment of their human right to a decent standard of living, for instance, is arbitrarily impacted by the social credit scores because those with low credit scores are denied access to government welfare or benefits. Their human right to work, while not being completely devalued, is arbitrarily limited because those with low social credit have no access to advantageous public sector employment. Equally, their children's human right to education can be unjustly curtailed by denying them access to good schools. Their enjoyment of their human right to healthcare is affected as their access to public health services is impeded. Even citizens' freedom of movement can be restricted because low social credit scores prevent individuals from purchasing certain travel services such as tickets for aeroplanes or fast trains (Xu et al. 2022: 2235). These measures do not necessary amount to human rights violations because red-listed citizens might still be able to access basic forms of provisions and services. Nonetheless, the limitations they experience related to their opportunities to enjoy their rights are unjustifiable because they are based on factors that are morally arbitrary and irrelevant, such as not opposing the rule of their autocratic government. Moreover, when information about an individual's personal opinions and behaviour is collated and combined in databases and used to affect their opportunities in society, this leaves little room for leading a private life and the enjoyment of the human right to privacy. Living a decent life as an autonomous individual is impossible under such circumstances of constant surveillance and assessment as well as coercion regarding personal choices (which reaffirms the function of human rights as protections of minimally decent lives outlined in Chapter 1). Such constant surveillance and assessment of actions is designed to control what people think and do, and therefore directly affects people's sense of self and their lives as a whole.

Financial credit scores are certainly also employed in democratic countries. However, even though these are not entirely unproblematic either,[3] politically motivated and constructed social credit schemes such as the Chinese system are imposed and controlled by autocratic regimes that do not follow the rule of law. That is to say, such regimes not only do not let people have a say about who is in charge. They also deny their subjects any real influence on the rules that are imposed on them and that they are expected to follow. Moreover, financial credit scores in democratic states do not make the enjoyment of human rights dependent on citizens' political views or personal affiliations. Their effects are normally limited to the economy and do not spill over into other social spheres, for example, the range of public services, employment, or educational opportunities that people have access to. Finally, and importantly, purely financial credit scores do not threaten individuals with public shaming or social isolation because others do not fear to be deemed

---

[3] For example, because these scores often are untransparent and those who are rated according to them have insufficient recourse to redress in case their evaluation contains errors.

guilty by associating with them (Tirole 2021: 2010). Overall, limited financial credit scores do not render human rights practically ineffective by attaching punitive costs to making autonomous choices that the government dislikes. These financial credit scores in democratic countries, even though they might not be unproblematic, are therefore not morally comparable to China's social credit system.

What is relevant to the topic of this book is that, although China's social credit system assesses many offline activities (e.g. traffic violations, defaulting on loans, physical movements), the internet and digital technology are central to the entire project. That is because citizens' online activities are easily traceable and digital technology is required to record and keep track of the vast amounts of data generated by the complex behaviour of hundreds of millions of citizens. One study of the Chinese social credit system suggests that, even though many Chinese citizens have in fact altered their behaviour in response to credit scores, they have done so more in response to rewards engendered by the system rather than the punishment that government-run scores threaten. This suggests that the scores currently function more according to positive incentives than fear and chilling effects (Kostka and Antoine 2019). A different study recorded generally favourable views of the social credit system among Chinese citizens. This study, though, also showed that there is generally little knowledge among citizens of how the system operates and suppresses political dissent – to a large extent because the government's own messaging about the system is positive and focuses on its social order and trust-building functions. However, once citizens were made aware of the system's political repression function, their support for it sank considerably (Xu et al. 2022).

The general support and the fact that citizens appear to respond more to rewards than to fear of punishment within the system might be surprising at first glance. However, to fully appreciate its effects, we have to see China's social credit system in conjunction with the ones outlined here. It is but one of several effective surveillance systems that together disincentivise unwanted behaviour (Kostka and Antoine 2019: 279). Even if China's social credit system is still in development, it gives a vivid idea of how an autocratic regime – if it has the resources and expertise – can use the internet and digital technology to achieve tight, all-encompassing, and preventive repression. This kind of digitally enabled repression allows autocratic governments to control their populations largely without fear and brutal human rights violations, and makes challenging their grip on power extremely difficult for opponents. In such a situation, the enjoyment or exercise of many human rights (e.g. to free speech, association, information, political participation) is suppressed, chilled, or used against people. Moreover, the full enjoyment of many other rights (e.g. to free movement, education, right to work, or public benefits) is denied to those who resist autocratic rule. Even when these infringements do not amount to human rights violations, political and social punishments for transgressing against the dictates of their unelected government turns people into second class citizens who have fewer opportunities than their obedient fellow citizens. Under digital authoritarianism, a decent life is not possible for people. They cannot fully exercise their autonomous agency, because their basic interests are only respected if they live in conformity with the commands of the regime and do not challenge its authority, and because (if they are aware of the surveillance capabilities of their government) they have to live with the constant concern that their digitally traceable and analysable behaviour will attract the disapproval of their rulers. Life as a morally equal member in such a society is made impossible because no civil society can exist. 'Autocrats learn to broaden internet censorship and weaken civil society. [...] The stronger internet censorship is, the weaker civil society becomes' (Chang and Lin 2020: 875). As all aforementioned practices make clear, the internet offers many new and highly effective methods for autocrats to oppress their own subjects, but if used in these ways, the internet facilitates the opposite of human progress.

6.1.4 *Interfering in Institutions and Lives Abroad*

While digital authoritarianism is effective in suppressing domestic dissent and opposition, the internet also gives autocrats entirely new opportunities to attack institutions and people in other countries.

The most infamous example of this is the digital disinformation operation associated with the Putin regime that is euphemistically named the Internet Research Agency (IRA), which was founded by Yevgeny Prigozhin (who also headed the Wagner mercenary group) and has operated at least since 2013. The agency has trained and paid more than a thousand online commentators to operate bots and to post messages on social media platforms such as Facebook, Twitter, and Instagram in Russia and abroad. The IRA's task was to covertly influence the outcomes of pivotal democratic decisions such as the UK's 2016 referendum on ending its membership in the EU and the 2016 US presidential elections, but also major elections in other democracies. To do so, the IRA was divided into separate departments that each focused on influencing discussions and events in assigned countries or regions. Individual commentators were paid to fulfil a range of tasks. If they acted as 'trolls' (i.e. persons posting inflammatory or upsetting comments online to elicit emotional responses in others), they had to post around fifty comments daily in news article comment sections. When assigned to Facebook forums, 'they were tasked with maintaining six Facebook pages, posting three times daily about the news, and discussing new developments in groups on Facebook twice daily, with a target of at least 500 subscribers by the end of the first month' (Dawson and Innes 2019: 246). And if they were assigned to Twitter, commentators were expected to operate ten accounts that each had at least 2,000 followers and to post 135 comments during a twelve-hour shift.

Sometimes the objective of these activities was to promote specific messages to give the impression that certain persons or political views and choices had significant popular support to sway democratic citizens to support them as well (Woolley and Guilbeault 2017). Other goals were targeting specific communities (e.g. African Americans) with divisive messages, voter suppression, promoting secession, and promoting certain political candidates (DiResta et al. 2019: 6–10). But the purpose of IRA operations was not always to make those who read the disingenuous expressions believe them. The messages posted were in fact often contradictory. Rather, the main aim seems to have been to create 'epistemic anarchy' (Dawson and Innes 2019: 254) by sowing confusion and disorientation among readers about what information could still be trusted. Moreover, even if citizens did not believe the false messages, their mere awareness of the circulation of disinformation could have the effect that they lost trust in their democratic institutions and processes. This is because knowing of the circulating falsehoods, citizens could be led to worry that their fellow democratic citizens might fall prey to and be manipulated by 'fake news' and misinformation (Rini 2021, Reglitz 2022). In pre-internet times, planting false information or increasing political polarisation in other democratic states was an extremely difficult objective for autocratic regimes. When this was attempted, it could mostly only be done indirectly by disseminating information elsewhere in the hope that news media in the target country would take up and relay this information to their own audiences (Moore 2019: 83). The internet, though, with its online discussion forums and social media platforms makes it incomparably easier to create epistemic confusion and to promote political strife abroad. This is because, given how these platforms currently operate, online disinformation attempts are technically simple and can have extremely wide reach. One analysis of the IRA's activities found that between its inception and 2018, it reached 126 million Facebook users, 20 million Instagram users, and 1.4 million Twitter users with more than 10 million tweets, 116,000 Instagram posts, 61,500 Facebook posts, and 1,100 YouTube videos (DiResta et al. 2019: 6–10). From the perspective of human rights, the goals of the IRA are clearly problematic. Its operations are yet another attempt by autocratic regimes to use the internet not to promote human rights, but to use foreign citizens' exercise of their human rights against them. Democratic citizens used social media and other online sources to connect with like-minded people, to express their opinions, and to obtain political information to form their own views so that they can participate in the democratic processes of their country. By spreading false information, simulating opinions and popular consensus (Woolley and Howard 2017), and by sowing distrust among voters, the Russian government used the human rights and freedoms respected in other countries to attack democratic citizens and institutions abroad.

But with the help of the internet, authoritarian states can also persecute their own citizens abroad. China, for example, reportedly monitors the online activities and expressions of opinions of its citizens in other countries (Xiao and Mozur 2022). When Chinese international students and citizens working abroad posted statements online that were critical of the Communist Party, or they supported views and causes that the regime disapproved of, their families or they themselves faced recriminations by Chinese authorities. The internet has therefore become a tool for the China regime to exert its authoritarian grip on its citizens around the world even when these are beyond its physical reach.

Other autocratic regimes, such as Iran, Saudi Arabia, and many others also utilise practices of digital authoritarianism to protect their power. One such case that attracted international attention and condemnation was that of the Saudi blogger Raif Badawi, who in 2014 was sentenced to prison and 1,000 lashes for 'insulting Islam through electronic channels' (Haidar 2016). Freedom House (2022) estimates that most internet users today live in countries where they cannot freely exercise their human rights on the internet and where their online activities are monitored by their oppressive governments. In attempts to mimic China's Great Firewall, an increasing number of states are also trying to manipulate the digital flow of information into their territories and to bring the internet infrastructure within their borders under their control to limit their citizens' exercise of human rights online. These efforts are leading to a 'Balkanisation' of the formerly global internet (Freedom House 2022: 11–16).

Russia and especially China employ the most resourceful and sophisticated versions of digital authoritarianism. They present the most striking examples of how states can use the internet to oppress their own citizens and to try to undermine the human rights of people in other countries as well. What is especially concerning from the perspective of human rights is that Russia and China are also at the forefront of exporting to other states their digital authoritarianism and the technology needed to enact it. According to Freedom House, until 2018 at least eighteen countries had installed surveillance software produced in China. Concerns about possible malignant covert capabilities of Chinese-produced telecommunications infrastructure technology has led a number of Western democracies, such as the US and the UK, to ban the use of Chinese 5G technology in their countries (Kelion 2020, The Guardian 2021). But China is not only exporting surveillance technology. It is also teaching other regimes the skills to use it. Until 2018, representatives of at least thirty-six governments had participated in 'trainings and seminars on new media and information management' led by Chinese officials (Freedom House 2018: 8). Russia, too, exports its surveillance technology. Almost all former Soviet republics as well as some countries in the Middle East and Latin America have acquired Russian SORM technology to be able to spy on their citizens (Polyakova and Meserole 2019: 10).

The export success of leading digital autocracies such as China and Russia signifies that globally there are at least two competing models of the internet and its governance because many states are willing to arbitrarily interfere in their citizens' access and use of the internet. One model enables the realisation of human rights online and the other prevents their exercise or even turns the use of human rights online against people. The model advocated by autocratic states such as China and Russia is one of cyber-sovereignty. According to this, states ought to have sovereignty of their cyberspace and internet just as they do over their territory. The primary motivation offered for this notion by its defenders is that states ought to respect each other's self-determination in cyberspace and interact internationally as equals in questions of internet governance. This concern for external sovereignty is justified by China, Russia, and others with reference to the dominant position of the US in shaping how the internet is governed and used. However, the concept of cyber-sovereignty is also used by authoritarian regimes to demand respect for their internal governance and control of the internet (Hong and Goodnight 2020: 16, 17). Against these claims of cyber-sovereignty, others have argued that concepts such as territoriality and authority are inappropriate to the domain of the internet as its very point is to bridge territorial boundaries and enable the global flow of information (Mueller 2020). From the perspective of human rights, what is crucial to note is that the sovereignty of states is conditional upon their respect for the human rights of their citizens and others. Therefore, even if the concept of cyber-sovereignty were to make sense, it could not (except in cases of exceptional emergencies) be used to justify general interferences with human rights of the kind discussed in this section.

Autocratic states today routinely limit internet freedom with the aim to secure their own illegitimate and arbitrary rule. Because it has been found that regimes that want to control their society's information environment tend to expand the internet rather than to prevent its spread, it has been argued that the internet is a 'repression technology' rather than a liberation technology (Rød and Weidmann 2015: 349). The only way to ensure that this is not the case is for states to respect people's vital interest to access and use the internet without arbitrary interference.

6.2 TEMPTING DEMOCRACIES

Autocratic regimes, though, are not the only ones that misuse the capabilities of the internet. Problematically, even though democracies have been argued to be the type of government that best respects the human rights of their citizens (Christiano 2011), that does not mean that they do not arbitrarily interfere with their citizens' access to and use of the internet. In contrast to autocratic states practising digital authoritarianism, though, most democracies do not routinely interfere with human rights such as free speech, free assembly, and accessing information freely online. Their main problem is their morally unjustifiable violation of people's privacy online. Democratic governments normally explain such privacy violations with the claim that these are necessary to protect national security, for example by identifying and pre-empting threats such as terrorism and intrusions by hostile foreign powers.

In June 2013, the revelations of Edward Snowden about the mass surveillance practices of American and British security agencies shocked many in the democratic world. Snowden, who worked as a computer security consultant for the US National Security Agency (NSA), in cooperation with *Guardian* journalist Glenn Greenwald, revealed that with the help of computer data analysis programmes called PRISM and XKeyscore, his former employer had gathered and analysed information about the phone calls, emails, and online activities (e.g. use of social media platforms) of millions of US Americans and foreigners. This was done, without the targets' knowledge, for the stated purpose of identifying threats to US national security (MacAskill and Dance 2013). The NSA also forced telecom companies such as Verizon to hand over metadata on the phone calls of millions of Americans and accessed the computer servers of the main internet companies (Google, Facebook, Microsoft, Apple, and others), bypassing encryption and other privacy protections with the help of these companies. In this way, in the month between 8 February and 8 March 2013, alone, the NSA collected 124.8 billion phone data items and 7.1 billion computer data items (Lyon 2014: 2, Henschke 2017: 28). Its PRISM programme allows the NSA to access the metadata and the content of internet communications directly from the servers of the companies holding this data. According to Greenwald and Snowden, the XKeyscore software gives

NSA data analysts real time access to anyone's internet activities (including IP addresses) anywhere around the world without prior authorisation or legal warrant. XKeyscore also allows them to search the contents of emails, websites, browsing histories, and personal chats for specific keywords (Greenwald 2013). The British government's General Communications Headquarters (GCHQ) on its part at the same time operated a computer programme called Tempora that secretly extracted vast amounts of internet data (for example, emails, search histories, social media activities, and phone calls) from internet backbone optic fibre-cables. Tempora stores this information for thirty days so it can be sifted and analysed (MacAskill et al. 2013). Mass data surveillance practices such as those of the NSA and GCHQ have been widely condemned as unjustifiable by many important institutions, such as the UN's Human Rights Council (UN 2014) because they are covertly and preventively conducted without the authorisation of, or oversight by, independent judicial authorities and mostly on people who have not done anything to justify becoming targets of such intrusions.

However, democratic governments and powerholders not only secretly monitor populations on a mass scale. They also use surveillance software to covertly and arbitrarily monitor individuals they deem problematic or to be of interest. In November 2022, the European Parliament commissioned a draft report describing and condemning the use of the Pegasus mercenary spyware by EU member-state governments in what it calls a 'full-blown European affair' (EU Parliament 2022: 3). The draft report sets out in detail the comprehensive capabilities of the software. It is said to

> Not only allow for real-time surveillance, but full, retroactive access to files and messages created in the past, as well as metadata about past communications. The surveillance can even be done at a distance, in countries anywhere in the world. Spyware can be used to essentially take over a smartphone and extract all its contents, including documents, images and messages. Material thus obtained can be used not only to observe actions, but also to blackmail, discredit, manipulate and intimidate the victims. Access to the victim's system can be manipulated and fabricated content can be planted. The microphone and camera can be activated remotely and turn the device into a spy in the room. All the while, the victim is not aware of anything. Spyware leaves few traces on the victim's device, and even if it is detected it is nearly impossible to prove who was responsible for the attack. (EU Parliament 2022: 3)

Moreover, this comprehensive spyware can be installed without requiring any interactions of the individual targeted with it. Naturally this software has been employed by authoritarian governments around the world as a powerful addition to their arsenal of tools of digital authoritarianism. But democratic states too have made use of the spyware. The EU Parliament's report, for instance, accuses the Polish government of having used it to spy on opposition politicians and the Hungarian government of having employed Pegasus to monitor lawyers, journalists, political activists, and opposition politicians without legal oversight or authorisation (Sherman 2022). Even European governments that were not found to have used the spyware are involved in its distribution by facilitating the trading of the software within their jurisdiction. The European Parliament's draft report therefore sees Europe as having become 'the hub for exports [of surveillance software] to dictatorships and oppressive regimes' (EU Parliament 2022: 3). There are therefore hardly any states, democratic or not, that are not demonstrably involved (directly or indirectly) in using the internet to spy on or oppress individuals and entire populations. Even if democratic states often seem to limit their misuse of online technologies to violating people's privacy, such transgressions as such present a very serious moral issue.

6.2.1 The Importance of Privacy for Minimally Decent Lives

To see the problem with states' routine practices of indiscriminately accessing individuals' internet activities and personal data, we have to consider why such activities and data are protected by the human right to privacy, and why the human right to privacy is of pivotal moral importance in the first place. Philosophers have different views on what makes the right to privacy so important. Generally, though, this right is seen as essential not because privacy is important as such, but because it is extremely useful for other things that we primarily value – for example, the exercise of other human rights such as our freedoms of opinion and conscience, for the development of a person's autonomy, and for trust and openness in political societies. The human right to privacy is therefore functionally a derivative right like the human right to free internet access. At its core, privacy as the object protected by this human right is morally essential because it is linked to personal information about us, our identity, who we are, what we think, feel, believe, and do, and to what extent others have access to this most intimate information about us. The human right to privacy is therefore generally concerned with the protection of that sort of personal information that has to do with the core of who we are: our self-identity. If this information involuntarily falls into the hands of others, we can become the victims of various kind of harms, misrecognitions, or mistreatments by others, such as identity-fraud, blackmail, public shaming, social exclusion, and political persecution (Henschke 2017: 50, 185).

How exactly privacy protects this link between personal information and identity is a matter of debate among philosophers. There are at least two main positions in this debate, one of which sees the human right to privacy justified because it gives us control over who can access personal information linked to our self-identity. The second one only takes privacy to be at stake when that information is actually accessed (rather than merely controlled) by others. According to Andrei Marmor, for instance, privacy is morally important enough to impose duties on others because it gives us a reasonable amount of control over how we present ourselves to others (Marmor 2015). Our right to control what others know about ourselves is not absolute, though. Such absolute control would allow us to deceive others, and is mostly not possible anyway in the real world that we inevitably share with others because, to interact with others in the physical world, we minimally have to be seen by them.[4] But having an effective degree of control over information about our self-identity is indispensable for a person's well-being, their ability to navigate the social world, and for having control over their social lives.

For example, if we could not conceal information about who we are from others it would be very difficult to establish and maintain special relationships with others. We share certain things about ourselves only with those who are close to us. How close they are to us normally depends on how much and what they know about our most intimate desires, beliefs, and behaviours. That is, the more intimate we are with someone, the more we normally reveal about ourselves to them (Marmor 2015, Henschke 2017: 41–43). But privacy is also essential for our ability to live with others in politically organised modern communities. If a government knows, for instance, its citizens' political and religious beliefs, moral or sexual beliefs, this seriously jeopardises their political agency. For example, the government can use this knowledge to pressure or manipulate individuals, or, even worse, to persecute and neutralise them (Véliz 2020: 133) – as shown by the example of Egyptian police using dating apps to 'hunt' LGBT individuals. And if citizens are aware that their government knows about their personal beliefs and thoughts, they might constrain or alter their behaviour, or they might feel threatened and observed (Henschke 2017: 41, Véliz 2020: 85, 94). Indiscriminate preventative mass surveillance by governments can therefore even problematically change the conditions and constitution of the public sphere. Where people used to interact and associate freely with others, they might now not say, do, or write certain things, or interact or

---

[4] Online, people can of course interact with each other under the cloak of anonymity. This tight control over how we appear to others that is possible online, but not offline, creates new risks and vulnerabilities that will be discussed in Chapter 8.

collaborate with others because they know their government is digitally collecting data on their actions (Stahl 2016). The enjoyment of many of our civil and political human rights (e.g. to freedom of expression, freedom of association, freedom of information, freedom of conscience and belief, the right to a family) therefore presuppose that we have an intact private sphere that is not generally accessible to others without our consent (UN 2015: 7, Véliz 2020: 208). Moreover, because people normally fundamentally disagree about what is good and right, they need a private space in which they can discover, test, and live out ideas that might not be shared by most of their fellow citizens. Otherwise, they are likely to face social pressure to conform to what most others think and do, and such social pressure undermines the pursuit and exercise of their individuality and autonomy as human beings (Henschke 2017: 41–43).

These important functions that the human right to privacy protects are of course exactly the reasons why for autocratic states the violation of their subjects' privacy is often an essential precondition of digital authoritarian practices. After all, autocratic regimes want to know who opposes their rule and neutralise their opponents. To do this, they need to know as much as possible about what their citizens think and believe. Privacy violations by different kinds of states and the effects these have on citizens help explain further why privacy has the status of a human right. The ability to conceal to a reasonable degree information about who we are and what we do, think, and believe is necessary for us as self-determined social beings for leading minimally decent lives. The thought of living in a panopticon where no privacy is possible is generally horrendous to people because in such a situation they must either at least outwardly adopt behaviour that is acceptable to those who watch them, or even have to adopt an identity that lets them act in conformity with the expectations of their watchers and at the same time endorse this sort of behaviour. Either limitation, though, frustrates and negates the very notion of autonomous agency that is part of the essence of what it means to be human. It is therefore not surprising that many of the most essential legal documents recognise a right to privacy, such as the Universal Declaration of Human Rights (§12), the International Covenant on Civil and Political Rights (§17, see UN 2015: 6), as well as the US Constitution's Fourth Amendment, which specifically protects an individual's private sphere from indiscriminate interference and surveillance (Henschke 2017: 25).[5]

---

[5] The Fourth Amendment states that 'the right of the people to be secure in their persons, houses, papers, and effects, against unreasonable searches and seizures, shall not be violated, and no Warrants shall issue, but upon probable cause, supported by Oath or affirmation, and particularly describing the place to be searched, and the persons or things to be seized' (US Congress 1791).

The importance that privacy has for our lives explains why mass surveillance practices such as those revealed by Edward Snowden have morally devastating effects on people. As the UN Special Rapporteur for the Promotion and Protection of the Right to Freedom of Opinion and Expression clarifies, in our digital age the human right to hold opinions without interference – one of the most important human rights for being an autonomous person, which depends on privacy – 'is not an abstract concept limited to what may be in one's mind' (UN 2015: 8). Rather, this right today also must be understood to protect people's email archives, online search history, and hard drives from arbitrary surveillance and interference because it would be unreasonable to expect people to avoid all these dominant tools used for accessing, sharing, and preserving information in forming and holding opinions about the world. If government agencies read citizens' emails, access and analyse their online search or browser histories, trace their location online, and keep a record of the online expressions of their views or who they maintain relationships with, this negatively affects the development, or at least the exercise, of their personality and agency.

Since Snowden's revelations, people have become increasingly aware of the fact that some of their online activities (e.g. posting in a public online forum or uploading private images online) will remain traceable for many years because of the practices of how such data is currently predominantly handled. However, other online activities that are not exercised in public (e.g. emails, online searches, online interactions through non-public channels) have to remain concealable for people lest they become distrustful of, and vulnerable to, their political institutions. The collection and accessing of personal data online is particularly problematic because it can be used to establish a virtual identity of people that is composed of information about themselves that they leave behind digitally. But such a virtual identity or profile renders permanently observable information about who people are and what they think and do. This is because the digitally gathered personal information does not degrade over time and the virtual profile of a person is expandable by combining it with other information (e.g. where they are and move to, where they live, what their health is like, see Henschke 2017: 55). A virtual identity therefore constitutes a very different account of a person than could be obtained by observing their actions offline. If I am seen by others in public, I necessarily reveal information about myself. But this knowledge of my actions and movements is limited to those who are around me, and their memory of the details of much of what I do will fade over time (Marmor 2015: 21). The information can of course be written down and passed on, but if it is restricted to my activities in the real world, it will in most cases remain much more limited than the information that can be gleaned from my online activities. This is the reason why online privacy violations are often much more consequential than when they occur in the offline world. Having control over who has access to the most intimate information about who we are, what we believe, and what we do in our personal lives – especially in its digital form – is therefore clearly necessary for a minimally decent life as an individual among others and in modern political societies.

As mentioned, though, other philosophers hold a different view of how privacy functions and what the right to it must protect. For them privacy is not violated when we lose control over our personal information, but only if that information is actually accessed by others against our will. To understand this point, we can imagine that I access my email account via a web browser in a public internet café. For some reason, I leave the café in a hurry and forget to log out of my email account. Someone else uses the internet terminal after me and finds the website and my email account open. In this situation, I have clearly lost control over the personal information contained in my email archive. However, if the person using the computer after me simply logs out of my email account without reading my emails before they do because they realise that it is unlikely that I intended to leave my account accessible, my privacy remains intact even though I have involuntarily lost control of some personal information. This view of privacy as only depending on whether personal information is actually accessed is shared, for instance, by former NSA director Keith Alexander, who argues that the mere collection of personal data about the online activities of citizens with the help of PRISM and XKeyscore did not constitute a violation of people's privacy (MacNish 2016: 2).

However, even though a loss of control over personal information does not always constitute a direct violation of privacy if that information is not accessed, such loss of control remains very much an issue related to, and a problem for, a person's privacy. That is because, if someone else obtains control over my personal information against my will, my privacy has been compromised and is no longer protected by my own choices. Whether or not my personal information is in fact accessed is now arbitrarily under the control of someone who should not have the power to make that decision. The human right to privacy is intended to give a person power over who accesses their personal information. If this was not the case, the right would not be needed since it would be practically ineffective. Moreover, in the case of the NSA and GCHQ mass surveillance practices revealed by Snowden, the question whether privacy violations occur at the point when a person is losing control over their personal information or only when this information is actually accessed by someone else is a moot point. This is because both NSA and GCHQ not only collected personal data from millions of people, but also accessed and analysed this information with the help of computer programmes (MacNish 2016: 14, 15). Even if we accept an 'access account' of privacy, this view therefore offers no justification for these mass surveillance practices.

The protection of personal identity-related information is also vital for people who have not violated any laws and whose governments follow the rule of law. Lack of concern about, or interest in, the practices revealed by Snowden sometimes takes the form that people who have nothing to hide do not have to be concerned about mass surveillance by governments. But such a response is problematic for at least two reasons. First, this stance acquiesces to governments secretly and coercively gaining access to a sphere and to personal information that they have no right to have. Second, such compromising of privacy leaves people's identity-related information at the mercy of the governments that gain control over it. Whether that information is then used to harm people is up to them. But whether democratic, rights-respecting regimes turn into oppressive ones or whether they start using the personal information they have collected on citizens against them is not in the hands of most individual citizens. The only way to safeguard people's personal information is to protect their right to privacy before it is compromised. This concern is captured by Edward Snowden's statement that 'when you say I don't care about the right to privacy because I have nothing to hide, that is no different than saying I don't care about freedom of speech because I have nothing to say or freedom of the press because I have nothing to write' (Rusbridger et al. 2015). The problem with this view is that, even though one might not have anything to say or write right now, one might be mistaken about this, or one might have something to say or write in the future. But without having a right to say or write freely, one will not be able to in the future when external circumstances (e.g. one's government) change.

Privacy is therefore crucial for many human rights and moral goods. It is a precondition for the development and exercise of personhood and individuality (Griffin 2008: 225–241); it is necessary for an open and active democratic society because the lack of privacy means that people are forced to reveal to the government or others involuntarily who they are; without an intact private sphere, people also have no possibility to act in ways that are socially or politically disapproved of without paying a heavy price for it. All these considerations present reasons why the indiscriminate and arbitrary mass online surveillance of innocent people by any state is morally difficult to justify and (except in exceptional circumstances) constitutes a human rights violation. Moreover, democratic states engaging in such practices undercut their own legitimacy because they violate the very principles that their rule is based on. Democratic governance is based on respect for the idea that everyone is morally equal and therefore must be treated with equal respect and concern, and that their fundamental rights must be respected by everyone else. By violating their citizens' privacy online without good reason, though, democratic governments do not treat them with the respect that they are entitled to as moral equals in whose name and for whose interest democratic power is exercised. The use of the Pegasus spyware is a clear case of an arbitrary interference with people's privacy online that is not done with their interests in mind but for the benefit of those in power who are using the spyware. But NSA and GCHQ-style mass surveillance practices also violate democratic principles because they were conducted without proper authorisation, justification, or oversight, and therefore amount to arbitrary exercises of power that do not adequately respect the rights of those who are spied upon.

6.2.2 Mass Online Surveillance and National Security

Those responsible for the mass surveillance in democratic states argue that, even though they have a moral cost, these privacy violations are ultimately in the interests and for the benefit of the citizens whose privacy is interfered with. They argue that such indiscriminate preventive surveillance is necessary as the only or most effective way to thwart attacks on the political community by those who want to harm it. Their claim, in essence, is that the loss of freedom (in the form of privacy) is worth the gain in (national) security. But even if that were so, it is not a conscious or voluntary trade that democratic citizens have made. After all, the violation of their privacy happened covertly (Xu et al. 2022: 2231), which is likely an indication that those monitoring them were concerned that too many citizens would not actually want to trade away their freedom in this way. If the practices revealed by Snowden had been democratically adopted, though, this would have not undermined their effectiveness. After all, the only alternative for people disagreeing with these measures would have been to stop using the internet in the most common ways they do today, which would have been impracticable for many.

The question about the effectiveness of public mass surveillance programmes is beside the point, though, because – covert or not – these practices cannot morally be justified by the legitimate interest of states to fulfil their obligation to protect national security and the basic security rights of their citizens. This is not because surveillance can never be morally justified because people have a human right to privacy. Privacy and security are not mutually exclusive, and the choice is not between always respecting privacy or not having to respect it at all. After all, there are tried and tested moral and legal principles and procedures for determining when and how states can legitimately intrude into the private sphere of individuals. Important institutions such as the UN Human Rights Council (UN 2014) and the European Court of Justice (Korff 2019: 137), though, have argued that practices such as those of the NSA and GCHQ failed to meet these principles and were therefore unjustified methods for the protection of national security.

To be morally justified, intrusions into the private sphere of individuals must pass a three-part test, as the UN Special Rapporteur for Protection of Freedom of Opinion and Expression explains (UN 2015: 11–12). Such privacy violations must be (1) *legally provided*. That means they must be authorised by legitimate and public laws and authorised on a case-by-case basis by an independent authority, which is normally a court or judge. They must further be (2) employed only *for justifiable reasons* such as the protection of, for example, people's rights and reputation, national security, public order, public health or morals. That means that privacy violations by states for the prevention of crimes can be justified under certain circumstances but spying on political opponents or citizens to prevent them challenging one's political power or privileges normally cannot. Finally, justified surveillance must be (3) *necessary and proportionate* as stated, for example, in General Comment No 31 on the International Covenant on Civil and Political Rights (UN 2014: 8). For a privacy violation to be *necessary*, it must be more than a merely useful or expedient way to achieve its goals. This is because violating someone's privacy presents a very serious interference with their lives that can only be justified for especially strong reasons. This normally means that violating someone's privacy must only be allowed if other measures are unlikely to achieve the necessary goal and if there is a reasonable chance the intrusion will achieve its aim. Surveillance and other privacy violations therefore cannot be routine practices because this would make them the rule rather than the exception. There is, though, no reason to think that the permanent surveillance of large numbers of or all citizens is necessary for any goal that is morally justified (UN 2015: 8). But even if privacy violations are justifiable, there are different methods for monitoring people, and not every kind of privacy violation is as necessary and justified as the others (Henschke 2018: 227). For example, instead of collecting metadata or analysing a person's emails and online activities, in-person surveillance can be sufficient to prevent a crime. Moreover, to prevent acts of terrorism, the surveillance of a limited number of suspicious individuals might be justifiable while the preventive online surveillance of large numbers of innocent people is not. In their attempts to justify mass online surveillance practices, though, public officials often downplay the effectiveness of non-digital monitoring methods (UN 2015: 12).

Finally, *proportionality* is a crucial but complex moral precondition of justified privacy intrusions. It is fundamentally a comparative notion: if something is a proportionate means, its benefits must outweigh its costs and its use must not lead to the destruction of the end it aims to protect (Henschke 2018). For example, fraudulent votes violate the democratic principle of giving every eligible citizen an equal chance to influence the outcome of elections. If voter fraud is indeed widespread it can undermine the legitimacy of elections. If its occurrence is proven likely to be widespread, stricter voter identification procedures might be justifiable to protect democratic procedures. But if voter fraud occurs only rarely and stricter voter identification rules would prevent significant numbers of citizens from voting, such requirements are disproportionate because they do more damage than good. That is because, by excluding more voters than preventing false votes, stricter voter identification requirements make the resulting electoral choice less of a genuine expression of the popular will than the few false votes that the requirements might prevent. Moreover, if they create voter apathy and distrust in the democratic procedures as a whole, such requirements can even lead to large numbers of people losing faith in their political system, in which case voter identification requirements seriously harm the very institutions they are intended to protect. To be proportionate, a means must be adequate to the threat it is supposed to counter. Since privacy protects vital moral goods and much is at stake when it comes to people's private sphere, violations of privacy must be as targeted and minimal as possible to ensure they are proportionate (i.e. that they do not cause more harm than good).

The basic moral issue with surveillance programmes such as PRISM, XKeyscore, and Tempora is that, in their attempts to catch those intending wrongdoing, they illegally, unnecessarily, and disproportionately violate the right to privacy of millions of innocent citizens. The mass surveillance of these programmes is not a defensive method to counter a known threat to people's rights and national security. Rather, they constitute an offensive or preventive attack on privacy to identify unknown perpetrators and potential harms (Rønn and Lippert-Rasmussen 2020: 187). This matters morally because if surveillance targets a known threat, it is easier to justify privacy intrusions. That is because their target has made themselves liable to the intrusions by attempting to harm others without justification. However, almost all people monitored by the NSA and GCHQ programmes have not done anything to justify such intrusions of their privacy. Instead, they are involuntarily made to pay a price for attempts to protect national security by having their online activities, and therefore their opinions, beliefs, interests, and interactions with others, covertly scrutinised and monitored by their government – even if these harms are not the intended goals of the surveillance practices. But such unintentional harming of innocent people as a lesser evil is justifiable only in exceptional circumstances (Rønn and Lippert-Rasmussen 2020: 189).

For example, in a war, civilians oppressed by a tyrant who live near a crucial military installation might be killed when that facility is bombed by forces trying to bring down that tyrant's regime. Their deaths as innocent bystanders might be justifiable if they are necessary and without reasonable alternatives to end the rule and human rights violations of their tyrannic government (Rønn and Lippert-Rasmussen 2020: 194). The mass surveillance of democratic citizens by the NSA and GCHQ, though, is not a situation of this nature. Such practices might be justifiable in case of a national emergency, for example, if they would have been necessary to prevent the collapse or destruction of an entire state and society, and not simply for preventing isolated acts of terrorism. But the threats that the PRISM, XKeyscore, and Tempora programmes have been said to counter were less urgent and emergent than that. Neither were these programmes very effective in achieving even their stated goals. According to the deputy director of the NSA at the time, the use of PRISM and XKeyscore might have at most foiled one concrete terrorist plot (Rønn and Lippert-Rasmussen 2020: 196). But even if these programmes would definitely have prevented several terrorist attacks, they would not have been justifiable as proportionate means for the protection of national security owing to their serious moral costs. Snowden's revelations confirmed the suspicions of many citizens and undermined the trust of others in their democratic authorities and their belief in a free society (Rønn and Lippert-Rasmussen 2020: 196). Moreover, the data gathered on people might have further harmful repercussions if it could be used against them by future government administrations or stolen by other, hostile forces. The practices of the NSA and GCHQ were also not justifiable because they did not meet the requirements of lawfulness and necessity. The privacy violations they committed were not authorised on a case-by-case basis by an independent oversight institution. Neither were these practices permanently needed as the only or uniquely effective means available to prevent isolated acts of terrorism – let alone the destruction of an entire society and states. The practices of the NSA and GCHQ were later declared to have been 'unlawful' by the US Court of Appeals (BBC News 2020) and the European Court of Human Rights, respectively (Casciani 2018).

Because privacy violations have serious moral costs, in non-emergency situations they must take place only on a transparent, public, legal basis and be individually approved by an independent oversight authority. Moreover, the target of these intrusions must be notified of having been surveilled after the fact and be provided with a chance to legally challenge the violations of their rights (UN 2014: 13–14). All these conditions are standard measures to safeguard the rule of law and to ensure that people's rights are not violated without adequate justification. There are therefore well-defined and proven procedures and requirements that, if followed and met, can justify the online surveillance of individuals or even groups of people. However, democratic governments must not be tempted to use online surveillance and privacy intrusions in disregard of these procedures as a seemingly expedient method to fulfil their obligation to protect national security or to break the law for their own benefit. The moral and political costs of mass online surveillance – if it is conducted covertly and preventively, on a mass scale, against innocent people, and without sufficient oversight – undermine the political legitimacy of democratic states. By using these practices, democratic states misuse the power vested in them by their citizens by violating their subjects' rights without proper justification and authorisation. All people have a human right to privacy because the protection of control over intimate information about who we are as individuals is crucial for the exercise of essential human rights, for the development of autonomy, and a minimally decent life in human societies. Indiscriminate mass online surveillance by any state not only presents a violation the human right to privacy, but also makes internet access unfree by arbitrarily interfering with it.

6.3 DUTIES OF STATES NOT TO THREATEN FREE INTERNET ACCESS

Many misuses of the internet exist only because autocrats are not accountable to their subjects and generally do not respect their human rights. But human rights are moral norms whose validity does not depend on the consent of autocratic regimes. The internet does not have to be a repressive technology. But for it to be a technology for the good, states must respect free internet access. The UN is therefore right to demand that states respect the offline rights of people online as well (UN 2016: 2). However, doing so is not sufficient to prevent the misuse of the internet. One important reason for considering digital authoritarian methods and online privacy violations is that they can help us identify obligations that states can be said to have to protect internet freedom as part of a new human right to free internet access. If states do not accept these duties, there is little chance of a free internet. The following list of duties has no claim to exhaustiveness and will have to be updated considering future technological developments and autocratic attempts to use the internet to secure illegitimate rule. However, if states were to respect the obligations set out here, the internet would become a relatively free space in which people could exercise their human rights.

Several of these duties that are part of the social guarantees that a human right to free internet must entail have also been advocated in documents by official institutions (e.g. UN 2014) or third section organisations (e.g. the Electronic Frontier Foundation's 13 *Principles on the Application of Human Rights in Communication Surveillance* (2015) or the Open Society Foundations' (2013) *Tshwame Principles on National Security and the Right to Information*). With regard to the distinction drawn in Chapter 5 between the general content of the human right to free internet access and its minimum core obligations, it is important to understand that – except for one – all duties of states mentioned here are minimum core obligations rather than duties that states can progressively realise. This is not because as negative duties of forbearance these are more pressing than positive duties of provision to help eliminate digital poverty discussed in Chapter 5. Rather, all but one of the listed duties are minimum core obligations because they are imminently realisable for all states. The obligations that states must keep internet access free with respect to their own actions can be divided into five categories.

6.3.1 *Cybersecurity Obligations*

The only duty of states that is not a core obligation because it is not feasible for all states right now is the positive obligation to protect their national cyberspace and critical digital infrastructure from foreign interference. Because of the importance of cybersecurity for people's opportunities to exercise their human rights online and for the fulfilment of the UN's Sustainable Development Goals, the World Economic Forum demands that the protection of digital systems and infrastructure from malicious attacks should be considered a public good akin to national defence. However, the provision of such measures and protections presupposes that states have access to the necessary technology and expertise, but, as we saw in Chapter 5, not all states have the resources even to connect many of their citizens to the internet. The costs of cybersecurity are indicated by the estimate that the value of the global cybersecurity market will reach USD $300 billion by 2024 (World Economic Forum 2019).

As part of cybersecurity considerations, states also have a duty to refrain from attacking the digital infrastructure of other states – especially if these attacks target civilian infrastructure and functions needed for the fulfilment of human rights (Kettemann 2017). However, even though there is a growing literature on cybersecurity (Christen et al. 2020, Shackelford 2020), the related duties are not the focus of this chapter because, as we saw, states' biggest threat to free internet access is their use of it to oppress and violate the human rights of their own populations. It is therefore states' duties to respect the free use of the internet domestically that we turn to now instead.

6.3.2 *Privacy and Data Storage*

To ensure that the internet does not become a repressive technology, states must not – without due cause and authorisation – violate the privacy of their citizens and citizens of other states by preventively monitoring people's online communications and activities. Any justifiable intrusions into the private sphere of people must meet the three standard tests of (1) legality, (2) legitimate cause, and (3) necessity and proportionality. To protect the most intimate and personal information of people, incursions must also be authorised on a case-by-case basis. For the same reason, there must also not be any unnecessary storage of personal data or metadata. Storage of such data is unnecessary when the information is protected by privacy considerations (meaning that collecting it requires people's consent), when there is no good reason why public authorities should preserve a record of it, or if states store personal information that they legitimately obtained for longer than is needed. The indiscriminate digital surveillance of a person not only violates their right to privacy, but (as we saw in Section 6.2) also their right to freely form and hold opinions, which according to the UN is absolute and therefore must never be violated by states or anyone else. The online surveillance of citizens who are in good standing therefore requires a particularly strong justification that is only possible on an individual basis and must be authorised by an independent political authority. Moreover, targets of surveillance must be informed after the fact and have access to effective remedies to contest and have confirmed the justifiability of their surveillance. Such remedies are effective when they are prompt, thorough, and conducted by impartial and independent institutions (UN 2015: 14).

Because of the durability of digitally collected and stored data, people should be entitled to have their unnecessary, outdated, or improperly obtained digitalised personal information deleted to avoid potential unjust discrimination. Such discrimination could occur if personal information held by states (e.g. information regarding ethnicity, religious beliefs, sexual orientation, or even evidence of debauchery during adolescence) irrelevantly affects people's opportunities or if personal data is misused by political institutions to treat individuals unjustly. The idea behind digital personal data expiration is the same rationale used to expunge certain entries in people's criminal records. But states' obligations to delete outdated personal information has to exceed recent attempts by the European Union in the form of its so-called right to be forgotten, since this law merely allows persons to have their personal data deleted in certain situations, if doing so is acceptable to those who collected the data (Custers 2022: 9–10). The law therefore gives insufficient power to individuals to protect their personal information, since – digitally preserved – this data does not degrade and can be used by computer algorithms in much more extensive ways than by human efforts to keep track of individuals. Such an effective right to have one's personal information deleted would present a new right rather than respect for existing offline rights in the online sphere.

States also must not legally ban encryption technology or require producers of digital technology to install 'backdoors' into devices and technology that encrypt data and messages, such as pseudonyms, VPNs, proxy servers, or P2P networks without a case-by-case justification and authorisation by independent oversight authorities such as courts (UN 2015: 5). As the UN Special Rapporteur explains, encryption today is an essential method for protecting privacy and free speech because, if used online without encryption, online activities leave traces that can be accessed and misused by states and others who might wish to harm internet users (UN 2015: 5). For the same reasons, states must also not force people to always be identifiable when they use the internet without sufficient, independent, and case-by-case authorisation. In this chapter, we have encountered several violations of this duty. There are, though, also other transgressions that the UN Special Rapporteur points to in his 2015 report on the importance of encryption and anonymity for human rights online. Iran, for instance, requires the registration of all IP addresses that are in use in its territory; Russia forces bloggers with more than 3,000 daily readers to register with the media regulator Roskomnadzor so they are known to the government; and the Chinese government requires internet users to register their real names when using certain websites so it can keep track of their activities. Moreover, Russia, China, and Iran all block, or try to monitor, the use of the Tor network whose function it is to make internet use untraceable (UN 2015: 18). The same report, though, also lists positive examples of anonymity protections by states. For instance, the Supreme Courts of the US, Canada, and South Korea have consistently protected the right to anonymous expression online or struck down laws of their states that tried to ban people from using the internet anonymously. The EU Court of Justice, too, generally protects the anonymity of internet users except for lifting such anonymity for justifiable causes such as the prosecution of crimes (UN 2015: 15–16). Moreover, the EU Parliament passed a draft law intended to protect privacy from artificial intelligence-based surveillance. The Artificial Intelligence Act aims to ban the routine use of 'real-time and remote biometric identification systems, such as facial recognition' and gait recognition because these present 'unacceptable risk' to citizens owing to detailed information they can reveal about individuals (EU Parliament 2023). Moreover, the UN report demands that states consult civil society actors and minority groups when they make laws to restrict the use of encryption and anonymity online to give a voice to those affected and possibly endangered by such restrictions (UN 2015: 19).

6.3.3 *Censorship*

States must not, without due cause and authorisation, shut down the internet fully or partly, or censor information online, throttle internet speeds, filter online search results, or even try to disconnect national internet backbone infrastructure from the global internet infrastructure network. Considering how people's opportunities to exercise their human rights are curtailed if the internet is shut down, generic justifications – such as the often used one of preventing the spread of fake news – are insufficient. This is because there are other, less intrusive measures available to address such issues (e.g. online media training of citizens, restrictions on the operations of private internet companies, or public information campaigns). Disconnecting the entire national internet infrastructure from global networks is practically always unjustifiable in light of the harm this causes (e.g. giving states effective ways to oppress their citizens by censoring information that governments deem dangerous to their rule). This is because such a step would only be justifiable if it were the only way to prevent the destruction of an entire state or society, which is an unlikely occurrence.

Online censorship measures, like surveillance, must be based on legitimate, public laws and be necessary and proportionate. There are legitimate reasons for censoring information online, for example to curb the spread of child pornography or incendiary speech, to prevent the grooming of people for terrorism, or for protecting people's reputation.[6] But even if censorship measures are enacted for these reasons, they require case-by-case authorisations by independent authorities to prevent their unjustified use by governments. Moreover, how censorship is conducted also matters for its moral justifiability. For example, the use of computer algorithms to remove online content has been found to be problematic. One problem with the use of algorithms for the detection and deletion of problematic content is that decisions of what information can justly be blocked often require judgements that these programmes are (so far) incapable of. For example, some images might

---

[6] These cases are discussed in Chapters 7 and 8.

contain artistic yet controversial content that is protected by free speech but are blocked because an algorithm is programmed to treat it as exploitative, incendiary, or copyright protected. Second, if programmed in non-transparent ways, algorithmic filters give those who programme them problematic abilities to block content that they deem undesirable but that they have no justifiable reasons to block. And third, algorithmic filtering requires the generalised monitoring of the online communications of vast numbers of innocent citizens and therefore can constitute unjustifiable surveillance. The European Court of Justice for this reason has denounced algorithmic filters as 'censorship machines' that are incompatible with the EU Charter of Fundamental Rights (Korff 2019: 139–142).

To ensure that states do not conduct unjustified forms of online censorship, they should be transparent about what information they block and ensure they are accountable to their citizens. Such accountability can be established when states cooperate with independent third-sector initiatives such as the Open Observatory of Network Interference (Burnett and Feamster 2013: 87). This NGO documents internet censorship internationally in a decentralised way by providing internet users with software that can probe and measure the blocking of websites and instant messaging services. The project has so far published over 545 million network measurements from more than 200 countries (OONI 2022). Beyond this, states should also establish and cooperate with independent censorship monitoring watchdog agencies that are free from government control and ensure that states do not impose unjustifiable restrictions on internet content on their populations.

6.3.4 *Manipulation*

States must not manipulate online content (e.g. search engine results) or employ sock puppets, bots, cyborgs,[7] and paid commentators to distract citizens or to distort the public political discourse domestically or abroad by publishing false or irrelevant information. The publication of correct and relevant information with the purpose of informing the public (e.g. about dangers to health and security or to inform oppressed populations in other, autocratic, countries) is certainly part of the duties of states. However, such communications must be made transparently and marked as coming from public authorities. There is never a justification for the covert misinformation of citizens by their own government or by other states because such manipulation

---

[7] Sock puppets are false online identities used for deceptive purposes. Cyborgs are social media accounts that are partly operated by humans and partly by bots.

violates the fundamental human rights to form opinions and to access information freely. Intentional misinformation therefore also undermines people's meaningful exercise of the human right to political participation.

States also must not use information that they collect on their citizens in arbitrary ways, for example for the purpose of coercing citizens to change their behaviour or to desist from acting contrary to the interests of those in power. Appropriately collected information can be used to sanction citizens; for example, a traffic violation record can justly be used to coerce citizens to pay a fine, or information on private debt may be used by a bank to evaluate the creditworthiness of a person. However, personal information is used arbitrarily if it is applied in irrelevant ways and, in particular, if it is used to violate citizens' rights or to manipulate their behaviour without reasonable cause. For instance, speeding tickets are not a justifiable reason to refuse bank loans and citizens' activities on social media and their political views do not constitute acceptable reason to limit their opportunities to enjoy their rights to free movement, a good education, or to receiving public services such as health care.

6.3.5 Export Controls

Finally, states should only permit export of digital technology that can be used to violate people's human rights (such as spyware) in specific limited circumstances where such transferred technologies are not used by states to violate people's human rights (Wagner 2012).

The draft report commissioned by the European Parliament has outlined what such a test for the justifiability of digital technology exports can look like. It called for a general moratorium on the export of spyware (such as Pegasus) that is only to be lifted on a case-by-case basis and when certain conditions are fulfilled (EU Parliament 2022: 148). These conditions are informed by decisions of the European Court of Justice and the European Court of Human Rights, which in turn closely track the conditions of legitimate justifications for surveillance that we considered in Section 6.2. The conditions that should apply for the authorisation of exporting digital technology that can be used to violate human rights include:

- a limited list of crimes that technology such as spyware may be used for,
- a limited list of authorities that are permitted to make use of the imported technology,
- a list of professions (lawyers, doctors, journalists, etc.) that must not be targeted with the technology,
- a merely temporary use of the imported technology,
- a case-by-case judicial authorisation before the technology is employed,

- the transparent use of imported technology that is to be ensured by the accountability of the institutions employing it to an independent audit body,
- a duty to notify the targets of surveillance after the fact as well as effective remedies for the target including the possibility of the deletion of irrelevant data. (EU Parliament 2022: 149–150)

These conditions are meant to ensure that any infringements of human rights such as privacy are as limited as possible and that there exists effective oversight for the employment of exported technology to prevent its arbitrary use. To operate effective export controls, states can also adopt legislation such as the Global Online Freedom Act that was introduced to, but has not been passed by, the US Congress. This act would require the government to establish a list of human rights-violating states to which exports of potentially oppressive digital technologies are banned and require domestic internet service companies that operate in states that violate free internet access to report on the steps they take to protect internet freedom in these countries (Freedom House 2018: 20).

6.4 CONCLUSION

For the internet to be truly free and to promote human rights and the progress of mankind, people must be able to access it without arbitrary interferences. In this, states have a dual role to play. They are the most powerful standard threats to free internet access where the technical requirements for such access already exist. Therefore, states must desist from obstructing people's online access. Yet states are also the primary duty bearers tasked with protecting internet freedom. The various forms of misuse of the internet by states canvassed in this chapter show that, as such, the internet does not promote human rights and well-being. Without the protection and the respect of states for free online access, the internet is bound to become the most finegrained and powerful technical medium of oppression that humanity has ever invented. Adopting and enforcing a human right to free internet access is therefore an important step that states must take to ensure that the internet is used as an empowering, rather than a repressive, technology. If states were to protect, rather than to arbitrarily interfere with, internet access, this would solve most issues discussed in this chapter. States are not the only active standard threat to free internet access. As Chapter 7 will show, private businesses also present such threats. However, as the practices of digital authoritarianism and Snowden's revelations demonstrate, states have the power to bend the operations of private companies to their will. States are therefore primary standard threats as well as duty-holders.

7

Private Companies as Standard Threats

As we saw in Chapter 6, states have the coercive and legal powers to shape and illegitimately interfere with internet access within their borders. The internet as a technological development started out as a publicly funded project – as the ARPANET developed by the US Department of Defense in the late 1960s. It was then extended to national and later to international academic and research institutions. However, from the late 1980s onwards, the internet's infrastructure and applications were expanded, and today are owned, predominantly by private enterprises (Leiner et al. 2009). Companies that run the physical infrastructure and network level of the internet include backbone operators (e.g. China Telecom, Verizon, AT&T, Deutsche Telekom), internet service providers (ISPs) (e.g. Comcast, Verizon, BT Group, Sky, Vodafone), and content delivery networks (e.g. Akamai, Fastly, Cloudflare, Amazon Web Services, which operate data centres or proxy services that ensure that content is online and services are quickly accessible to end-users). At the application/content level, internet-based business (e.g. Amazon, Apple, Google, Microsoft, Netflix) sell products that people can use or consume, and they provide platforms (e.g. Facebook with WhatsApp and Instagram, TikTok, YouTube by Google, Reddit) that people can use to create and publish their own content (Economides 2016, Greenstein 2020).

Because private companies sell much of people's experiences of the internet as products and services, they have enormous power to shape people's access and use of the internet. Given this position, private corporations can undermine people's free use of their human rights online. Because they primarily strive to create profits rather than to enable people's enjoyment of their rights, these corporations standardly also pose threats to online access. They influence the ways in which people can access and use the internet so that it maximises their financial gain – even if this creates vulnerabilities for their customers or society at large. States on their part impose legal rules that shape and limit the operations of private companies within their jurisdiction. As we saw in Chapter 6, both autocratic and democratic states in violation of their human rights obligations abuse their coercive power to force private businesses to compromise people's human rights either to secure their rule or to protect their national security. As explained, this interference of states with free internet access is morally unacceptable. But private companies too have moral obligations to respect human rights in their business activities and cannot simply pursue their profit maximisation agenda any way they want.

The human rights obligations of private companies have been outlined in the United Nations' (UN) *Guiding Principles on Business and Human Rights* (hereafter 'the Guiding Principles') that 'apply to all States and to all business enterprises, both transnational and other, regardless of their size, sector, location, ownership and structure' (UN 2011b: 1). The UN established these principles in recognition of the fact that, even though international human rights law applies to states as the primary addressee of people's human rights claims, the activities of private businesses also have profound impact on people's rights. The core demand of these Guiding Principles is that 'Business enterprises should respect human rights. This means that they should avoid infringing on the human rights of others and should address adverse human rights impacts with which they are involved' (UN 2011b: 13).Because international human rights law is only binding on states, the Guiding Principles do not create legal human rights obligation but 'a global standard of expected conduct for all business enterprises wherever they operate' (UN 2011b: 13). However, they also reaffirm that states as primary duty-holders according to international human rights law have a legal duty to 'respect, protect and fulfil human rights and fundamental freedoms' (UN 2011b: 1) – an understanding of rights that reflects Henry Shue's explanation of the duties entailed by rights that we covered in Chapter 1. As part of this legal obligation, 'states must protect against human rights abuse within their territory and/or jurisdiction by third parties, including business enterprises' (UN 2011b: 3). To that end, states are to 'enforce laws that are aimed at, or have the effect of, requiring business enterprises to respect human rights' (UN 2011b: 4).

The Guiding Principles confirm that private companies have the moral obligation to respect human rights that should become a legal obligation through national legislation within states. Whether businesses are *legally* bound to respect human rights therefore depends on states' willingness to fulfil their primary human rights obligations (Jørgensen 2019: 350). Even where states do not create the necessary laws (or even try to violate human rights with the help of businesses), though, private companies are still expected to fulfil their moral obligation to respect human rights (UN 2011b: 13). However, to know what states ought to do to protect human rights online from the activities of businesses, we have to understand how businesses affect the human rights of people online and internet access in the first place. More specifically, we need to understand which of these impacts are morally arbitrary interferences in the sense that they cannot be justified, so that people need to be protected by states from these activities of private businesses.

With respect to the operations of private companies that are involved in the provision of internet services, there are three fundamental issues that negatively affect people's human rights when they access and use the internet. First, there is the question of how businesses that provide internet information services treat data streams. Data traffic can be treated equally, or different data can be treated differently, for example, to generate more profits by giving preferential treatment for the data of those willing to pay for this. This is the issue of (inter)net neutrality. Second, there is the question of how personal data that end-users produce when they do things online is treated by those who handle this information. This has become known as the problem of 'surveillance capitalism' (Zuboff 2019). Finally, there is the question how those companies who provide virtual spaces that are used by most internet users, and which significantly shape their experiences of the internet, treat not only their users' data, but also the latter's opportunities to exercise their human rights online. This concerns the question how to regulate the dominant social media platforms (SMPs) that can exclude people from their privately owned virtual forums and determine what people can do and say on them. This chapter looks at these three pressing issues to determine how private companies currently unjustifiably interfere with people's internet access and use, and thereby objectionably compromise their human rights. Once these problems have become clear, we can formulate what concrete steps states should take in fulfilment of their obligations to protect human rights online from the profit-maximising operations of private companies over which they have jurisdiction.

7.1 PRIVATE DATA HARVESTING

This section first describes the problem of the collection of private user data by internet-based businesses, then explains the moral problems with these practices, and finally outlines plausible obligations of states in the form of solutions that can tackle these issues.

7.1.1 *Facts about Data Harvesting*

As we saw in Chapter 6, when we use the internet, unlike with most actions in the physical world, we leave observable and analysable traces in the form of data behind. This data can reveal much about us and it can be collected not only by states, but also first and foremost by those private companies that own the infrastructure and applications that make up much of the internet today. And companies do collect user data on a massive scale with the aim to commodify it to make a profit. This practice has been called 'surveillance capitalism' by Shoshana Zuboff (2019).

For example, when I search a term on Google, Google can (via my IP address or my Google accounts that I am logged into) record my interest in that term or topic. That is, when you search Google, 'Google searches you' (Zuboff 2019: 262). When I purchase something online, my willingness to spend money on this product is thereby known to the seller and others who collect information on my transaction and add it to the virtual data profiles they are building about all their customers. When I watch videos on TikTok or view photos on Instagram, the companies who operate these platforms can keep track of my preferences. And if I write a post online, my expression is preserved for others to read. Personal information about myself is especially attractive for those who want to sell me things based on my preferences and beliefs. The more they know about me, the more they can customise the information about their products for me through targeted advertising. The idea behind targeted advertising is that it is more effective than traditional, indiscriminate advertising via TV, radio, or billboards. On these, a company buys time or space to send the same advertisements to many people without detailed knowledge about its effectiveness in convincing their audience to purchase their product. Targeted advertising promises to be more effective because it can be sent to those who appear most likely to purchase a product based on knowledge about their individual preferences.

As Zuboff explains, in the early 2000s, Google was looking to start making profits because its internet search service alone was not profitable. It discovered that, if it recorded personal data from its users, Google could sell this information to product companies that could then buy advertisement space on Google's websites (and later on other websites too) and have their products appear more prominently in Google search results (Zuboff 2019: 74–96). Since then, the collection and sale of personal information to enable predictions about potential customers' choices based on what is known about their beliefs and preferences has become the dominant profit model on the internet. The more personal data is harvested, the more can be known and inferred about people's beliefs and preferences. The more these are known, the more individuals can be targeted by companies who want to sell their products to them. But the point of personal data collection is not simply to predict people's behaviour. Rather, the goal is also to alter it. By showing people more of what they like, or products similar to the ones they have purchased, they can be incentivised to buy another product, watch another video, read another article or post, or to post messages themselves (Zuboff 2019: 293–309). To maximise the profits that they make from collecting and marketizing personal information, internet companies such as Google, Facebook, and Amazon are ever increasing the ways in which they monitor people's actions and harvest their users' personal data. Data collection is no longer limited to internet searches or online product purchases. Instead, personal information is gained by data transfer from all 'smart' devices (such as TVs, household appliances, health data trackers, and devices such as Amazon's Alexa) and from smartphone apps that standardly require a range of permissions to operate properly (Zuboff 2019: 262–269). Firms participating in surveillance capitalism also want to maximise user engagement to make users do more things on their websites because additional activities generate more engagement of other users and/or more personal data that can be sold for more profit. Users of these online-based services have been willing to reveal all this information about themselves in exchange for apparently free personalised experiences and services that fulfil their needs for recognition and support. This came at a time when many publicly funded services had increasingly been reduced even in the most developed states since the 1990s and especially the financial crisis of 2008, when states spent enormous sums of public money to bail out private banks and their clients (Zuboff 2019: 256). Paying with personal data for using online applications is also attractive as these provide novel, convenient, and often useful services such as Google Maps, personalised videos, news feeds, or other information.

Today, enormous amounts of data are harvested by surveillance capitalist companies and stored by data brokers. For example, the data broker Experian aggregates data on more than 1 billion people and businesses and its competitor Axicom holds more than 10,000 data points on 2.5 billion consumers in sixty-two countries (Véliz 2024). This personal data reveals more about people than could previously be known about anyone except by the individuals themselves. It either contains direct knowledge about people or allows knowledge about them through inferences by algorithms. For example, Facebook has patented algorithms that can infer people's relationship status from the number of times they visit their friends' profiles. Computer algorithms are sets of rules designed to execute computations, such as calculations or data processing, that perform specific tasks or solve specific problems. Facebook has also developed an algorithm that can predict whether people are experiencing significant life events based on their recorded locations and credit-card transactions (Deibert 2019: 27). People's sexual preferences can now be inferred by algorithms from their music tastes (Véliz 2024). One 2015 academic study even showed that Facebook's algorithm can better judge the personality of its users than their colleagues (based on ten 'Likes'), their friends (based on seventy 'Likes'), their family members (based on 150 'Likes'), and even their spouses (based on 300 'Likes', see Youyou et al. 2015: 1037). In 2017, an internal Facebook report showed that by monitoring the photos and posts of teenagers in real time, the company can identify which of them feel insecure, worthless, or in need of a confidence boost (Levin 2017). The most intimate details about persons can therefore be gleaned from their online activities and be employed in the drive for profits. For companies that specialise in surveillance capitalism, their users are therefore first and foremost 'eyeballs attached to a wallet' (Balkin 2021: 92) rather than people whose human right to privacy must be respected.

The biggest internet-based companies have by now been fined in powerful democracies for their misuse of personal data. For instance, in March 2023, TikTok was fined GBP £12.7 million by public authorities in the UK for allowing up to 1.4 million UK children below the age of thirteen to access the platform without parental consent. On the platform, children's activities are tracked and profiled like those of all users, which can result in them being shown inappropriate content (McCallum et al. 2023). In August 2023, TikTok was also fined EUR €345 million by the Irish Data Protection Commission for a lack of transparency to children concerning how their personal data was used. In 2020, for instance, TikTok violated the EU's General Data Protection Regulation (GDPR) by making the accounts of teenagers public by default when they registered on the platform (Gerken and McMahon 2023). In January 2023, Irish authorities followed EU guidance and imposed a EUR €390 million penalty on Facebook's parent company Meta for using its users' data by default for targeted advertising purposes, which violates the EU's GDPR (Vallence 2023). In May 2023, Facebook owner Meta was hit with the record fine of EUR €1.2 billion by the same regulator for violating the same EU data protection regulation by transferring the data of Facebook users from Europe to the US where US intelligence agencies could access the data owing to weaker US privacy protection laws (McCallum 2023). And in November 2022, US authorities fined Google USD $391.5 million for tracking the location of users who had opted out of its location services (BBC News 2022). However, instead of protecting user data from misuse by private companies, states have also collaborated with these businesses to obtain personal information on citizens that states themselves are legally banned from collecting. For example, in 2018 the Trump administration bought access to commercial databases on the movements of millions of US mobile phones after it was banned by the US Supreme Court from gathering this data itself (Véliz 2024). These cases shows that personal data harvesting by private companies does not just create transparent customers whose preferences can be exploited for profit. The practice can also help create transparent citizens who become vulnerable to the abuse of state powers.

7.1.2 *The Problems with Data Harvesting*

The obvious primary problem with the current practice of personal data harvesting is that it compromises people's privacy. By knowingly or unwittingly revealing even the most intimate personal information about themselves, people also effectively create power over themselves for private companies, public authorities, and others who could illegitimately exploit this knowledge about their personal lives and preferences to use it against their interests. As discussed in Chapter 6, privacy is an important human right that is meant to give people control over their personal information and thereby about how they appear to others. This control is essential for private and public purposes. In the private sphere, privacy allows persons to develop and exercise their personality without being scrutinised by others. The ability to conceal personal information from others is also a precondition for establishing different levels of intimacy with other people depending on how much we reveal about ourselves (Marmor 2015). In the public sphere, privacy is important to avoid unnecessary conflicts that are more likely to occur the more people know about each other. Being able to remain anonymous is also essential for speaking out freely, for criticising powerholders without fear of retaliation, and for freely associating with others without fear of being monitored. Conversely, the less people can express themselves without public scrutiny, the more reasons they have to conform to social or political expectations, and to censor what they say and do in public (Véliz 2024). In the economic sphere, the more private companies know about people, the more they can try to influence them. Businesses can use personal information to coax people into purchasing things or paying higher prices for products that they otherwise would not have bought or paid if their preferences were unknown to the seller.

However, targeted ads and product recommendations are appreciated by many consumers. If they want to give up their privacy by agreeing to give away their personal data to companies to receive more personalised recommendations, people should be free to engage in such trade. And in fact surveillance capitalism companies argue that their users freely consent to the collection and use of their data. People do so, these companies argue, because they accept the privacy policies and terms of service (ToS) of the commercial websites and online businesses that they use. The problem with this claim of voluntary transactions in the form of personal data for improved services is that to be genuinely voluntary such agreements must meet certain conditions, which they do not in current surveillance capitalism practices. First, to freely agree to contracts, people must know what they are specifically agreeing to. That is why children who are unable to understand the complexities of transactions cannot agree to enter economic contracts. Second, people need to have reasonable alternatives to an agreement that they strike or, if there are no such alternatives, their situation must not be exploited by others. This is why contracts made under duress are void and why price gouging (i.e asking unreasonable or unfair prices during times of emergencies such as natural catastrophes, accidents, or other events that put people into extreme need) is illegal. The issue with most agreements between internet businesses and their users is that they do not meet either of these necessary conditions for at least three reasons.

The first problem with the contracts that underpin mass personal data harvesting by surveillance capitalism businesses is that there are too many privacy policies for individuals to scrutinise. Already in 2008, when this business model was in its infancy, one study estimated that the time required of an individual for a reasonable reading of all privacy policies that they encountered in one year would amount to seventy-six full working days (Zuboff 2019: 32). Today, people can come across dozens of websites that all want to know how they can use their personal data. Privacy agreements also cannot be individually negotiated but are of the 'take it or leave it' sort. Moreover, agreements that users have accepted once can be changed spontaneously by companies (Véliz 2022). All of this means that internet-based companies and their consumers are not negotiating privacy agreements on equal ground. Instead, companies alone have the power to shape these contracts.

The second problem with today's standard privacy policies and ToS is that these are designed only to protect the interests of businesses, and to obscure the purposes for which the collected data will be used. What these agreements are not designed to promote is users' ability to make informed choices about contracting with private companies for using their services. Privacy policies and ToS are as a matter of course extremely long and written in specialised legalistic terms that are incomprehensible to most who accept them. This was demonstrated in one experiment, in which researchers tested how many of their more than 500 participants either read or ignored the privacy policies and ToS of a fictitious SMP (Obar and Oeldorf-Hirsch 2020). Participants were asked to consider whether they would use the offered services. To do so, they were first shown a 'click-join' clickwrap that gave participants the option to accept or decline the service's privacy policy and ToS. Acceptance at this stage allowed them to bypass reading the entire agreements. If they declined, participants were then shown a privacy policy and asked to reject or accept it. Subsequently, participants were also asked to review the ToS. The privacy policy was 7,797 words long, the ToS 4,316 words, and both were modified versions of LinkedIn's policies in order to be of comparable length to agreements actually used by large online corporations. The ToS also contained two 'gotcha' clauses that were formulated to be highly objectionable and likely to be rejected if they were read. One clause asked participants to agree to the fictitious SMP's sharing of their personal data with the NSA and other foreign security agencies. The other clause was more extreme and asked participants to agree to give up their first-born child to the SMP. Under the assumption of the average reading speed of educated citizens of 250–280 words per minute, it should have taken participants between twenty-nine and thirty-two minutes to read the privacy policy and between five and seventeen minutes to read the ToS (Obar and Oeldorf-Hirsch 2020: 133, 134). The results clearly showed that the vast majority of participants ignored the privacy policy and ToS: 75 per cent skipped reading the privacy policy by accepting the clickwrap. Those who rejected the clickwrap and who were shown the privacy policy on average only spent seventy-three seconds (instead of twenty-nine to thirty-two minutes) reading it. Moreover, the average time participants spent on reading the ToS was fifty-one seconds (instead of fifteen to seventeen minutes). Unsurprisingly, in reading the ToS, 98 per cent of participants missed the two 'gotcha' clauses that they would very likely have rejected if they had become aware of them. A similar result about the ineffectiveness of standard personal data policies occurred in a separate test when a US software company offered its customers USD $1,000 by including this information at the very end of their ToS. Only those who read the full agreement text would have known to claim the money. As the company reported, within four months, 3,000 people downloaded their ToS but only one person claimed the offered sum (Deibert 2019: 29). These results clearly suggest that the length and frequency of personal data agreements make them unreasonably demanding by design so that users cannot consent to them in a meaningfully informed way.

The lack of informed consent that this 'end-user choice' model of privacy intentionally gives rise to has objectionable consequences for those who accept standard privacy policies and ToS. First, owing to the nature of these contracts, users lack the knowledge needed to assess the risks of future harm that can derive from giving up their personal data as well as the ability to understand what data can be extracted from them. Shorter and clearer statements of these points would be required for people to have a reasonable chance to know about the risks to which they agree. Second, users cannot know how the data they give to companies can be used and combined to draw inferences about them because information about the capabilities of commercial algorithms are essential secrets of the companies whose business is based on them. Third, because data harvesting happens automatically and non-transparently, users are unaware how companies can design their websites and applications to maximally extract data from them. Fourth, companies can shape users' behaviours, elicit their emotions, and use their cognitive limitations in ways not explicitly explained in data agreements to entice their users to give up more data. Finally, the agreements between internet companies and their users do not involve others about whom information can be gleaned or inferred from the collected user data. This means that parties whose privacy is affected by the agreements between data-collecting businesses and their consumers are not given a say in or notified about what happens to their information (Balkin 2020: 16–17). If informed consent is needed for valid contracts, the standard ToS and privacy policies used today are designed to prevent rather than to facilitate it. To be clear, these practices are not necessary but chosen by companies to maximise their profits.

To make matters worse, the third problem with current data harvesting agreements is that internet users have no real option not to use the services that force them to give up information about themselves. As we saw in Chapters 3 and 4, internet access has become necessary for having adequate opportunities to exercise most of our vital human rights. In digitalised societies, people must use privately owned internet platforms and applications to fully participate in society (Véliz 2022). To avoid being socially or politically excluded, people must use online services for professional and social communications. However, the collection of personal data online is so ubiquitous that even the most privacy-minded people cannot entirely avoid having to give up their personal data (Williams and Raekstad 2022: 428–429, Balkin 2020: 13). It has been argued that we are witnessing a privacy paradox in how people behave in digitalised society. This is because people generally claim that they value their privacy even though they are willing to give up personal data to use the services of surveillance capitalism companies (Obar and Oeldorf-Hirsch 2020). However, the lack of alternatives to fully participate in society by exercising our human rights online resolves this apparent paradox. That is, people might well want to protect their privacy, but the price they have to pay to do so by staying offline has become too high – especially when the apparent benefits of using online services are directly salient while the risks and harms involved in having one's personal data collected are rendered invisible by obscure, unreasonably long, and ubiquitous data collection agreements (Véliz 2024). Because of this lack of reasonable alternatives, there is a problematic asymmetry of power in the interactions between internet-based companies and their users in that people have no effective choice about, and control over, the terms of their surveillance (Williams and Raekstad 2022: 431–432). 'Users are forced to give up access to their data if they want to utilise the internet and other modern technological appliances, and thus they are forced to subject themselves to the uncontrolled power of surveillance corporations with respect to their data' (Williams and Raekstad 2022: 435). This, though, presents a violation of people's privacy because the space in which people can protect their personal information has been unacceptably limited by companies' personal data harvesting policies (Marmor 2015: 14). Even though the use of online services and applications cannot reasonably be avoided, businesses use this fact to extract not only some, but a maximal amount of data from their users.

This lack of alternatives, the obscurity of the terms of the agreements and their implications, the sheer number of agreements to which people are asked to consent, and the effort that would be required to read these policies thoroughly show that people's acceptance of businesses' unnecessary collection of their personal data cannot plausibly be interpreted as voluntary, informed, or morally acceptable. This is not a minor issue about the internet. Rather, current personal data harvesting practices in fact constitute a serious human rights issue. To understand this, we have to recall that this book argues that free internet access must be a human right because it has become necessary for having adequate opportunities to exercise our human rights. But having one's personal data harvested inevitably, maximally, and without genuine informed consent makes the practically indispensable use of most essential internet services unfree. This matters greatly for the quality of internet access as well because, if using most essential online services compromises our privacy, accessing the internet most of the time has the consequence of compromising our freedoms. However, both privacy and free internet access are necessary conditions of leading minimally decent lives in our digital age. Both should therefore be accepted as human rights. But the current practices of surveillance capitalism companies effectively force internet users to choose between two things that are necessary elements of minimally good lives today: adequate control over their personal information and having adequate opportunities to exercise their human rights. This unnecessary and forced choice to give up at least one condition of decent lives in digitalised societies explains the moral problem at the heart of the private data harvesting practices of surveillance capitalism.

7.1.3 Solutions to Private Data Harvesting

States could change the current situation and require private companies by law to protect their users' personal data. In line with the Guiding Principles, because privacy is a human right and free internet access should be a human right, states should also accept human rights obligations to create such laws. There are at least two legal changes that states should enact that would protect both internet users' privacy and free internet access from arbitrary interference by private companies in their pursuit of profit.

First, public authorities should legally force internet-based companies to give their users a clear and effective way to avoid the collection of their personal data (Williams and Raekstad 2022: 435). Given the ubiquity of user agreements online, not having one's personal data harvested should therefore be the default setting so that users actively have to choose to consent to the collection of their data (Véliz 2020: 156). Users should not be prompted to make a choice when they access websites or services but rather merely be offered the choice to opt in on websites. This is because prompting people to choose still requires users to read privacy policies or might lead them to accidentally agree to data collection. Moreover, being prompted on every website to make a choice can become a nuisance rather than helpful. Article 25 of the EU's GDPR presents one of the currently most serious attempts by public authorities to enforce 'data protection by design and by default' (Proton 2023). However, this legislation still allows companies to prompt users to make a choice that makes it by design complicated to opt out of the collection of data. Website operators should be free to make their users aware that consenting to data collection can lead to a more personalised experience. But, if they do, people should be informed in clear, simple, and short terms what their data can subsequently be used for. Moreover, there should be legal limits on data harvesting from children and severely mentally disabled people because they are unlikely to be able to provide informed consent (Williams and Raekstad 2022: 435).

Such effective legal personal data protection would resolve, to a significant extent, the problem of internet access made unfree through personal data harvesting because internet users would have a genuine alternative to using online services under the surveillance of those who provide the services. Their choice to having their data collected would be more informed because privacy policies and ToS would be more informative and manageable. Since users would not be prompted to make a choice about data collection, theirs would be an unforced decision. However, even making opting out of data collection the default would leave a residual issue. There would still be the question of how data can be used that is being generated because people have opted into the harvesting of their personal information. If there are no limits to its possible uses, the data of those who opt in can still be sold on to others, used to infer information about people or others they interact with, and possibly even accessed by public authorities that have no right to access this information about their citizens. The second measure that public authorities should therefore take to regulate not only the collection, but also the permitted usages, of data is to replace the current 'end-user choice' model to privacy with a fiduciary model that forces those who collect personal data to treat it in ways that are compatible with the interests of their users (Balkin 2020).

The fiduciary model of protecting personal information is used standardly in situations where there are significant asymmetries in knowledge and power between two parties, and the stronger party implicitly or explicitly invites the weaker one to trust it with its information. These asymmetries in power and knowledge make the weaker party vulnerable to coercion or abuse by the stronger one. The fiduciary model is accordingly intended to make the stronger party accountable to the weaker one by imposing special obligations on the more powerful side (Balkin 2020: 13–14). The model is applied to regulate, for example, the professional interactions between lawyers or physicians and their clients. Facebook or Google are certainly not lawyers or doctors to their users. However, because of the lack of alternatives to using their products and their control over the design of their services, these internet-based companies (that currently are among the most valuable ones in the world) have more power and knowledge over their users than the other way around. Moreover, because online activities can be meticulously recorded and considering the inferential power of their algorithms, these businesses are able to collect much more personal information about their users than doctors or lawyers know about their clients. But the greater the asymmetries of knowledge and power and the resulting vulnerabilities, the greater the need for the protection of the weaker party. Therefore, applying the fiduciary model would be appropriate for regulating the agreements between internet companies and their clients even though these businesses do not offer services that have traditionally been thought to require confidentiality (Balkin 2020: 26).

The fiduciary model is based on three duties. First, the more powerful party has a duty of confidentiality with respect to their customers' data. Second, it has a duty of care to keep that data safe. Finally, it also has a duty of loyalty towards its clients to not betray their trust or manipulate them (e.g. by exploiting people's general psychological weaknesses), which is to say that it must use the data to act in the interest of its clients. To be meaningful, the legal scholar Jack Balkin argues, these fiduciary duties must 'run with the data', which is to say that data-harvesting companies should only be permitted to pass on personal data to other companies (e.g. data brokers or advertisers) if these are equally bound by the same duties (Balkin 2020: 14). Only in this way are the customers of companies that collect data appropriately protected from the profit interests of other firms that they do not directly engage with but that can obtain access to their information. The benefits of the fiduciary model therefore exceed the direct relations between internet-based companies and their users, and has certain systemic benefits. Other data handlers such as ISPs would be bound by the same model, and data brokers that have no contractual relationship with internet users would nonetheless have obligations to those who opt into having their data collected (Balkin 2020: 17). Owing to the large numbers of internet users who would become protected by the fiduciary model, it would also force companies to act not simply in line with their own profit motives, but also in the interest of the public as a whole. That is because personal data could no longer be used by these companies to target individual users with political or health information, which might be false or planted by hostile agents (such as the Russian Internet Research Agency). Moreover, applying the fiduciary model to the handling of personal information collected online would protect the contacts of users about whom information could be inferred. Finally, the fiduciary model would also protect the public from over-reach by governments because these could no longer simply purchase access to personal information about their citizens from data harvesters and brokers. Rather, the duties of confidentiality and care that private companies would acquire towards their customers would require governments to obtain warrants for (and therefore impose legal oversight on) their accessing of sensitive data about their citizens generated by internet-based businesses (Balkin 2020: 17–19).

The application of fiduciary obligations to the use of personal information online also aligns with the professional rights of internet-based companies that arise from the human right to free internet access. Just as journalists have professional rights to protect their sources from powerful parties so they can fulfil their valuable functions for society, analogously internet service and applications providers with fiduciary obligations towards their clients should have rights to protect the personal information of users from powerful agents that have illegitimate interests in gaining access to this data. If internet-based companies do not have such rights, they cannot provide their essential services in a safe way for their clients. In this case, these firms cannot effectively protect their users' human rights from abuses by states, as they are obligated to do according to the Guiding Principles. The human right to free internet access would therefore provide a direct moral justification for assigning fiduciary professional privileges and obligations to those who generate and handle internet users' personal information as part of their business operations.

Imposing fiduciary obligations would end the enormously profitable business of selling personal information for commercial reasons in its current shape. However, this does not mean that targeted advertising would no longer be possible at all. It would remain permissible in the form of 'contextual' advertising that only makes recommendations based on the limited localised activities of internet users (e.g. recommendations in product searches). The information that contextual advertising depends on, though, must no longer be used to create virtual data profiles of consumers that are used to target and monitor them in other ways. Current 'behavioural' advertising that relies on generating such personal information profiles and on tracking people's online activities would be impermissible. At least, it could no longer be employed to elicit or change certain behaviours of people because doing so is incompatible with companies' duty of loyalty towards their users (Balkin 2020: 28). Targeted behavioural advertisement of the kind that currently dominates would then have the same moral status as spam messages.

Applying the fiduciary model to contractual relations between surveillance capitalism companies and their users would upend their core business model, which currently counts among the most profitable in the world. However, morally speaking, the protection of human rights and the minimally decent lives of internet users far outweigh the interests of companies to maximise their profits. The entire purpose of changing the default on personal data collection and introducing the fiduciary model is to change the business model of internet businesses and to make them 'trustworthy stewards of personal data' (Balkin 2020: 26). Internet businesses can still be extremely profitable under such new rules. In July 2023, the European Court of Justice ruled that in line with the EU's GDPR, businesses must not target users with personalised ads based on combined personal data without their consent. In response, from November 2023 Meta offered its EU users an ad-free subscription alternative to its standard personalised ad-based service (Milmo 2023). Profitable internet-based businesses therefore do not have to harvest their clients' personal data.

Private companies are not free to operate in whichever ways maximise their profits and those of their investors. Thus they also do not experience conflicting duties towards their investors because businesses must operate within the limits set by human rights. For instance, businesses are generally not allowed to externalise costs of their operations (e.g. pollution or unsafe working conditions) on others (Balkin 2020: 23–24). In the same way, the Guiding Principles demand that businesses must not violate people's human rights in their striving for profits. The profit interests of investors are therefore limited by the human rights of people. That is, the human rights to free internet access and to privacy constrain which data harvesting and handling practices are morally permissible. Accordingly, any frustrated profit interests are morally insignificant compared with the protection of people's human rights. The Guiding Principles therefore plausibly require of states to regulate online personal data businesses by requiring them to operate an 'opt-out by default practice' and to accept fiduciary obligations towards the data of their users. Both changes to the status quo are needed to ensure that internet access and use is free for people who must use the internet to have adequate opportunities to exercise their human rights.

7.2 REGULATING SOCIAL MEDIA PLATFORMS

Among the biggest harvesters of personal information are SMPs. Besides currently making internet access and use unfree by conducting unnecessary, unconstrained, and ubiquitous surveillance, these private companies have additional, problematic impacts on the human rights of their users. In this section, we look at these biggest private internet companies and their complex relationship with human rights and internet access. We will first consider how they arbitrarily interfere with human rights and internet access beyond personal data harvesting. These impacts further explain why SMPs need to be regulated by states. Subsequently, we analyse the conflicting values and objectives that are at stake in the regulation of SMPs, and which are difficult to balance. Finally, the section ends by outlining suggestions for how to regulate SMPs to keep internet access free and to protect people's exercise of human rights from unjustified interference by these businesses.

Many of the biggest internet businesses are, or operate, SMPs. Examples are Meta's Facebook, Instagram, and WhatsApp; Alphabet's YouTube; TikTok; and X (formerly Twitter). Platforms are businesses that bring together users to enable and manage positive network effects between them. Positive network effects occur when the value of a service is increased by other people's use of it (Franck and Peitz 2019: 13). For instance, Facebook does not simply offer a space where people can read newsfeeds. It more fundamentally offers a virtual place where people can congregate to interact with each other. Similarly, Amazon's marketplace is a virtual bazaar where buyers and sellers come together to do business. The more people interact with each other on platforms, the greater the positive network effects from which each of them can benefit. The greater the network effects of a platform, the more value and interest they hold for users who look for the same purpose in a platform, and the more users are drawn to it. SMPs are spaces specifically designed for social interactions that are not direct economic transactions.

SMPs such as Facebook, Instagram, and TikTok have acquired enormous social and political importance in digitalised societies. They have expanded the scope of democratic participation by expanding people's ability to join their society's public sphere (Smith and Niker 2021: 64). They have also enabled people for the first time to form something that has similarities to a global public forum (e.g. the formation of the European anti-Transatlantic Trade and Investment Partnership movement discussed in Chapter 3). Moreover, in many digitalised societies, most people use SMPs to obtain political information (Shearer and Matsa 2018). In January 2023, almost 60 per cent of the world's population was using SMPs, including 83 per cent of the populations of Northern and Western Europe and almost 74 per cent of people in North America (Statista 2023). Their popularity is the reason why SMPs have become some of the most valuable businesses on the planet as advertisers buy advertising space and use the platforms' knowledge about its users to target their products individually. As discussed in Chapter 3, SMPs have vastly increased people's opportunities to exercise many crucial political human rights (e.g. free speech and free assembly) and offer forums for advocating for better protection of civil human rights (e.g. legal equality, security of person). Because having adequate opportunities to exercise these rights today requires access to these platforms, their positive network effects are one important reason public authorities should recognise a human right to free internet access. However, in their current form SMPs do not only have benign effects on human rights. Without additional regulation through law, they also have great powers to undermine their users' human rights (Jørgensen 2019: 346–347). The question of how to legally regulate SMPs is therefore a matter of ensuring that internet access remains free from arbitrary interference by the private companies whose business is based on these platforms. There are at least three ways in which currently under-regulated SMPs objectionably can interfere with human rights.

7.2.1 *Social Media Platforms' Interferences with Human Rights*

First, SMPs have not only enhanced opportunities for positive or useful free speech. They have also provided unparalleled opportunities to disseminate abusive speech – such as speech that expresses hate towards vulnerable groups and can incite violence against them; speech that defames, that promotes violent extremism, or that consists of revenge pornography (Oliva 2020: 608). All these forms of abusive speech may violate various human rights that people have (e.g. to equal dignity, security of person, respect for their reputation, a fair trial, and freedom from discrimination), and which must be protected online as offline (UN 2016: §1). Besides these offences, SMPs also enable forms of extreme speech, that is 'speech that expresses hostility to basic commitments of liberal democracy' (Howard 2024: 183), as well as misinformation that can threaten entire public goods such as public order, public health, and democratic processes.

For example, false information, intentionally or unintentionally spread, can undermine efforts to protect public health. This became evident during the COVID-19 pandemic when misinformation about the virus, its origin, and the vaccines developed against it led to a denial of the dangerousness of the virus, attacks on ethnic groups, and vaccine scepticism (Parmet and Paul 2020, Shelton 2020). Politically, even though SMPs offer spaces that fulfil the function of a virtual public sphere, they can be misused to enable authoritarian practices even within democratic states. Because the internet provides unprecedented amounts of information, people have to select the information they consume in some way. Unfortunately, studies have shown that emotionally charged, divisive information (such as hate speech, conspiracy theories, or fake news) are more likely to attract people's attention and to spread more quickly than messages based on rational, deliberate engagement (Deibert 2019: 31). Because of this tendency of speech that appeals to people's non-rational capacities, according to Freedom House, anti-democratic forces in democracies have used SMPs effectively in five major ways to undermine democratic values and processes. These tactics comprise 'propagandist news, outright fake news, paid commentators, bots (automated accounts)' (Freedom House 2019: 6), and the hijacking of real social media accounts.

Some of these tactics, as we saw in Chapter 6, are also deployed by autocratic governments to secure their rule. However, SMPs also give political forces in democracies the opportunity to use elements of the digital authoritarianism playbook. For example, in 2018 Twitter announced that 9–15 per cent of its accounts were operated by bots and Facebook deleted 1.3 billion fake accounts (Deibert 2019: 32). SMPs are not themselves the reason why anti-authoritarian movements have appealed to citizens. The more fundamental grounds of the success of these factions range from 'ethnic divisions to anxiety about crime to the weakness of the political opposition' (Beauchamp 2019). However, SMPs have greatly enhanced anti-democratic tactics in ways that were unthinkable before. Online mobs can 'amplify conspiracy theories, inflammatory views, and misleading memes' (Freedom House 2019: 7) and in this way reach large amounts of people. But SMPs do not simply function like megaphones for anti-democratic messages; they also enable new tactics. In Brazil, for example, the movement supporting Jair Bolsonaro used specialised software to collect mobile phone numbers, then added them to WhatsApp groups, and used these to target citizens based on their location, income, and gender with conspiracy theories (Freedom House 2019: 7–8).

Like autocrats, anti-democratic forces in democracies can succeed by simply spreading their often false or misleading messages without having to rely on people believing that information. Simply by becoming public knowledge, incorrect or misleading messages cause confusion, disorientation, and distrust among citizens who are unable to fact-check all information they read. Moreover, research has shown that emotionally charged messages are generally difficult to counter once they have become widespread even if they are false and there is ample counter-evidence. The minimal effect of this sort of information is that it leads to a flattening of the epistemic landscape (4) and 'epistemic anarchy' (Dawson and Innes 2019: 254) by sowing confusion among citizens about what sources of information can still be trusted at all. But misinformation can have the further effect of creating distrust among citizens when they come to fear that others believe the lies that they themselves have encountered but not bought into (Rini 2021, Reglitz 2022). Citizens who are affected in these ways can be motivated to withdraw from public political discourse entirely or to retreat to their own political group and thereby shut themselves off from democratic dialogue and discussion. Because dialogue, willingness to consider the arguments of others, and having a sufficiently overlapping view of what is factually true are essential conditions of democratic politics and non-oppressive political public participation, SMPs have not simply promoted people's opportunities to participate in the public sphere. Instead, they have also lowered the quality of the discourse that occurs in their virtual forums, and likely helped worsen political polarisation in democratic societies.

SMPs have played this ambiguous, simultaneously enabling and worsening role for public discourse and the public sphere because they suffer from a structural problem of improperly regulated information markets. The flaw of such markets is that the economic incentives they create for competitors in them do not align with those of citizens and the public. Companies in insufficiently regulated information markets under-produce informational goods that are useful for human rights and democratic politics (e.g. information that supports democratic values, culture, and political knowledge). This is because information businesses cannot appropriate all value of these goods. For example, while information-producing businesses incur the costs of producing valuable information, they cannot monetise the effects of citizens becoming more educated, better informed, and more motivated to be engaged in civil society. At the same time, private companies in the information market have incentives to over-produce harmful information (e.g. extreme speech, fake news, or conspiracy theories) because such information generates a lot of attention and therefore more profit for them (Balkin 2021: 81–82). Without appropriate regulation, SMPs have therefore a strong motivation to enable the misuse of human rights such as free speech because doing so maximises their users' engagement with their product. That is, it improves their bottom line at the expense of individuals whose rights come under attack and of the public that suffers the consequences of misinformation and manipulation spread through these platforms.

Second, SMPs not only offer opportunities to use human rights online. Because they are private businesses that determine the rules of membership and conduct on their platforms, they also have enormous powers over who can exercise their human rights and how in the virtual spaces they create. SMPs generally have incentives to expand their userbase as far as possible. However, this can also have the effect of limiting the exercise of users' options on the platforms. This happens, for example, when SMPs adopt ToS or 'community standards' that prohibit certain content, which is permissible according to the human right to free speech, but that might create obstacles for the platform's business interests in countries where this content is banned or deemed problematic. Facebook's ban of nudity on its platforms is a case in point (Jørgensen 2019: 359). From the perspective of, for example, the human right to free speech, Facebook's community standards that prohibit certain content that is permissible according to international human rights law therefore appear as problematic, arbitrary interferences with people's exercise of this human right. Moreover, SMPs also seem to arbitrarily interfere with the human right to free association when they ban certain people from using their platforms because these are deemed to have violated the platform's ToS. The most prominent example of this is Facebook's and Twitter's ban of Donald Trump after the attacks of his supporters on the US Capitol on 6 January 2021. From this perspective, SMPs do not simply appear as enablers, but also as arbitrary inhibitors of people's human rights.

Third, the business model of SMPs has led to a decline of important local journalism. Local newspapers and TV stations are crucial institutions of the democratic public sphere that depend on advertising revenue, which has become largely appropriated by SMPs because of their greater reach and ability to customise ads to individuals, as explained in Section 7.1. For example, a report of the UK's House of Commons states that, because of this development, more than 300 local UK newspapers closed between 2009 and 2010 (UK Government 2023: 5). Local journalism and news, though, perform crucial functions for human rights by providing information needed for holding local power holders to account, by reporting on local events, by encouraging local participation (for example in elections) by building community cohesion and pride of place, and by increasing understanding among intercultural communities (UK Government 2023: 7). SMPs have therefore undermined a source of news that is essential for the usefulness of people's human right to free information.

7.2.2 What Is at Stake in Regulating Social Media Platforms

The impacts of SMPs on human rights are too powerful and ambiguous, and the interests of these companies diverge too much from those of individual users and democratic publics, to leave it up to SMPs to regulate themselves. However, appropriately regulating these companies is a difficult task because there are many complex and sometimes conflicting considerations to weigh. Only certain regulations will protect the positive functions that SMPs have for human rights and public discourse while at the same time counteracting their destructive effects. Less well-designed regulation, on the other hand, is likely to impede SMPs' useful functions as a side-effect of attempts to protect human rights and the public sphere. This section therefore outlines those functions and effects of SMPs that should be protected in attempts to create necessary legal rules that force them to respect human rights and safeguard public discourse.

What appears problematic from the perspective of free internet access is that SMPs have significant power over people's human rights (e.g. to free speech and free assembly) because these companies practise something that can be understood as a kind of 'devolved law enforcement' (Oliva 2020: 613). On their platforms, as private agents SMPs are police, judge, jury, and executioner with respect to the enforcement of their own community standards, and thereby affect people's opportunities to use their human rights online. Fundamentally, social media companies have the power to decide which content to publish and which people to ban from their platforms because they have the same legally protected editorial rights as traditional mass media such as newspapers or TV and radio stations. All these media possess editorial rights because these rights enable them to fulfil crucial functions for public discourse and the public sphere. There are at least four essential services that SMPs provide in this respect. First, SMPs facilitate public participation in the arts, in culture, and in politics. Second, they organise the public conversation so that those with the same interests or similar perspectives can identify and affiliate with each other. Third, SMPs curate public opinion by allowing their users to express certain, but not other, points of view (Balkin 2021: 75) and, finally, in doing so they create a particular experience for their users (Bhagwat 2021: 111). All these functions are important as they help realise crucial purposes or 'values' of free speech. These purposes or values partly justify why we have a human right to free speech in the first place. They centrally include:

(1) democratic participation via public opinion, which enables citizens to hold those in powerful positions to account,
(2) the production of a democratic culture that creates the meanings that 'construct us as individuals' (Balkin 2021: 77),
(3) the growth and spread of knowledge that enables social and technological progress (Balkin 2021: 78).

In other words, traditional news media and SMPs provide services that help us realise the purposes of our human right to free speech and their editorial powers are indispensable for fulfilling these functions (Bhagwat 2021: 112). This means that taking editorial rights away from SMPs would turn them into virtual public noticeboards for publishing the views of members of the public and thereby undermine the functions they can currently perform. A functioning modern public sphere, though, requires more than public opinion noticeboards and permitting members of the public to speak. Without any mediating institutions such as mass media, there are simply too many voices that would seek to attract attention and people would have little access to services that specialise in providing reliable information. For this reason, a functioning public sphere relies not simply on an unfettered marketplace of ideas but rather on intermediary institutions that provide information and present coherent points of view on matters of public importance.

Because there are too many facts to research and report as well as many diverging but not unreasonable points of view, a multitude of such institutions is required to represent various perspectives that people use to inform themselves. To fulfil their functions, intermediary institutions have to be guided by professional norms and need to be publicly trusted, which is increasingly difficult in a situation in which the internet enables everyone who can go online to become their own source of information. But without such intermediary institutions, free speech becomes a 'rhetorical war of all against all' (Balkin 2021: 79) that undermines the crucial purposes of free speech we encountered earlier, that is, public participation, production of culture and meaning, and the creation and dissemination of knowledge. Importantly, in our digital age, traditional mass media (even if they now have online presences) are no longer sufficient as intermediary institutions. That is because they are largely channels that allow people to participate only indirectly, while SMPs allow individuals to get involved directly in the public sphere. Even though the power of SMPs to exclude content and people seems arbitrary at first sight, there are therefore good reasons not to simply force them to permit all content and all speakers on their platforms.

On the other hand, leaving these platforms to publish whatever they want in whatever way they please can also undermine the very values and purposes of free speech if, for example, the published content violates people's rights, consists of false information, or threatens processes of political participation and accountability. More generally, the editorial rights of the dominant SMPs clash with the democratic idea that people should have roughly equal political influence on the collective decision-making process (Christiano 2008). SMPs exercise editorial discretion via the use of algorithms (e.g. Facebook's News Feed or YouTube's video recommendations) that determine the order in which platform users encounter information. This gives those in control over the algorithm (similar to all those who own powerful private news businesses) enormous power to shape public discourse and opinion (Aytac 2024). It is this outsized political influence of those who control algorithms that curate platform content that can objectionably limit the effectiveness of the freedom of expression of those whose views are either deprioritised and made less visible by platform algorithms or who are excluded from using platforms altogether. Some regulation is clearly needed to protect human rights online and internet access from arbitrary interferences. However, such regulation should leave intact SMPs' ability to provide important opportunities for people's fundamental interests and essential functions for the public sphere.

A different yet equally pressing challenge with respect to regulating SMPs is that effective regulation can give too much power over human rights to the regulating public authorities. This challenge cannot easily be avoided. Either we let social media companies define their own rules for what can be said on their platforms or we let the state make the decisions for them through legislation. Therefore, the real question is not *whether* but *how* to distribute the power of deciding about people's opportunities to exercise their human rights online between different public and private governance institutions (Langvardt 2021: 289). However, there are good reasons not to allow public authorities directly to set all the rules of what is permitted on social media and what is not.

First, for the state to be able to enforce legislation on social media content, it would have to monitor people's speech in these spaces to identify which expressions violate the rules. But as we saw in Chapter 6, ubiquitous public monitoring of people's speech is highly problematic because it gives states too much information about individuals, because doing so makes citizens vulnerable to the powers of the state, and because it can have chilling or self-censorship effects. Second, if governments have control over the content published on social media, this can give them the opportunity to abuse this power to spread messages that are to their benefit. Third, because democratic states have strong protections of free speech (as they should), they have to expect that removals of content from platforms will be met with legal challenges from those whose expressions have been blocked. These legal processes take time, and therefore any legitimate and urgent moderation of content (e.g. to eliminate anti-democratic propaganda and empirically false information that could endanger public health, elections, or the safety of people) would take much longer than if this were left up to private parties that have editorial powers (Balkin 2021: 86). Finally, states certainly have the task of protecting the human rights of people online. Generally, though, their protective measures should not go so far as to select what citizens are allowed to read online (Bhagwat 2021: 113–114), thereby compromising people's human right to free information. States should therefore not have the editorial powers of traditional mass media and SMPs. The functions that editorial rights serve are better fulfilled by non-state agents that do not have the coercive powers of public authorities. Moreover (as we will see in Section 7.2.3), states have other options to protect the human rights of people than to assume full editorial powers over SMPs. SMPs in effect have power over people's opportunities to exercise important human rights such as free speech, free assembly, and free information on their platforms. However, allowing SMPs to have this power has to be understood as a strategic choice, the alternative to which is to let public authorities enforce their own rules for participation in the public sphere. This, though, would create the risk of states over-reaching and limiting people's rights more than is necessary or legitimate to protect human rights online if this serves the authorities' own interests.

Moreover, there can be good reasons for restricting participation in certain public spaces. For example, private companies might create certain virtual spaces for particular groups, such as children or members of the LGBTQ community, and exclude others from these spaces to provide safe environments where members of these groups are free from the standard attacks and manipulation attempts to which they are unfortunately subject (Oliva 2020: 618–619). States, on the other hand, could not easily exclude people on such grounds because they must treat citizens equally in a way that private parties do not (even though private businesses also must not arbitrarily discriminate against people). What is important, though, is that while there is just one state per country that enforces the same laws on everyone, there can be many SMPs. This means that people's exclusion from one or a few SMPs does not prevent them from exercising their human rights online elsewhere. After all, the internet offers virtually unlimited virtual space in which new groups, websites, and platforms can be created that those excluded from other virtual venues can join. Generally, one important consideration that alleviates the concern about SMPs' power to exclude people is that these private businesses have the general incentive to have as many members as possible. This is because having more members strengthens their business's network effects as greater participation makes their services more attractive to other people. If SMPs are in the advertising business, more members also means greater profits for them as advertisers can reach more people on a platform. SMPs therefore do not have the general tendency or motivation to exclude people from their virtual forums.

For these reasons, even though the exercise of people's human rights might be curtailed by some SMPs, it is unlikely that their opportunities are thereby objectionably limited absolutely or overall. There can also be good reasons for excluding people from platforms, for example if this is necessary to protect the rights of others. However, letting states decide either to force SMPs to host all persons and content, or for states themselves to determine who and what can be hosted on SMPs, is not a cost-free choice but instead comes with its own significant downsides. On balance, it seems therefore reasonable to accept SMPs' powers to curate content and to determine their own community standards rather than giving such powers to public authorities. When they possess editorial rights, SMPs are better placed than governments to realise the values that partly justify our human rights to free speech and free assembly, and to provide important services for a functioning public sphere. Attempts to regulate SMPs should therefore be done with full awareness that stripping them of certain capacities simultaneously transfers these powers to public authorities. That is, such regulations must be balanced appropriately to have the effect of protecting and enhancing human rights online and keeping internet access free. If they are not well balanced, such rules risk simply creating different, and in some cases worse, threats to free internet access and human rights by giving states too much power over both.

7.2.3 *Human Rights-Guided Regulations for Social Media Platforms*

SMPs need regulation to align their incentives with those of their users and the public at large. More specifically, an appropriate set of rules for SMPs has to achieve several things at the same time. First, it must make states act on their legal human rights obligations to turn private businesses' moral human rights obligations into legal duties, as demanded by the Guiding Principles. Second, it must enable SMPs to limit individuals' exercise of human rights on these platforms in legitimate ways so that the platforms can fulfil their important functions for the public sphere and for human rights (i.e. free speech, free association, and free information) overall. They are needed as curators of public opinion and thereby help create a public sphere that is as free as possible from state interference. Third, an appropriate set of regulations must ensure the conditions under which the limiting of individual persons' human rights by SMPs is unproblematic because it does not objectionably affect people's overall opportunities to exercise their human rights online. This requires that people have sufficient alternative options to the platforms from which they might be banned. Only if this is ensured can internet access and use still be considered 'free' for them. Considering these complex requirements, we can identify at least four rules that states should enforce on SMPs.[1]

7.2.3.1 International Human Rights Principles as Boundaries of Acceptable Speech on Social Media Platforms

Whatever else the ToS of SMPs entail, these companies must be required to take steps to protect the human rights of people from violations committed on, or enabled by, their platforms. Their community standards must contain a 'bottom floor' of permissible speech that defines which content clearly violates human rights and is therefore disallowed. For this purpose, it is helpful that the UN's international human rights treaties provide guidance for how to determine when limitations of human rights are justifiable. States should use this guidance to specify what rules SMPs must adhere to. Even though this limits their editorial rights, such restrictions are justifiable because these editorial powers are themselves morally not more important than the human rights that they are supposed to help promote, and which need protecting from certain content (Bhagwat 2021: 118).

Most relevant in the essential UN human rights treaties for specifying a bottom floor of permissible speech on SMPs is Article 19.3 of the International Covenant on Civil and Political Rights (ICCPR, UN 1966a). This states that restrictions on free speech are justifiable if they fulfil the '3-step test' (Oliva 2020: 617) of being (1) legal/provided by law, (2) used for legitimate purposes

---

[1] Even though there might well be alternative realisations of the following four rules, any shape of SMP regulation would have to fulfil the desiderata set out by these rules to make the operations of SMPs compatible with human rights and to protect their users from undue influence by governments and SMPs themselves.

(e.g. rights/reputation of others, national security, public order, public health and morals), and (3) necessary – which includes the requirements of proportionality and minimality. The conditions of justified limits on free speech are therefore not coincidentally the same as the ones for legitimate restrictions on people's human right to privacy that we encountered in Chapter 6. Moreover, the UN Special Rapporteur on the Promotion and Protection of the Right to Freedom of Opinion and Expression clarifies that legitimate purposes for restricting free speech include

> Child pornography (to protect the rights of children), hate speech (to protect the rights of affected communities), defamation (to protect the rights and reputation of others against unwarranted attacks), direct and public incitement to commit genocide (to protect the rights of others), and advocacy of national, racial or religious hatred that constitutes incitement to discrimination, hostility or violence (to protect the rights of others, such as the right to life). (UN 2011a: §25)

As the legal scholar Thiago Dias Oliva points out, many categories of speech that are already banned on major SMPs correspond to these legitimate aims of limiting speech (Oliva 2020: 618). Using Article 19.3 of the ICCPR as a basis for laws that regulate speech on SMPs would be a principled way for states to discharge their human rights obligations without overstepping their authority and their own duties to respect human rights. But it would also have advantages for SMPs themselves if they chose to adopt rules in line with Article 19.3 voluntarily. First, using human rights law as grounds for determining permissible content would base the decisions of these companies on internationally agreed upon principles. This would offer SMPs protection from arbitrary requests by governments that do not themselves respect human rights or are trying to curtail these rights, such as requests by states to block certain content unfriendly to them (Oliva 2020: 622). Adopting Article 19.3 would also provide SMPs with principled reasons to reject anti-democratic tactics employed by governments, for example in Brazil and Mexico, that have used anti-censorship laws to prevent SMPs from blocking false content friendly to their regime (Freedom House 2021: 15). Second, employing Article 19.3 as a basis for their community rules could provide guidance for SMPs on how to balance differing national laws with their own commercial interests. Different countries have different laws on free speech. In the US, for example, there are few limits on free speech,[2]

---

[2] Even in the US, though, the Constitution's First Amendment allows the restriction of free speech and editorial rights for urgent social goals if restrictions are narrowly tailored (i.e. specific and limited), for example if such speech constitutes hate speech that incites violence or false commercial speech that deceives (Bhagwat 2021: 129).

while the EU takes a more permissive line concerning what kind of speech is unprotected as it violates people's rights.[3] If SMPs were to adopt Article 19.3 as the standard for specifying which speech they do not permit, they would be able to fulfil their universal moral obligation to respect human rights in their business practices also in those states that might insufficiently protect human rights or that have a much wider interpretation of permissible free speech (Oliva 2020: 619–620).

From a moral perspective, it is important to consider that free speech is not an absolute human right but rather an entitlement worthy of respect because and if it fulfils certain ends. The permissible exceptions contained in Article 19.3 are therefore not in conflict but in alignment with the purposes of free expression. The right to free speech that imposes a duty on others to respect a person's expression is either (non-instrumentally) justified because giving people the freedom to express their beliefs and opinions is necessary for respecting their moral equality as persons. We cannot claim to respect others as equal but not generally give them an opportunity to speak their mind. Alternatively, free speech can be (instrumentally) justified because it promotes important goods such as the ones discussed in Section 2.2. To recall, free speech is (among other things) essential for (1) democratic participation via public opinion, which enables citizens to hold those in powerful positions to account, (2) the production of a democratic culture that creates the meanings that 'construct us as individuals' (Balkin 2021: 77), and (3) the growth and spread of knowledge that enables social and technological progress (Balkin 2021: 78). However, speech that is either extreme, hateful, or false and as such dangerous cannot claim to deserve the status of protected speech according to either the instrumental or non-instrumental route.

The non-instrumental argument does not protect extreme, hate, or false and as such dangerous speech because such expressions either violate the speaker's duty to respect other people's rights (e.g. to moral equality and dignity) or because the expressions endanger other people's rights (e.g. to safety of person or their reputation). In the latter case, the harms of speech must be balanced against the rights of others that it might violate and, if the danger to others is likely, serious, and predictable, the rights to be protected arguably outweigh the importance of the speech that would cause the harm. Hardly any rights are absolute, and free speech too is not more important that the protection of

---

[3] As explained in Chapter 3, this is one of the reasons why having a stand-alone human right to internet access can protect online access in cases where specific rights (most prominently free speech), which internet access as an entitlement would otherwise be subsumed under, are legitimately restricted in certain situations.

people's other human rights (Howard 2024: 184–185). If free expression has the essential (non-instrumental) purpose of respecting people's moral equality by permitting their expressions, speech that either denies other's moral equality and dignity or that endangers other's rights therefore undercuts its own justification. The instrumental argument does not protect extreme speech either because there is little to learn from, for example, neo-Nazis and white supremacists or others who deny the moral equality of people they despise. That there is nothing to learn from hate speech is especially salient in online echo chambers or social media where people seek out and are being shown predominantly views to which they are already sympathetic. But even if there were something to be learned from extreme or dangerous speech, there must be a trade-off between the alleged benefits of being exposed to extreme speech and the likely harms that such speech causes. If these harms are clearly foreseeable or very likely, the speech causing them cannot be deemed morally worthy of protection (Howard 2024: 185–186). One important harm of extreme speech (e.g. in the form of online harassment and trolling) is that it can have chilling effects on its victims. When it does, it lessens the benefits that free expression can have for everyone because it reduces the voices present in the public exchange of opinions (Langvardt 2021: 290).

Restrictions on free speech that are in line with Article 19.3 of the ICCPR also do not undermine the effectiveness of editorial rights of SMPs. That is, imposing regulations on SMPs that limit problematic speech do not prevent these businesses from fulfilling the important functions that they provide for individuals and the public (i.e. facilitating public participation, structuring public conversations, curating public opinion, and creating particular experiences for their users). These functions can also be performed when SMPs are forced by law to exclude certain forms of speech, to label some content as uncontroversially false, or even to include factual non-ideological content that helps to counter misinformation that can undermine human rights or important public interests (e.g. public health information or information for the effective conduct of elections, Bhagwat 2021: 120, 137). Fully unproblematic from the human rights perspective is a legal requirement that SMPs remove bots and fake accounts from their forums. These do not constitute the genuine speech of any person but rather undermine people's rights to free information and political participation because the main purpose of bots and fake accounts is normally to manipulate and misinform (Benkler et al. 2018: 368).

There are, however, important caveats on the permissibility of blocking certain speech or people from SMPs. This is because the Guiding Principles specify that states must ensure that people have access to remedies if their human rights are violated (UN 2011b: 1). In many cases, those affected by having their content removed or being themselves blocked by SMPs will dispute that they violated the platform's community standards. Appropriate regulation must therefore ensure that platforms adhere to certain procedural rules even when they have editorial powers to moderate content and exclude people. First, SMPs must not arbitrarily exclude people and must execute their own ToS neutrally (Bhagwat 2021: 124). Creating safe spaces for marginalised people who are vulnerable and often victims of attacks by others (e.g. ethnic minorities, children, LGBTQ communities) is not an arbitrary exclusion. However, excluding people simply because one dislikes them is unjustifiable (Bhagwat 2021: 126). Second, SMPs must be transparent about their community standards and how they enforce them, so people understand what rules they must abide by. Third, SMPs must notify those who have their speech taken down just as those whose privacy is compromised by state surveillance must be informed about the infringements of their rights. Without such notifications, people might not be aware that their rights have been curtailed and are consequently unable to challenge the decision. Fourth, there must be some channel of appeal for those who want to challenge the decisions of SMPs (Bhagwat 2021: 124). This is important because content moderation decisions cannot be expected always to be correct. Facebook's CEO Mark Zuckerberg once admitted that Facebook's content moderators at the time had a 10 per cent error rate (Langvardt 2021: 296). SMPs should have the editorial powers to exclude content that violates their rules and people who do not abide by these rules, but they must not do so non-transparently or arbitrarily. One of the reasonable provisions of the EU's Digital Markets Act (European Union 2022) is therefore to force SMPs to offer their users channels to appeal exclusionary decisions. It is important for public authorities to enforce regulation of this kind because, even though it is essential that SMPs have adequate content moderation and channels of appeal, operating these mechanisms is costly for them and therefore reduces their profits (Balkin 2021: 81).

7.2.3.2 Breaking Up the Current Oligopoly of Dominant Social Media Platforms

Besides enforcing a bottom floor of permissible speech to protect human rights from abuse, legal rules for SMPs must also address other problems with the status quo. For this purpose, Jack Balkin (2021) suggests a three-pronged approach outlined in this section and Sections 7.2.3.3 and 7.2.3.4. First, the argument that people's human rights are not objectionably limited if they are excluded from SMPs depends on them having adequate opportunities to join comparable platforms. Moreover, the claim that SMPs can play an important role in constituting the public sphere and realising the ends of free speech is predicated on there being a multitude of them. The problem with the status quo is that there are currently but a few major companies that dominate the market of online platforms. However, for SMPs to reflect different perspectives and in that way to promote public participation, for their owners to not have a problematically large influence on public opinion through the power of the algorithms that curate platform content, and to present different sources of knowledge for the public, there needs to be a significant number of platforms (Balkin 2021: 76–77). Instead, at present a few powerful platforms dominate the online public sphere by enforcing their community standards on vast numbers of people. One significant risk inherent in the status quo is therefore that some individuals who own SMPs use their power to publicly promote their private interests. This becomes clear if we imagine that a company such as Facebook were to use its editorial freedom before an important election to favour the political messages and perspective of one particular political party. Because of its power, Facebook would no longer fulfil an important service in the public sphere. Instead, the company would undermine the very purposes for which it has editorial rights in the first place since there are too few sufficiently influential alternative platforms that could represent alternative perspectives (Langvardt 2021: 277–278). One important goal of social media regulation must therefore be to increase the number of influential platforms that curate viewpoints, shape public opinion, and represent a diversity of perspectives.

Balkin (2021: 91) argues that in the US, which is the home to many of the most powerful SMPs and where the most dynamic innovations in this sector take place,[4] competition law provides a crucial tool for the government to change the status quo. Competition law could be used in several ways with the aim to protect the quality of the public sphere and, we can add with a view to the human rights angle of this book, to ensure adequate opportunities for people to exercise their freedoms online. Competition law could be used to produce a multitude of smaller SMPs, for example, by protecting start-up companies that could challenge the dominance of current forerunners through innovations from being bought up early in their development by their biggest competitors. Facebook, for instance, achieved its dominant market position to a significant extent by buying other companies, including WhatsApp and Instagram. Moreover, competition law should be used to separate different functions of businesses that they currently control under one roof, such as content delivery, content moderation, advertisement brokering, and

---

[4] At least innovation under democratic political governance.

advertisement publication.[5] If these tasks were performed by separate companies in different markets, their individual powers would be less significant and there would no longer be an oligopoly of companies that dominate the online public sphere.

One worry might be that even then network effects would still lead people to gravitate back to a few platforms. However, if competition laws created a SMP landscape populated by genuinely different platform services and experiences, different communities might well prefer certain platforms over others, or they might join several platforms – especially if they can link content between different platforms (Balkin 2021: 80–81). From the human rights perspective, what is crucial is that a multitude of platforms offers people alternatives to exercise their freedoms online even if they are excluded from some virtual forums (Bhagwat 2021: 112–113). In that sense, these individuals' internet access and use would not be arbitrarily constrained because there would be sufficient alternatives available to them.

Two other, more fundamental, concerns about the proposal of creating a multitude of privately owned SMPs by breaking up the current oligopoly of platforms are the following. First, such an outcome would not address the issue of the problematically large influence of SMP owners on public discourse and opinion based on algorithmic curation. Second, breaking up the current oligopoly of platforms might be thought to be undesirable since it would increase the fragmentation of the public sphere as people would have many more platforms into which they sort themselves (Aytac 2024). One alternative approach towards ending the problematic concentration of power in the hands of the owners of SMPs that aims to address these two problems is proposed by the political theorist Ugur Aytac. Instead of breaking up currently dominant platforms, his proposal is to legally require SMPs of a certain size to incorporate citizen boards of governance. These boards would operate at the national level and consist of a few dozen citizens who are selected for multi-year terms through stratified random sampling. The citizens (who would receive compensation for their services) would be supported by a dozen experts from relevant fields such as software engineering, law, and other disciplines. The task of these citizen boards of governance would be to determine the way that platform algorithms operate and, in that way, separate editorial powers from profit interests. Specifically, citizens supported by experts would be given the authority to determine what algorithmic rules are used to curate content on SMPs (Aytac 2024). Importantly, this solution would also leave intact the vast user

---

[5] For an argument for enforcing a content moderation option by independent, non-platform services, see Article 19 (2021).

communities of existing SMPs, which is seen as important for an integrated public sphere that can collectively deliberate on political issues.

However, there are several reasons why Balkin's suggestion of breaking up the existing platform oligopoly is preferable to introducing citizen boards of governance into the structure of the currently dominant SMPs. First, the desire to create an online public sphere that is as unified as possible through a limited number of SMPs (or possibly even one) is undesirable. Before the internet, democracies did not have one unified public sphere. Rather, their public sphere consisted of various overlapping public discourses of different social groups. These debated political issues among themselves and sometimes with each other. Without the internet, a single public debate involving everyone simply was not feasible. Despite the internet's unique opportunities for people to interact, it is questionable that political issues can be debated among millions of citizens in one single discussion or in one virtual forum. Even individual SMPs currently do not present unified discourses as users sort themselves into specific groups and communities on these platforms. Neither would such a singular public debate be desirable as it would likely drown out the voices of minorities and marginalised groups. However, if a singular unified discourse on one platform is not desirable, enabling citizens to select themselves into a larger number of SMPs that all offer different environments and user experiences is not problematic from a democratic perspective. As long as debates that happen within these platforms can influence each other, membership in different platforms does not have to lead to an unprecedented fragmentation of the public sphere. Inter-platform exchanges would especially be facilitated by forcing SMPs to allow users to link their different platform accounts so that they could import content from one to the other.

Second, concerns about undue political influence of those who control platform algorithms can be mitigated if there is public demand for a platform experience that prioritises democratic interactions and undistorted information over entertainment and reaffirming users' existing perspectives. In a market that is open to genuine competition among SMPs, it is conceivable that there will be contenders that offer specifically democratic and human rights promoting features. As their selling points, such platforms could have, for instance, the facilitation of democratic discourse that is free from algorithmic distortion based on platform owners' profit interests, from government influence, from misinformation, and from user attacks on each other. SMPs that have community rules that disallow dangerous speech and false information, and that allow users to up-vote popular content would seem well positioned to attract democratically minded citizens, journalists, and democratic parties that want to engage in free and open discussions. Public sphere-enabling SMPs of this kind could therefore carve out for themselves a specialised niche in a non-oligopolised market.

Third, a strategy based on legally requiring social media companies to yield the central part of their corporate power to citizen boards of governance would have to challenge the shareholder primacy doctrine in corporate law (Aytac 2024). According to this dominant legal view, the primary purpose and responsibility of corporations is to benefit their shareholders. Introducing citizen boards of governance instead would change the business model of SMPs by forcing these companies to work for the public good – a change that is likely to meet with significant corporate and legal resistance. Even though they are privately owned, SMPs indeed fulfil important public purposes as virtual forums for public debate. However, if there was a genuinely competitive market in SMPs, states could incentivise private SMPs to operate for profit while furthering public goals and values without having to interfere with their shareholder primacy. This could be done by offering either public grants for emerging companies or tax breaks for established SMPs that voluntarily subjected themselves to certain requirements. Public financial support could be given to companies that, for instance, commit themselves to forms of algorithmic curation that prioritised civil public discourse, that allowed regular public scrutiny of their algorithms, commit themselves to enforcing international human rights principles for the regulation of free speech via their community standards, and that had transparent community standard enforcement procedures with possibilities for appeal for users whose content was blocked. SMPs that transparently used their businesses for the free exercise of human rights would still be run for private profit. However, their explicit purpose would not be to concentrate political influence but to facilitate democratic exchange on a voluntary basis.

Breaking up the current oligopoly of SMPs would therefore present a way out of the seeming dilemma that control over public discourse either lies with the government or with private corporations that have the sole purpose of maximizing profits. The use of existing laws would create a situation in which private firms would facilitate online public discourse, but not simply for private profit. Instead, the business model of at least some SMPs could be expected to voluntarily have as an important purpose the promotion of human rights and the public good. That is because their business model would be supported and incentivised by public authorities that do not control the terms of the public sphere or monitor the activities of democratic citizens. Balkin's suggestion is therefore a more desirable way to ensure that SMPs do not interfere with the free access and use of the internet than alternative proposals (such as citizen boards of governance or forcing SMPs to host all content and people).

7.2.3.3 Enforcing Fiduciary Relationships between Platforms and Users

As we saw in Section 7.1, SMPs currently see personal data as a financial asset to be exploited, not something to be respected as part of users' privacy. Current market incentives in fact incentivise them to eliminate their users' privacy as much as possible. Consequently, SMPs cannot be expected voluntarily to respect people's privacy online (Jørgensen 2019: 356–358). Balkin's second suggestion is therefore to combine competition law that aims to create smaller platforms with enforcing fiduciary obligations on platforms to protect their users' personal data. This would achieve multiple aims. First, as explained in Section 1.1, it would protect users' human right to privacy because SMPs could no longer exploit this information for profit without restraint because they would acquire duties of care, confidentiality, and loyalty towards their clients. Because there would be a multitude of SMPs, each of them would also likely collect less personal data on individuals overall (Balkin 2021: 84–85). In combination with the partition of different parts of current SMPs' business into separate companies, this would weaken each platform's position as an advertiser. Consequently, local news services could be expected to regain some attractiveness as advertising spaces, which would make local journalism more viable again. Moreover, since SMPs could no longer sell information about their users to third parties that did not themselves accept fiduciary obligations towards that data, platform users would no longer become individually identifiable targets of political manipulation or other forms of disinformation (Balkin 2020:18).

7.2.3.4 Imposing Distributor Liability for Published Content on Social Media Platforms

Balkin's final suggestion links up with the first policy for the regulation of social media companies, which requires them to determine a bottom floor of speech that is permissible on their platforms. The way to do this effectively would be to enforce a particular form of legal liability for content carried by SMPs, that is 'intermediary' or 'distributor' liability (Balkin 2021: 93). There are different ways of holding to account those who publish their own or other's content. They can have 'publisher' or 'strict' liability when it is appropriate to hold them legally responsible for what they publish. For example, newspapers can be liable for the harmful or illegal consequences that can be causally attributed to something they published. Alternatively, those distributing content can be granted immunity from the consequences of what they distribute if such immunity helps them perform important functions. Bookshops, for example, would be unlikely to be willing to sell any material that might cause them legal problems if they were held liable for the content of the books they sell. In fact, they might not sell many books at all, which would reduce the information that circulates in society. Similarly, Section 230 of the US Communications Decency Act of 1996 currently still gives computer service providers legal immunity from liability for the content provided by third parties. The successful intention of this law was not to stifle the development of the still nascent internet infrastructure and services, which would likely have unfolded much less rapidly if those selling internet services had to fear legal repercussions for all content they carried.

However, the situation in 2024 is very different, and the internet by now has reached large parts of humanity and provides countless services that are improved by constant innovations. Despite the changed situation, enforcing publisher liability on SMPs would still be morally questionable because SMPs are not co-authors of content that might violate the rights of others or undermine public interests (Howard 2024: 188). However, SMPs are not simple conduits for the content of others either. They use their editorial freedoms to curate and present the content of others in particular forms, for example by using algorithms that create personalised news or video feeds, and by setting ToS that determine what can and cannot be published in the first place. SMPs therefore causally contribute to the violations of human rights or threats to vital public interests that occur in their virtual spaces. They are not bookshops or newspapers but rather like curators of art galleries who choose the way in which they present the objects they display (Howard 2024: 187–188). Especially because SMPs are given the protected freedom to decide (within limits) what content they publish, the appropriate response to questions of liability cannot be that they are completely absolved from all responsibilities for the consequences of their choices. That is, editorial freedom 'cuts in favor of, not against, platform liability' (Bhagwat 2021: 130).

Rather than strict or no responsibility, the appropriate kind of liability to enforce on SMPs is distributor liability (Bhagwat 2021: 132). This requires SMPs to take down within a reasonable timeframe content that violates the rights of others or public laws once they have been notified of it. If they do not, SMPs would otherwise become legally liable for the problematic content that they failed to remove. This notice period takes into account that it is unlikely that even technologically powerful SMPs are able to detect all problematic content of others before or immediately after it is published on their platforms (Bhagwat 2021: 131). The EU, for instance, as part of its Digital Services Act, has enforced 'notice-and-takedown' regulations on SMPs operating in its territory. How such rules are formulated is important because if they are too strict they are likely to lead to 'collateral censorship', as SMPs also remove content that might be permissible to minimise possible legal risks (Oliva 2020: 629). However, as a general approach to the regulation of SMPs, distributor or intermediary liability is a crucial instrument to ensure that SMPs' moral obligations to protect human rights from violations committed on their virtual premises are transformed into legal duties.

All four regulatory measures discussed here when combined would ensure that internet access is free from arbitrary interference by SMPs. They would also make sure that, where the use of human rights has to be limited, for example for the purpose of protecting the human rights of others or important public interests, this is done in line with Article 19.3 of the ICCPR and therefore justifiably so. At the same time, the four rules suggested in this section recognise and respect the important functions that SMPs play in the realisation of essential human rights (e.g. free speech and free information) and the maintenance of a free public sphere. The power of SMPs and the problems they are causing are something new. However, the four suggested measures are familiar and proven regulatory instruments that would help address the problems currently posed by SMPs for human rights and free internet access. The real question is therefore – as always with respect to human rights – whether there exists sufficient political will to implement these rules.

7.3 (INTER)NET NEUTRALITY

SMPs are essential for most people's experience of the internet, and it is therefore necessary to regulate them appropriately so that people can exercise their human rights online and access the internet without arbitrary interference. SMPs operate at the content/application layer of the internet. However, internet access can be arbitrarily interfered with at the more fundamental network level as well, where data is transmitted via internet infrastructure such as broadband cables. As we saw in Chapter 6, autocratic states such as China exploit this fact to keep their citizens from accessing certain information and to hide other content by blocking it or slowing it down, thereby making it harder to access (Roberts 2018: 62). However, in all countries there are private companies, namely ISPs, whose business consists in the delivery of data to and from different IP addresses. They can treat internet data packets in different ways, for example by blocking, filtering, throttling, or prioritising certain data. More specifically, ISPs can deliberately control internet traffic flows by employing a type of data processing called deep packet inspection. This enables ISPs to identify what information is contained in the data that they transmit via their internet infrastructure (Belli 2016: 18–19). As private companies, ISPs also have an incentive to treat data traffic differently if this increases their profits.

Because of the interests that private and public agents have in controlling and discriminating between internet traffic flows, since the early 2000s democratic states have been under pressure to adopt and protect the principle of 'internet' or 'net neutrality'.[6] The principle's aim is to guarantee 'that Internet users maintain the ability to choose freely how to utilise their own Internet connection, *without undue interferences* from public or private entities' (Belli, de Filippi 2016: 3, emphasis added) by ensuring that 'Internet traffic shall be treated in a non-discriminatory fashion so that Internet users can freely choose online content, applications, services and devices without being influenced by discriminatory delivery of Internet traffic' (Belli, de Filippi 2016: 2).

However, some data discrimination is generally accepted as necessary, for example for maintaining the functionality of networks by managing data flows to avoid or resolve data congestion, or for the purpose of blocking harmful data such as malware and spam (Belli 2016: 16). A crucial question from the perspective of the human right to free internet access is therefore when interference with data traffic is arbitrary, and thus morally objectionable. To allow a principled distinction between legitimate and arbitrary forms of data discrimination, this section first looks at the question why net neutrality matters, second at the different purposes that net neutrality is supposed to achieve, and finally proposes a particular human rights-promoting interpretation of this principle.

7.3.1 *The Problem of Net Neutrality*

At a basic level, ISPs operate in a market where they contract with both internet content/application providers as well as internet end-users. If they were allowed to charge either or both parties to deliver certain data in a preferential way, ISPs could generate profits beyond what they earn for the standard delivery of internet data from content/application providers to end-users.

ISPs have various options for treating data preferentially/non-neutrally. First, ISPs could offer various tiers of quality of service with those tiers that transfer

---

[6] The term 'internet neutrality' is sometimes used to clarify that the principle does not apply to non-internet services that can also be offered through broadband infrastructure, that is specialised services (McDiarmid and Shears 2016: 39) – for more explanation see Footnote 7. To stay in line with the terms of the public debate of our topic, in this book I will use the term 'net neutrality'.

data faster being more expensive while all content/application providers can purchase any quality of service. Second, ISPs could charge different content/application providers different prices for the same data delivery services (e.g. by charging the wealthiest corporations more than smaller ones). Third, ISPs could impose auctions for the exclusive delivery of a particular application or content per industry segment (e.g. video-streaming) so that only the highest bidder has its content delivered to the end-users of the ISPs. Fourth, as a specific version of the first method, if users pay for a limited amount of data (so that extra costs apply for data used beyond the cap or data used beyond that limit is slowed down – as is common with mobile internet data plans), ISPs can exempt the data of specific content providers from counting towards the data cap in what is known as 'zero-rating' (Maroni 2021). In contrast, genuinely neutral treatment of internet data only occurs where there is either no discrimination in the transmission of data at all or where the data of some content or applications (e.g. particularly popular ones) get preferential treatment but at no extra cost (Economides 2016: 815).

Whether data is delivered preferentially matters enormously for how people use the internet. As Roberts puts it, the delay in the delivery of data acts like a 'tax' on that content (Roberts 2019: 25) that has significant effects on the choices of internet users: 'research shows that increasing load times by as little as 100 milliseconds reduces the amount of time people spend on a site, how much they buy, and whether they come back' (van Schewick 2016: 4). Moreover, according to research by Google, 53 per cent of mobile broadband users leave a website that takes longer than three seconds to load (UNESCO 2023: 92). However, if we want people to be able to use the internet effectively and securely, as explained earlier, some data discrimination is needed and therefore desirable for network maintenance and security purposes. The real question is therefore not whether data discrimination occurs at the network level of the internet. Rather, the issue is for what purposes data is treated differently. This, though, is not a technical question but rather a normative one because it requires us to specify what functions and goals the internet and the data that is transmitted through it are to achieve (Sandvig 2007: 136). This also becomes clear when considering that autocratic states place no value on the neutral treatment of data at all. They instead use the fact that data on the internet can be treated differently to manipulate and control their subjects because the things autocrats value the most are their own rule and privileges. If we think that net neutrality and the non-discriminatory treatment of data is important, we therefore have to explain what this principle is important for. More specifically, as the Body of European Regulators for Electronic Communications (BEREC, the organisation in which the national regulators of the telecommunication markets of the EU member states co-operate) argues, to be acceptable, any discriminatory treatment of data has to be undertaken for legitimate purposes, and must be necessary and proportionate as a means for achieving these purposes (BEREC 2012). The reasoning here is the same that underpins exceptions to the human rights to privacy and free speech that we have discussed in this chapter and in Chapter 6. The default should be for ISPs to treat all data in non-discriminatory fashion (net neutrality) unless they have good grounds not to do so. There are several reasons why different internet data should sometimes be treated in non-neutral ways but why it otherwise should be transmitted in non-discriminatory fashion.

7.3.2 Purposes for Treating Internet Data Neutrally and Differentially

The first purpose that is generally accepted as a legitimate reason why some data can be slowed down or even be blocked is the maintenance and security of the networks of which the internet consists. There is no reason to think that data that has the aim of harming internet users or of contacting them in unsolicited and undesirable ways should be treated equally to other data. ISPs therefore not only protect their own interests, but also those of all internet users if they block malware such as computer viruses and spam messages. These are standard threats against safe internet access that ISPs as part of the service they provide must address. Moreover, ISPs can be justified in routinely slowing down certain data during peak times when this is necessary for preventing or resolving data congestion issues on their networks, and if this is done by type of data (e.g. bandwidth throttling for *all* video-streaming traffic or *all* online game traffic, Belli 2016: 18) rather than sources of data. Such security and network maintenance goals are necessary forms of data discrimination because without guaranteeing them there is no functioning or safe internet that can serve the purposes we want it to fulfil.

A second category of goals for neutral or differential treatment of data is economic ones. Here, the first reason offered in favour of treating data traffic non-neutrally is the profit motive of ISPs: by charging more for preferential data delivery, they can improve their bottom line. However, morally speaking, the goal of profit maximisation is as such negligible because the interests of some to become ever richer are not more important than the interest of all end-users to freely use the internet to exercise their human rights. A more normatively relevant justification for wanting to generate more profits via the differential delivery of data is that in this way ISPs could obtain a fairer share of the profits that the internet engenders. Currently, vast profits are made by application/content providers such as Facebook, Google, and Amazon that for their business rely on the services of ISPs, which are forced to deliver all data neutrally because of net neutrality rules. If ISPs were instead allowed to charge major application/content providers more for delivering their data to their customers, ISPs would receive a greater share of internet-generated revenues (Comeig et al. 2022). Indirectly, the profit motive of ISPs might be relevant if it also benefits end-users. In this respect, some economists and ISPs have argued that allowing ISPs to charge more for preferential delivery of content might improve 'consumer welfare' by making internet access and data use cheaper for end-users and by providing ISPs with funds they can use to expand and enhance their existing internet infrastructure. However, these arguments appear at best inconclusive – in part because governments in most developed countries have embraced net neutrality rules so that there have not been many opportunities to study the effects of data discrimination in practice (Economides 2016, Greenstein et al. 2016).

An economic argument in defence of net neutrality rules is that non-discriminatory delivery of data is essential for innovation in internet content and applications by keeping the entry barriers for new developers low (van Schewick 2010). If ISPs had been permitted to charge higher prices for preferential delivery of data from the early stages of the global diffusion of the internet, it stands to reason that only those with sufficient funds would have been able to offer new online applications and services, that only those that use prioritised services would have been widely adopted, and that innovative activity would have been slower overall because fewer developers would have been able to compete in the market. Net neutrality rules therefore have been and remain important for offering a level playing field for all those who want to develop new online applications, content, or services, and for allowing end-users to freely choose between these. This level playing field for innovative economic activity has also been important from the perspective of human rights because it has enabled tech entrepreneurs to develop applications and services that now offer new and unprecedented ways to exercise and promote human rights (McDiarmid and Shears 2016). We encountered examples of this in Chapters 3 and 4 such as people's abilities to document and distribute human rights violations on social media, to use social media to express their views, to use online sources such as Wikipedia to access information, to use FinTech to participate in the economy, or eHealth and eLearning tools to access medical and educational services. Insofar as net neutrality promotes innovation in online content and applications, economic arguments for net neutrality can therefore have direct relevance for human rights as well.

This last economic argument points towards the third category of reasons in the debate of net neutrality, which is human rights considerations. Morally speaking, the impact that the neutral or preferential delivery of data has on people's human rights is the weightiest reason for net neutrality, and economic reasons are most relevant when they matter for human rights, as just explained. The most serious problem of data discrimination is that it causes serious collateral damage for people's opportunities to exercise their human rights online beyond the problem of stifled innovation (van Schewick 2015: 15). If some content is delivered faster, or accessing it is more costly in terms of time and money, this incentivises people to use the internet in certain ways. If higher costs are attached to some data (e.g. by asking fees for preferential treatment of data or through zero-rating, van Schewick 2016: 3), end-users are steered towards the less costly prioritised content (van Schewick 2015: 15).

However, the internet's beneficial potential for human rights is fundamentally based on its open architecture. Its networks provide channels for individuals to exchange information with each other. More specifically, the novelty about the internet as a mass medium, which is decisive for making human rights more effective, is that it permits everyone not simply to be a receiver, but also a sender of information (van Schewick 2010). The opportunity to send data can be used for different purposes, though. It can be used in productive ways that have positive externalities for others and society overall (e.g. when people create websites, share knowledge, blog about politics, or document and disseminate evidence of rights abuses). These are the kinds of uses that are generally most relevant and beneficial for human rights. Alternatively, the internet can be used for consumptive purposes to produce commodities (e.g. online shopping or entertainment). Such uses mostly benefit the producers of products and their consumers, but not others outside these transactions. Data discrimination, though, 'favours listening over speaking, consuming over producing, and consumptive uses over communicative uses' of the internet (van Schewick 2010: 364). That is because it is producers of consumption goods, rather than individual citizens, who have the money needed to pay for prioritised content delivery, which is to the detriment of individuals' use of human rights. In their attempts to maximise profits, ISPs therefore have inherent incentives to favour content and applications whose value they can appropriate rather than those kinds of data, such as most data that is relevant for human rights, that create unobservable value and positive externalities for others and society (van Schewick 2010: 364).

Violations of the net neutrality principle for the sake of maximising profits are therefore arbitrary interferences with people's free internet access. This is because if data that is created by the exercise or is relevant for the use of, human rights (i.e. 'human rights data') is blocked, slowed down, or made harder to find to increase profits for some, people's opportunities to exercise their human rights online are negatively affected. The problem becomes clear when we consider the positions of the different parties affected by the discriminatory treatment of data. From the perspective of the sender, unnecessary data discrimination creates two classes of speakers: those who can pay for preferential treatment (e.g. wealthy individuals and large companies) and those who cannot (who are often those holding unpopular or new viewpoints, e.g. activists and artists). In such a situation, non-commercial content will be less attractive for end-users because there are higher costs attached to its use compared with commercial content whose prioritisation is more likely to be paid for (van Schewick 2015: 15). This means that people's opportunities to express themselves, to participate in cultural activities and politics, or generally to use the internet productively in ways that benefit others are reduced or devalued (van Schewick 2010: 364). From a recipient's perspective, non-necessary data discrimination negatively affects the free choice of information. If ISPs do not have to treat all data equally, they can in effect restrict 'my ability to educate myself, my ability to contribute to a discussion on [a] subject, and my ability to make informed decisions' (van Schewick 2010: 365). In this way, ISPs even obtain power over the shape of the public discourse by influencing what information citizens are likely to access, which would make them 'gatekeepers of what circulates online' (Maroni 2021: 528). As a side-effect of efforts to maximise private profits, non-necessary internet traffic differentiation has to be seen as creating 'new forms of exclusion from society [...] based on commercial interests' (Maroni 2021: 534) that are detrimental to human rights. Respecting net neutrality is therefore necessary to create an internet in which 'freedoms have a chance to materialise' (Maroni 2021: 534) and can be freely exercised.

These reasons for treating internet traffic the same or differently that we have just canvassed help us identify when data discrimination can be seen as permissible rather than arbitrary interferences with free internet access and human rights online.

7.3.3 *A Human Rights-Promoting Interpretation of Net Neutrality*

How should data be treated on the internet? There are several legitimate objectives to consider when answering this question. Some of them require that data is treated discriminatorily, some require that data is treated equally. There can therefore be no single rule that achieves all objectives, which is to say that absolute net neutrality is not a plausible policy. Instead, a combination of measures is needed to achieve all goals at the same time (Bauer and Obar 2014). The primary aim of any set of regulations about internet data treatment has to be to protect free internet access and the use of human rights online because these considerations are morally more important than private profit motives as such or the increase of consumer welfare when this pertains to optional, non-essential uses of the internet (e.g. for entertainment and convenience-enhancing purposes). A human rights-promoting scheme of rules on the treatment of data on the internet that keeps access free from arbitrary interference by ISPs would entail the following directives:

First, at the network level of the internet, by default ISPs should have to treat all traffic equally, which includes a ban on the practice of zero-rating. Only this rule safeguards the internet as a 'decentralised environment for social [, political,] and cultural interaction in which anyone can participate' (van Schewick 2010: 359), where marginalised voices meet powerful ones on an equal footing, and where concentrations of power through the ability to purchase better delivery of information are thwarted. General net neutrality also ensures a level playing field for innovations in online applications and content that is relevant for human rights.[7]

Second, deviations from net neutrality are permissible where these are necessary and proportionate means for ensuring the management and security of internet networks, that is for resolving of network congestion and for blocking malware and spam.

Third, if discriminatory treatment of data becomes necessary for managing network traffic, and when human rights-data therefore comes into competition with other (e.g. commercial) data, the moral importance of human rights justifies rules that require ISPs to prioritise certain data that is relevant for the exercise of human rights. Such an online equivalent of 'must-carry' rules could apply to the data of specifically recognised activities or services that are highly relevant for human rights,[8] such as government websites that provide public information or services, publicly accredited education and healthcare providers, cultural institutions such as museums, and media presences of public broadcasters. The mandated prioritisation of human rights-data would

---

[7] To be effective, this default also requires a clear separation of regular internet traffic from so-called specialised services that have the purpose of guaranteeing the quality of particular communications (e.g. voice-over-IP for telephony services). These operate through closed, private virtual or physical networks that are separate from internet networks but share the same physical infrastructure and are exempt from net neutrality rules. If these services are not kept separate from regular internet traffic or are expanded at the expense of internet traffic bandwidth, they would externally 'degrade the capacity of […] Internet access […] as a whole' (Sørensen 2016: 104).

[8] 'Must-carry' rules force cable TV networks to broadcast licensed local TV stations owing to limited broadcast frequencies available and/or the monopolised position of cable TV networks (Bhagwat 2021: 108).

not objectionably interfere with the freedom of ISPs because, according to the Guiding Principles, as private companies they have obligations to ensure their business operations do not harm human rights. Just like other firms, ISPs' freedom to conduct business is morally limited by the rights of people and important public interests (e.g. to public order, public health, or national security, see Maroni 2021: 534).

Finally, net neutrality rules do not have to apply to how ISPs must treat the data of the most powerful internet-based corporations, which the EU's Digital Markets Act identifies as 'gatekeepers' (European Commission 2023c) based on their dominant market position. From the perspective of human rights, allowing ISPs to charge these gatekeepers more for an equal (but not for better/preferential) delivery of their content can be justifiable because it does not impose additional costs on citizens for exercising their rights online. These gatekeepers normally provide free services (Facebook, Google, TikTok) or morally non-essential services (Amazon, Netflix). On the other hand, though, if ISPs make it more expensive for mega-corporations to transmit their content with equal quality of service as everyone else to end-users, this could address ISPs' claim that they deserve a greater share of internet-generated profits as a matter of fairness. More importantly, though, such a rule would also enable them to generate the funds that they claim they require to expand their fixed and mobile broadband infrastructure, which would in turn benefit people's opportunities to use the internet for exercising their human rights online.

However, even if other rules would be more effective in achieving the legitimate purposes of data traffic management, any scheme of regulations should give priority to the use of human rights online over the maximisation of profits and consumption because human rights data is morally more important than other uses of data. Only in this way can public authorities ensure that they perform their obligations to protect human rights from private companies and to keep internet access free from being arbitrarily constrained by businesses.[9]

---

[9] In 2019, the UK Labour Party as part of its parliamentary elections campaign adopted the pledge to nationalise the country's broadband infrastructure and to offer free, high-speed broadband access to all households by 2023 (BBC News 2019). Public broadband ownership has also been advocated for by others, for example, for the purpose of 'curbing the domination of tech companies and enabling the popular control of digital services' (Muldoon 2022). There might be other good reasons for states to take into public ownership their country's broadband infrastructure such as generating revenue through usage collected from internet businesses. Moreover, public ownership can come in different shapes such as municipal broadband networks and privately run municipal networks (see European Commission 2022b). There are also, though, reasons against taking broadband infrastructure out of private hands because doing so might, for example, make it extremely easy for governments to monitor citizens' use of the internet. It might be objected that (as we saw in Chapter 6) private

7.4 CONCLUSION

In this chapter, we have considered the most important ways that private companies, which have established and now own large parts of the network and application/content levels of the internet, can arbitrarily interfere with, and therefore undermine, people's free access and use of this important medium. However, as the UN has clarified, private corporations have moral obligations to respect human rights in their business activities and states have obligations to convert these duties into legal regulations. This chapter has identified some of the main ways in which private businesses currently arbitrarily interfere with people's human rights online as well as the obligations that public authorities have to keep internet access and use free. States can fulfil their duties by creating legally binding regulations that set boundaries for the attempts of companies to maximise profits using the internet. Here, we have focused on three standard threats to free internet access that corporations currently pose for free internet access and use.

First, the extremely lucrative business of surveillance capitalism is not compatible with people's human right to privacy. Internet users have no realistic options to avoid having to accept the dominant internet corporation's one-sided, privacy destroying policies and ToS. Because internet that is free from arbitrary interference and privacy are both necessary elements of decent lives, public authorities should enforce fiduciary obligations on private data handling firms. The fiduciary model is a familiar instrument designed to protect weaker parties from stronger ones that could abuse their informational advantage. Fiduciary obligations entail duties of care, confidentiality, and loyalty for the handling of personal data. Imposing these rules would upend one of the currently most profitable business models in the world. However, surveillance capitalist firms' interest in profit is morally insignificant compared with the human rights of people that states must protect.

Second, SMPs are some of the dominant and most powerful private players in the online sphere. Their arbitrary interferences with people's human rights are not limited to compromising their users' privacy, though. Rather, in their

---

ownership did not keep the US NSA and the UK GCHQ from forcing private companies to hand over their users' data to the government either. These companies, though, could at least have appealed to independent courts to protect their clients against illegitimate mass surveillance. However, what is decisive from the perspective of the human right to free internet access is whether public broadband ownership is necessary for the free use of human rights online. Because net neutrality has been successfully implemented in many countries, this does not appear to be the case. This book will therefore not engage in the debate about private versus public internet infrastructure ownership.

current form, these giant corporations also have too much power over other human rights, such as free speech and free information. SMPs fulfil important functions in the public sphere. As editors or curators of cultural, social, and political perspectives they are intermediary institutions that help shape public opinion. Their powers to exclude certain expressions and persons from their private forums that today make up a significant part of the virtual public sphere are currently problematic because these corporations have become too few and powerful for people to have adequate opportunities to join alternative platforms if they or their views are refused representation on the dominant SMPs. On the other hand, SMPs also have the ability and obligation to ensure that the speech that occurs in their spaces does not violate people's rights. States therefore ought to impose regulation on SMPs that does several things at once. Public authorities should require SMPs to adopt Article 19.3 of the ICCPR as a bottom floor of permissible free speech. SMPs on their part should voluntarily adopt the article's reasoning so they can make principled decisions as to which content to permit even if states ask them for too much or too little content exclusion. To hold SMPs to account for any non-compliance with these minimum standards, public authorities should impose intermediary or distributor liability of the platforms. This would require SMPs to take down human rights-violating content within a certain notice period or otherwise make them legally liable for it. Beyond this, though, states should use legal instruments such as competition law to break up the existing oligopoly of SMPs. Only if there is a multitude of SMPs can the ends of free speech and other human rights be realised. In the current situation, people do not have an adequate range of options if they or their speech is excluded from the major platforms because the latter have editorial or curatorial rights to set their own ToS.

Finally, at the network level of the internet, public authorities should impose a human rights-promoting interpretation of net neutrality on ISPs. These should by default have to treat all data traffic equally unless discrimination is necessary or targets the most powerful gatekeeper content/application providers. Charging the biggest corporations more to treat their data equally would enable ISPs to generate funds they can use to maintain, enhance, or expand their existing broadband infrastructure in ways that do not negatively affect individuals' internet access or their human rights online. According to this model, exceptions to net neutrality are acceptable if they are necessary and serve maintenance and security purposes or if they are designed to prioritise human rights-data traffic during times of network congestion.

Public authorities have all these duties to regulate private businesses because they have obligations to protect human rights from firms' profit motives and activities. The specific duties of states that this chapter identified are the protection of people's right to freely access the internet without thereby having to compromise their privacy, the guarantee of an adequate range of virtual platforms where people can exercise their human rights, and to ensure that the data that people generate or seek out is treated equally by ISPs without additional costs of any kind. Implementing the obligations does not impose unacceptable costs on private companies. After all, their interest in profit maximisation is outweighed by the moral urgency of people's human rights.

All duties that arise from the human right to free internet access for public institutions have as their main obstacle resistance against political regulations by powerful corporate interests. Lack of political clout is particularly a problem for developing nations. It is likely that internet businesses would shun these countries if they tried on their own to end surveillance capitalism or enforce a breaking up of the services of SMPs within their territory. The situation of developing countries with respect to free internet access is like that of their position in the global garment trade. Allowing powerful foreign businesses to manufacture their products in human rights-violating conditions means that these countries are not properly protecting the human rights of their citizens against corporate interests. However, if these states were to ban the problematic production practices, foreign investment and domestic jobs would disappear leaving their citizens even worse off. For this reason, the primary responsibility for changing human rights violating business practices lies with those powerful states where the global corporations are based. These states, which also benefit the most from the companies' operations, must protect the human rights of people in other nations too from unjustifiable business practices of the companies that they have jurisdiction over. This, again, is not a matter of technological feasibility but of political will. The UN Guiding Principles, though, are – as we saw – quite clear that all states have obligations under international human rights agreements to prevent human rights abuses everywhere by companies within their jurisdiction.

In Chapter 8, the final chapter, we will consider what further obligations public authorities have as part of the human right to free internet access to protect end-users from the standard threats posed by the actions of other internet users.

8

Other Internet Users as Standard Threats

Chapters 6 and 7 have explained how states and private companies pose standard threats to free internet access, and what public authorities have to do to protect internet users from these powerful agents. But even if the dangers posed by states and businesses were resolved, there would still be at least one other significant group of agents that generally poses threats to free internet access and to the unimpeded use of human rights online. That group consists of internet users themselves. Sadly, there is a long list of ways in which individuals (who do not operate in the name of states or private businesses) misuse the internet and the possibilities it offers to harm or violate the rights of other people online. Examples of such 'individual digital harms' include online fraud and other cybercrimes such as identity theft, the distribution of child and revenge pornography, and 'doxing' (the act of illicitly publishing personally identifiable information online). Moreover, there are important individual digital harms in the form of various kinds of dangerous speech such as threats of death, rape, or injury; incitement of racial hatred and violence; the dissemination of fake news and conspiracy theories; cyberbullying; and trolling.

Although all these digital harms are morally objectionable, not all of them are illegal. In many countries harmful speech (e.g. trolling, certain forms of cyberbullying, unspecific calls for violence, and the dissemination of conspiracy theories) is protected by free speech rights. Even though they are undesirable, it is important that many instances of harmful speech are not legally punishable. As we saw in Chapter 1, not everything that is morally objectionable (e.g. the breaking of moral rules such as the rule not to lie or the violation of moral rights such as the trust among friends or of a romantic partner) is appropriately subject to public coercion. People have the liberty to make mistakes, to believe things they accept, and to say things that are objectionable if they do not violate others' legally protected rights. For this they might be liable to various kinds of criticism. But to make their errors a matter for legal sanctions would cause more harm than good because most would probably refrain from many things people normally do to avoid punishment in case they commit mistakes. On the other hand, people have no general right to be insulated from things they do not approve of or are offended by. The free exercise of our rights, online and offline, will inevitably lead to some forms of harm that we cause to others. However, many individual digital harms mentioned earlier (e.g. child pornography, death and rape threats, or harms specifically engendered by the internet and digital technology such as revenge pornography) constitute clear violations of the moral and legal rights of people and are therefore not protected by free speech rights.

Because of the severity of illegal digital harms committed by individuals, it is crucial that public institutions protect internet users not only from abuses of state power and the power of private companies, but also from arbitrary interferences with each other's internet access and use. However, in protecting individuals' rights from harm that they might cause each other, states also have to respect people's rights, the legitimate exercise of which can be the cause of harm that is not properly subject to legal sanctions. To understand what public authorities must do as part of a human right to free internet access to counter online harms and rights violations committed by individual internet users against each other, it is useful to consider three general conditions that must be met for people to enjoy any rights anywhere (which is to say offline and online).

1. Rights enforcement: The rights of individuals must be enforced by public authorities from attacks by other individuals and rights violations must be punished. As the UN General Assembly's 2016 unbinding resolution clarifies, it considers it a duty of member states to ensure that 'the same rights that people have offline must also be protected online' (UN 2016: 2). For example, as a basic condition of their legitimate authority over us, within their jurisdictions, states must protect our basic human liberties such as those to life, bodily integrity, and liberty. If a fellow citizen wants to deprive us of these, the state should intervene and to punish those who violate our rights. If it does not do that, it fails to fulfil one of the fundamental tasks and reasons that we grant states coercive power and legal authority over us for in the first place (Reglitz 2015).

2. Environment: The environment in which people live and exercise their rights must be protected from predicable dangers and harms that are not posed by other individuals but by larger structural forces. In Chapters 6 and 7 we saw that free online access and the exercise of human rights online is only possible if states as well as businesses do not arbitrarily interfere with our access and use of the internet. Because states and private

companies currently do not follow this demand, they presently create an online environment in which people are unjustifiably restricted in their access to, and use of, the internet. Equally, individuals can only safely live and be guaranteed enjoyment of their human rights in a natural environment that is not polluted, destroyed, or otherwise uninhabitable. That is why environmental protection regulations are essential for ensuring that with their operations businesses do not undermine the rights of people. Moreover, climate change is not merely a meteorological issue but rather an urgent moral one, in part because it poses a great danger to our human rights and those of future generations (Caney 2010, Moellendorf 2014).

3. Education and resources: Finally, individuals need certain resources and skills to be able to exercise and protect their rights. For example, we have a human right to education (in part) because, without basic knowledge about our world and our options, many of the freedoms we have in our personal lives would be of little practical use to us. This book argues that internet access is a resource needed today for our human rights to be of adequate worth. Similarly, without knowledge of health risks such as sexually transmittable diseases and to how prevent acquiring them, people are unable to protect their health from these avoidable harms. Equally, knowledge and availability of contraception methods is essential for having an effective choice about having children.

If any of these three conditions are not met, people's rights are not adequately protected because they lack important guarantees and means to actually enjoy their (human and other) rights. That is why (as explained in Chapter 1) public authorities are obligated to provide certain social guarantees against what regularly threatens our rights. Individuals pose standard threats to each other's rights online if their behaviour is left unchecked and/or if they have to operate in an environment that is not conducive to the enjoyment of rights. This chapter will therefore address all three necessary conditions of the enjoyment of our rights online to explain what public authorities have to do to protect free internet access from transgressions by individuals. The chapter will conclude with a summary of the identifiable duties that public authorities can be said to have to mitigate the standard threats to free internet access and rights enjoyment online posed by individual internet users for each other.

8.1 ONLINE RIGHTS ABUSES AND ENFORCEMENT

Rights are social guarantees against standard threats. The most basic protection we need from public authorities for our rights is security guarantees against attacks by other people. Physical security is also one of three basic rights that Henry Shue identifies whose fulfilment is a condition of the enjoyment of (at least most) other rights (Shue 2020). Online, individuals routinely become the victims of individual digital harms done to them by other individuals. Examples include, as mentioned, cybercrime, child and revenge pornography, personal threats, dangerous incitement of racial hatred and violence, the dissemination of fake news and conspiracy theories, cyberbullying, and trolling. Some harms, such as trolling and some forms of cyberbullying and hate speech are permissible in many countries because the right to free expression is seen to outweigh the moral relevance of the harms they cause.

For the purposes of outlining the duties of states to protect the rights of internet users from violations by other individuals, it is therefore helpful to focus on those harms that constitute clear violations of rights, and which public authorities are dutybound to police. Among these are cybercrimes; the distribution of child and revenge pornography; specific threats of murder, rape, injury; and detailed incitements of violence towards individuals. None of these are protected by the human right to free speech. As explained in Chapter 7 (2.3.1), the human right to free expression does not protect all speech. According to Article 19.3 of the International Covenant on Civil and Political Rights (ICCPR), free expression can be justly limited if this is necessary and proportionate for pursuing legitimate goals such as the protection of the rights of others (including their reputation) and important social goods (e.g. public health, public order, national security). Public authorities are therefore justified in prosecuting a significant range of harmful online speech acts. In analysing the duties of states concerning the protection of rights online, we will abstract from the problems of mass surveillance by states, digital authoritarianism, surveillance capitalism, and concentrated social media platform (SMP) power because these have been addressed in the previous chapters. What we are interested in here instead are the standard threats that individuals would be exposed to in a world in which free internet access is already free from arbitrary interferences by states and businesses.

The German 2018 Network Enforcement Act, the European Union's 2020 Digital Services Act (crucial parts of which only came into effect in August 2023), and the UK's proposed Online Safety Bill all indicate that the most powerful public institutions have only recently begun systematically and legally to address many online harms by requiring SMPs to censor and take down certain forms of harmful speech that are deemed impermissible. The US (home to the leading SMPs outside China) has not even passed a national law that specifically addresses and limits illegal online content. Nonetheless, morally it is quite uncontroversial that states have duties to protect their citizens' rights from online attacks by other individuals. It does not matter whether a person threatens to kill, rape, or maim another online rather than in a written letter, that someone tries to defraud another using a phishing email rather than visiting their physical doorstep, or that child and revenge pornography are shared online rather than through physical compact discs. As a condition of legitimately wielding coercive power over their citizens, states must protect people from such attacks and prosecute those committing offences. However, as mentioned earlier, the difference between legal and illegal content as well as having to protect people's rights online has posed particular difficulties for public authorities. To understand these challenges, it is useful to take a brief look at the case of a German law that is specifically intended to tackle dangerous online speech. Even though the law has the important purpose of protecting people online, it has been criticised for its scope as well as for the means it employs to achieve its ends.

Germany is at the forefront of enforcing individual rights online by punishing impermissible speech online. Modern German history includes the Nazi tyranny that essentially rested on stirring up and exploiting ethnic and religious hatred among citizens. In part motivated by the country's genocidal recent past, in 2018 the German government introduced the Network Enforcement Act (NEA) (Bennhold 2018). At its core, this law enforces distributor liability on SMPs with more than 2 million users (Wikipedia 2023c). The law threatens such platforms with fines (a maximum of EUR €50 Million) if they do not take down within seven days content that clearly or likely violates German free speech laws. As such, the purpose of the law reflects important arguments in Chapter 7 (Section 7.2.3.4) that SMPs should be forced to remove content they host that clearly is not protected by the human right to free speech. However, the German NEA has been widely criticised because of the extensive notion of punishable speech specified by the German criminal code that it enforces. According to the German criminal code (which also reflects the country's experience with National Socialism) illegal speech acts are any incitements of hatred that offend human dignity based on the target's ethnic, national, racial, or religious features; the denial of the Holocaust; the public display of Nazi symbols; and defiling the memory of the dead (Glaun 2021). But critics, such as the international human rights organisation Article 19, have criticised the German criminal code and the NEA for its criminalisation of 'prohibitions of "defamation of religion", broad concepts of "hate speech", and criminal defamation and insult' (Article 19 2017: 2). Article 19 and others reject the German criminal code's notion of impermissible speech as incompatible with the protections offered for free expression by ICCPR Article 19 because it criminalises forms of speech that Article 19 argues must be considered permissible, such as some forms of defamation, insults, and even certain forms of hate speech. Moreover, because what counts as illegal content according to the NEA is defined in broad and vague terms, Article 19 and other critics of the law (such as the UN Special Rapporteur on the Promotion and Protection of the Right Freedom of Opinion and Expression) fear that it leads to an over-censoring of legitimate free speech by SMPs, which are exercising caution about what they publish to avoid significant fines (UN 2017). The German law and the criticism it has received therefore exemplify the difficult balance that public authorities have to strike between protecting people from individual digital harms and respecting people's rights.

However, Germany is also a particular case of rights protection online because its criminal agencies do not only rely on the co-operation of SMPs to identify and punish offenders. Instead, German law enforcement agencies have established their own departments (such as the Central Point of Contact for Criminal Content on the Internet (FRA 2023) of the Federal Criminal Police Office (BKA), the Center for Combating Cybercrime (ZIT) at the Prosecutor General's Office Frankfurt am Main (ZIT 2023), and other German state-based agencies such as the Centre for Combating of Hate Crimes on the Internet (ZHIN 2023) of the state of Lower Saxony or the Reporting Centre for Cybercrime (BKA 2023) of the state of North Rhine-Westphalia) that prosecute child pornography, darknet criminality, cybercrimes, and online hate speech. Prosecutors of these agencies identify criminal online speech acts, such as death threats, and take those committing them to court. If legally convicted, offenders face fines of several thousand Euros for their illegal online speech acts. Even though prosecutors cannot punish all offences in this way, their aim is to generally change the behaviour of online users as potential attackers learn that they risk being criminally charged and fined for illegal online speech. By clamping down on punishable online speech, public law enforcement agencies hope to protect citizens rights and free speech by defending those who are silenced by online hate speech. According to the *New York Times*, more than 1,000 people were in this way charged with and fined for online-speech related crimes in Germany between 2018 and 2022 (Satariano and Schuetze 2022). However, the operations of these new internet crime prosecution agencies have faced criticism. One important objection relates, again, to the broad definition of illegal speech in the German criminal code that these agencies are enforcing, and which according to critics renders as offences expressions that should be legal according to ICCPR Article 19. Another point of criticism pertains to reports of criminal investigations into citizens whose online expressions cannot be deemed illegal even according to the extensive definitions of illegal speech of the German code. In one such instance, a citizen's house was raided by police in search of evidence after they had posted online the insult 'dick' directed at a local public official (Satariano and Schuetze 2022). The way that illegal online speech is prosecuted, and the legal safeguards there are against prosecution failures, therefore matter decisively for protecting people's rights from law enforcement overreach.

Despite clear problems with the way individuals' rights are defended from online attacks in Germany, an important point to be taken from the German case is that states are capable of protecting people from harmful and illegal online speech if they are willing to strike a plausible balance between the protection of rights and free expression. If public authorities define and prosecute impermissible speech too broadly, this leads to over-censorship of protected speech – either because it is directly banned or because online service providers take down permissible speech because they want to minimise their risk of being fined for distributing illegal content. If states define impermissible speech too narrowly, though, the rights of those who become victims of illegal speech are infringed without consequences. As we saw in Chapter 7 (Section 7.2.3.1), not enforcing bans on impermissible speech online can also be a tactic of governments to create a climate of misinformation and aggression that is favourable to those in power but inhospitable to free public discourse. In any case, if illegal speech is not policed, the likely effect is that people's rights (such as free expression) and democratic values suffer as those who are attacked withdraw from public discourse. This explains why the non-enforcement or very permissive interpretations of free speech are not morally neutral political choices. Any laws and attempts to protect individuals' rights online can of course be abused by states to silence critics and to persecute dissenters. However, this risk does not undermine the argument that public authorities, as a matter of safeguarding existing rights online as well as the human right to free internet, ought to try to enforce their citizens' human rights on the internet in accordance with the spirit and letter of international human rights law.

8.1.1 *Rights Enforcement and Online Anonymity*

As we have seen, some public authorities have begun to attempt to prosecute illegal speech online and to force SMPs to better protect the rights of their users. Many states such as the US (Holpuch 2023) and the UK (Hall 2023) indeed already punish other cybercrimes such as child and revenge pornography. However, states face specific challenges when they try to protect human rights online from attacks by individuals because the internet has proven to be a sphere that is more difficult for public authorities to police than their physical jurisdictions. Cyberspace remains an environment that is conducive for individual acts of harm because 'it is a space that sprawls jurisdictions, it develops at a faster pace than regulation, and it allows great degrees of anonymity and secrecy for those wanting to commit wrongdoing with impunity' (Trengrove et al. 2022: 1). Online anonymity in particular poses complex challenges for public authorities. If perpetrators of online attacks on others' rights only provide non-identifying information, their identity cannot be directly known. Currently, many dangerous and illicit online speech acts are in fact committed by people who do *not* hide their identity. This is because the public nature of their attacks increases their standing among like-minded others. But if public authorities were (as they ought) to begin prosecuting publicly committed online rights violations as is happening in Germany, it can be expected that an increasing number of such offences will be committed anonymously as attackers try to avoid legal punishments.

But internet user anonymity is not simply a problem for states because it makes those violating individual rights difficult to identify. Rather, anonymity is a complex issue because it is also a particularly valuable feature for everyone. Simply imposing a duty on all internet users to be permanently identifiable therefore does not provide a plausible solution because such a step would cause more moral harm than good. As explained in Chapter 6, states must generally permit anonymity and promote data encryption because banning them in general would be disproportionate and overall harmful for people and their rights. Chapters 6 and 7 have shown that ensuring privacy is essential for individuals' ability to protect themselves from the illegitimate interests of states and businesses, and for developing their own personality. Positively, being anonymous in public (either offline or online) offers a way for people to exercise their autonomy while protecting their privacy and identity. In writing anonymously or by using pseudonyms, people can present socially useful or novel ideas, arguments, or factual knowledge while protecting themselves from those whose interests are set back by such expressions. Negatively, though, anonymity enables those who harm others to avoid accountability for their actions (Véliz 2019: 644, 645). The internet therefore creates specific challenges that require technological solutions to protect both rights and anonymity. In what follows, we consider two such technical mechanisms that have been proposed as solutions for simultaneously protecting rights and user anonymity. These examples also show, though, that there are no easy solutions to this problem, and that all efforts are likely to face their own challenges.

The first of these technological solutions is proposed by Carissa Véliz and takes the form of an international databank of non-public or unlinked pseudonyms (Véliz 2019: 652). According to this proposal, internet users would either have to use identifying information or pseudonyms when active online.

If they choose to use pseudonyms to protect their identity, internet users would have to register their pseudonyms with a politically independent, international pseudonym agency. This specialised institution would in turn have fiduciary responsibilities to protect the information about its users' real identities. However, if an internet user commits offences online, public authorities could contact the databank with a request for the identifying information connected to the pseudonym that was used for committing the rights violations. As a consequence of abusing their anonymity for committing offences, internet users could also lose (at least temporarily) the option of using online pseudonyms at all so that they would have to conduct their online activities without the protection of anonymity. Véliz plausibly argues that such a pseudonym databank would have to be an international agency because national pseudonym databanks would not protect but undermine anonymity in autocratic nations by centrally holding identifying personal information about all citizens who are active online.

Véliz's proposal is designed to protect both individual rights and anonymity in a balanced way. However, her solution would likely encounter at least two significant obstacles. First, as with all international governance agencies, it would be difficult to ensure the databank's political independence from powerful states. States would likely have to provide the funds to set up and operate the pseudonyms databank. Moreover, states would have to co-operate with and accept the authority of the databank for the system to work. However, the realities of international power politics (e.g. the non-recognition of the International Criminal Court by powerful countries such as the US, Russia, and China) suggest that an authoritative and politically independent pseudonym databank is unlikely to become a reality in our world of competing and often human rights-disregarding nation states. Second, even if an independent pseudonym databank could be established, it would present an extremely tempting target for data theft for all kinds of agents (such as autocratic as well as democratic governments, criminal actors, and powerful commercial enterprises) that have an interest in identifying online users. Data that has been collected can be stolen. In this way, the mechanism of a pseudonym databank would create new vulnerabilities for individuals that currently do not exist and that might be avoidable with other solutions.

One alternative approach called the 'login trap' has been suggested by the German think tank D64 – Centre for Digital Progress (D64 2021). This organisation campaigns for changing internet politics and the internet itself in line with basic liberties. The login trap was incorporated into the 2021 coalition treaty of the German government to be tested as a solution to the prosecution of online crimes in a way that protects internet user anonymity. The procedure operates analogously to judicial warrants that lift the privacy of particular suspects to enable the prosecution of crimes. Under the login trap proposal, internet users generally retain their anonymity. However, if a person commits offences in online forums (e.g. in the form of illegal speech), other internet users can report these to criminal prosecutors who in turn can supply the evidence to a court to obtain a warrant for the lifting of the offender's anonymity. The prosecutors can then use this warrant to require platform operators to help identify the suspect by providing them with the offender's IP address. Online platform operators can obtain the suspect's IP address when the suspect logs into their platform user account the next time. In this way, the offender's identity can be found out using an individual authorisation from an independent judicial authority. This process avoids a general ban on online user anonymity and the need to record the identifying information of all internet users. For these reasons, the login trap offers a solution that is superior to an international pseudonym databank. However, the login trap, too, encounters challenges.

First, to work as intended, the system presupposes public authorities that respect the rule of law and the separation of powers, and states that are motivated to protect rather than to undermine their citizens' rights. As we saw in Chapter 6, today even established democracies are tempted to violate the privacy and anonymity of their citizens so that this might seem an unrealistic precondition. On the other hand, in this chapter, for the sake of the argument we suppose that states actually protect rather than compromise free internet access for their citizens by fulfilling the obligations set out in Chapter 6 so that we abstract from this complication. Moreover, all democratic goods (such as an independent judiciary, free and fair elections, and a free press) are only protected if they have the support of governments and are defended by widespread public support. There are many instances that show that such political and popular support for democratic institutions is possible. The condition of political support is therefore not a fatal one for the login trap. A second, more inherent issue with the login trap might be that over time perpetrators of online harm and crimes might become more technologically savvy in their attempts to avoid identification. They might, for instance, increasingly use virtual private networks (VPNs) to avoid detection of their IP address. However, the ensuing technological arms race would be nothing new or unexpected, and public authorities would have to try to refine their methods to identify individual offenders.

More important for our present discussion is the point that the two examples highlight general criteria for how public authorities should go about the prosecution of online attacks on individual rights. States and public authorities have clear obligations to protect their citizens and users from attacks by other individuals. But in doing so, they must follow human rights principles. These require that the prosecution efforts of public authorities are legally authorised, minimally intrusive, necessary, proportionate, and pursue legitimate aims. This importantly means that enforcement practices ought to be maximally protective of internet user anonymity. The details of which solution meets these requirements best are to a significant extent a matter of what is technologically possible. However, the two suggestions canvassed here indicate that the matter of enforcing human rights online while generally respecting internet user privacy and anonymity is a technical 'how-best-to' issue rather than a normative 'whether-or-not' question. Human rights-respecting and properly motivated governments can work with online service providers to ensure that illegal speech does not undermine individual rights and public discourse online. The first condition of securing internet users' rights online, then, is that these rights are being enforced and their violations policed by public authorities that are properly motivated, checked by independent institutions such as courts, and use methods of rights enforcement that are respectful of the very rights they aim to protect.

8.2 ONLINE MISINFORMATION, POLARISATION, AND AN ENVIRONMENT CONDUCIVE FOR RIGHTS

A second condition of people's enjoyment of their rights is that individuals live in an environment that is favourable to the protection and use of their rights. This regards their physical (i.e. ecological) as well as socio-political environments. Chapters 6 and 7 set out duties for public authorities to protect the socio-political environments of internet users from unjustifiable encroachments by states and private companies. Beyond this, though, secure rights enjoyment also requires an adequate *informational* environment. It is this informational environment that the human right to free internet access aims to protect. The informational environment encompasses all sources that can introduce information into the public sphere that are subject to regulation by the government. However, beyond the informational environment, people also inhabit social environments that can either be conducive or detrimental to their rights. As we will see in this section, social and informational environments affect each other (e.g. when political divisions lead opponents to willingly promote misinformation or when misinformation deepens political divisions). Moreover, the informational environment of digitalised societies today is relevant for this chapter because, if the informational environment is unprotected and polluted by 'bad' information, it can cause individuals to attack the rights of others online. Political violence generally has often been motivated by false claims about the victims (e.g. in the Middle Ages that Jewish people poisoned communal wells, according to the Nazis that the Jews orchestrate a global cabal to achieve world domination, or the belief of the perpetrators of recent mass shootings that Muslims and other non-white immigrants are trying to replace native white populations in Western countries). Political divisions and rights violations are therefore important reasons for widely shared concerns that the internet has worsened the informational environment in democratic societies by creating or exacerbating problems such as political polarisation and misinformation (owing to echo chambers, filter bubbles, and the spread of fake news and online conspiracy theories).

Worries about attacks on individuals' rights motivated by false information are not unfounded because empirical observations show that political polarisation and misinformation reduces people's willingness to act civilly towards others and to be open to respectful interactions with them. For example, a 2021 survey by the Pew Research Center on the state of online harassment in the US found that 41 per cent of Americans reported experiencing some form of online harassment (physical threats, stalking, sustained harassment, sexual harassment, offensive name-calling, purposeful embarrassment) (Vogels 2021: 4). Importantly, 20 per cent of Americans (half of those reporting harassment) said that they have been harassed because of their political views (Vogels 2021: 5). Moreover, questions of sexual identity are known to be highly political topics, and roughly 70 per cent of surveyed non-binary Americans have experienced (often extreme kinds of) online harassment (Vogels 2021: 8). This link between political polarisation and aggression is unsurprising if one considers that online hate speech has important benefits for those who attack others verbally online. Expressing negativity towards perceived opponents can, for example, signal one's group membership and promote in-group cohesion. In these ways, social media communications have been found to have important identity- and group-affirming functions (Lupu et al. 2023: 1). Correspondingly, the philosopher Elizabeth Anderson argues that many seemingly absurd political statements that people endorse or promote online (such as insults, conspiracy theories, or fake news) should not be understood as statements of belief. Rather, if people make such statements in a political context, this 'may signal whose side one is on, who is the enemy, or doesn't belong, who is illegitimate, who is superior to whom' (Anderson 2021: 23). As such, online actions that are harmful to others can have a crucial 'identity-expressive' function for those committing attacks on others. Political divisions and strife are therefore relevant for understanding many instances of harmful and rights-disrespecting online behaviour.

If the internet really leads to an increase in political polarisation and misinformation, and if political polarisation and misinformation motivate people to violate each other's rights online, public authorities have reasons to combat these harms to reduce such attacks. More problematically for the argument of this book, though, if it is inevitable that the internet creates an information environment that is hostile to the protection of individual rights, the argument for the human right to free internet access would be a tragic one. This is because it would mean that those who use the internet to increase their opportunities to enjoy their rights at the same time face greater risks of attacks on their rights when they are online. Even worse, people's rights might become more endangered even if they choose not to go online. This is because as long as others use the internet, they can be affected by online misinformation and become motivated to express negative attitudes or violate the rights of those who remain offline whom they perceive as opponents. In this case, the internet would inevitably have a Janus-faced role for human rights: it enhances them but at the same time inevitably makes them less secure.

However, this negative techno-deterministic view of the internet's effects on the information environment of digitalised societies is unfounded, as we will see in the following sections. Because it has become the dominant medium for sharing and obtaining information, the internet certainly plays a role in problems such as political polarisation and misinformation. But the best available evidence also shows that the internet is not the primary or sole cause of these issues. Rather, there are larger societal trends and factors (e.g. socio-economic inequality, the behaviour of political elites, socio-political uncertainty, as well as inadequate education) that drive developments such as increased political antagonism and the spread of false information. Even though the internet has enabled new ways of sharing false information and finding people who have ill intentions towards others, it is for the most part merely the medium through which general societal developments operate and express themselves. This also means that simply trying to 'fix' the internet is unlikely to address the more deeply rooted problems of political divisions, misinformation, and increasing attacks and hostility among internet users. To understand how states can better protect individuals' rights and improve the informational environment of their citizens, it is therefore necessary for us to look at the issues of political polarisation, misinformation, echo chambers, filter bubbles, fake news, and online conspiracy theories.

8.2.1 Media Policy Failures and Importance of Independent Public Service Broadcast

Informational environments can be conducive or detrimental for the enjoyment of rights depending on how much false information they contain. When considering the role that the internet plays for the informational environment, the first important point to note is that the internet is but one – if crucial – component of that environment. Other vital elements of a free society's informational environment entail traditional mass media such as newspapers, television, radio stations, as well as government-operated news sources. All of them supply people with information that shapes their personal views and goals. For people to live together peacefully and co-operatively, they do not have to agree on their community's goals or on what is good and right. However, they have to share a minimum view of what is factually the case in their world to be able to openly communicate, debate, and co-operate with each other (Rosa 2022: 22–23). If citizens disagree too much about common goals, common threats, or about important events, they are unlikely to share enough beliefs about the world and to sufficiently trust others to co-operate with them. Instead, they are more likely to retreat to the social group they identify with and to act with hostility towards those they perceive as their political opponents. The information that is provided to citizens by all elements of the informational environment therefore matters tremendously for whether a society functions co-operatively, and for how individual citizens perceive and treat each other.

When we consider the informational environments of leading democracies during the last few decades it becomes clear that these suffered from informational distortions long before the internet became widespread. This matters because, even if the internet might have exacerbated the spread of false or skewed information, important causes of these problems precede it. Tackling online information problems will therefore not fix a society's informational environment nor is a focus on the internet alone likely to heal political divisions and the deeply felt antipathy that motivates some to dislike and/or attack others. As to the main causes of worsening information environments, the media and communication theorist Des Freedman (2021) identifies four regulatory media policy failures that have occurred since 1980 in leading democracies. All these developments (some, but not all, related to the internet) have exacerbated political divisions, conflict, and hostility among different political factions and have made co-operation and acceptance of differences less likely.

The first regulatory policy failure of many democratic states has been their failure to address concentrated private media ownership in television, radio, and online information businesses. In a 2016 study of thirty countries, the top ten media content companies 'account for an average of 67 percent of national market share while the top four digital platforms account for a whopping 88 percent of their national media markets' (Freedman 2021: 414). The problem with concentrated private media ownership is that it gives an outsized voice and disproportionate political influence to those who own these outlets. The concept of private media ownership has been justified with claims that such a regime best promotes innovation in information markets and the profitability of information services. Private media ownership has also been defended as a way for their owners to realise their free speech rights. But in hindsight, the values of free speech, innovation, and financial viability have been undermined by the increased concentration of privately owned media. For example, the benefits of free speech (such as better information for individual and societal decisions) have been hampered rather than promoted by the reduction of competitive informational sources that can present distinct viewpoints and interests to citizens who necessarily have limited attention. Those few information services that have acquired dominant positions (e.g. TV businesses such as Fox News in the US, and print media such as the *Daily Mail* in the UK and *Bild* in Germany) have done so often by employing tactics of division rather than dispassionate reporting. The dominant position of leading private media outlets has in turn provided their owners with a previously unknown agenda-setting and -influencing power that would not be possible in a more diverse and less concentrated media landscape (Freedman 2021: 413–414). As we saw in Chapter 7, mass media outlets with editorial rights are important for curating distinct perspectives. However, in pluralistic democracies, concentrated media ownership is unlikely to reflect realistically existing viewpoints within societies.

The second policy failure identified by Freedman concerns the lack of regulation of Big Tech companies that was one of the topics of Chapter 7. As explained in that chapter, the dominant position of a few online platforms and services is detrimental for people's opportunities to exercise their human rights. But the concentrated power of the few dominant Big Tech platforms is also problematic from the perspective of the informational environment because these dominant internet businesses have acquired and oligopolised the editorial and creative gatekeeping functions of traditional mass media. The biggest online platforms now control and shape vast amounts of information that citizens have access to in ways that maximise their profits (Freedman 2021: 414). As we saw in Chapter 7, these companies present information using algorithmic content curation based on the personal information harvested from users with the goal of maximising engagement with their services. Their aim in doing so is not to help people become better informed and to make better choices. Whether the information presented is conductive or detrimental to the enjoyment of individual rights is not a primary concern or goal of these private online information businesses. Instead, SMPs have 'gamified' communication to maximise user engagement. By adding features such as 'likes', 'retweets', and 'upvoting', the companies incentivise users to seek rewards such as maximising the attention their communications receive from others (Nguyen 2021). Empirical research has shown, though, that emotionally charged message (especially against other groups of people) are likely to receive the most attention (Rathje et al. 2021). Moreover, as we saw in Chapter 7, SMPs allow (or do not effectively remove) content that is not protected by free speech rights. The informational environment therefore suffers from the dominance of businesses that promote political divisions (rather than co-operative interactions or information communications) as collateral damage of their pursuit of profit.

The third policy mistake of democratic governments has been their failure to protect (and instead to rather undermine) the operations of the free press. In important democracies such as the US and the UK, governments have used legislation (such as the US's Espionage Act and the UK's 2016 Investigatory Powers Act) to interfere with the work of journalists when they co-operated with whistle-blowers or when their work was perceived to go against national security goals. As we saw in Chapter 6, in democracies such as Hungary, Mexico, and Poland, governments have used the Pegasus spyware to actively violate the rights of journalists and their sources without independent judicial oversight or legitimate cause. The actions of many democratic governments have therefore obstructed the legitimate work of members of the free press. The work of journalists, though, is essential for holding governments to account and for enabling journalists to provide citizens with information that scrutinises the actions of powerholders. The free press is therefore essential for a functioning informational environment that provides essential resources for the formation of personal and public opinion.

The final media policy failure diagnosed by Freedman regards democracies' failure to sufficiently support and protect independent public service broadcasters (PSBs) (Freedman 2021: 416). The idea behind a PSB, such as the UK's BBC, is to provide the populace with impartial and accurate information on political and societal matters based on politically independent reporting. But the ability of PSBs to fulfil their functions is essentially based on their financial and editorial independence. These are normally secured through institutional independence and a financing model that raises funds directly from the public, and in this way makes PSBs independent of the will of political powerholders or private funders. However, in countries such as the US, PSBs are traditionally underfunded and therefore unable to serve the informational needs of the public. In 2011 and 2012, the per capita spending on public media outlets in the US was USD $3 compared to USD $100–177 in the UK, Germany, and Scandinavia (Benson et al. 2017: 4). In other democracies such as Hungary and Poland, PSBs have become co-opted by the government. Rather than holding officeholders to account, they are instead misused to propagate information that favours the government. Even the British BBC has become increasingly subject to government influence because its leading officials are appointed by the government. Moreover, the government has tried to find ways to replace the BBC's licence fee-based funding model with alternatives that would make the broadcaster less independent and less capable of questioning the actions of those in power (Freedman 2019). Through underfunding or government co-optation, PSBs in many democracies have been prevented from performing their essential task to be independent (and therefore publicly trusted) sources of information that can hold the powerful to account and to inform the public. Political independence and impartial informing of the population is feasible for PSBs, though, if their work is enabled by sufficient political will and democratic support (Benson et al. 2017: 14).

Once we consider the effects of the internet on the informational environment of modern societies, we see that PSBs today fulfil another crucial role besides independent and impartial reporting. An intact informational environment is as essential for the functioning of democracies as is an intact ecological environment or national security. This is because, as previously mentioned, to co-operate and co-exist peacefully, citizens must sufficiently trust each other and share enough beliefs about what the world is like. These essential resources of mutual trust and informational common grounds are threatened if citizens have too widely diverging views about facts, if most information they have access to is shaped and distorted to benefit the particular interests of those who control the information, or if people have lost trust in their dominant informational sources. The internet has allowed everyone who can access it with minimal skills to become the sender of information. In the resulting deluge of information, citizens must be able to identify commonly relied upon and trusted sources of information. The more sources of information there are, the less individuals are capable of assessing the quality of, and the interests behind, each source. The more informational sources there are, the less citizens also have reasons to believe that they consume the same information as their fellow citizens. The over-abundance of information enabled by the internet therefore makes it more difficult for people to share informational common ground with others and to trust that others share their views about the world.

Importantly, the nature of its source matters a great deal for the quality and trustworthiness of information. If, for example, private media ownership is accepted as a way for the owners of media businesses to realise their right to free expression, it must be expected that the information disseminated by these companies reflects and promotes the owner's particular interests rather than constituting an impartial reporting of facts. Therefore, the only source of information that can be independent of particular interests by design is one that the public funds itself. Privately owned news media fulfil an important function by mapping out particular viewpoints on political matters. Private media businesses can also adopt professional journalistic standards in search of consumers who have a demand for accurate reporting. However, as we saw in Chapter 7, profit motives and other private agendas mean that the interests of private media owners and the interest of the public in accurate information diverge or only align if the business owner wants them to. Dispassionate reporting is often therefore eschewed in favour of disseminating what maximises profits or benefits the company's owners in other ways. Moreover, privately owned news media that have to generate profits often do not represent the perspectives of marginal societal groups because these represent fewer potential consumers. Mainstream private news media are often therefore less attractive to marginal societal groups. Structurally, only a PSB that is sufficiently insulated from government influence can service the public's interest in impartial information and is likely to represent the perspective of all parts of society. Only an information provider that is publicly known to be independent can become a trusted source for a sufficiently large part of a population to create the 'social' (Sunstein 2017: 137) or 'national glue' (House of Lords 2022: 10) that is needed for public trust and co-operation. If, on the contrary, most citizens only trust particular news sources that represent the world in incompatible perspectives, they are unlikely to have sufficient informational common ground and mutual trust to work together for the common good.

The uniquely positive effects of PSBs have been repeatedly confirmed by empirical research. According to studies of news media, countries with strong PSBs tend to have citizenries with 'high levels of political knowledge, voting, and democratic engagement' (Neff and Pickard forthcoming). Moreover, the presence of and trust in PSBs encourage 'higher levels of news consumption, and shrinks the knowledge gap between economically advantaged and disadvantaged citizens' (Neff and Pickard forthcoming). PSBs have also been found to be able to create informational common ground by mitigating the effects of political selective exposure to partisan news sources (Bos et al. 2016). That is, even if people consume partisan news sources with different leanings, if they also rely on information from PSBs, their views of what is factually the case overlap significantly with that of others whom they politically disagree with. PSBs can therefore be important for bridging political divides by providing common informational points of reference among members of different political factions.

The importance of PSBs in societies in which the internet has become widespread has increased compared with their role in offline societies. PSBs (as long as they are politically and financially independent) structurally were always the only informational sources that were impartial by design. But in societies in which most people obtain their information from a myriad of online sources, PSBs obtain the role of essential common informational anchor points. PSBs have therefore taken on a crucial role for creating the public trust that counters the political divisions and strife which often result from the consumption of highly diverse and divisive informational sources that people encounter offline and online. If a state cares about protecting its citizens' rights online, it has to ensure that its citizens share sufficient common ground. Only such informational common ground motivates citizens to co-operate and to tolerate political and moral disagreements that they have with each other. Informational environments of free societies in the age of the internet that are conducive to individual rights therefore require changes to the currently prevailing media landscapes. Even though all four regulatory failures identified by Freedman are relevant for this, the focus in this section has been on the less obvious requirement for an independent, impartial, and widely trusted common source of information – a role that structurally can only be fulfilled by a PSB. A well-funded, politically independent PSB alone is not sufficient to overcome political and societal conflicts and to guarantee a functioning informational environment. However, because of their structural features, PSBs must be seen as an essential and necessary condition of functioning informational environments and political co-operation in our digital age.

8.2.2 *Political Polarisation and the Internet*

Political divisions and hostility among people provide powerful motivations for individuals to attack other internet users. Even if PSBs can have a unifying effect on a society's informational environment, there have been widespread concerns that the internet inevitably has led to an increase of political polarisation. The internet has the essential strength that it allows people to exchange information and to associate with others. As we saw in Chapters 3 and 4, this is in part why access to the internet should be recognised as a human right. But strong public concerns have emerged that by allowing like-minded people to come together online, the internet has also hardened political divisions as it has become less necessary for people to engage with those whom they do not agree with (Haidt 2016). However, increased political tribalism and social pressures to affirm their group membership by expressing negativity towards outsiders (Lupu et al. 2023: 1) can motivate people to attack others offline and online. To better safeguard individual rights, it is therefore necessary to understand to what extent the internet promotes political polarisation and what can be done about increased political hostility in general.

When considering 'political polarisation' it is important to distinguish between 'issue polarisation' (i.e. disagreement about political questions) and 'affective polarisation' (i.e. dislike and disapproval of other political groups). Empirical studies of US voters have found no clear evidence that 'issue polarisation' has markedly risen on average among most of the population throughout the last decades. Instead, disagreements about political questions have increased among political elites and the most politically active engaged citizens (Benkler et al. 2018: 301–302). For example, a 2020 poll by the Carr Center for Human Rights Policy of Harvard University found that a vast majority of US Americans agree on key political issues such as affordable health care, the importance of protecting private data, the need to protect democratic processes, racial equality, women's right to abortion, and the need to better regulate social media companies (Carr Center 2022). Internationally, data from the World Value Survey provides some support for the thesis that the Left/Right polarisation in high-income democracies has even slightly decreased in the past decades (Arguedas et al. 2022: 21). However, empirical research has also found that affective polarisation (i.e. the strength of dislike of political opponents) has indeed increased among citizens in democracies such as the US and the UK in recent decades (Arguedas et al. 2022: 22). The question of interest for our discussion is whether the internet is the cause of this increase in affective polarisation. Greater dislike for political opponents is after all likely to also increase the motivation of polarised citizens to act aggressively towards perceived opponents.

There are several considerations, though, that speak against a causal responsibility of the internet for recent increases in affective polarisation. First, an important 2017 study of political attitudes of US voters found that affective polarisation has increased in recent times, mostly among people who were aged seventy-five years or older and the least likely to use the internet and social media. Even though indirect effects of the internet (e.g. views or stories that circulate online first and are then reported in offline media consumed by senior citizens) could not be ruled out by the authors, the study's findings 'argue against the hypothesis that the internet in general or social media in particular are the main drivers of increasing polarization' (Boxell et al. 2017: 3). Second, the increase of affective polarisation found internationally varies among different countries and different times. This observation contradicts 'the notion that a single universal cause – for example the spread of the internet – is driving polarisation everywhere' (Arguedas et al. 2022: 22). Affective polarisation is problematic, though, because it reduces people's willingness to co-operate with those outside their group, lowers their acceptance of democratic results that realise the goals of political opponents, and can increase motivation to act with hostility towards others. One study of the effects of affective polarisation shows that it indeed increases support for political violence among those polarised. This is because intense aversion towards political opponents can lead strongly partisan persons to view their perceived enemies as less than human and motivate partisan political groups to act on their feelings of dislike (Piazza 2023). It is therefore important to understand the most likely causes of this increase in affective polarisation because only if these are understood can we hope to resolve the problem.

Researchers have identified plausible explanations of the origins of increased political polarisation other than people's use of the internet. For instance, in recent decades in the US, voters have increasingly clearly associated themselves with distinct political parties so that fewer voters are uncertain about, or willing to switch, their political affiliation. It has been argued that this increased political sorting alone, without an underlying change of opinions about political issues, is sufficient to cause more negative views of members of other political groups (Mason 2016, Benkler et al. 2018: 306). That is, the more people's identities and views align closely with one political group, the more strongly they distinguish between those within and outside their group. Disagreement with others is no longer seen as limited to one or a few political questions, but as affecting one's entire outlook on life. Another crucial driver of affective polarisation is the behaviour of political elites and the way they communicate with their audiences, for example by using certain political 'cues' (Arguedas et al. 2022: 25) or by articulating clear differences in political debates (Heiberger et al. 2022). To increase their support, leading politicians such as Donald Trump have increasingly used and normalised incendiary language and promoted divisive positions (such as climate change denial and blaming migrants for voters' economic woes). Political strategies that purposefully employ tactics of division and antagonisation among citizens have therefore plausibly played an important role in enhancing negative attitudes among members of different political groups.

Other causes for increases of political antipathy and resentment have been suggested as well. For example, 'a large body of empirical and theoretical work has demonstrated that inequality and polarization correlate and are likely causally linked' (Stewart et al. 2021: 3). According to these studies, the connection between a rise in material inequality and affective polarisation is based on a growth of intergroup conflict in response to people's deteriorating socio-economic situation. As people's own situation becomes worse or threatened, they join forces (and increasingly identify) with people with whom they share similar concerns and challenges. This distinction between those within one's group and those outside it who are likely seen as partly responsible for one's own problems can lead to 'economic discrimination' (Stewart et al. 2021: 3), which in turn can again worsen socio-economic inequality. In such a situation, the concerns and challenges of outsiders are devalued and the willingness to support them diminishes. Examples of familiar political narratives that justify negative attitudes and a lack of solidarity towards other groups include those of 'welfare scroungers', 'economic migrants', and 'the elite'. Theoretical research suggests that the only way to prevent polarisation in deteriorating socio-economic circumstances and existing wealth inequality is a 'high degree of redistribution' in the form of public goods (Stewart et al. 2021: 6). However, if affective polarisation has already become entrenched, the most likely way for a society to overcome polarisation is to experience economic 'shock' or 'catastrophe' (Stewart et al. 2021: 7) that affects a great majority of the population and in this way creates new grounds for solidarity.

All these non-internet based explanations for the rise of affective political polarisation are good news for the argument for a human right to free internet access because they show that giving people online access does not alone and necessarily lead to an increase in affective polarisation. However, even though the internet might not be primarily responsible for increasing affective political polarisation, it might nonetheless contribute significantly to its rise. This would go against the view that the internet is good for the realisation of human rights because by increasing political polarisation, the internet would contribute to an informational environment (that can be a significant factor in creating a negative socio-political environment) in which rights would be less secure against politically motivated attacks by others. Three of the main issues that are thought to show the internet's involvement in recent rises of political polarisation are the phenomena of echo chambers, filter bubbles, and fake news. Therefore, we will next consider to what degree these phenomena present concerns not only for political polarisation, but also for hostility among internet users.

8.2.3 *Echo Chambers, Filter Bubbles, and Fake News*

An echo chamber is the phenomenon of an informational space in which a person's views are reflected back to them in the information they access, and which insulates them from views that diverge from their own opinions. Filter bubbles refer to situations in which the algorithms of search engines and social media feeds function as informational filters that show users more of the things that they are already interested in with the aim of maximising user engagement. Even though the outcome of filter bubbles is thought to be similar to that of echo chambers in that people become insulated from views that diverge from their own, the reasons why a person might be trapped in an echo chamber or a filter bubble differ. Filter bubbles are algorithmically generated and therefore only occur online. The reasons why someone occupies an informational echo chamber can vary, though, and echo chambers can consist of offline media channels as well (e.g. when a person only reads print media or TV programmes that promote their preferred perspective). Unlike the case of algorithmically generated filter bubbles, people can build their own echo chambers that confirm their views by avoiding other informational sources (Arguedas et al. 2022: 10, 11). However, it is feared that both echo chambers and filter bubbles drive affective polarisation and political divisions because they prevent people from engaging with alternative views and the perspectives of those with whom they disagree. After all, people are less likely to empathise or compromise with those they disagree with if they have no understanding of the concerns relating to their opponents' viewpoints. The resulting affective polarisation can increase people's willingness to attack and violate the rights of their perceived opponents whom they might come to see as having lower moral status.

However, empirical research finds that only a small percentage of populations in Western democracies are caught in echo chambers and that filter bubbles are a theoretical rather than actual phenomenon (Stark and Stegmann 2020: 44). For example, recent studies of the British public suggest that merely 6–8 per cent of the population is likely to occupy partisan echo chambers. Moreover, in other democracies too, only a small minority of about 5 per cent of the population consume partisan information from a single news source. The number of people who rely exclusively on partisan news sources is highest in the US where about 10 per cent of the population falls into this category. In all countries studied, the number of people who regularly consume no online news sources at all is larger than that of those trapped in echo chambers (Arguedas et al. 2022: 13). Moreover, most internet users report that they use several SMPs and sources other than the internet to access information (Dutton et al. 2019: 235). These findings contradict concerns that online echo chambers drive political polarisation that can lead to hostilities and attacks among citizens and internet users.

Importantly, people who occupy informational echo chambers most likely do so because of their own choice. This becomes clear when considering that on the supply side, in democracies, the free press and uncensored internet mean that there is no problem of a supply of diverse information (Arguedas et al. 2022: 17). Citizens of states that employ digital authoritarianism, on the other hand, can be trapped in echo chambers created by their own governments as autocrats try to ensure that their subjects do not encounter information that goes against the government's interests. On the demand side, the distribution of different informational sources has also become much more effective with the internet, which allows citizens to access an enormous range of available information more easily than ever before. Moreover, empirical studies find 'no support for the filter bubble hypothesis' (Arguedas et al. 2022: 5). Rather, people's self-reported use of search engines and social media is found to expose them to slightly more and more diverse news sources than people who do not use such online resources (Stark and Stegmann 2020: 45). This increase in the diversity of consumed informational sources is thought to be due to the tendency of search engines algorithms to return results to queries that users themselves would not otherwise have accessed ('automated serendipity'). Moreover, the algorithms of non-news focused SMPs expose users to news articles that they would otherwise not encounter ('incidental exposure').

Both features of algorithms broadly align with, and promote the profit interests of, Big Tech platforms because they increase user engagement. This happens when users spend more time on a platform because automated serendipity and incidental exposure contribute to a more varied experience as they occasionally encounter unrequested information that is interesting to them. This means that the algorithmic curation of information on online platforms is geared towards presenting people with diverse information rather than showing them ever more of the same information. The main reason why a minority of people occupy echo chambers is therefore most likely because they choose to do so to avoid information that contradicts their views and as such does not fit comfortably with their established beliefs and opinions (Arguedas et al. 2022: 18). People who are found to be particularly prone to such self-selection into echo chambers are those who hold strong political views and have lower levels of income and education (Arguedas et al. 2022: 19). Research that studied the viewing choices of 1,181 adult US YouTube users in the second half of 2020 confirms this view. In 2020, YouTube was 'the most widely used social media platform in the United States' (Chen et al 2023: 1). According to the study, the vast majority of users who watched extremist or 'alternative' YouTube videos did so because they subscribed to the YouTube channels disseminating this content. These users also exhibited high prior levels of racial and gender resentment. Only 3 per cent of participants who did not subscribe to such channels were recommended extremist or 'alternative' content by the platform algorithm, leading the researchers to conclude that 'unsolicited exposure to potentially harmful content on YouTube in the post-2019 era is rare' (Chen et al 2023: 2).

Nonetheless, as discussed in Chapter 7, under certain circumstances algorithms have been found to indirectly contribute to an increase in affective polarisation without creating echo chambers. This can occur when the algorithmic curation of information favours topics or opinions that are highly emotionally charged or controversial since these, as mentioned earlier, tend to increase the engagement of users with SMPs. By prominently presenting such content, algorithms do not directly trap people in echo chambers by reinforcing existing views. However, algorithmic curation that favours divisive and emotional content can 'lead to an overrepresentation of radical viewpoints and arguments in the political discourse' (Stark and Stegmann 2020: 45) and thereby distort people's perception of the actual political climate, which in turn can increase their negative attitude towards other political groups. Importantly, though, international studies of polarisation find that in countries with well-established PSBs, the formation of echo chambers is mostly prevented by people's trust in and use of these public goods (Arguedas et al. 2022: 5). People who include in their media diet an impartial public news provider avoid an exclusively partisan informational environment. On the other hand, because people can choose to consume highly partisan offline media (e.g. if no comprehensive public service broadcast is available to them), the internet is not required for them to self-select into occupying echo chambers. The importance of PSBs in preventing people from inhabiting echo chambers further supports the argument made earlier about the decisive role that these public goods play in creating a healthy informational environment in digitalised societies.

Fake news has become another important concern that is thought to increase the number of misinformed and manipulated citizens. Fake news is information that is made to look like genuine news, is presented in highly emotional terms to attract attention, but contains falsehoods. Even though the popular concern about fake news is that it manipulates internet users because they come to believe the false information it contains, there is little evidence that those who consume fake news mistake it for genuine information. Empirical studies and surveys show that fewer people than commonly thought are exposed to fake news (Allcott and Gentzkow 2017, Grinberg et al. 2019), that only a small number of people actually share fake news (Guess et al. 2019), and that many people are confident in their ability to identify false information online (Barthel et al. 2016).

However, there are other ways than actual acceptance of fake news as true in which these falsehoods can contribute to polarisation and political hostility. First, public knowledge of the circulation of fake news can lead people to worry about others believing false information. Such concerns can increase distrust of other citizens' competence and political choices. This in turn can undermine citizens' acceptance of democratic processes and results as they fear their fellow citizens have been manipulated by fake news (Rini 2021, Reglitz 2022). Moreover, as we saw in Chapter 7, even if people can correctly identify fake news, its existence can lead them to develop a general scepticism of their informational environment as they are no longer certain which informational sources to trust. Such a 'flattening [of] the epistemic landscape' (Levy 2024) is fatal for public discourse and political co-operation because democratic citizens must be able to rely on information to make political choices. If they are generally confused about what to believe, they are likely to either withdraw from political engagement entirely or to seek orientation within their own group alone. Either response to the contamination of the informational environment by fake news would make increases in political divisions and polarisation more likely. Finally, fake news can worsen affective polarisation because its dissemination can be a non-optional way for members of some political groups to demonstrate their political affiliation and allegiances. Most people do not share fake news for fear of damaging their reputation (Altay et al. 2022). However, if people feel they are forced to share fake news to signal their support for their own group, this can count as a reason for others outside their group not to engage with them, which exacerbates political divides. One study of 51,537 Twitter users found that in groups where fake news circulates online, those who do not share these falsehoods indeed experience a reduction of social interactions with other group members over time (Lawson et al. 2023). The sharing of fake news can therefore be seen as an act of expressive responding (rather than actual endorsement) that is essential for affirming membership in certain political groups. The study therefore empirically confirms Elizabeth Anderson's argument noted earlier that many divisive political online speech acts ought to be interpreted not as an assertion of facts but as an expressive signalling of social and political group affiliation.

There are therefore reasons to believe that, just like echo chambers, fake news does not itself generate political polarisation. However, by generating distrust among citizens and in sources of information, and by constituting a way to signal group membership, false information shared online can exacerbate existing political divisions and antipathies. Fake news is an internet-enabled phenomenon that negatively affects the informational environment (that can negatively affect the socio-political environment) in ways that are detrimental for the enjoyment of individuals' rights even if the internet is not the ultimate cause of the political divisions that it helps to ferment.

8.2.4 Conspiracy Theories

A final online misinformation issue to be covered here that contributes to an informational environment that is not conducive to mutual respect for individual rights is conspiracy 'theories' that circulate online. Conspiracy 'theories' are 'attempts to explain the ultimate causes of significant social or political events and circumstances with claims of secret plots by two or more powerful actors' (Douglas et al. 2019: 4). However, since these 'theories' do not employ scientific theoretical methods but are speculative (Cassam 2019: 16), they will here be referred to as 'conspiracy narratives'. And since advocates of such narratives do not work with or accept the adequacy of falsifiable evidence as standards for testing the plausibility of their conspiratorial narratives, they are here identified as 'conspiracy users' rather than 'conspiracy theorists'.

The worry about conspiracy narratives that are propagated online is that they cause political divisions that can misinform citizens and motivate them to attack other internet users whom they see as conspiring against them. Conspiracy narratives have also often been found to be the pivots around which echo chambers form (Cinelli et al. 2022: 1). More generally, conspiracy narratives are a matter of concern since their acceptance has been shown to be connected to various harms (Douglas et al. 2019: 17–21). For example, those who believe in conspiracies often change their political views and develop negative attitudes against those they believe are implicated in conspiracies (e.g. anti-Semitism, hatred of immigrants, hatred of individual politicians or political elites). Conspiracy users who accept health-related conspiracies have been found to make health-related choices that are harmful to themselves or others (e.g. rejecting contraception or vaccines). Acceptance of other conspiracies (e.g. about climate change) has been found to lead to science denial, therefore making it more difficult to build support for addressing societal challenges. Moreover, conspiracism is linked to, and has been used to justify, acts of violence against minorities and opponents (e.g. white supremacist beliefs were the alleged motive behind the 2019 killing of fifty-one people in two mosques in Christchurch, New Zealand, and Anders Breivik's mass shooting of sixty-nine participants at a Work Youth League's summer camp in Norway in 2011).

There are many concerning reports of how widely conspiracy narratives are accepted among democratic citizens. Many of these are based on US polling data. For example, according to one 2020 poll of 1,583 registered US voters,

50 per cent of Donald Trump supporters thought that leading Democratic politicians were involved in child sex trafficking rings. According to a different 2021 poll of 19,399 US Americans, almost one-fifth of the US population and about one-quarter of those identifying as Republicans believed in the QAnon conspiracy narratives (PRRI 2021). A 2023 poll of 981 US adults suggested that 30 per cent of Americans (including 68 per cent of Republicans) believed that Joe Biden won the 2020 presidential election because of voter fraud (Monmouth 2023). These numbers indicate that a sizeable minority of the US population accepts unsubstantiated and even extremely implausible claims about large-scale conspiracies. Moreover, other surveys show that Americans see the internet as central to this situation. According to a 2021 poll, 73 per cent of Americans think conspiracy narratives are out of control. And in a 2018 poll, 59 per cent of surveyed Americans expressed concern that belief in conspiracy narratives has increased in the past twenty-five years, and 77 per cent say they think that social media and the internet are responsible for this increase (Uscinski et al. 2022: 1–2).

However, even though empirical research finds that the internet plays some role in the proliferation of conspiracy narratives, researchers have not found evidence that it has caused a new crisis of mass conspiracy narrative acceptance. To understand whether there has been an increase in the number of conspiracy users in recent years, one group of researchers studied survey data about beliefs in conspiracy narratives spanning more than half a century. In their studies, they considered, for instance, how many Americans believe in forty-six conspiracy narratives over different time spans (starting with the acceptance of various John F. Kennedy assassination conspiracies across fifty-five years to belief in COVID-19 conspiracies across seven months in 2020 and 2021) and how many Europeans accepted six different conspiracy theories between 2016 and 2018. Neither of these studies produced compelling evidence that the share of populations in the Western democracies that accepts conspiracy narratives has increased over time, which contradicts the claim that the internet is at fault for a new crisis in mass conspiracy belief (Uscinski et al. 2022: 2; for more support for this conclusion, see Uscinski and Parent 2014).

Moreover, researchers have repeatedly found that not all people are equally susceptible to accepting conspiracy narratives. Rather, available evidence 'strongly suggests that conspiracy [narratives] must align with a person's existing set of predispositions to be adopted' (Douglas et al. 2019: 12). Conspiracy narratives can fulfil several functions for a person, and the reasons why someone adopts a conspiratorial mindset can therefore be complex. For example, these stories can provide apparent causal explanations for people who seek certainty, meaning, and patterns in significant, large-scale events

(Douglas et al. 2019: 7, Enders et al. 2023). For people who cannot tolerate randomness or unpredictability as explanations of such events, conspiracies can fulfil a psychologically important explanatory function. Especially for people with a 'paranoid social cognition' who are hyper-vigilant towards possible ill intentions of others, these narratives therefore fulfil the need to resolve 'subjective feelings of uncertainty, for instance about the self or the surrounding social environment' (Prooijen and Jostmann 2013: 110, Douglas and Sutton 2023: 273). Additionally, acceptance of conspiracy narratives has been found to be stronger in those who are affected by the Dunning–Kruger effect and over-estimate their own ability to understand complex causal phenomena (Douglas et al. 2019: 7).[1] Furthermore, for people who feel powerless and a lack of agency, conspiracy narratives can offer a way to explain their situation by identifying those responsible for their lack of control and in that way lead to a feeling of empowerment (Prooijen 2018). Conspiratorial beliefs are therefore also 'correlated with alienation from the political system and anomie – a feeling of personal unrest and lack of understanding of the social world' (Douglas et al. 2019: 8). Finally, empirical research has found that 'higher levels of conspiracy thinking correlate with lower levels of education and lower levels of income' (Douglas et al. 2019: 10), which suggests that those who have received more education have better cognitive tools to resist conspiracy narratives. Based on all these findings (and even though the studies they are based on often only reveal correlations), it is therefore plausible to think that, even though people can come to accept conspiracy narratives for different reasons, not everyone is equally prone to become convinced by them. This insight also speaks against the claim that the internet is responsible for an increase in conspiracism because internet use does not seem sufficient for most people to come to accept conspiracy narratives. Rather, conspiracy narratives seem particularly convincing to people who have certain personality traits and dispositions.

The role of the internet in the spread of conspiracy narratives is further qualified when considering that these are not merely promoted online. Rather, important politicians have directly or indirectly advanced conspiracies for their own political gain. Donald Trump, for instance, has endorsed narratives such as that of a 'deep state' in the US government that acts to thwart the

---

[1] 'The Dunning–Kruger effect is a cognitive bias in which people with limited competence in a particular domain overestimate their abilities. It was first described by Justin Kruger and David Dunning in 1999. Some researchers also include the opposite effect for high performers: their tendency to underestimate their skills. In popular culture, the Dunning–Kruger effect is often misunderstood as a claim about general overconfidence of people with low intelligence instead of specific overconfidence of people unskilled at a particular task' (Wikipedia 2024b).

will of the American people. He has also not disavowed the QAnon narrative according to which he was working to undo a child sex trafficking network of his political opponents. Moreover, conspiracy narratives have been promoted widely on popular privately owned offline media channels such as Fox News that aired Tucker Carlson's repeated claims of a great replacement conspiracy. According to this narrative, Democratic politicians are trying to supplant the white American population with immigrants from other ethnicities and religions (Birchall and Knight 2022: 598). For example, an important study of the disinformation campaign about fraudulent mail-in ballots in the run-up to the US 2020 presidential election found that unjustified concerns and false claims about voter fraud were primarily driven by political elite figures (especially Donald Trump) and partisan offline mass media (especially Fox News). Online disinformation via social media, on the other hand, merely played a secondary role (Benkler et al. 2020). Moreover, radio hosts and conspiracy entrepreneurs such as Alex Jones have established entire businesses based on promoting conspiracies such as the claim that the 2012 Sandy Hook school shooting massacre was a fake orchestration by the US government to justify limiting people's constitutional right to bear arms (Williamson 2021). The prominence of these offline media show that the internet is unlikely to be the only pathway through which conspiracy narratives have been promoted in the recent past.

It is nonetheless clear that the internet has played an important role in the dissemination of conspiracy narratives. This is because the internet, which provides unprecedented opportunities for exchanging and searching information, has made it easier for conspiracy users to find and connect with each other. Online venues such as SMPs have also made it easier for them to share and consume conspiracy narratives (Birchall and Knight 2022: 585–586). The internet as a medium has therefore 'contributed to an intensification of emerging trends and processes – such as polarization, populism, and post-truth politics' (Birchall and Knight 2022: 598). Indirect support for this claim is provided by the fact that social media companies such as YouTube have attempted with some success to reduce the spread of conspiracy videos promoted by their algorithms (Nicas 2020). Such attempts are important because a 2023 study by the Center for Countering Digital Hate found that thirteen- to seventeen-year-old teenagers, and especially those who are heavy social media users, are more likely to accept conspiracy narratives than the average US citizens (Center for Countering Digital Hate 2023). These teenagers are persons whose education is not completed and whose personality is not yet fully formed. As such, they have fewer cognitive tools than adults to resist conspiracy narratives. And because they use the internet more often than older adults, it is particularly important that social media companies prevent the dissemination of conspiracy narratives via their platforms even if conspiracy narratives shared on them do not influence the majority of the population.

The internet's relevance for conspiracy narratives is therefore similar to the role it has played for affective polarisation and echo chambers: the internet is not the sole or main cause of these issues that can put individuals' rights at risk, but it has provided new venues and opportunities for their spread and, in some cases, their exacerbation.

8.2.5 *Summary: Problematic Online Phenomena and the Environment of Rights*

Individual rights require an environment that is conducive to their protection or else they are threatened by preventable and expectable threats. Ecological hazards such as pollution and climate change are familiar environmental threats to individual rights. But also the informational environment that surrounds people has important effects on whether or not their rights are respected. If people are misinformed so that they see others as opponents and threats to their interests, this can move them to harm and to violate the rights of others. The quality of people's informational environments is therefore linked with (and partly constitutive of) the quality of their socio-political environments. In this section, we have considered various informational problems associated with the internet that could lead individuals to attack other people offline as well as online in the ways outlined in Section 8.1. Politically polarised citizens, misinformed by conspiracy narratives that circulate in echo chambers and by fake news shared in their own political community, can be motivated by false information to attack those whom they perceive as political opponents. The question this section has investigated is whether the internet inevitably creates informational hazards such as echo chambers, filter bubbles, and fake news that contribute to political polarisation, which in turn can motivate rights violations–or whether there are other reasons for increases in affective polarisation.

What we have found is that, according to empirical research, even though the internet contributes to increases in political polarisation, it is not the ultimate cause of it. That is, rather than directly leading to the affective polarisation of large parts of the public, the internet offers new ways for polarised citizens to find and join with like-minded others. As such, the internet is a vehicle and medium in which political divisions play out. However, the internet is not the ultimate reason why people in many Western democracies increasingly feel antipathy towards their political opponents. The causes of this development that have been suggested are linked to deeper and more long-term social trends such as increased political sorting, growing socio-economic inequality and uncertainty as well as the increasingly hostile and antagonistic strategies of political factions and leading politicians. Similarly, even though the internet has provided new opportunities for echo chambers and conspiracy narratives to thrive, there is no decisive evidence to show that the internet is an essential cause of them. Instead, it mainly appeals to those who are already predisposed to these kinds of misinformation, who appear to self-select into echo chambers and to adopt conspiratorial explanations that circulate online.

Attempts to create an environment in which people are less likely to violate others' rights will therefore certainly require technological and legal changes to the way that the internet is currently used – especially by SMPs. Many of these (e.g. ending surveillance capitalism and the algorithmic manipulation based on it, enforcing limits to free speech on SMPs, highlighting disputed information online, and enforcing distributor liability on social media businesses) were discussed in Chapter 7. However, beyond these changes to the dominant way in which the internet is currently monetised, states will have to address offline challenges to informational environments. Among the measures discussed in this section are the creation and protection of PSBs that can establish common informational ground among citizens and the establishment of a more diverse, less concentrated, and therefore more democratic media landscape that is free from the dominance of a few privately owned media businesses. The current oligopolies of private media give their owners an outsized voice and influence on the political process and the information that is available to all citizens. But beyond the informational environment, states also have to address problems in the social environments of people (e.g. by reducing socio-economic inequality (Stewart et al. 2021), providing more opportunities for democratic participation to combat feelings of anomie and powerlessness (Prooijen 2018), and improving norms of political competition and communication), insofar as these exacerbate political polarisation that can in turn motivate people to harm each other. All these changes are plausibly required to better protect people's individual rights from offline and online attacks by others. Moreover, states have to empower individuals themselves to protect their own rights by providing them with the right education and skills to do so. These are the measures we now turn to in Section 8.3.

8.3 EMPOWERING INDIVIDUALS WITH SKILLS AND EDUCATION

The internet is essential for our opportunities to enjoy and use our human rights today. However, it is also a dynamic and complex environment that differs from the physical-social one that we grow up in as human beings. We all need certain skills and knowledge to navigate different aspects of our lives. Voters have to know their political options, citizens have to know their rights to defend them from others and their government, and people generally have to be aware of the opportunities they are free to pursue in life and require skills training to make the most of their talents and ambitions. Equally, internet users need certain skills and knowledge about the internet to use it safely and to protect their rights from attacks by others.

To understand this point better, it is helpful to consider Thomas Christiano's explanation of the concept of informational power. According to him, this kind of power has two dimensions. First, people possess informational power to the extent that they are able to seek out and understand the information that they require to form opinions and to advance their own interests as well as the common good (Christiano 2022: 116). Second, people have informational power to the extent that they can disseminate information to others (Christiano 2022: 117). To these two, we can add a third, essential, dimension based on the standard threats to free internet access posed by states and private companies that we discussed in Chapters 6 and 7. That is that people have informational power to the extent that they can control how much of their personal information can become known by others. Informational power has important moral and political significance. People are morally equal, they have equal human rights, and under democratic governance they should have political influence on the collective decisions of their political community (Christiano 2008). But realising all these ideals (moral equality, human rights, democratic equality) presupposes that people's informational power is not too unequal. If informational power is unequally distributed, those with more informational power have objectionably greater opportunities to promote and use their rights. In light of this role of informational power, one important purpose of the human right to free internet can be understood as ensuring that everyone has an adequate amount of informational power, and that differences in this power among people are not excessive. People today need online access to have a minimal guaranteed level of informational power; that is to say, adequate opportunities to search, obtain, send, and conceal information relevant for the enjoyment of their human rights. Moreover, those with insufficient informational power are at risk of being wrongfully manipulated by others who have greater informational power. Christiano defines 'wrongful exploitation' as a process in which those with greater informational power exploit known weaknesses of others to make them act in line with the interests of the manipulator. In cases of wrongful exploitation, 'one person or group sets in motion processes of influencing people's minds that take advantage of flaws in the recipients' rational capacities. Minds are changed in such a way that the appreciation of reasons is set back either intentionally or at least is welcomed' (Christiano 2022: 111). Examples of using natural weaknesses of human rationality include the deliberate use of false claims or information, the appeal to emotions such as anger and pride to undermine another person's use of rational deliberation, and the use of quick, unsubstantiated inferences that remain unnoticed (e.g. 'all politicians are equally corrupt so that no politician can be trusted and voting is pointless').

Risks of wrongful exploitation and unequal opportunities to realise human rights based on unequal informational power also help explain some of the problems we encountered earlier. For example, the disproportionate informational power of the owners of private media businesses dominating the media landscape in most Western democracies allows them to exert outsized influence on political processes, agendas, and decisions. Moreover, unequal informational power explains in part what is problematic with personal data harvesting and the resulting practices of micro-targeting and algorithmic manipulation of internet users by surveillance capitalist companies that know more about their users than they might know about themselves. The surveillance of individuals by powerful agents is nothing new. However, the algorithmic influencing of internet users' choices presents a novel, distinctive problem because of the sheer scale of information that is available to these businesses about their users' personal preferences and features (Christiano 2022: 114). Accordingly, as we saw, one thing that is required to change the informational power imbalance between big tech companies and their users is to reduce the power of these corporations by ending surveillance capitalism through the imposition of fiduciary duties on companies that collect personal user information.

However, another essential measure that is required for reducing informational power imbalances between individuals and governments as well as private corporations is an increase in people's own informational power. This is because some algorithmic sorting of information is needed for people to navigate the internet effectively and for them to make use of our human rights online. Even if surveillance capitalism were to end, algorithms would still be needed for presenting information to us and to tailor information according to our interests – with the decisive difference that personal information about our interests would no longer be collected and sold to other parties. Moreover, even in a world that was free of personal data harvesting, misinformation would still be present online. People would still encounter fake news, conspiracy narratives, inaccurate or flawed individual opinions, and fraud attempts online. For this reason, training individuals to have greater informational power to enable them to distinguish 'good' from 'bad' information is important regardless of the existence of surveillance capitalism. Consequently, public authorities ought to provide education to improve their citizens' informational power and to help them protect their rights when they use the internet. In what follows, we consider some of the most relevant skills that public education should train people to have.

8.3.1 Cybersecurity Awareness

Among the individual digital harms mentioned at the outset of this chapter are various cybercrimes that are standard threats when engaging with the internet. To enable internet users to protect themselves from cybercrime, it is therefore important that they know of the risks to their security and rights that they face online owing to the attempts of criminals to harm them (Hargittai and Micheli 2019: 115). They have to be aware of safety and security issues such as viruses, spyware, and phishing messages, as well as of practices to avoid these. Among the latter are installing and updating anti-virus software; updating operating system software; using complex passwords or password managers; enabling 2-factor authentication protection; spam and other email filters, internet browser add-ons; blocking unsolicited contact attempts and not sharing personal identifying information publicly online; and using secured broadband networks only.

However, researchers have found that mere awareness of cybersecurity threats is insufficient for most internet users to take the actions required for protecting themselves. Even though many people are aware of the threats they face to their security online, only some of them take appropriate measures to mitigate security risks to themselves and others. Instead, they do not employ sufficiently strong password protection, do not install antivirus software, and use sensitive personal data on public computers and free open networks such as unsecured Wi-Fi networks. However, studies of cybersecurity behaviour suggest that the more cybersecurity training people receive (e.g. as part of their formal education), the more likely they are to take adequate action to protect themselves against cybercrime (Zwilling et al. 2022: 91). There are therefore evidence-based reasons for arguing that public authorities have an obligation to make cybersecurity awareness training part of public education curriculums and to offer other ways (e.g. free online training opportunities such as self-guided online courses) for citizens to learn how to protect themselves from security risks online. Senior citizens have been found to be the group that is most vulnerable to cybercrime. However, cybercrime awareness and security skills training have also been shown to significantly improve their ability to recognise and protect themselves against online frauds and other crimes (Blackwood-Brown et al. 2021).

8.3.2 *Internet Search Skills*

Digital harms such as echo chambers or fake news can affect internet users who do not know how to search effectively for information online or how internet search engines work. Without the appropriate knowledge, people might therefore not have access to the information that is relevant for them or trust information that is untrustworthy. Researchers have found that (besides a lack of interest in politics) what makes people most vulnerable to involuntarily becoming trapped in echo chambers is a lack of internet search skills (Dutton et al. 2019: 243). To avoid this pitfall, internet users have to know how to find and evaluate information online. This entails knowing which search tools are available, not overly trusting the results of individual search engines, and knowing how to evaluate search results for quality, credibility, completeness, accuracy, validity, and relevance (Hargittai and Micheli 2019: 113). Empirical studies have found that most internet users say that they are concerned about the trustworthiness of the information they encounter online (Dutton et al. 2019: 236). People who know how online search tools work and what their limitations are have been found to be more likely to revise search terms they use, to fact-check information they are presented with, to use multiple search engines, and to consult a greater variety of online sources (Dutton et al. 2019: 241, 243). Training people's online search skills therefore enables them to avoid digital harms such as echo chambers and misinformation more reliably.

8.3.3 *News Media Literacy*

News media literacy is the 'ability to analyze, evaluate, and process mediated messages, as well as the creative or production skills necessary to self-expression and participation in democratic life' (Craft et al. 2017: 391). If people are news media literate, they know how to check the credibility of news sources and to evaluate whether information they read follows adequate and critical reporting standards. Moreover, media-literate internet users are also aware of the commercial context of news production and who owns the businesses whose products they consume. This sort of literacy has been found to reduce people's vulnerability to digital harms such as conspiracy narratives: 'the greater one's knowledge about the news media – from the kinds of news covered, to the commercial context in which news is produced, to the effects on public opinion news can have – the less likely one will fall prey to conspiracy theories' (Craft et al. 2017: 396).

News media literacy generally works by increasing people's scepticism about the news sources and news content they encounter. However, news media literacy alone is unlikely to be sufficient to overcome the reasons (discussed earlier) why people are attracted to skewed reporting and misinformation, such as paranoid social cognition, the effects of socio-economic inequality, political uncertainty, and affective polarisation. Moreover, if news media literacy focuses exclusively on scepticism towards news content and does not also teach people about reliable informational sources, news media literacy training can also have detrimental effects and lead, for example, to a general distrust of all news reporting (Benkler et al. 2018: 378). If news media literacy is taught in an empowering way, though, such training plausibly provides internet users with skills that help them resist digital harms such as fake news and conspiracy narratives.

8.3.4 *Privacy Literacy*

As we saw in previous chapters, a loss of privacy and the harvesting of personal information makes internet users vulnerable to the power of governments and private companies. But loss of control over privacy and personal data also makes internet users susceptible to attacks by other individuals because of their personal views or attributes. For these reasons, knowing how to protect one's privacy online is of paramount importance for all internet users.

'Critical privacy literacy' has been used as a concept to describe people's ability to protect their personal information online (Masur 2020). To acquire this ability, as a first step people have to understand why protecting their privacy is important for them (Hargittai and Micheli 2019: 114). Internet users have to know what risks they expose themselves to if they do not protect their personal information. They also have to know what information about them requires particular concern and protection (e.g. sexual and political preferences, relationship status, health problems, financial information) and how their own online behaviours and activities can endanger their own privacy. As a second step, internet users need to become familiar with relevant facts about privacy threats on the internet. They have to understand, for instance, who wants to collect their personal information and for what purposes, how these agents collect information about them, and what their own privacy rights are. Finally, internet users must learn how to manage threats to their privacy and what they can do to protect their personal information online (Masur 2020: 260–262). These skills include adopting a parsimonious approach to revealing personal data, choosing privacy-friendly platforms and applications (such as Firefox for web browsing, DuckDuckGo for online searches, Signal for messaging, VPNs for anonymous browsing), using the privacy settings of platforms and applications, employing pseudonyms and 'social steganography' (hiding messages and meanings in information that one shares) in risky public settings (Hargittai and Micheli 2019: 114–115, Masur 2020: 261–262).

Critical privacy literacy is crucial for increasing people's informational power because it helps them to use the internet without revealing personal data to others who otherwise would gain an informational advantage over them. However, as we saw in Chapter 7, the currently dominant internet business model of surveillance capitalism makes it extremely difficult for internet users to protect and hide their personal information. Many services and applications on the internet are only usable if people give up their personal data. Moreover, how this data is used by algorithms is difficult to comprehend (Masur 2020: 263). It has therefore been argued that under surveillance capitalism, critical privacy literacy cannot be limited to privacy skills and awareness training. Rather, raising people's awareness of the ubiquitous risks to our privacy must also include educating people to become politically active in demanding changes to the status quo. People ought to be educated to become advocates for altering the basic conditions under which most of us use online services and applications so that these become more conducive to protecting our privacy. Critical privacy literacy, though, requires comprehensive training, and public authorities should therefore make it part of public education curriculums as a matter of priority (Masur 2020: 265). This links up with the duties of states to provide social guarantees against the standard threats posed by private enterprises to free internet access that were discussed in Chapter 7, because stopping the arbitrary interference of private companies with internet access and use requires extensive democratic support. Those benefiting from surveillance capitalism will use political pressure and try to influence people to resist legislation, forcing them to change their business models. Only a well-informed populace that understands why protecting privacy from powerful corporate and government interests is important will be able to resist corporate lobbyism.

8.3.5 Algorithmic Awareness

Increasing the informational power of internet users essentially also requires that they have 'algorithmic awareness'. Such awareness entails knowledge of how algorithms influence what information people see online and that people's experience of the internet differs because it is customised according to their personal preferences. Only in this way can people adjust their expectations and understanding of what they see online and adopt strategies that sidestep the limits on what information they are presented with by curating algorithms (Hargittai and Micheli, 2019: 113–114). Algorithmic awareness therefore entails adequate online search skills as well as critical privacy literacy.

To understand the vital role of algorithmic awareness is to grasp that it is an indispensable precondition of personal and political autonomy in our digitalised societies. At the personal level, internet users need to understand how algorithms operate to be able to interpret information that they encounter online correctly. For example, the development of individually usable artificial intelligence has recently taken great steps forward with the release of large language models such as ChatGPT. But users of such applications have to know, for instance, that these algorithms are trained on enormous amounts of data that enable them to create content by predicting the most likely combination of information that is requested by a user. That is, chat bots do not possess genuine intelligence and do not understand the information they process. The results they present their users with are therefore not always reliable, are framed by the limits of their programming, and as such are not generally trustworthy in terms of quality, accuracy, and completeness. Moreover, online environments that are curated by algorithms can lead people to mistake statistical information and correlations for reliable evidence of causal connections. People unfamiliar with the limitations of algorithms might therefore accept certain information as genuine explanations rather than undertaking the more difficult task of establishing sound causal connections or finding reliable evidence for themselves. Over-reliance on algorithmic curation can therefore lead people to draw false conclusions on matters that are important for their personal lives (e.g. information related to health, safety, education, or career choices). Inaccurate information, though, ultimately undermines the formation of their own views and preferences. The operations of algorithms can therefore be a threat to the autonomy of internet users when people are not aware that algorithms only present information selectively and arranged in specific ways (Coeckelbergh 2023: 1347–1348). Algorithmic awareness has therefore become a necessary condition 'for an enlightened and rewarding online life' (Gran et al. 2021: 1792).

However, the problem of algorithmic ignorance also has an important political dimension because the information people encounter online contributes to the formation of their political views as well. Being an informed citizen today requires that people know that algorithms present politically relevant information to them in ways that do not always reflect the best available evidence or does not represent a nuanced coverage of different opinions on a particular subject. Algorithmic awareness therefore greatly affects people's informational power. If they do not know how algorithms work, internet users' political agency can be reduced when they are badly informed, hardly informed, or misinformed by information that has been algorithmically curated and tailored to them. Without algorithmic awareness, there is therefore a 'greater risk of reinforcing whatever democratic deficit existed in the first place, weakening the condition for an informed public and democratic participation' (Gran et al. 2021: 1792), as those who are algorithmically aware have better skills to search and find information relevant to them.

The need for algorithmic awareness training was demonstrated in a study of a representative sample of 1,624 Norwegian citizens that tested the respondents' awareness of how algorithms work. The Norwegian population provides a useful testing ground because Norway is presently one of the most digitally developed societies. For example, in 2019, 98 per cent of the Norwegian population had internet access and 95 per cent owned a smartphone (Gran et al. 2021: 1782–1783). If the population of Norway is not algorithmically aware, it is plausible to infer that people in digitally less developed societies are unlikely to have a better understanding of how algorithms operate and what limitations they impose on how we consume information online. It is therefore of importance that the Norwegian study found that a sizeable minority of respondents (41 per cent) 'perceive that they have no awareness of algorithms' (Gran et al. 2021: 1784). One important factor that predicts whether people are aware of algorithms is their level of education. The more education a respondent has, the more likely they are to understand that and how algorithms influence their experiences on the internet. Moreover, 'the higher the awareness of algorithms, which correlates with [...] higher levels of education, the more negative are the attitudes towards them' (Gran et al. 2021: 1792).

Algorithmic awareness for these reasons is crucial for people's informational power. Only if internet users are aware of how algorithms work do they know how to find and send information online in a way that empowers them. The moral problem with informational power imbalances that derive from unequal algorithmic awareness is therefore that such imbalances lead to an 'uneven distribution of data and knowledge, between those who have the means to question the processes of datafication and those who lack the necessary resources' (Gran et al. 2021: 1792). As with the other skills discussed in this section, though, there is evidence that informational power can be increased by education.

In this section, we have considered a non-exhaustive list of examples of internet skills and knowledge that affect people's informational power. Having more of these skills increases people's ability to find information, to disseminate information, and to protect their personal information from others.

All these dimensions of informational power are indispensable for people's ability to use the internet to exercise their human rights online safely without putting themselves at unnecessary risk of being manipulated or of being attacked by other internet users. As we saw, informational skills and power can be increased through training. Considering the crucial role that online skills training has for the protection and enjoyment of human rights online, training in the form of public education and freely available learning opportunities for citizens is therefore an obligation for public authorities.

8.4 DUTIES OF PUBLIC AUTHORITIES AND CONCLUSION

Besides (digital) poverty, states, and private companies, other internet users pose standard threats to free internet access. Similar to states, internet users in this respect have a dual role. States, to recall, are primary duty-holders with respect to human rights and free internet access; yet at the same time they also constitute some of the main, regularly expectable threats to free internet access. Individual internet users, similarly, are the bearers of human rights and are entitled to free internet access; yet at the same time at least some internet users pose threats to others' free use of the internet and rights online. Public authorities therefore have obligations to protect individuals' rights online as much as offline and to make sure that citizens lack reasons to attack one another. The particular obligations that public authorities have to protect individuals' free internet use and rights online from each other follow from the conditions that must obtain in general for people to be able to securely enjoy their rights. These conditions include the enforcement of rights, a physical, socio-political, and informational environment that is conducive to rights, and the skills and knowledge that individuals require to make use of and defend their rights. Each of these conditions requires the support and protection of public authorities.

With respect to the first condition, we have seen that states have to defend internet users against online attacks on their rights by prosecuting individuals who commit punishable offences. Not all harmful speech is a criminal offence, but not all speech is permissible and must be endured either. States ought to hold to account individuals who overstep the line of what is acceptable and who commit dangerous speech acts online. If they do not, states do not in fact protect free speech but instead allow the most threatening speakers to dominate online interactions and to silence others. In enforcing rights online, though, public authorities face the particular difficulty of identifying offenders without thereby negating or jeopardising general internet user anonymity. The ability to speak in public without being identifiable is morally too important for public authorities to undermine it even for the important purpose of protecting people's rights. The question of how general online anonymity can be safeguarded while identifying those who commit punishable offences online is largely a technological question and challenge. What is clear, though, is that public authorities have an obligation to enforce and protect the rights of internet users online.

The second condition of secure rights enjoyment is the most complex one. That is because the environments in which people's rights are enjoyed or violated have many components. Moreover, the quality of these environmental components often also influences whether individuals threaten each other's rights. In this chapter we have focused on the informational environments of digitalised societies because this book argues for a right to free internet access and the internet is the dominant informational medium of our time. Moreover, the informational environment has a crucial influence on other components of people's environment, such as the socio-economic and-political conditions in which they live. We have focused especially on political polarisation as this issue is strongly affected by the information to which people have access. Moreover, affective polarisation in particular has been found to be an important cause of politically motivated attacks of citizens on each other. We have seen that phenomena associated with the internet that have been blamed for recent increases in affective polarisation such as echo chambers, fake news, and conspiracy narratives are indeed linked to political polarisation. This is hardly surprising since today almost every societal development, good or bad, is communicated through the internet and because the internet provides more opportunities than ever before to communicate societal changes.

However, the empirical research that we have considered also suggests that, contrary to popular opinion, the internet is not the primary cause of people's self-sorting into echo chambers, their sharing of fake news, their attraction to conspiracy narratives, or the growing political disaffection of political factions towards each other. The underlying causes of these issues go beyond the internet and concern macroscopic societal trends and changes. It is with respect to shaping and changing these trends and developments that public authorities have obligations so that individuals do not inhabit environments that move them to violate each other's rights and to arbitrarily interfere with others' internet use. If, for example, the sharing of fake news and the seeking out of echo chambers is particularly motivated by increases in affective polarisation, states ought to counteract the causes of affective polarisation. If the worsening of affective polarisation is rooted in increased socio-economic inequality and insecurity as well as in more divisive and confrontational tactics that are utilised by political elites and leaders, states have obligations to reduce this inequality and to inform the public and political leaders about the importance of the norms of civility and respectfulness in political contests. If affective polarisation is also driven by media landscapes that are dominated by a few privately owned information businesses rather than by independent PSBs, states have duties to establish and respect independent public service broadcasting as well as to regulate and change the current media environment so that it better serves everyone's interests as well as democratic values. And insofar as a lack of control is an important motive for people to accept conspiracy narratives, states ought to provide more opportunities for people to become involved and to participate in political decisions. None of this means that there is no need to change the status quo of how the internet is run for profit today and used by public authorities to monitor their citizens. As the previous chapters show, such changes to how states and businesses use the internet are very much straightforward demands deriving from the human right to free internet access. However, with respect to the informational and other components of the environment in which people exercise their rights, the obligations of states are far-reaching because the societal factors that cause political polarisation and motivate individuals to attack each other are extensive as well.

Finally, states have duties to ensure that citizens have the education and skills required to safely use the internet and to protect their rights while being online. The secure use of the internet is only possible if people are aware of and know how to protect themselves from cybercrime, unwanted intrusions into their privacy, misinformation, and the presentation of information that is skewed by algorithmic curation that serves the interests of those who own these programmes. Effective internet skills alone are unlikely to protect most individuals from avoiding all digital harms. After all, unless they are computer experts, they might still fall prey to the latest elaborate tricks of cybercriminals, and without structural changes to the way in which Big Tech companies run their services it is difficult for people to avoid all unwanted harvesting of their personal information. However, crucial digital skills that ought to be taught as part of public education curriculums and by providing public resources for citizens outside education systems have been shown to reduce individuals' vulnerabilities to digital harms such as cyberscams, misinformation, and algorithmic manipulation. Public authorities can therefore do much to help people to help themselves to protect their rights online.

If states fulfil their obligations concerning all three dimensions of the secure enjoyment of rights, it is plausible to hold that attacks on, and violations of internet users' rights by, other internet users will become much less common. Just as in the case of the other standard threats discussed in Part II of this book, addressing risks posed by other individuals is insufficient to guarantee free access to and use of the internet. The standard threats discussed in the previous chapters must be met for this as well. However, without ensuring that internet users are reasonably safe from other individuals' arbitrary interference with their rights online, the objects of the human right to free internet access are unachievable. Improvements to the current state of the cyberspace, which often appears to be a free-for-all,[2] seem well within the range of what is feasible for properly motivated states.

---

[2] Sometimes, cyberspace is referred to as an online Wild West. However, the analogy of the Wild West is deficient in at least one important respect. In the nascent USA, the Wild West was only part of the territory and citizens were able to escape its lawlessness by moving to the already established eastern US states. The same is not true for the internet where their rights currently are not properly enforced in a great majority of spaces. I thank Art Held for this point.

Conclusion

This book has investigated the moral importance of the internet from the perspective of human rights. However, human rights are not the only things that matter morally. A full account of justice requires more than human rights. Neither are rights the only things affected by the internet that matter morally. Despite their urgency and forcefulness, human rights are merely minimal demands and standards of justice. As a matter of justice, though, we must also ensure that people live more than minimally decent lives. We must ensure, for example, as John Rawls puts it, that the benefits and burdens of social cooperation are fairly shared among people (Rawls 1999). And we must address harms that threaten to befall people that do not affect their rights (e.g. unjust personal attitudes such as sexism and racism).

C.1 LIMITATIONS OF THE BOOK

Because human rights are not all that matters morally, there are also many effects of the internet that are morally important that exceed the scope of this book, which is limited to the internet's relevance for human rights. Each of these issues presents an important topic for further inquiry. The following examples are mentioned to indicate some of the limits of the discussion of this book and the need for further research.

C.1.1 *Internet, Information Communication Technologies, and Climate Change*

Climate change poses the most serious threat to the long-term survival and flourishing of humanity. As has been established beyond reasonable doubt, with human-caused greenhouse gas (GHG) emissions, humanity is increasing the Earth's average global temperature significantly beyond pre-industrial levels. With the climate policies currently in place, the planet is on course for an increase of at least 2.7 °C. This would significantly affect all of our species. The 'human climate niche', which is optimal for human existence and flourishing, has been found to contain 'a primary peak of population density at a mean annual temperature (MAT) of ~13 °C and a secondary peak at ~27 °C' (Lenton et al. 2023: 1237). Living in temperatures outside this ideal niche leads to negative consequences such as lower health, higher mortality, and displacement as people migrate to regions that are more hospitable to human life. According to the most recent estimates, 'the worst-case scenarios of ~3.6 °C or even ~4.4 °C global warming could put half of the world population outside the historical climate niche, posing an existential risk. The ~2.7 °C global warming expected under current policies puts around a third of the world population outside the niche' (Lenton et al. 2023: 1243). What is relevant for the argument of this book is that internet use contributes to global warming because it requires energy for the production and operating of the data centres, network infrastructures, and end devices that physically constitute this network of networks. To understand the internet's impact (and more generally that of information communication technologies (ICTs) on the climate), the following facts are useful:

- According to estimates for 2023 by the International Energy Agency (IEA), data centres and data transmission networks were responsible for circa 1 per cent of energy-related global GHG emissions (Rozite et al. 2023).
- According to a meta-analysis of studies of the climate impacts of ICTs, in 2020 the global 'carbon footprint of ICT, including TVs and other consumer electronics [equates to] 2.1–3.9 per cent of global GHG emissions (Freitag et al. 2021: 3).
- In 2019, the French non-profit climate change think tank The Shift Project estimated that pornography accounted for almost a third of global online video streaming (The Shift Project 2019). The energy needed for this data traffic generated as much carbon dioxide (CO_2) as the entire country of Belgium in one year (Griffiths 2020).
- According to 2022 estimates, 'it seems that a value of 1 kWh [Kilowatt hour] per GB could be a reasonable approximation of the current energy cost of data. Using that estimate, we can now more easily compare the energy use of data with other human activities. For instance, a two-hour movie in 4K resolution is about 7 GB, or approximately 7 kWh of energy, comparable to a 45-minute car drive' (Bonetti 2022).
- On the other hand, the growth of internet use has been accompanied by greater energy efficiency so that energy use has not increased

proportionally with global internet traffic. According to the IEA, 'since 2010, the number of internet users worldwide has more than doubled, while global internet traffic has expanded 25-fold' (Rozite et al. 2023). However, the estimated amount of energy consumed by ICT use globally has only increased from 800 TWh (terawatt hours) in 2010 to 916 TWh in 2020. During the same period, the total carbon footprint of the global ICT sector is estimated to have increased from 720 megatonnes CO_2e (CO_2 equivalent) to 763 megatonnes (Malmodin et al. 2024: 11).

The reason that this book has not engaged with the emissions impact of the internet is that humanity must in any case transition to green, sustainable energy if we want to prevent a hothouse Earth that would leave only a few areas hospitable for human life. As the figures given here indicate, internet use makes up a non-negligible but minor contribution to global warming. The energy use needed for its operation has become more efficient. Moreover, climate emissions caused by internet use are not luxury emissions (i.e. emissions generated by the production, use, or consumption of unnecessary things such as bitcoin, private yachts and aeroplanes, and factory farming; see Shue 1993) – at least if the internet is used to exercise human rights. In these cases, internet access and use are not luxuries, but rather practically indispensable for the protection of some of our morally most urgent interests. The supreme danger of climate change is therefore not an argument against the human right to free internet access. The reasoning in this regard is analogous to that about the moral importance of human development and its impact on the climate. People in developing countries have a right to human development and the fulfilment of their human rights. As long as not all energy use is environmentally sustainable, human development will involve creating GHG. However, this is not a reason to deny people their opportunities for development when humanity can instead reduce other optional emissions (Moellendorf 2014). In the same way, the internet is morally too important to deny people a right to access it when there are other (luxury) emissions that can be cut instead.

C.1.2 *Internet Addiction and Other Types of Digital Addiction*

Even though internet addiction, or problematic internet use, is not recognised as a disorder by the World Health Organization, it has been a long-standing concern about the internet. Internet addiction disorder 'can be defined as a lack of control in the use of the Internet, in such a way that it impacts the personal life of the user' (Lozano-Blasco et al. 2022: 1). More specifically, problematic internet use is characterized by:

> (1) impaired control over internet use, (2) increased priority of internet use that leads to the neglect of other life domains and (3) the continuation or escalation of internet use despite negative consequences [and] associated with a variety of negative mental health outcomes, e.g. depression and anxiety […], affective and obsessive-compulsive symptoms […], Attention Deficit Hyperactivity Disorder (ADHD) […] or social withdrawal, distress and familial conflicts […]. (Augner et al. 2023: 1)

It might be argued that the more widespread problematic internet use is, the more it diminishes the overall positive value of the internet for people. However, when consulting empirical studies on the problem, it appears that internet use does not as such and inevitably lead to internet addiction for the vast majority of users.

According to one large and recent meta-analysis of 495 peer-reviewed articles containing 504 studies involving about 2 million individuals in sixty-five countries, 'global pooled prevalence estimates were 26.99% […] for smartphone addiction, 17.42% […] for social media addiction, 14.22% […] for Internet addiction, 8.23% […] for cybersex addiction, and 6.04% […] for game addiction. Higher prevalence of digital addiction was found in Eastern Mediterranean region and low/lower-middle income countries' (Meng et al. 2022: 1). Even though the authors of the meta-analysis acknowledge the limitations of their study owing to factors such as limited data from low-income countries, their findings show that there is a clear connection between the prevalence of digital addiction and a low quality of life. 'Participants with economic or social disadvantages are more likely to use digital media to build connections, self-medicate, reduce stress, and alleviate mood as an escape from the unsatisfied outer environment' (Meng et al. 2022: 9). If this connection between socio-economic deprivation and digital addiction is correct, this suggests that it is not the use of the internet itself that leads to addictive use. Rather, other factors such as socio-economic disadvantage are essential for explaining why a minority of people engage in problematic internet use. Moreover, other empirical studies stress that 'the addictive use of the Internet is associated with interpersonal problems, depression, anxiety […], perceived stress, difficulties in resilience […], and traits such as psychological inflexibility, experiential avoidance and emotional instability […]' (Lozano-Blasco et al. 2022: 6). It therefore appears that besides societal factors, there are frequently personal ones that lead some people to become addicted to internet use.

These insights are important for the book's purposes because they suggest that the availability of the internet alone does not necessarily or equally pose a risk to all people for developing forms of digital addiction. Instead, in most cases other contributing factors have to be present for problematic internet use to occur. Therefore, the problem of internet addiction and other forms of digital addiction does not undermine the argument for the human right to free internet access. Even though internet addiction disorder presents a serious problem for those affected by it, it does not constitute an inevitable downside that has to be weighed against the benefits that internet access offers for our human rights. Further discussions of this problem can therefore be bracketed here.

C.1.3 *Internet Use and User Attention*

Another concern that is frequently cited as a serious potential downside of internet use even by those who recognise the internet's positive potential (e.g. Cruft 2024) is that extensive internet use might negatively affect users' attention and ability to focus. As with the problem of internet addiction, one might worry that – if internet use as such is likely to lead for many to a reduction of their ability to focus and pay attention – this would constitute a significant harm of internet use that has to be weighed against its benefits.

When considering this issue, it is important to note right from the start that, according to the non-profit organisation CHADD (Children and Adults with ADHD – a leading US charity dedicated to helping people suffering from attention deficit hyperactivity disorder), internet use does not cause ADHD. This is because ADHD is a lifelong medical condition, the causes of which are thought to be genetic or related to exposure to risks in the womb or at a young age (Love 2022).

However, studies suggest that people who suffer from ADHD are particularly prone to developing problematic or addictive internet use. Both problematic internet use and ADHD are associated with attention deficit, hyperactivity, and impulsivity (Augner et al. 2023: 1). What is particularly challenging for those who suffer from ADHD is not internet use as such, but rather the attention-grabbing design of many apps and websites that employ, for example, instant action–reward mechanisms to 'hook' users to their services. 'Here, a *trigger* initiates an *action*, i.e. open a website, follow a link, click a button, respond to a message, or download an app. Developers connect the action to a (variable) *reward* for reinforcement. [...] Small investments by the user aim to "hook" them to the app. The aim is above all to create new habits, i.e. "habit-as-a-routine"' (Augner et al. 2023: 11). Researchers think that sufferers of ADHD are particularly vulnerable to such mechanisms because ADHD symptoms are thought to be the result of a 'reward regulation deficit [that is caused by] dopaminergic dysfunctions' (Augner et al. 2023: 11). It is therefore the design of online services that aim to capture the valuable and scarce resource of user attention that presents a particular challenge for those who already have difficulties focusing their attention. These correlations between ADHD symptoms and internet addiction have been found in Asian (Augner et al. 2023) as well as non-Asian contexts (Panagiotidi and Overton 2018).

Other studies, though, suggest that – even though high internet use does not lead to people suffering from ADHD – it might cause ADHD-like symptoms in them. One study followed more than 2,500 ninth-grade US students over almost two years to investigate the effect that frequent digital media use had on their attention. The study included only participants without known ADHD symptoms and found that 'high-frequency use of multiple forms of modern digital media was associated with increased odds of ADHD symptom occurrence over a 24-month period of midadolescence' (Ra et al. 2018: 258). To explain this association between frequent digital media and the occurrence of attention deficits, those conducting the study point to the features of common digital media:

> [M]odern media devices immediately notify users when new text messages, social media postings, or videogame play invitations arrive. Exposure to such notifications may draw attention away from focal tasks. Frequent distractions could disrupt normative development of sustained attention and organization skills. Additionally, modern media platforms provide instantaneous access to highly stimulating experiences and rapid feedback in response to user input. (Ra et al. 2018: 261)

Empirical studies of internet use and attention deficits therefore suggest a vital role for the way that digital devices and online services such as websites and apps operate to capture the attention of their users. This, though, also suggests that it is not primarily internet use as such, but rather the way that internet use is often operationalised by digital service providers for the purpose of profit maximisation that can lead to attention deficits in users, especially younger ones. Even though this problem is an important subject for further studies (e.g. to determine whether the harm done to users is serious enough to require public authorities to intervene to protect internet users), it is not serious enough to endanger the argument for the human right to free internet access, and is therefore not within the remit of this book.

C.1.4 *Global Beauty Norms and Online Misogyny*

Beyond these issues, there are other examples of morally relevant effects of the internet that are not primarily human rights-related, and therefore beyond the scope of this work. For example, the internet and the global sharing of videos and photos it enables has been argued to be partly responsible for the emergence of a common global beauty standard. The beauty norms involved in this standard appear to be no longer simply of regional or aesthetic relevance but rather have acquired a moral quality. That is, adherence to and fulfilment of the standard promise rewards while divergence from it is seen as a moral failure of a person. Because its norms are extremely demanding, often impossible to fulfil for individuals, and attach moral praise and blame to something for which such judgements are inappropriate, the emerging global beauty standard constitutes a moral problem (Widdows 2018).

Another example is the spread of misogynistic attitudes online as exemplified by Andrew Tate. Tate is a social media personality and self-proclaimed misogynist who advocates norms of masculinity that express and endorse male supremacy, aggression, emotional rigidity, and hypersexuality (Verma and Khurana 2023). His rise as a celebrity would be hardly imaginable without the opportunities that the internet offers individuals for creating and sharing content online. Another instance of how the internet can help spread misogyny is the phenomenon of involuntary celibate men (known as 'incels'). These are mostly under thirty years old, use the internet as a crucial medium for communicating their views, and view sex as a right that they are entitled to but deprived of (O'Donnell and Shor 2022). Incels have been found to generally support violence against women and others as a legitimate way to draw attention to their grievances, and some of them have committed deadly attacks on random co-citizens (e.g. the case of Alek Minassian who killed ten pedestrians with a car in Toronto in 2018 or the 2014 Isla Vista killings perpetrated by Elliot Rodger, who shot to death six people before killing himself).

The demanding and harmful effects of the rise of a common, moralised, global beauty standard and the ease with which misogynistic attitudes and aggression can spread online most certainly present extremely serious problems associated with the internet. However, just like ICT emissions, problematic internet use, and attention deficits, they do not constitute significant reasons against recognising a human right to free internet access and are therefore not pursued further here. Instead, over-demanding beauty norms and misogyny are issues that ought to be addressed by education and critical discussion of the harms they involve. They might also in certain cases fall under the need to regulate dangerous online speech on social media platforms, as was discussed in Chapter 7.

C.1.5 *Responses to Violations of Free Internet Access*

The book also does not provide details about how states and other agents should respond if the human right to free internet access is violated. This might seem surprising given the specific role of human rights as matters of international concern that obligate the international community to protect these universal entitlements everywhere. One reason for this omission is that it is normally difficult to say in the abstract what responses to specific human right violations would be appropriate. The answer to this question will have to take into account moral considerations, such as proportionality, which require knowledge of the features of the individual case. Concrete judgements about individual cases often exceed the scope of moral philosophy, and therefore this book. However, what can be said at this point is that it is difficult to see how violations of the human right to free internet access could justify extreme responses such as military interventions. That is because such violations of free internet access and use will rarely lead to immediate grievous harm. Any serious harm that they cause would therefore likely be outweighed by military conflict that has the purpose of reinstating free internet access. As we saw in Part II, interference with free internet access and use can indeed have devastating consequences for human rights and threaten minimally decent lives. Any adequate response to online censorship, mass online surveillance, and online manipulation, though, has to employ justifiable means.

Proportionate responses could, for example, entail measures that restrict the violating party's ability to interfere with free internet access and use. Chapter 6 outlined, for example, strong restrictions on the export of surveillance technology to prevent unjustified violations of free internet use in the first place. Moreover, a 2017 proposal to AFRINIC (the Reginal Internet Registry for Africa) suggested that the agency should stop allocating new IP addresses for one year to governments that unjustifiably enforce internet shutdowns on their populations (Digital Watch 2017). Even though the proposal was ultimately rejected, such a step could cause significant problems for regimes that violate internet freedom, as the strongly negative response of African governments to the proposal indicates (McCarthy 2017). Private companies on their part should refuse to co-operate with, and acquiesce to the demands of, governments that would require the companies to commit or enable violations of free internet use. For example, in 2017 Cambridge University Press reversed its initial compliance with the Chinese government's demands to take down hundreds of journal articles that were deemed undesirable by the regime (BBC News 2017). Moreover, the big tech giants Google and Facebook have for some time accepted the blocking of their services in China by the Great Firewall because they refuse to co-operate with the censorship requirements of the Chinese government. However, since the institution of these bans on their services, there have also been reports from time to time that both companies have become more open to abiding by the regime's demands in order to gain access to the lucrative Chinese market (Isaac 2016, Nossel 2018). Such a decision, though, would be incompatible with the human right to free internet access and the companies' moral obligations to respect human rights in their business dealings outlined by the UN *Guiding Principles on Business and Human Rights* (UN 2011b), which we discussed in Chapter 7.

C.1.6 *Legitimate Restrictions on the Human Right to Free Internet Access*

Finally, the book does not establish a comprehensive list of cases of justified restrictions of free internet access and use. It seems clear, though, that there are plausible cases in which internet access and/or use can legitimately be restricted for certain purposes and people, and that – consequently – the human right to free internet access (as most other human rights) is not an absolute right.

Examples of justifiable restrictions discussed throughout the book include the blocking of online content on social media platforms to protect human rights and the unequal treatment of internet traffic for purposes such as network security and management. Beyond these cases, it is also plausible to think that restricting internet access for children to protect them from harmful content is justifiable, just as limiting children's access to TV programmes and bank accounts are reasonable steps to prevent them from harm that they are unable to grasp. Moreover, some restrictions of internet use also seem plausible for incarcerated criminals if continued access to certain online sites or applications would enable them to continue criminal activities. This does not mean, though, that there is a straightforward case for denying imprisoned criminals all internet access – especially if such access might allow them to stay connected to society while being confined to prison.

It is important to note, though, that complete internet shutdowns seem justifiable only in theory as legitimate means to protect people's rights or other goods such as national security. To see this, we can appreciate that the case of complete internet shutdowns is similar to that of indiscriminate mass online surveillance. The threat needed to justify an extreme measure such as complete internet shutdowns as a proportionate and necessary response would have to be massive or even existential to warrant its impact on all the human rights and other freedoms affected. In contrast, temporary and local restrictions of particular online applications or content might be justifiable if these are necessary and likely successful means for preventing serious harm (e.g. violent protests or attacks on individuals or groups). However, such limited measures would not constitute complete or even partial internet shutdowns. More work is needed to specify when and why restrictions of free internet access and use can be compatible with the human right to free internet access (see e.g. Thumfart 2024). But such plausible restrictions concern the implications, rather than the justifiability or demands, of that right.

C.2 A NEW HUMAN RIGHT

Despite these restrictions of its scope, this book has presented a detailed, empirically informed justification for the demand that public authorities recognise a new human right to free internet access. The internet has become too important for the enjoyment of our existing human rights to leave online access up to the profit motives of private companies or the financial means of individuals. Moreover, unjustifiable interferences with individuals' access and use of the internet have become too commonplace and are too damaging to vital interests and fundamental rights of people to allow them to continue. The answer to these problems is the recognition and enforcement of a human right to free internet access because such an entitlement guarantees both online access and use without objectionable restrictions. This new human right also has implications for many much-discussed issues such as the (domestic and global) digital divide, digital authoritarianism, the permissibility of online mass surveillance, online misinformation, net neutrality, social media platform regulation, and dangerous online speech. Recognition of and respect for this right would provide effective protection from the harms associated with digital poverty and unfree internet use because rights are enforceable claims to social guarantees against standard threats. The human right to free internet access is also useful for those to whom it is denied because it provides a normative goal and an argumentative resource against those who interfere with it.

In the introduction, we encountered six demanding tests that James Nickel specifies for determining whether something qualifies as a human right. These tests are important because they prevent us from problematically expanding the entire category of human rights, thereby making it less urgent and authoritative. According to the first test, all human rights must be relevant for people's most fundamental and morally urgent interests. Throughout this book (in particular in Chapters 3 and 4), we have seen that internet access today is relevant for very morally important things, namely the enjoyment and protection of our existing human rights. To be more precise, internet access has become practically and systemically indispensable for having adequate opportunities to exercise our human rights. Where internet access is already widespread, the effectivity and practical worth of human rights are objectionably curtailed for those who involuntarily remain offline. Without being able to access the internet, people can no longer live in a satisfactory way in digitalised societies because online access is necessary for entering and participating in cyberspace. This does not mean that people generally can be forced to, or have a duty to, use the internet (Kloza 2024). As with many other rights (e.g. to free speech, free assembly, free information), the point of a novel right to internet access is to guarantee protected opportunities, not to create an obligation to exercise it. Its purpose is to make sure that those who want to use the internet can do so. We also saw that in developing nations, internet access can make the difference between people having some or no level of enjoyment of their human rights. This does not mean that digital options provide sufficient opportunities for all human rights. The full realisation and guarantee of human rights plausibly require in-person provision of, for example, health care and education. However, where this is not immediately possible, internet-based options can be the only feasible ones. As internet adoption rates increase in these regions, so does the importance for people's adequate opportunities to use their human rights vis-à-vis their fellow citizens who already have online access. Either way, internet access has become indispensable for our human rights today.

Nickel's second test demands that human rights provide social guarantees against substantive and recurring threats to the urgent interests that human rights protect, rather than ineffective measures against rare dangers. This follows from Shue's understanding of rights as social guarantees against standard threats that are 'ordinary' (rather than exceptional), 'serious' (rather than trivial), and 'remedial' (instead of unavoidable) (Shue 2020: 32). In Part II we saw that, without appropriate protections (such as those demanded by the human right to free internet access), people face standard threats from poverty, states, private companies, and other internet users to their access and use of the internet. Chapters 5–8 therefore spelled out feasible social guarantees that properly motivated public authorities can and should offer to protect people from a lack of, and arbitrary interferences with, online access and use. What is decisive for effective protections, this book argues, is the necessary political will and popular support they require. Their technical and financial viability, on the other hand, is generally not in question.

Because human rights matter to all people, the third test requires that the urgent interests that human rights protect must be of universal importance rather than of merely national or local relevance. The human right to free internet access meets this requirement because its justification rests on the usefulness of the internet for our political, civil, socio-economic, and cultural human rights around the globe. In that way, the right is relevant because it protects those universal urgent interests that are the objects of existing human rights.

According to the fourth test, human rights must be necessary for their objects so that no weaker norm (e.g. helping people to help themselves or voluntary aid of others) could provide the needed protections. Throughout this book, we have seen indeed that for multiple reasons only a human right is adequate to the task of protecting free internet access and use. The internet is a medium the establishment of which requires technological know-how and substantial financial resources. In the context of those who are currently digitally left behind, public institutions must step in where individuals either do not have the means or are not attractive enough as customers for private enterprises to develop currently missing internet connections. The empowering effects that the internet can have for human rights make online access a proper matter of international concern. Where individuals are unable to afford internet access, their government has an obligation to provide a sufficient level of access for them, and where entire countries are unable to guarantee online access for their citizens, the international community has a moral obligation to step in to ensure universal connectivity. Additionally, because abuses of the internet with the aim to control, oppress, or monitor people are extremely threatening to individual autonomy and effective political participation, they generate obligations for states to not arbitrarily interfere with people's internet access and to not support such interferences by other agents. Importantly, subsuming the good of internet access under any existing human right offers insufficient protection because almost all human rights can legitimately be curtailed in certain circumstances. Denying a person internet access, though, always affects not just one but most of their human rights. Moreover, there is no existing human right that specifically guarantees people access to the important social realm of cyberspace. Both the harms of lacking internet access and of unprotected internet access and use justify the claim that free internet access must be its own human right.

The fifth test demands that the fulfilment of human rights must not cause unjustifiable financial or moral burdens on others. This follows from the structure of rights that necessarily impose burdens on others, and these burdens must be justifiable to those who are put under an obligation to provide or respect the objects of the rights in question. As outlined in Part II, the general content of the human right to free internet access does not generate unjustifiable burdens for public authorities or individuals. The right secures a level of digital sufficiency and adequacy rather than what is maximally possible in terms of internet connectivity. Part II also discussed invasions of internet users' privacy by states and private companies that today are the norm when people access and use the internet. However, neither these privacy violations nor online attacks on internet users by other individuals are necessary consequences or part of the experience of the internet. Rather, they present standard threats from which public authorities ought to protect their citizens. Moreover, the profit interests of private companies do not outweigh the moral importance of people's human rights. Therefore, the human right to internet access does not entail unavoidable monetary and moral costs for those who have to provide or respect free internet access.

The last of Nickel's tests of human rights states that these must all be feasible for the majority of countries. If this was not the case, most states would become liable to criticisms that they have not realised something that they lack the means to guarantee (Nickel 2007: 78–86). With this in mind, the global standard of provision of internet connectivity that was outlined in Chapter 5 is partly determined with a view to meeting this requirement. To recall, one desideratum of the provisions that the human right to free internet access demands was that these are feasible for most states right now. This was one reason for choosing 2 GB of data for no more than 2 per cent of a country's monthly gross national income per capita, universal 4G mobile broadband coverage, availability of a smartphone, and the teaching of basic digital skills. All present feasible obligations for most states right now. Chapter 5 also specified minimum core obligations for those states unable to meet these requirements, but most states are capable of doing more. Moreover, abstaining from arbitrarily interfering with internet access and use is a matter of political will rather than technical feasibility for states. Concerning the passing of legislation to protect citizens against unjustifiable limitations or violations of people's internet access and use by private companies, it is the most powerful states, home to the most powerful internet corporations, that have to take the lead in regulating the Big Tech industry.

The fact that the human right to free internet access can meet all of Nickel's tests of human rights demonstrates the importance, urgency, and feasibility of public authorities recognising this universal entitlement. The internet is no longer a luxury, but a basic, non-optional utility and infrastructure for a decent life in digitalised societies. However, it is a technological means whose empowering potential is contingent and fragile. As a technology, the internet can be put to good and bad uses. Its negative potential for human rights and progress is as devastating as its positive potential is powerful. Free access and use of the internet therefore requires adequate protections by public authorities. The proposed human right provides such protections as well as a normative standard and a positive global vision that, if respected, can ensure that the internet becomes indeed a liberation technology that promotes human development and progress. The book therefore calls for public authorities to recognise, respect, and defend a new universal entitlement with the following content, or one that is equivalent in spirit:[1]

Article X

1. Everyone shall have the right to access and use the internet without arbitrary interferences by any other party. Free internet access offers uniquely powerful means for the use and protection of most human rights, it enables participation in cyberspace where a significant share of human interactions take place and unparalleled amounts of information are stored, and therefore can promote the progress of humanity overall.
2. This right shall entail the provision of the technological means and skills needed for guaranteed, meaningful access to the internet that is of sufficient quality for people to effectively make use of their human rights; moreover, the right shall guarantee the absence of unjustifiable restrictions or interruptions to people's exercise of their familiar freedoms (such as those to free expression, free information, free association) online.
3. Any justified restrictions of the right (e.g. temporary localised restrictions of internet access and use, censorship, surveillance and other denials of privacy) must conform to the familiar requirements of acceptable restrictions of human rights. This means that they must be:
    a. Provided by public law and subject to review by independent judicial bodies;
    b. Necessary, proportionate, and minimal;
    c. Undertaken for legitimate ends (e.g. for the protection of the rights and reputation of others; network maintenance and security; the protection of national security, public health, or public order).

Respect for free internet access is necessary for having adequate opportunities to exercise our human rights today, to make the internet a technology of liberation and progress, and to prevent it from being used as a uniquely powerful

---

[1] See Alexandria Poole's analogous case for a Sustainable Development Goal 18 (Poole 2018).

tool of oppression. The human right to free internet is an argumentative resource and normative goal for all those fighting against digital oppression and for the ability to use their rights online. But it also provides a standard of what states and the international community must guarantee in terms of digital connectivity for all human beings who want to participate online. If the human right to free internet access is recognised and respected, the internet will look very different from what we are used to today. The realisation of this right, though, is an important part of a global vision of the internet that promotes the good and progress of humankind. Losing the fight for the internet against forces that want to use it to manipulate, subdue, and exploit is something that humanity cannot afford. Too much is at stake here because the internet is too powerful a medium to be left to those who want to benefit only themselves and their interests. Recognising and defending this right would have the potential to make the world better for all with the help of the internet. The values and demands included in this idea are not optional. Instead, they necessarily follow from the premise that everyone possesses equal moral dignity and is entitled to live a decent life today in societies that are ever-more characterised by the information flows and connections made possible by the internet.

Bibliography

A4AI. 2017. *Affordability Report 2017*. Available at https://a4ai.org/research/affordability-report-2017/.
A4AI. 2018. *Closing the Investment Gap: How Multilateral Development Banks Can Contribute to Digital Inclusion*. Available at https://a4ai.org/news/closing-the-investment-gap-the-critical-role-of-development-banks-to-advance-digital-inclusion/.
A4AI. 2019. *Affordability Report 2019*. Available at https://a4ai.org/research/affordability-report/affordability-report-2019/.
A4AI. 2020a. *Affordability Report 2020*. Available at https://a4ai.org/research/affordability-report-2020/.
A4AI. 2020b. *Meaningful Connectivity. A New Target to Raise the Bar for Internet Access*. Available at https://a4ai.org/meaningful-connectivity/.
A4AI. 2020c. *Lowering Prices for Marginalised Users*. Available at https://a4ai.org/research/lowering-prices-for-marginalised-users/.
A4AI. 2020d. *Eliminating Luxury Taxation on ICT Essentials*. Available at https://a4ai.org/research/eliminating-luxury-taxation-on-ict-essentials/.
A4AI. 2021a. *Affordability Report 2021*. Available at https://a4ai.org/research/affordability-report/affordability-report-2021/.
A4AI. 2021b. *A Policy Guide: Toward Meaningful Connectivity*. Available at https://a4ai.org/meaningful-connectivity/.
Access Now. 2023. *Keep It On*. Available at www.accessnow.org/keepiton/.
Allcott, Hunt, Matthew Gentzkow. 2017. 'Social Media and Fake News in the 2016 Election,' *Journal of Economic Perspectives* 31(2): 211–236.
Allen-Ebrahimian, Bethany. 2016. 'The Man Who Nailed Jello to the Wall,' *Foreign Policy*. Available at https://foreignpolicy.com/2016/06/29/the-man-who-nailed-jello-to-the-wall-lu-wei-china-internet-czar-learns-how-to-tame-the-web/.
Altay, Sacha, Anne-Sophie Hacquin, Hugo Mercier. 2022. 'Why Do So Few People Share Fake News? It Hurts Their Reputation,' *New Media & Society* 24(6): 1303–1324.
Alyukov, Maxim. 2022. 'Propaganda, Authoritarianism and Russia's Invasion of Ukraine,' *Nature Human Behaviour* 6: 763–765.
Anderson, Elisabeth. 2021. 'Epistemic Bubbles and Authoritarian Politics' in Elizabeth Edenberg, Michael Hannon (eds.), *Political Epistemology* (Oxford: Oxford University Press): 11–30.

Antara. 2021. *BTS Development in 3T Areas Prioritises Sustainable Energy: BAKTI*. Available at https://en.antaranews.com/news/203305/bts-development-in-3t-areas-prioritizes-sustainable-energy-bakti.

APT. 2023. *ATP Report on Best Practice of Connectivity – Village Broadband Internet Project (Net Pracharat) of Thailand*. Available at www.apt.int/Publications.

Arguedas, Amy Ross, Craig T. Robertson, Richard Fletcher, Rasmus K. Nielsen. 2022. 'Echo Chambers, Filter Bubbles, and Polarisation: A Literature Review,' *Reuters Institute at the University of Oxford*. Available at https://reutersinstitute.politics.ox.ac.uk/sites/default/files/2022-01/Echo_Chambers_Filter_Bubbles_and_Polarisation_A_Literature_Review.pdf.

Article 19. 2017. *Germany: The Act to Improve Enforcement of the Law in Social Networks*. Available at www.article19.org/resources/germany-act-improve-enforcement-law-social-networks-undermines-free-expression/.

Article 19. 2021. *Watching the Watchmen. How to Regulate Content Moderation While Protecting Freedom of Expression*. Available at www.article19.org/wp-content/uploads/2023/02/Watching-the-watchmen-UPDATE-Jan2023-P04.pdf.

Augner, Christoph, Thomas Vlasak, Alfred Barth. 2023. 'The Relationship between Problematic Internet Use and Attention Deficit, Hyperactivity and Impulsivity: A Meta-Analysis,' *Journal of Psychiatric Research* 168: 1–12.

Australian Communications and Media Authority. 2022. *The Regional Broadband Scheme*. Available at www.acma.gov.au/regional-broadband-scheme.

Australian Government. 2021. *Universal Service Guarantee (USG) – 3 September 2021*. Available at www.infrastructure.gov.au/department/media/publications/universal-service-guarantee-usg-3-september-2021.

Aytac, Ugur. 2024. 'Digital Domination: Social Media and Contestatory Democracy,' *Political Studies* 72(1): 6–25.

Aytac, Ugur. 2024. 'Big Tech, Algorithmic Power, and Democratic Control,' *Journal of Politics*: 1–37.

Balkin, Jack M. 2020. 'The Fiduciary Model of Privacy,' *Harvard Law Review Forum* 134(1): 11–33.

Balkin, Jack M. 2021. 'How to Regulate (and Not to Regulate) Social Media,' *Journal of Free Speech Law* 1(1): 71–96.

Bamford, Roxanna, Georgina Hutchinson, Benedict Macon-Cooney. 2021. *The Progressive Case for Universal Internet Access: How to Close the Digital Divide by 2030* (London: Tony Blair Institute for Global Change).

Barthel, Michael, Amy Mitchell, Jesse Holcomb. 2016. 'Many Americans Believe Fake News Is Sowing Confusion,' *Pew Research Center*. Available at www.pewresearch.org/journalism/2016/12/15/many-americans-believe-fake-news-is-sowing-confusion/.

Bastick, Zach. 2017. 'Digital Limits of Government: The Failure of E-Democracy' in Alois A. Paulin, Leonidas G. Anthopoulos, Christopher G. Reddick (eds.), *Beyond Bureaucracy. Towards Sustainable Governance Informatisation* (Cham: Springer): 3–14.

Bauer, Johannes M., Jonathan A. Obar. 2014. 'Reconciling Political and Economic Goals in the Net Neutrality Debate,' *The Information Society* 30(1): 1–19.

Bauerly, Brittney Crock, Russell F. McCord, Rachel Hulkower, Dawn Pepin. 2019. 'Broadband Access as a Public Health Issue: The Role of Law in Expanding

Broadband Access and Connecting Underserved Communities for Better Health Outcomes,' *Journal of Law, Medicine & Ethics* 47(2): 39–42.
BBC News. 2017. *Cambridge University Press Reverses China Censorship Move*. Available at www.bbc.com/news/business-40998129.
BBC News. 2019. *General Election 2019: Labour Pledges Free Broadband for All*. Available at www.bbc.co.uk/news/election-2019-50427369.
BBC News. 2020. *NSA Surveillance Exposed by Snowden Ruled Unlawful*. Available at www.bbc.com/news/technology-54013527.
BBC News. 2022. *Google to Pay Record $391m Privacy Settlement*. Available at www.bbc.co.uk/news/technology-63635380.
BBC News. 2023. *What Is the Emergency Alert System and When Will We Get Messages?* Available at www.bbc.co.uk/newsround/65026368.
Beauchamp, Zach. 2019. 'Social Media Is Rotting Democracy from Within,' *Vox*. Available at www.vox.com/policy-and-politics/2019/1/22/18177076/social-media-facebook-far-right-authoritarian-populism.
Beitz, Charles. 2009. *The Idea of Human Rights* (Oxford: Oxford University Press).
Belli, Luca, Primavera De Filippi. 2016. 'General Introduction: Toward a Multistakeholder Approach to Net Neutrality' in Luca Belli, Primavera De Filippi (eds.), *Net Neutrality Compendium. Human Rights, Free Competition and the Future of the Internet* (Cham: Springer): 1–7.
Belli, Luca. 2016. 'End-to-End, Net Neutrality and Human Rights' in Luca Belli, Primavera De Filippi (eds.), *Net Neutrality Compendium. Human Rights, Free Competition and the Future of the Internet* (Cham: Springer): 13–29.
Bellingcat. 2023. *About*. Available at www.bellingcat.com/about/.
Benda, Natalie, Tiffany Veinot, Cynthia Sieck, Jessica Ancker. 2020. 'Broadband Internet Access Is a Social Determinant of Health!' *American Journal of Public Health* 110(8): 1123–1125.
Benkler, Yochai, Robert Faris, Hal Roberts. 2018. *Networked Propaganda. Manipulation, Disinformation, and Radicalization in American Politics* (Oxford: Oxford University Press).
Benkler, Yochai, Casey Tilton, Bruce Etling, Hal Roberts, Justin Clark, Robert Faris, Jonas Kaiser, Carolyn Schmitt. 2020. 'Mail-In Voter Fraud: Anatomy of a Disinformation Campaign,' *Berkman Klein Center for Internet & Society*: Research Publication No. 2020-6. Available at http://dx.doi.org/10.2139/ssrn.3703701.
Bennhold, Katrin. 2018. 'Germany Acts to Tame Facebook, Learning from Its Own History,' *New York Times*. Available at www.nytimes.com/2018/05/19/technology/facebook-deletion-center-germany.html.
Benson, Rodney, Matthew Powers, Timothy Neff. 2017. 'Public Media Autonomy and Accountability: Best and Worst Policy Practice in 12 Leading Democracies,' *International Journal of Communications* 11: 1–22.
BEREC. 2012. *Summary on BEREC Positions on Net Neutrality*. Available at www.berec.europa.eu/en/document-categories/berec/opinions/summary-of-berec-positions-on-net-neutrality.
Bergin, Julia, Louisa Lim, Nyein Nyein, Andrew Nachemson. 2022. 'Flicking the Kill Switch: Government Embrace Internet Shutdowns as a Form of Control,' *The Guardian*. Available at www.theguardian.com/technology/2022/aug/29/flicking-the-kill-switch-governments-embrace-internet-shutdowns-as-a-form-of-control.

Bergin, Julia, Louisa Lim. 2022. 'When Internet Shutdowns Spill over Borders,' *The Guardian*. Available at www.theguardian.com/technology/2022/aug/29/when-internet-shutdowns-spill-over-borders.

Bervell, Brandford, Hosam Al-Samarraie. 2019. 'A Comparative Review of Mobile Health and Electronic Health Utilization in Sub-Saharan African Countries,' *Social Science & Medicine* 232: 1–16.

Bhagwat, Ashutosh. 2021. 'Do Platforms have Editorial Rights?' *Journal of Free Speech Law* 1(1): 97–138.

Bhat, Irfan Ahmad, Imran Hafeez, Muzaffar Zargar, Nasir Shamas, Afaq Jalali. 2020. 'Managing STEMI & Other Time Sensitive Cardiac Emergencies by Using Smart Phones – A Study Utilizing Social Media As Tool to Integrate Local Health Network in Remote Areas of India – Save Heart Initiative,' *European Heart Journal* 41(2): ehaa946.3475.

Bibby, Jo, Cara Leavey. 2020. 'Learning from Lockdown. How Can We Build a Healthier Future Post-COVID-19?' *The Health Foundation*. Available www.health.org.uk/publications/long-reads/learning-from-lockdown.

Bill & Melinda Gates Foundation. 2023. *Global Libraries*. Available at https://billgatefoundation.org/What-We-Do/Global-Development/Global-Libraries.html.

Birchall, Clare, Peter Knight. 2022. 'Do Your Own Research: Conspiracy Theories and the Internet,' *Social Research* 89(3): 579–605.

BKA. 2023. *Cybercrime*. Available at www.bka.de/EN/OurTasks/AreasOfCrime/Cybercrime/cybercrime_node.html.

Blackwood-Brown, Carlene, Yair Levy, John D'Arcy. 2021. 'Cybersecurity Awareness and Skills of Senior Citizens: A Motivation Perspective,' *Journal of Computer Information Systems* 61(3): 195–206.

BMBF. 2021. *Initiative Digitale Bildung*. Available at www.bildung-forschung.digital/digitalezukunft/de/bildung/initiative-digitale-bildung/initiative-digitale-bildung.html.

BMBF. 2023. *DigitalPakt Schule*. Available at www.digitalpaktschule.de/.

BMBWF. 2023. *Digitale Grundausbildung*. Available at www.bmbwf.gv.at/Themen/schule/zrp/dibi/dgb.html.

Boeing, Geoff. 2020. 'Online Rental Housing Market Representation and the Digital Reproduction of Urban Inequality,' *Economy and Space* 52(2): 449–468.

Bonetti, Stefano. 2022. 'Could Video Streaming be as Bad for the Climate as Driving a Car? Calculating Internet's Hidden Carbon Footprint,' *The Conversation*. Available at https://theconversation.com/could-video-streaming-be-as-bad-for-the-climate-as-driving-a-car-calculating-internets-hidden-carbon-footprint-194558.

Booth, Robert. 2023. 'Automated UK Welfare System Needs More Human Contact, Ministers Warned,' *The Guardian*. Available at www.theguardian.com/society/2023/may/22/automated-uk-welfare-system-needs-more-human-contact-ministers-warned.

Bos, Linda, Sanne Kruikemeier, Claes de Vreese. 2016. 'Nation Binding. How Public Service Broadcast Mitigates Political Selective Exposure,' *PLoS One* 11(5): e0155112.

Boxell, Levi, Matthew Gentzkow, Jesse M. Shapiro. 2017. 'Is the Internet Causing Political Polarization? Evidence from Demographics,' *National Bureau of Economic Research*: Working Paper 23258.

BPB. 2023. *Wahl-O-Mat*. Available at www.bpb.de/themen/wahl-o-mat/.

Braumüller, Heike. 2018. 'The Little We Know: An Exploration Literature Review on the Utility of Mobile Phone-Enabled Services for Smallholder Farmers,' *Journal of International Development* 30(1): 134–154.
Brecht, Bertolt. (2003). 'The Radio as an Apparatus of Communication' in Anna Everett and John T. Caldwell (eds.), *New Media: Theories and Practices of Digitextuality* (New York: Routledge): 29–32.
Broadband Commission. 2017. *Digital Health: A Call for Government Leadership and Cooperation between ICT and Health*. Available at https://broadbandcommission.org/publication/digital-health/.
Broadband Commission. 2019. *Connecting Africa through Broadband. A Strategy for Doubling Connectivity by 2021 and Reaching Universal Access by 2030*. Available at www.broadbandcommission.org/publication/connecting-africa-through-broadband/.
Broadband Commission. 2020. *The State of Broadband: Tackling Digital Inequalities: A Decade for Action*. Available at https://broadbandcommission.org/publication/the-state-of-broadband-2020/.
Broadband Commission. 2021a. *The State of Broadband: People-Centred Approaches for Universal Broadband*. Available at https://broadbandcommission.org/publication/state-of-broadband-2021/.
Broadband Commission. 2021b. *21st Century Financing Models for Bridging Broadband Connectivity Gaps*. Available at https://broadbandcommission.org/publication/21st-century-financing-models/.
Broadband Commission. 2022. *2025 Broadband Advocacy Targets/Target 2: Make Broadband Affordable*. Available at www.broadbandcommission.org/advocacy-targets/2-affordability/.
Buchanan, Allen. 2013. *The Heart of Human Rights* (Oxford: Oxford University Press).
Bundesagentur für Arbeit. 2021. *Mehrbedarfe für digitale Endgeräte für den Schulunterricht*. Available at www.arbeitsagentur.de/datei/weisung-202110004_ba147174.pdf.
Bundesnetzagentur. 2023. *Internet und Telefon: Versorgung*. Available at www.bundesnetzagentur.de/DE/Vportal/TK/InternetTelefon/Versorgung/start.html/.
Burnett, Sam, Nick Feamster. 2013. 'Making Sense of Internet Censorship: A New Frontier for Internet Measurement,' *ACM SIGCOMM Computer Communication Review* 43(3): 84–89.
Burns, Anthony. 2016. '"Happy Slaves?" The Adaptation Problem and Identity Politics in the Writings of Amartya Sen,' *International Journal of Social Economics* 43(12): 1178–1193.
Bychawska-Siniarska, Dominika. 2017. 'Protecting the Right to Freedom of Expression under the European Convention on Human Rights. A Handbook for Legal Practitioners,' *Council of Europe*. Available at https://rm.coe.int/handbook-freedom-of-expression-eng/1680732814.
Calı, Başak. 2020. 'The Case for Meaningful Access to the Internet as a Human Right in International Law' in Andreas von Arnauld, Kersin von der Decken, Marti Susi (eds.), *The Cambridge Handbook of New Human Rights: Recognition, Novelty, Rhetoric* (Cambridge: Cambridge University Press): 276–283.
Caney, Simon. 2005. *Justice beyond Borders. A Global Political Theory* (Oxford: Oxford University Press).
Caney, Simon. 2010. 'Climate Change, Human Rights, and Moral Thresholds' in Stephen M. Gardiner, Simon Caney, Dale Jamieson, Henry Shue (eds.), *Climate Ethics: Essential Readings* (Oxford: Oxford University Press): 163–177.

Caputi, Theodore L., Alicia L. Nobles, John W. Ayers. 2019. 'Internet Searches for Sexual Harassment and Assault, Reporting, and Training Since the #MeToo Movement,' *JAMA Internal Medicine* 179(2): 258–259.

Carr Center. 2022. 'Reimagining Rights and Responsibilities in the United States,' *Harvard University*. Available at https://carrcenter.hks.harvard.edu/reimagining-rights-responsibilities-united-states.

Carter, Meg. 2014. 'How Twitter May Have Helped Nigeria Contain Ebola,' *BMJ* 349: g3946.

Casciani, Dominic. 2018. 'Edward Snowden Surveillance Powers Ruled Unlawful,' *BBC*. Available at www.bbc.com/news/uk-45510662.

Cassam, Quassim. 2019. *Conspiracy Theories* (Cambridge: Polity Press).

Center for Countering Digital Hate. 2023. *Belief in Conspiracy Theories Higher among Teenagers than Adults, as Majority of Americans Supports Social Media Reform, New Polling Finds*. Available at https://counterhate.com/blog/belief-in-conspiracy-theories-higher-among-teenagers-than-adults-as-majority-of-americans-support-social-media-reform-new-polling-finds/.

Cerf, Vinton G. 2012. 'Internet Access Is Not a Human Right,' *New York Times*. Available at www.nytimes.com/2012/01/05/opinion/internet-access-is-not-a-human-right.html.

CESCR. 1990. *General Comment No. 3: The Nature of States Parties Obligations*. Available at https://tbinternet.ohchr.org/_layouts/15/treatybodyexternal/Download.aspx?symbolno=INT%2FCESCR%2FGEC%2F4758&Lang=en.

CESCR. 2000. *General Comment No. 14: The Right to the Highest Attainable Standard of Health*. Available at https://tbinternet.ohchr.org/_layouts/15/treatybodyexternal/Download.aspx?symbolno=E%2FC.12%2F2000%2F4&Lang=en.

Chang, Chun-Chih, Thung-Hong Lin. 2020. 'Autocracy Login: Internet Censorship and Civil Society in the Digital Age,' *Democratization* 27(5): 874–895.

Chen, Annie Y., Brendan Nyhan, Jason Reifler, Ronald E. Ronaldson, Christo Wilson. 2023. 'Subscriptions and External Links Help Drive Resentful Users to Alternative and Extremist YouTube Channels,' *Science Advances* 9(35): eadd8080.

Christen, Markus, Bert Gordjin, Michele Loi (eds). 2020. *The Ethics of Cybersecurity* (Cham: Springer Open).

Christiano, Thomas. 2008. *The Constitution of Equality: Democratic Authority and Its Limits* (Oxford: Oxford University Press).

Christiano, Thomas. 2011. 'An Instrumental Argument for a Human Right to Democracy,' *Philosophy & Public Affairs* 39(2): 142–176.

Christiano, Thomas. 2022. 'Algorithms, Manipulation, and Democracy,' *Canadian Journal of Philosophy* 52(1): 109–124.

Cinelli, Matteo, Gabriela Etta, Michele Avalle, Alessandro Quattrociocchi, Nicolo Di Marco, Carlo Valensise, Alessandro Galeazzi, Walter Quattrociocchi. 2022. 'Conspiracy Theories and Social Media Platforms,' *Current Opinions in Psychology* 47: 101407.

Citizens Online. 2023. *What We Do*. Available at www.citizensonline.org.uk/what-we-do/.

City Bar Justice Center. 2020. *Homeless Need Internet Access to Find a Home*. Available at www.citybarjusticecenter.org/news/homeless-need-internet-access-to-find-a-home-the-city-bar-justice-center-documents-lack-of-technology-in-nyc-homeless-shelters/.

City of Boston. 2023. *BPL Outdoor Spaces*. Available at www.boston.gov/bpl-outdoors.

Clément, Dominique. 2018. 'Human Rights or Social Justice? The Problem of Rights Inflation,' *International Journal of Human Rights* 22(2): 155–169.

Coeckelbergh, Mark. 2023. 'Democracy, Epistemic Agency, and AI: Political Epistemology in Times of Artificial Intelligence,' *AI & Ethics* 3: 1341–1350.
Coleman, Eli, Esther Corona-Vargas, Jessie V. Ford. 2021. 'Advancing Sexual Pleasure as a Fundamental Human Right and Essential for Sexual Health, Overall Health and Well-Being: An Introduction to the Special Issue on Sexual Pleasure,' *International Journal of Sexual Health* 33(4):473–477.
Comeig, Irene, Klaudijo Klaser, Lucía D. Pinar. 2022. 'The Paradox of (Inter)Net Neutrality: An Experiment on Ex-Ante Antitrust Regulation,' *Technology Forecasting & Social Change* 175: 121405.
Confused.com. 2023. *Data Usage Calculator*. Available at www.confused.com/mobile-phones/mobile-data-calculator.
Council of Europe. 2018. *Online Participation in Culture and Politics: Toward More Democratic Societies?* Available at https://rm.coe.int/second-thematic-report-based-on-the-indicator-framework-on-culture-and/16808d2514.
Craft, Stephanie, Seth Ashley, Adam Maksl. 2017. 'News Media Literacy and Conspiracy Theory Endorsement,' *Communication and the Public* 2(4): 388–401.
CrowdJustice. 2023. *How It Works*. Available at www.crowdjustice.com/how-it-works/.
Crisp, Roger (ed.). 2014. *Griffin on Human Rights* (Oxford: Oxford University Press).
CRTC. 2023. *Broadband Fund: Closing the Digital Divide in Canada*. Available at https://crtc.gc.ca/eng/internet/internet.htm.
Cruft, Rowan. 2024. 'Is There a Human Right to Internet Access?' in Carissa Véliz (ed.), *The Oxford Handbook of Digital Ethics* (Oxford: Oxford University Press): 63–82.
Custers, Bart. 2022. 'New Digital Rights: Imagining Additional Fundamental Rights for the Digital Era,' *Computer Law & Security Review* 44: 105636.
D64. 2021. *The Login Trap: Combating Hate Speech without Mass Surveillance*. Available at https://d-64.org/wp-content/uploads/2022/01/D64-LoginTrap.pdf.
Dawson, Andrew, Martin Innes. 2019. 'How Russia's Internet Research Agency Built Its Disinformation Campaigns,' *The Political Quarterly* 90(2): 245–256.
De Hert, Paul, Dariusz Kloza. 2012. 'Internet (Access) as a New Fundamental Right. Inflating the Current Rights Framework?' *European Journal of Law and Technology* 3(3): 1–23.
De Schutter, Olivier. 2010. 'The Emerging Human Right to Land,' *International Community Law Review* 12(3): 303–334.
De Vries, Bouke. 2022. 'Should Autists Have Cultural Rights?' *Human Rights Review* 23(2): 205–219.
Deibert, Ronald J. 2019. 'The Road to Digital Unfreedom: Three Painful Truths about Social Media,' *Journal of Democracy* 30(1): 25–39.
Deng, Xin, Dinge Xu, Miao Zeng, Yanbin Qi. 2019. 'Does Internet Use Help Reduce Rural Cropland Abandonment? Evidence from China,' *Land Use Policy* 89: 104243.
Deutscher Bundestag. 2020. *Drucksache 19/22750. Entwurf eines Gesetzes zur Ermittlung von Regelbedarfen und zur Änderung des Zwölften Buches Sozialgesetzbuch sowie des Asylbewerberleistungsgesetzes*. Available at https://dserver.bundestag.de/btd/19/227/1922750.pdf.
Digital Inclusion. 2023. *About Us*. Available at https://digital-inclusion.lu/about-us/.
Digital Watch. 2017. *AFRINIC Rejects Proposal to Stop Allocating IP Addresses to Governments That Shut Down Internet Access*. Available at https://dig.watch/updates/afrinic-rejects-proposal-stop-allocating-ip-addresses-governments-shut-down-internet-access.

DiResta, Renee, Kris Shaffer, Becky Ruppel, David Sullivan, Robert Matney. 2019. 'The Tactics & Tropes of the Internet Research Agency,' *Congress of the United States*. Available at https://digitalcommons.unl.edu/senatedocs/2/.

Douglas, Karen M., Joseph E. Uscinski, Robbie M. Sutton, Aleksandra Cichocka, Turkay Nefes, Chee Siang Ang, Farzin Deravi. 2019. 'Understanding Conspiracy Theories,' *Political Psychology* 40(1): 3–35.

Douglas, Karen M., Robbie M. Sutton. 2023. 'What Are Conspiracy Theories? A Definitional Approach to Their Correlates, Consequences, and Communication,' *Annual Review of Psychology* 74: 271–298.

Dragu, Tiberiu, Yonatan Lupu. 2021. 'Digital Authoritarianism and the Future of Human Rights,' *International Organization* 75(4): 991–1017.

Dutton, William H., Bianca C. Reisdorf, Grant Blank, Elizabeth Dubois, Laleah, Fernandez. 2019. 'The Internet and Access to Information about Politics. Searching Through Filter Bubbles, Echo Chambers, and Disinformation' in Mark Graham, William H. Dutton (eds.), *Society and the Internet: How Networks of Information and Communication Are Changing our Lives* (Oxford: Oxford University Press): 228–247.

Dutton, William H. 2023. *The Fifth Estate: The Power Shift in the Digital Age* (Oxford: Oxford University Press).

Dzopko, Ike. 2020. *Parallel Wireless Partners GIFEC to Roll-Out of 2000 OpenRAN Sites Across Ghana*. Available at http://dlvr.it/RVVdsj.

Eagleton-Pierce, Matthew. 2001. 'The Internet and the Seattle WTO Protests,' *Peace Review* 13(3): 331–337.

Economides, Nicholas. 2016. 'Economic Features of the Internet and Network Neutrality' in Yann Bramoullé, Andrea Galeotti, Brian W. Rogers (eds.), *The Oxford Handbook of the Economy of Networks* (Oxford: Oxford University Press): 810–822.

EducationSuperHighway. 2021. *No Home Left Offline: Bridging the Broadband Affordability Gap*. Available at www.educationsuperhighway.org/no-home-left-offline/.

EIFL. 2023. *Digital Skills and Inclusion Through Libraries in Uganda*. Available at www.eifl.net/eifl-in-action/digital-skills-and-inclusion-through-libraries-uganda.

Electronic Frontier Foundation. 2015. *13 Principles on the Application of Human Rights in Communication Surveillance*. Available at https://necessaryandproportionate.org/13-principles/.

Ellis-Petersen, Hannah. 2020. 'Many Lives Have Been Lost: Five-Month Internet Blackout Plunges Kashmir into Crisis,' *The Guardian*. Available at www.theguardian.com/world/2020/jan/05/the-personal-and-economic-cost-of-kashmirs-internet-ban.

Emmaüs Connect. 2023. *Nous Pouvons Faire Reculer L'exclusion Numérique et Sociale*. Available at https://emmaus-connect.org/.

Enders, Adam M., Joseph E. Uscinski, Michelle I. Seelig, Casey A. Klofstad, Stefan Wuchty, John R. Funchion, Manohar N. Murthi, Kamal Premaratne, Justin Stoler. 2023. 'The Relationship between Social Media Use and Beliefs in Conspiracy Theories and Misinformation,' *Political Behavior* 45(2): 781–804.

EQUALS. 2022. *EQUALS Global Partnership*. Available at www.equalsintech.org/.

Ermoshina, Ksenia, Benjamin Loveluck, Francesca Musiani. 2022. 'A Market of Black Boxes: The Economy of Internet Surveillance and Censorship in Russia,' *Journal of Information Technology & Politics* 19(1): 18–33.

EU Parliament. 2022. 'Committee of Inquiry to Investigate the Use of Pegasus and Equivalent Surveillance Spyware.' Available at https://media.euobserver.com/281e6 fa170b4673bc87da11181f30041.pdf.

EU Parliament. 2023. *EU AI Act: First Regulation on Artificial Intelligence*. Available at www.europarl.europa.eu/news/en/headlines/society/20230601STO93804/eu-ai-act-first-regulation-on-artificial-intelligence.

European Commission. 2017. *G20 Leaders' Declaration: Shaping an Interconnected World*. Available at https://ec.europa.eu/commission/presscorner/detail/en/STATEMENT_17_1960.

European Commission. 2020a. *Digital Education Action Plan 2021–2027*. Available at https://education.ec.europa.eu/focus-topics/digital-education/action-plan.

European Commission. 2020b. *Digital Education Action Plan – Action 7*. Available at https://education.ec.europa.eu/focus-topics/digital-education/action-plan/action-7.

European Commission. 2021a. *Broadband Coverage in Europe 2020. Executive Summary*. Available at https://digital-strategy.ec.europa.eu/en/library/broadband-coverage-europe-2020.

European Commission. 2021b. *Digital Economy and Society Index (DESI) 2021*. Available at https://ec.europa.eu/newsroom/dae/redirection/document/80563.

European Commission. 2022a. *Broadband Glossary*. Available at https://digital-strategy.ec.europa.eu/en/policies/broadband-glossary.

European Commission. 2022b. *Broadband: Investment Models*. Available at https://digital-strategy.ec.europa.eu/en/policies/broadband-investment-models.

European Commission. 2023a. *WiFi4EU*. Available at https://digital-strategy.ec.europa.eu/en/activities/wifi4eu.

European Commission. 2023b. *Broadband in Finland*. Available at https://digital-strategy.ec.europa.eu/en/policies/broadband-finland.

European Commission. 2023c. *Questions and Answers: Digital Markets Act: Ensuring Fair and Open Digital Markets*. Available at https://ec.europa.eu/commission/presscorner/detail/en/qanda_20_2349.

European Union. 2021. *Sweden – National Digitalisation Strategy for the School System*. Available at https://digital-skills-jobs.europa.eu/en/actions/national-initiatives/national-strategies/sweden-national-digitalisation-strategy-school.

European Union. 2022. *The Digital Markets Act*. Available at https://digital-markets-act.ec.europa.eu/index_en.

Eurostat. 2023. *Key Figures on European Living Conditions. 2023 Edition*. Available at https://ec.europa.eu/eurostat/en/web/products-key-figures/w/ks-hc-23-001.

Evans, Olaniyi. 2018. 'Connecting the Poor: The Internet, Mobile Phones and Financial Inclusion in Africa,' *Digital Policy, Regulation and Governance* 20(6): 568–581.

Fayoyin, Adebayo. 2016. 'Engaging Social Media for Health Communication in Africa: Approaches, Results and Lessons,' *Journal of Mass Communication & Journalism* 6(6): 1–7.

FCC. 2021. *Fourteenth Broadband Development Report*. Available at www.fcc.gov/reports-research/reports/broadband-progress-reports/fourteenth-broadband-deployment-report.

FCC. 2023a. *Lifeline Program for Low-Income Consumers*. Available at www.fcc.gov/general/lifeline-program-low-income-consumers.

FCC. 2023b. *Affordable Connectivity Program*. Available at www.fcc.gov/acp.

FCC. 2023c. *Universal Service*. Available at www.fcc.gov/general/universal-service.

FEMA. 2023. *Emergency Alerts*. Available at www.ready.gov/alerts.

FFC. 2024. *The FCC Is Taking Steps to Wind Down the Affordable Connectivity Program.* Available at www.fcc.gov/fcc-taking-steps-wind-down-affordable-connectivity-program.
Flusser, Vilem. 2022. *Communicology: Mutations in Human Relations?* (Redwood City: Stanford University Press).
Fox, Stacy. 2016. 'An Equitable Education in the Digital Age: Providing Internet Access to Students of Poverty,' *Journal of Education & Social Policy* 3(3): 12–20.
FRA. 2023. *Central Reporting Unit for Criminal Content on the Internet.* Available at https://fra.europa.eu/en/promising-practices/central-reporting-unit-criminal-content-internet.
Franck, Jens-Uwe, Martin Peitz. 2019. 'Market Definition and Market Power in the Platform Economy,' *Centre on Regulation in Europe (CERRE).* Available at https://cerre.eu/wp-content/uploads/2020/05/report_cerre_market_definition_market_power_platform_economy-1.pdf.
Freedman, Des. 2019. '"Public Service" and the Journalism Crisis: Is the BBC the Answer?' *Television & New Media* 20(3): 203–218.
Freedman, Des. 2021. 'Media Policy Failures and the Emergence of Right-Wing Populism' in Howard Tumber, Silvio Waisbord (eds.), *The Routledge Companion to Media Disinformation and Populism* (London: Routledge): 411–419.
Freedom House. 2018. *Freedom of the Net 2018: The Rise of Digital Authoritarianism.* Available at https://freedomhouse.org/report/freedom-net/2018/rise-digital-authoritarianism.
Freedom House. 2019. *Freedom of the Net 2019: The Crisis of Social Media.* Available at https://freedomhouse.org/report/freedom-net/2019/crisis-social-media.
Freedom House. 2021. *Freedom of the Net 2021: The Global Drive to Control Big Tech.* Available at https://freedomhouse.org/report/freedom-net/2021/global-drive-control-big-tech.
Freedom House. 2022. *Freedom of the Net 2022: Countering an Authoritarian Overhaul of the Internet.* Available at https://freedomhouse.org/report/freedom-net/2022/countering-authoritarian-overhaul-internet.
Freitag, Charlotte, Mike Berners-Lee, Kelly Widdicks, Bran Knowles, Gordon S. Blair, Adrian Freitag. 2021. 'The Real Climate and Transformative Impact of ICT: A Critique of Estimates, Trends, and Regulations,' *Patterns* 2(9): 1–18.
Future.Now. 2023. *The FutureDotNow Coalition.* Available at https://futuredotnow.uk/about-us/.
Gartner. 2022. *Press Release: Gartner Says Global Smartphone Sales Grew 6% in 2021.* Available at www.gartner.com/en/newsroom/press-releases/2022-03-01-4q21-smartphone-market-share.
Gerken, Tom, Liv McMahon. 2023. 'TikTok fined €345m over Children's Data Privacy,' *BBC.* Available at www.bbc.co.uk/news/technology-66819174.
Gershon, Ilana, Amy Gonzales. 2021. 'You Got a Hole in Your Belly and a Phone in Your Hand: How US Government Phone Subsidies Shape the Search for Employment,' *New Media & Society* 23(4): 853–871.
GIFEC. 2019. *Source of Fund.* Available at https://gifec.gov.gh/source-of-fund/.
Gilabert, Pablo. 2024. 'Inclusive Dignity,' *Politics, Philosophy & Economics* 23(1): 22–46.
Glaun, Dan. 2021. 'Germany's Laws on Hate Speech, Nazi Propaganda & Holocaust Denial: An Explainer,' *PBS.* Available at www.pbs.org/wgbh/frontline/article/germanys-laws-antisemitic-hate-speech-nazi-propaganda-holocaust-denial/.

Good Things Foundation. 2020. *Digital Inclusion in Health and Care*. Available at www.goodthingsfoundation.org/research-publications/digital-inclusion-health-and-care-lessons-learned-nhs-widening-digital/.
Good Things Foundation. 2021a. *National Device Bank*. Available at www.goodthingsfoundation.org/national-device-bank/.
Good Things Foundation. 2021b. *Future Digital Inclusion*. Available at www.goodthingsfoundation.org/what-we-do/our-partnerships/digital-skills-safety/future-digital-inclusion/.
Government of Canada. 2022. *Universal Broadband Fund*. Available at https://ised-isde.canada.ca/site/high-speed-internet-canada/en/universal-broadband-fund.
Government of Chile. 2023. *BiblioRedes*. Available at www.biblioredes.gob.cl/quienes-somos.
Government of the People of Rwanda. 2023. *Digital Ambassadors Programme*. Available at https://minict.prod.risa.rw/projects/digital-ambassadors-programme.
Graham, Mark. 2019. 'The Internet at the Global Economic Margins' in Mark Graham, William H. Dutton, Manuel Castells (eds.), *Society and the Internet: How Networks of Information and Communication are Changing our Lives* (Oxford: Oxford University Press): 265–280.
Gran, Anne-Britt, Peter Booth, Tania Bucher. 2021. 'To Be or Not to Be Algorithm Aware: A Question of a New Digital Divide?' *Information, Communication & Society* 24(12): 1779–1796.
Greenstein, Shane, Martin Peitz, Tommaso Valletti. 2016. 'Net Neutrality: A Fast Lane to Understanding the Trade-Offs,' *Journal of Economic Perspectives* 30(2): 127–150.
Greenstein, Shane. 2020. 'The Basic Economics of Internet Infrastructure,' *Journal of Economic Perspectives* 34(2): 192–214.
Greenwald, Glenn. 2013. 'XKeyscore: NSA Tool Collects "Nearly Everything a User Does on the Internet",' *The Guardian*. Available at www.theguardian.com/world/2013/jul/31/nsa-top-secret-program-online-data.
Griffin, James. 2008. *On Human Rights* (Oxford: Oxford University Press).
Griffith, Sarah. 2020. 'Why Your Internet Habits Are Not as Clean as You Think,' *BBC*. Available at www.bbc.com/future/article/20200305-why-your-internet-habits-are-not-as-clean-as-you-think.
Grinberg, Nir, Kenneth Joseph, Lisa Friedland, Briony Swire-Thompson, David Lazer. 2019. 'Fake News on Twitter during the 2016 US Presidential Election,' *Science* 363(6425): 374–378.
GSMA. 2017. *Accelerating Affordable Smartphone Ownership in Emerging Markets*. Available at www.gsma.com/mobilefordevelopment/wp-content/uploads/2018/08/Accelerating-affordable-smartphone-ownership-in-emerging-markets-2017_we.pdf.
GSMA. 2020. *Global Mobile Trends 2020. New Decade, New Industry?* Available at https://data.gsmaintelligence.com/api-web/v2/research-file-download-old?file=c5f35990dcc742733028de6361ccdf3b&download.
GSMA. 2021. *The State of Mobile Internet Connectivity 2021*. Available at https://data.gsmaintelligence.com/research/research/research-2021/the-state-of-mobile-internet-connectivity-2021.
GSMA. 2022. *The Mobile Economy 2022*. Available at https://data.gsmaintelligence.com/research/research/research-2022/the-mobile-economy-2022.

The Guardian. 2021. *US Bans China Telecom Over National Security Concerns.* Available at www.theguardian.com/us-news/2021/oct/27/us-bans-china-telecom-from-operating-over-national-security-concerns.

The Guardian. 2022. *White House Announces Internet Program for Low-Income Americans.* Available at www.theguardian.com/us-news/2022/may/09/biden-internet-discount-program-low-income.

Guess, Andrew, Jonathan Nagler, Joshua Tucker. 2019. 'Less Than You Think: Prevalence and Predictors of Fake News Dissemination on Facebook,' *Science Advances* 5(1): 1–8.

HaDEA. 2020. *WiFi4EU.* Available at https://hadea.ec.europa.eu/programmes/connecting-europe-facility/wifi4eu_en.

Haidar, Ensaf. 2016. 'The First 50 Lashes: A Saudi Activist's Wife Endures Her Husband's Brutal Sentence,' *The Guardian.* Available at www.theguardian.com/world/2016/may/17/raif-badawi-saudi-blogger-lashes-prison-ensaf-haidar.

Haidt, Jonathan. 2016. 'Why Social Media Is Terrible for Multiethnic Democracies,' *Vox.* Available at www.vox.com/policy-and-politics/2016/11/15/13593670/donald-trump-social-media-culture-politics.

Hall, Rachel. 2023. 'Stephen Bear Jailed for 21 Months for Sharing Sex Video without Consent,' *The Guardian.* Available at www.theguardian.com/uk-news/2023/mar/03/stephen-bear-jailed-21-months-sharing-sex-video-without-consent-georgia-harrison.

Hamilton, Alexander, James Madison, John Jay. 2008. *The Federalist Papers* (Oxford: Oxford University Press).

Hampton, Keith N., Laleah Fernandez, Craig T. Robertson, Johannes M. Bauer. 2020. 'Broadband and Student Performance Gaps,' *Quello Center at the Michigan State University.* Available at https://quello.msu.edu/broadbandgap/.

Haq, Riaz. 2016. *Smartphones for Pakistan's Poor to Close Digital Divide.* Available at www.riazhaq.com/2016/10/smartphones-for-pakistans-poor-to-close.html.

HarassMap. 2023. *HarassMap. Stop Sexual Assault Together.* Available at https://harassmap.org/en.

Hardill, Irene, Roger O'Sullivan. 2018. 'E-Government: Accessing Public Services Online: Implications for Citizenship,' *Local Economy* 33(1): 3–9.

Hargittai, Eszter, Anne Marie Piper, Meredith Ringel Morris. 2019. 'From Internet Access to Internet Skills: Digital Inequality among Older Adults,' *Universal Access in the Information Society* 18(4): 881–890.

Hargittai, Eszter, Marina Micheli. 2019. 'Internet Skills and Why They Matter' in Mark Graham, William H. Dutton (eds.), *Society and the Internet: How Networks of Information and Communication are Changing our Lives* (Oxford: Oxford University Press): 109–124.

Harter, Fred. 2023. 'Record Number of Countries Enforced Internet Shutdowns in 2022 – Report,' *The Guardian.* Available at www.theguardian.com/global-development/2023/feb/28/internet-shutdowns-record-number-countries-2022-report.

Heiberger, Raphael, Silvia Majo-Vazquez, Laia Castro-Herrero, Rasmus K. Nielsen, Frank Esser. 2022. 'Do Not Blame the Media! The Role of Politicians and Parties in Fragmenting Online Political Debate,' *International Journal of Press/Politics* 27(4): 910–941.

Hennen, Leonhard. 2020. 'E-Democracy and the European Public Sphere' in Leonhard Hennen, Ira van Keulen, Iris Korthagen, Georg Aichholzer, Ralf Lindner,

Rasmus Øjvind Nielsen (eds.), *European E-Democracy in Practice* (Cham: Springer Open): 47–91.

Henschke, Adam. 2017. *Ethics in an Age of Surveillance* (Cambridge: Cambridge University Press).

Henschke, Adam. 2018. 'Are the Costs of Metadata Worth It? Conceptualising Proportionality and Its Relation to Metadata' in Daniel Baldino, Rhys Crawley (eds.), *Intelligence and the Function of Government* (Melbourne: Melbourne University Press): 221–242.

Hinson, Robert, Robert Lensink, Annika Mueller. 2019. 'Transforming Agribusiness in Developing Countries: SDGs and the Role of FinTech,' *Current Opinions in Environmental Sustainability* 41: 1–9.

Hjort, Jonas, Jonas Poulsen. 2019. 'The Arrival of Fast Internet and Employment in Africa,' *American Economic Review* 109(3): 1032–1079.

Hohfeld, Wesley. 1919. *Fundamental Legal Conceptions as Applied in Juridical Reasoning* (New Haven: Yale University Press).

Holpuch, Amanda. 2023. 'Woman Is Awarded $1.2 Billion in "Revenge Porn" Lawsuit,' *New York Times*. Available at www.nytimes.com/2023/08/15/us/houston-texas-revenge-porn.html.

Hopgood, Stephen. 2013. *The Endtimes of Human Rights* (Ithaca: Cornell University Press).

Hong, Yu, Thomas Goodnight. 2020. 'How to Think about Cyber Sovereignty: The Case of China,' *Chinese Journal of Communication* 13(1): 8–26.

House of Lords. 2022. 'Licence to Change: BBC Future Funding,' *UK Parliament House of Lords Communications and Digital Committee*. Available at https://committees.parliament.uk/publications/23091/documents/169130/default/.

House of Lords. 2023. 'Digital Exclusion,' *UK House of Lords Communications and Digital Committee*. Available at https://committees.parliament.uk/committee/170/communications-and-digital-committee/news/196028/the-government-has-no-credible-strategy-to-tackle-digital-exclusion/.

Howard, Jeffery W. 2024. 'Extreme Speech, Democratic Deliberation, and Social Media' in Carissa Véliz (ed.), *The Oxford Handbook of Digital Ethics* (Oxford: Oxford University Press): 181–200.

IFLA. 2014. *Sri Lankan E-Library Nenasala Program Receives International Access to Learning Award*. Available at www.ifla.org/past-wlic/2014/ifla80/node/624.html.

iMlango. 2022. *iMlango Endline Report*. Available at www.imlango.com/overview.

India Telecom. 2022. *PM-WANI Central Registry*. Available at https://pmwani.gov.in/wani.

Indian Express. 2021. *UP Government Launches Massive Drive to Distribute Free Tables, Smartphones to 1 Crore Students*. Available at www.newindianexpress.com/nation/2021/dec/25/up-government-launches-massive-drive-to-distribute-free-tablets-smartphones-to-1-crore-students-2399690.html.

Ingiyimbere, Fidèle. 2017. *Domesticating Human Rights. A Reappraisal of Their Cultural-Political Critiques and Their Imperialist Use* (Cham: Springer).

Internet Freedom Foundation. 2021. *The PM-WANI Scheme: An Explainer*. Available at https://internetfreedom.in/pm-wani-explainer/.

Isaac, Mike. 2016. Facebook Said to Create Censorship Tool to Get Back into China, *New York Times*. Available at www.nytimes.com/2016/11/22/technology/facebook-censorship-tool-china.html.

ITU. 2018. *Digital Skills Toolkit*. Available at www.itu.int/en/ITU-D/Digital-Inclusion/Youth-and-Children/Pages/Digital-Skills-Toolkit.aspx.

ITU. 2019. *BTS for Rural, Remote and Border of Indonesia*. Available at www.itu.int/net4/wsis/archive/stocktaking/Project/Details?projectId=1514829358.

ITU. 2020. *Connecting Humanity: Assessing Investment Needs of Connecting Humanity to the Internet by 2030*. Available at www.itu.int/en/mediacentre/Pages/PR16-2020-ITU-publishes-Connecting-Humanity-study.aspx.

ITU. 2021a. *Measuring Digital Development: Facts and Figures 2021*. Available at www.itu.int/itu-d/reports/statistics/facts-figures-2021/.

ITU. 2021b. *Press Release: 2.9 Billion People Still Offline*. Available at www.itu.int/en/mediacentre/Pages/PR-2021-11-29-FactsFigures.aspx.

ITU. 2021c. *Policy Brief: The Affordability of ICT Services 2021*. Available at http://handle.itu.int/11.1002/pub/81c276fe-en.

ITU. 2023a. *Measuring Digital Development: Facts and Figures 2023*. Available at www.itu.int/itu-d/reports/statistics/facts-figures-2023/.

ITU. 2023b. *Digital Development Dashboard*. Available at www.itu.int/en/ITU-D/Statistics/Dashboards/Pages/Digital-Development.aspx.

Jaeger, Paul. 2022. *Disability and the Internet* (Boulder: Lynne Rienner Publishers).

Jasmontaite, Lina, Paul de Hert. 2019. 'Access to the Internet in the EU: A Policy Priority, a Fundamental, a Human Right or a Concern for eGovernment?' in Ben Wagner, Matthias Kettemann, Kilian Vieth (eds.), *Research Handbook on Human Rights and Digital Technology* (Cheltenham: Elgar Publishing): 157–179.

Jørgensen, Rikke Frank. 2019. 'When Private Actors Govern Human Rights' in Ben Wagner, Matthias C. Kettemann, Kilian Vieth (eds.), *Research Handbook on Human Rights and Digital Technology* (Cheltenham: Edgar Elgar Publishing): 346–363.

Kalia, Heidi, Finn Tarp. 2019. 'Can the Internet Improve Agricultural Production? Evidence from Viet Nam,' *Agricultural Economics* 50(6): 675–691.

Kalid, Saifuddin, Mette Pedersen. 2016. 'Digital Exclusion in Higher Education Contexts: A Systematic Literature Review,' *Procedia – Social and Behavioural Sciences* 228: 614–621.

Kant, Immanuel. 1785. 'Groundwork of the Metaphysics of Morals' in Mary Gregor (trans.), *Practical Philosophy* (Cambridge: Cambridge University Press, 1996): 37–108.

Kant, Immanuel. 1795. 'Toward Perpetual Peace' in Mary Gregor (trans.), *Practical Philosophy* (Cambridge: Cambridge University Press, 1996): 311–351.

Kelion, Leo. 2020. 'Huawei 5G Kit Must be Removed from UK by 2027,' *BBC News*. Available at www.bbc.co.uk/news/technology-53403793.

Kerala High Court. 2019. W.P(C). No. 19716/2019-L. Available at www.livelaw.in/pdf_upload/pdf_upload-364655.pdf.

Kettemann, Matthias. 2017. 'Ensuring Cybersecurity through International Law,' *Revista Espanola de Derecho Internacional* 69(2): 281–289.

King, Gary, Jennifer Pan, Margaret E. Roberts. 2013. 'How Censorship in China Allows Government Criticism but Silences Collective Expression,' *American Political Science Review* 107(2): 326–343.

Kloza, Dariusz. 2024. 'The Right Not to Use the Internet,' *Computer Law & Security Review* 52: 105907.

Korff, Douwe. 2019. 'First Do No Harm: The Potential of Harm being Caused to Fundamental Rights and Freedoms by State Cybersecurity Interventions' in

Ben Wagner, Matthias Kettemann, Kilian Vieth (eds.), *Research Handbook on Human Rights and Digital Technology* (Cheltenham: Edward Elgar Publishing): 129–155.

Kostka, Genia, Lukas Antoine. 2019. 'Fostering Model Citizenship: Behavioral Responses to China's Emerging Social Credit Systems,' *Policy & Internet* 12(3): 256–289.

Kwauk, Christina, Jenny Perlman Robinson. 2016. 'Worldreader: Creating a Culture of E-Reading around the World,' *Brookings – Centre for Universal Education*. Available at www.brookings.edu/wp-content/uploads/2016/07/FINAL-Worldreader-Case-Study.pdf.

Landemore, Hélène. 2013. *Democratic Reason: Politics, Collective Intelligence, and the Rule of the Many* (Princeton: Princeton University Press).

Langvardt, Kyle. 2021. 'Can the First Amendment Scale?' *Journal of Free Speech Law* 1(1): 273–302.

Lawson, M. Asher, Shikhar Anand, Hemant Kakkar. 2023. 'Tribalism and Tribulations: The Social Costs of Not Sharing Fake News,' *Journal of Experimental Psychology: General* 152(3): 611–631.

Lee, Myunghee, Amanda Murdie. 2020. 'The Global Diffusion of the #MeToo Movement,' *Global Gender & Politics* 17(4): 827–855.

Leiner, Barry M., Vinton G. Cerf, David D. Clark, Robert E. Kahn, Leonard Kleinrock, Daniel C. Lynch, Jon Postel, Larry G. Roberts, Stephen Wolff. 2009. 'A Brief History of the Internet,' *ACM SIGCOMM Computer Communication Review* 39(5): 22–31.

Lenton, Timothy M., Chi Xu, Jesse F. Abrams, Ashish Ghadiali, Sina Loriani, Boris Sakschewski, Caroline Zimm, Kristie L. Ebi, Robert R. Dunn, Jens-Christian Svenning, Marten Scheffer. 2023. 'Quantifying the Human Cost of Global Warming,' *Nature Sustainability* 6(10): 1237–1247.

Levin, Sam. 2017. 'Facebook Told Advertisers It Can Identify Teens Feeling "Insecure" and "Worthless,"' *The Guardian*. Available at www.theguardian.com/technology/2017/may/01/facebook-advertising-data-insecure-teens.

Levy, Neil. 2024. 'Fake News: Rebuilding the Epistemic Landscape' in Carissa Véliz (ed.), *The Oxford Handbook of Digital Ethics* (Oxford: Oxford University Press): 103–120.

Liao, S. Matthew, Adam Etinson. 2012. 'Political and Naturalistic Conceptions of Human Rights: A False Polemic?' *Journal of Moral Philosophy* 9(3): 327–352.

Liao, S. Matthew. 2015a. 'Human Rights as Fundamental Conditions for a Good Life' in in Rowan Cruft, S. Matthew Liao, Massimo Renzo (eds.), *Philosophical Foundations of Human Rights* (Oxford: Oxford University Press): 79–100.

Liao, S. Matthew. 2015b. *The Right to be Loved* (Oxford: Oxford University Press).

Liu, Zhiqiang, Naixin Yan. 2020. 'On the Right to a Happy Life as a Human Right,' *Journal of Human Rights* 19(6): 819–836.

Local Government Association. 2017. *Health and Wellbeing in Rural Areas*. Available at www.local.gov.uk/health-and-wellbeing-rural-areas.

Love, Todd. 2020. 'Internet Addiction and ADHD,' *CHADD*. Available at https://chadd.org/adhd-news/adhd-news-adults/internet-addiction-and-adhd/.

Lozano-Blasco, Raquel, Alberto Quilez Robres, Alberto Soto Sánchez. 2022. 'Internet Addiction in Young Adults: A Meta-Analysis and Systematic Review,' *Computers in Human Behavior* 130: 107201.

Lu, Catherine. 2021. 'World Government,' *Stanford Encyclopaedia of Philosophy*.
Lund, Stine, Ida Marie Boas, Tariku Bedesa, Wondewossen Fekede, Henriette Svarre Nielsen, Bjarke Lund Sørensen. 2016. 'Association between the Safe Delivery App and Quality of Care and Perinatal Survival in Ethiopia: A Randomized Clinical Trial,' *JAMA Pediatrics* 170(8): 765–771.
Lupu, Yonatan, Richard Sear, Nicolas Velásquez, Rhys Leahy, Nicholas Johnson Restrepo, Beth Goldberg, Neil F. Johnson. 2023. 'Offline Events and Online Hate,' *PLoS One* 18(1): e0278511.
Lyon, David. 2014. 'Surveillance, Snowden, and Big Data: Capacities, Consequences, Critique,' *Big Data & Society* 1(2): 1–13.
MacAskill, Ewen, Julian Borger, Nick Hopkins, Nick Davies, James Ball. 2013. 'GCHQ Taps Fibre-Optic Cables for Secret Access to World's Communications,' *The Guardian*. Available at www.theguardian.com/uk/2013/jun/21/gchq-cables-secret-world-communications-nsa.
MacAskill, Ewen, Gabriel Dance. 2013. 'NSA Files: Decoded. What the Revelations Mean for You,' *The Guardian*. Available at www.theguardian.com/world/interactive/2013/nov/01/snowden-nsa-files-surveillance-revelations-decoded#section/1.
MacNish, Kevin. 2016. 'Government Surveillance and Why Defining Privacy Matters in a Post-Snowden World,' *Journal of Applied Philosophy* 35(2): 417–432.
Makina, Daniel. 2019. 'The Potential of FinTech in Enabling Financial Inclusion' in Daniel Makina (ed.), *Extending Financial Inclusion in Africa* (London: Academic Press): 299–318.
Malmodin, Jens, Nina Lövehagen, Pernilla Bergmark, Dag Lundén. 2023. 'ICT Sector Electricity Consumption and Greenhouse Gas Emissions – 2020 Outcome,' *Telecommunications Policy* 48(3): 102701.
MAMPU. 2021. *Internet Center*. Available at www.malaysia.gov.my/portal/content/30639.
Marler, Will. 2023. '"You Can't Talk at the Library": The Leisure Divide and Public Internet Access for People Experiencing Homelessness,' *Information, Communication & Society* 26(7): 1303–1321.
Marmor, Andrei. 2015. 'What Is the Right to Privacy?' *Philosophy & Public Affairs* 43(1): 3–26.
Maroni, Marta. 2021. 'An Open Internet? The Court of Justice of the European Union between Net Neutrality and Zero Rating,' *European Constitutional Law Review* 17(3): 517–537.
Martin, David, Jefferson Chase. 2017. 'App Pairs German Voters with Political Parties,' *DW*. Available at www.dw.com/en/german-election-wahl-o-mat-app-pairs-voters-with-political-parties/a-40301081.
Mason, Lilliana. 2016. 'Why Are American So Angry this Election Season? Here's New Research That Explains It,' *Washington Post*. Available at www.washingtonpost.com/news/monkey-cage/wp/2016/03/10/why-are-americans-so-angry-this-election-season-heres-new-research-that-helps-explain-it/.
Masur, Philipp K. 2020. 'How Online Privacy Literacy Supports Self-Data Protection and Self-Determination in the Age of Information,' *Media and Communication* 8(2): 258–269.
Mathiesen, Kay. 2012. 'The Human Right to Internet Access: A Philosophical Defense,' *International Review of Information Ethics* 18: 9–22.

McCallum, Shiona. 2023. 'Meta: Facebook Owner Fined €1.2bn for Mishandling Data,' *BBC News*. Available at www.bbc.co.uk/news/technology-65669839.
McCallum, Shiona, Tom Gerken, Zoe Kleinman. 2023. 'TikTok Fined £12.7m for Misusing Children's Data,' *BBC News*. Available at www.bbc.co.uk/news/uk-65175902.
McCarthy, Kieren. 2017. 'AFRINIC Shuts Down IP Address Shutdown Over Internet Shutdowns,' *The Register*. Available at www.theregister.com/2017/06/09/afrinic_shuts_down_internet_shutdown_proposal/.
McDiarmid, Andrew, Matthew Shears. 2016. 'The Importance of Internet Neutrality to Protecting Human Rights Online' in Luca Belli, Primavera De Filippi (eds.), *Net Neutrality Compendium: Human Rights, Free Competition and the Future of the Internet* (Cham: Springer): 31–41.
McMahan, Jeff. 2010. 'Humanitarian Intervention, Consent, and Proportionality' in N. Ann Davis (ed.), *Ethics and Humanity: Themes from the Philosophy of Jonathan Glover* (Oxford: Oxford University Press): 44–72.
MCMC. 2019. *Pusat Internet Continues to Uplift Local Communities*. Available at www.mcmc.gov.my/en/media/press-releases/pusat-internet-continues-to-uplift-local-communiti.
MCMC. 2023. *National Broadband Initiative*. Available at www.mcmc.gov.my/en/sectors/broadband/national-broadband-initiative.
Meng, Shi-Qui, Jia-Lu Cheng, Yang-Yang Li, Xiao-Qin Yang, Jun-Wei Zheng, Xiang-Wen Chang, Yu Shi, Yun Chen, Lin Lu, Yan Sun, Yan-Ping Bao, Jie Shi. 2022. 'Global Prevalence of Digital Addiction in General Population: A Systematic Review and Meta-Analysis,' *Clinical Psychology Review* 92: 102128.
Mihelj, Sabina, Adrian Leguina, John Downey. 2019. 'Culture Is Digital: Cultural Participation, Diversity and the Digital Divide,' *New Media & Society* 21(7): 1465–1485.
Mill, John Stuart. 2012. *On Liberty* (Cambridge: Cambridge University Press).
Milmo, Dan. 2023. 'Facebook and Instagram Users in Europe Can Pay for Ad-Free Versions,' *The Guardian*. Available at www.theguardian.com/technology/2023/oct/30/meta-facebook-instagram-europe-pay-ad-free.
MINTIC Colombia. 2015. *Vive Digital Para la Gente*. Available at https://mintic.gov.co/portal/vivedigital/612/w3-propertyvalue-19436.html.
MINTIC Colombia. 2016. *Internet Móvil Para los Colombianos Más Necesitados*. Available at https://mintic.gov.co/portal/715/w3-article-16860.html.
MINTIC Colombia. 2018. *Puntos Digitales*. Available at https://mintic.gov.co/portal/vivedigital/612/w3-propertyvalue-669.html.
Moellendorf, Darrel. 2014. *The Moral Challenge of Dangerous Climate Change* (Cambridge: Cambridge University Press).
Monmouth. 2023. *Most Say Fundamental Rights under Threat*. Available at www.monmouth.edu/polling-institute/reports/monmouthpoll_US_062023/.
Moore, Martin. 2019. *Democracy Hacked: How Technology Is Destabilising Global Politics* (London: Oneworld).
Moyn, Samuel. 2018. *Not Enough: Human Rights in an Unequal World* (Cambridge, MA: Harvard University Press).
Mozorov, Evgeny. 2011. *The Net Delusion: The Dark Side of Internet Freedom* (New York: Public Affairs).
Mueller, Milton L. 2020. 'Against Sovereignty in Cyberspace,' *International Studies Review* 22 (4): 779–801.

Muldoon, James. 2022. 'Data-Owning Democracy or Digital Socialism?' *Critical Review of Social and Political Philosophy*: 1–22.
NCES. 2018. *A Description of U.S. Adults Who Are Not Digitally Literate*. Available at https://nces.ed.gov/pubs2018/2018161.pdf.
Neff, Timothy, Victor Pickard. Forthcoming. 'Funding Democracy: Public Media and Democratic Health in 22 Countries,' *The International Journal of Press/Politics*: 1–27.
Net Pracharat. 2018. *The Village Broadband Internet Project*. Available at https://npcr.netpracharat.com/Netpracharat_EN/one-page/.
New York State. 2021. *Certify for Weekly Unemployment Insurance Benefits*. Available at https://dol.ny.gov/unemployment/certify-weekly-unemployment-insurance-benefits.
Nguyen, C. Thi. 2021. 'How Twitter Gamifies Communication' in Jennifer Lackey (ed.), *Applied Epistemology* (Oxford: Oxford University Press): 410–436.
Nicas, Jack. 2020. 'Can YouTube Quite Its Conspiracy Theorists?' *New York Times*. Available at www.nytimes.com/interactive/2020/03/02/technology/youtube-conspiracy-theory.html.
Nickel, James. 2007. *Making Sense of Human Rights* (Oxford: Blackwell Publishing).
Nickel, James. 2010. 'Indivisibility and Linkage Arguments: A Reply to Gilabert,' *Human Rights Quarterly* 32(2): 433–440.
Nickel, James. 2016. 'Can a Right to Health Care be Justified by Linkage Arguments?' *Theoretical Medicine and Bioethics* 37(4): 293–306.
Nickel, James. 2022. 'Linkage Arguments For and against Rights,' *Oxford Journal of Legal Studies* 42(1): 27–47.
Nielsen, Rasmus Øjvind, Hennen, Leonhard, Iris Korthagen, Georg Aichholzer, Ralf Lindner. 2020. 'Options for Improving e-Participation at the EU Level' in Hennen, Leonhard, Ira van Keulen, Iris Korthagen, Georg Aichholzer, Ralf Lindner, Rasmus Øjvind Nielsen (eds.), *European E-Democracy in Practice* (Cham: Springer): 329–359.
Not An Atlas. 2023. *This Is Not an Atlas: Mapping Sexual Harassment in Egypt*. Available at https://notanatlas.org/maps/mapping-sexual-harassment-in-egypt/.
Nossel, Suzanne. 2018. 'Google Is Handing the Future of the Internet to China,' *Foreign Policy*. Available at https://foreignpolicy.com/2018/09/10/google-is-handing-the-future-of-the-internet-to-china/.
Nussbaum, Martha. 1997. 'Capabilities and Human Rights,' *Fordham Law Review* 66(2): 273–300.
Nussbaum, Martha. 2000. *Women and Human Development. The Capabilities Approach* (Cambridge: Cambridge University Press).
NYC. 2021. *New York City to Close Digital Divide for 1.6 Million Residents, Advance Racial Equality*. Available at www.nyc.gov/office-of-the-mayor/news/724-21/new-york-city-close-digital-divide-1-6-million-residents-advance-racial-equity.
Obar, Jonathan A., Anne Oeldorf-Hirsch. 2020. 'The Biggest Lie on the Internet: Ignoring the Privacy Policies and Terms of Service Policies of Social Networking Services,' *Information, Communication & Society* 23(1): 128–147.
O'Donnell, Catharina, Eran Shor. 2020. '"This Is a Political Movement, Friend": Why "Incels" Support Violence,' *British Journal of Sociology* 73(2): 336–351.
OECD. 2016. *Ministerial Declaration on the Digital Economy ('Cancun Declaration')*. Available at https://legalinstruments.oecd.org/api/print?ids=343&lang=en.

OECD. 2019a. *OECD Reviews of Digital Transformation: Going Digital in Columbia. Chapter 3: Fostering the Digital Transformation among Individuals, Firms and the Government*. Available at www.oecd-ilibrary.org/sites/5786e2c8-en/index.html?itemId=/content/component/5786e2c8-en.

OECD. 2019b. *Educating 21st Century Children: Emotional Well-Being in the Digital Age. Chapter 11: Fostering Digital Literacy and Well-Being*. Available at www.oecd-ilibrary.org/sites/23ac808e-en/index.html?itemId=/content/component/23ac808e-en.

OECD. 2020. *Making the Most of Technology for Learning and Training in Latin America*. Available at www.oecd.org/publications/making-the-most-of-technology-for-learning-and-training-in-latin-america-ce2b1a62-en.htm.

Ofcom. 2023a. *Online Nation. 2023 Report*. Available at www.ofcom.org.uk/research-and-data/online-research/online-nation.

Ofcom. 2023b. *Social Tariffs: Cheaper Broadband and Phone Packages*. Available at www.ofcom.org.uk/phones-telecoms-and-internet/advice-for-consumers/costs-and-billing/social-tariffs.

Ofcom. 2023c. *What Is 4G?* Available at www.ofcom.org.uk/phones-telecoms-and-internet/advice-for-consumers/advice/what-is-4g.

OHCHR. 2018. *Statement on the Visit to the United Kingdom, by Professor Philip Alson, United Nations Special Rapporteur on Extreme Poverty and Human Rights*. Available at www.ohchr.org/en/statements/2018/11/statement-visit-united-kingdom-professor-philip-alston-united-nations-special?LangID=E&NewsID=23881.

Ohm, Paul. 2016. 'We Couldn't Kill the Internet If We Tried,' *Harvard Law Review* 130(2): 79–85.

Oliva, Thiago Dias. 2020. 'Content Moderation Technologies: Applying Human Rights Standards to Protect Freedom of Expression,' *Human Rights Law Review* 20(4): 607–640.

O'Neill, Onora. 2005. 'The Dark Side of Human Rights,' *International Affairs* 81(2): 427–439.

O'Neill, Onora. 2009. 'Kant: Rationality as Practical Reason' in Alfred R. Mele, Piers Rawling (eds.), *The Oxford Handbook of Rationality* (Oxford: Oxford University Press): 93–109.

OONI. 2022. *About*. Available at https://ooni.org/about/.

Open Society Foundations. 2013. *Global Principles on National Security and the Right to Information (Tshwame Principles)*. Available at www.justiceinitiative.org/publications/global-principles-national-security-and-freedom-information-tshwane-principles.

Optus. 2023. *Power Their Potential*. Available at www.optus.com.au/living-network/donate-your-data.

Oxfam. 2022. *Policy Paper: Inequality Kills. Executive Summary*. Available at www.oxfam.org/en/research/inequality-kills.

Panagiotidi, Maria, Paul Overton. 2018. 'The Relation between Internet Addiction, Attention Deficit Hyperactivity Symptoms and Online Activities in Adults,' *Comprehensive Psychiatry* 87: 7–11.

Parmet, Wendy E., Jeremy Paul. 2020. 'COVID-19: The First Posttruth Pandemic,' *American Journal of Public Health* 110(7): 945–956.

PatientsLikeMe. 2023. *Patients Like Me*. Available at www.patientslikeme.com/.

Perugini, Nicola, Neve Gordon. 2015. *The Human Right to Dominate* (Oxford: Oxford University Press).

Pettit, Philip. 2010. 'A Republican Law of Peoples,' *European Journal of Political Theory* 9(1): 7–94.
Piazza, James A. 2023. 'Political Polarization and Political Violence,' *Security Studies* 32(3): 476–504.
Pogge, Thomas. 2009. 'Kant's Vision of a Just World Order' in Thomas Hill (ed.), *The Blackwell Guide to Kant's Ethics* (Oxford: Blackwell Publishing): 196–208.
Pollicino, Oreste. 2020. 'The Right to Internet Access. Quid Iuris?' in Andreas von Arnauld, Kersin von der Decken, Marti Susi (eds.), *The Cambridge Handbook of New Human Rights: Recognition, Novelty, Rhetoric* (Cambridge: Cambridge University Press): 263–275.
Polyakova, Alina, Chris Meserole. 2019. 'Exporting Digital Authoritarianism: The Russian and Chinese Models,' *Brookings*. Available at www.brookings.edu/research/exporting-digital-authoritarianism/.
Poole, Alexandria. 2018. 'Where is SDG 18? The Need for Biocultural Heritage in the Sustainable Development Goals,' *Environmental Values* 27(1): 55–80.
Prooijen, Jan-Willem van, Nils B. Jostmann. 2013. 'Belief in Conspiracy Theories: The Influence of Uncertainty and Perceived Morality,' *European Journal of Social Psychology* 43(1): 109–115.
Prooijen, Jan-Willem van. 2018. 'Empowerment as a Tool to Reduce Belief in Conspiracy Theories' in Joseph E. Uscinski (ed.), *Conspiracy Theories and the People Who Believe Them* (Oxford: Oxford University Press): 432–442.
Proton. 2023. *General Data Protection Regulation. Article 25: Data Protection by Design and Default*. Available at https://gdpr.eu/article-25-data-protection-by-design/.
PRRI. 2021. *New PRRI Report Reveals Nearly One in Five Americans and One in Four Republicans Still Believe in QAnon Conspiracy Theories*. Available at www.prri.org/press-release/new-prri-report-reveals-nearly-one-in-five-americans-and-one-in-four-republicans-still-believe-in-qanon-conspiracy-theories/.
Q Costa Rica 2018. *Claro and Cable Vision Join Costa Rica's 'Connected Homes' Project*. Available at https://qcostarica.com/claro-and-cable-vision-join-costa-ricas-connected-homes-project/.
Queralt, Jahel. 2016. 'A Human Right to Financial Inclusion' in Helmut P. Gaisbauer, Gottfried Schweiger, Clemens Sedmak (eds.), *Ethical Issues in Poverty Alleviation* (Cham: Springer): 77–92.
Ra, Chaelin K., Junhan Cho, Matthew D. Stone, Julianne De La Cerda, Nicholas I. Goldenson, Elizabeth Moroney, Irene Tung, Steve S. Lee, Adam M. Leventhal. 2018. 'Association of Digital Media Use with Subsequent Symptoms of Attention-Deficit/Hyperactivity Disorder among Adolescents,' *JAMA* 320(3): 255–263.
Ramesh, Reethika, Ram Sundara Raman, Matthew Bernhard, Victor Ongkowijaya, Leonid Evdokimov, Anne Edmundson, Steven Sprecher, Muhammad Ikram, Roya Ensafi. 2020. 'Decentralised Control: A Case Study of Russia,' *Network and Distributed Systems Security (NDSS) Symposium 2020*. Available at www.ndss-symposium.org/ndss-paper/decentralized-control-a-case-study-of-russia/.
Rankin, Jennifer. 2022. 'Three Men Found Guilty of Murdering 298 People in Shooting Down MH17,' *The Guardian*. Available at www.theguardian.com/world/2022/nov/17/three-men-found-guilty-of-murdering-298-people-in-flight-mh17-bombing.
Rathje, Steve, Jay J. van Bavel, Sander van der Linden. 2021. 'Out-Group Animosity Drives Engagement on Social Media,' *Proceedings of the National Academy of Science* 118(26): e2024292118.

Rawls, John. 1999. *A Theory of Justice* (Cambridge, MA: Harvard University Press).
Rawls, John. 2001. *Justice as Fairness: A Restatement* (Cambridge, MA: Harvard University Press).
Rawls, John. 2005. *Political Liberalism. Expanded Edition* (New York: Columbia University Press).
Raz, Joseph. 1986. *The Morality of Freedom* (Oxford: Clarendon Press).
Raz, Joseph. 2010. 'Human Rights in the Emerging World Order,' *Transnational Legal Theory* 1(1): 31–47.
Reeves, Anthony R. 2015. 'Standard Threats: How to Violate Basic Human Rights,' *Social Theory & Practice* 41(3): 403–434.
Reglitz, Merten. 2015. 'Political Legitimacy without a (Claim-) Right to Rule,' *Res Publica* 21(3): 291–307.
Reglitz, Merten. 2019. 'A Kantian Argument against World Poverty,' *European Journal of Political Theory* 18(4): 489–507.
Reglitz, Merten, Abraham Rudnick. 2020. 'Internet Access as a Right for Realizing the Human Right to Adequate Mental (and Other) Health Care,' *International Journal of Mental Health* 49(1): 97–103.
Reglitz, Merten. 2022. 'Fake News and Democracy,' *Journal of Ethics and Social Philosophy* 22(2): 162–187.
Republic of Indonesia. 2022. *Akselerasi BTS 4G Desa 3T, Dirut BAKTI: Target Tahap 1 Tercapai 86%*. Available at www.kominfo.go.id/content/detail/41232/siaran-pers-no-144hmkominfoo42022-tentang-akselerasi-bts-4g-desa-3t-dirut-bakti-target-tahap-1-tercapai-86/0/siaran_pers.
Republic of the Philippines. 2023. *Free WiFi for All*. Available at https://dict.gov.ph/freewifi/.
Rini, Regina. 2021. 'Weaponized Skepticism' in Elizabeth Edenberg, Michael Hannon (eds.), *Political Epistemology* (Oxford: Oxford University Press): 31–48.
Roberts, Margaret E. 2018. *Censored: Distraction and Diversion Inside China's Great Firewall* (Princeton: Princeton University Press).
Rød, Espen Geelmuyden, Nils B. Weidmann. 2015. 'Empowering Activists or Autocrats? The Internet in Authoritarian Regimes,' *Journal of Peace Research* 52(3): 338–351.
Rodrik, Dani. 2011. *The Globalization Paradox: Democracy and the Future of the World Economy* (London: W. W. Norton).
Rønn, Kira Vrist, Kasper Lippert-Rasmussen. 2020. 'Out of Proportion? On Surveillance and the Proportionality Requirement,' *Ethical Theory & Practice* 23(1): 181–199.
Rosa, Hartmut. 2022. 'Social Media Filters and Resonances: Democracy and the Contemporary Public Sphere,' *Theory, Culture & Society* 39(4): 17–35.
Rotondi, Valentina, Ridhi Kashyap, Luca Maria Pesando, Simone Spinelli, Francesco C. Billari. 2020. 'Leveraging Mobile Phones to Attain Sustainable Development,' *Proceedings of the National Academy of Science* 117(24): 13413–13420.
Rozite, Vida, Emi Bertoli, Brendan Reidenbach. 2023. 'Data Centres and Data Transmission Networks,' *International Energy Agency*. Available at www.iea.org/energy-system/buildings/data-centres-and-data-transmission-networks.
Ruijgrok, Kris. 2017. 'From the Web to the Streets: Internet and Protests under Authoritarian Regimes,' *Democratization* 24(3): 498–520.
Rusbridger, Alan, Janine Gibson, Ewen MacAskill. 2015. 'Edward Snowden: NSA Reform in the US Is Only the Beginning,' *The Guardian*. Available at www.theguardian.com/us-news/2015/may/22/edward-snowden-nsa-reform.

Salim, Ruhul, Shamsul Arifeen Khan Mamun, Kamrul Hassan. 2016. 'Role of Communication Technologies in Broadacre Agriculture in Australia: An Empirical Analysis Using Panel Data,' *Agricultural and Resource Economics* 60(2): 243–264.

Sandvig, Christian. 2007. 'Network Neutrality Is the New Common Carriage,' *Info* 9(2/3): 136–147.

Satariano, Adam, Christopher F. Schuetze. 2022. 'Where Online Hate Speech Can Bring the Police to Your Door,' *New York Times*. Available at www.nytimes.com/2022/09/23/technology/germany-internet-speech-arrest.html.

Schewick, Barbara van. 2010. *Internet Architecture and Innovation* (Cambridge: MIT Press).

Schewick, Barbara van. 2015. *The Case for Meaningful Network Neutrality Rules*. Available at https://law.stanford.edu/wp-content/uploads/2023/11/Schewick2015TheCaseForMeaningfulNNRules.pdf.

Schewick, Barbara van. 2016. *Comments on BEREC Guidelines on the Implementation by National Regulators of European Net Neutrality Rules, BoR (16) 94*. Available at www.berec.europa.eu/sites/default/files/files/document_register_store/2020/6/BoR_PC_10_%2819%29_47_2_B._S._2.pdf.

Schwartz, John. 1996. 'Court Upholds Free Speech on Internet, Blocks Decency Law,' *Washington Post*. Available at www.washingtonpost.com/archive/politics/1996/06/13/court-upholds-free-speech-on-internet-blocks-decency-law/02e2ecfd-50c0-4d36-8d11-b78cdc3ad8e3/.

SCOTUS. 2017. *Packingham vs State of North Carolina* 15-1194. Available at www.supremecourt.gov/opinions/16pdf/15-1194_08l1.pdf.

Sen, Amartya. 1981. *Poverty and Famines: An Essay on Entitlement and Deprivation* (Oxford: Oxford University Press).

Sen, Amartya. 2001. *Development as Freedom* (Oxford: Oxford University Press).

Sen, Amartya. 2005. 'Human Rights and Capabilities,' *Journal of Human Development* 6(2): 151–166.

Sen, Amartya. 2010. 'The Mobile and the World,' *Information Technologies and International Development* 6 (SE): 1–3.

Shackelford, Scott. 2020. *Governing New Frontiers in the Information Age. Toward Cyber Peace* (Cambridge: Cambridge University Press).

Shandler, Ryan, Daphna Canetti. 2019. 'A Reality of Vulnerability and Dependence: Internet Access as a Human Right,' *Israel Law Review* 52(1): 77–98.

Shandler, Ryan, Michael L. Gross, Daphna Canetti. 2020. 'Can You Engage in Political Activity Without Internet Access? The Social Effects of Internet Deprivation,' *Political Studies Review* 18(4): 620–629.

Shearer, Elisa, Katerina Eva Matsa. 2018. 'News Use Across Social Media Platforms 2018,' *Pew Research Center*. Available at www.journalism.org/2018/09/10/news-use-across-social-media-platforms-2018/.

Sheehey, Maeve. 2021. 'Teen Who Recorded George Floyd's Murder Awarded Pulitzer Special Citation,' *Politico*. Available at www.politico.com/news/2021/06/11/darnella-frazier-george-floyd-pulitzer-prize-493496.

Shelton, Taylor. 2020. 'A Post-Truth Pandemic?' *Big Data & Society* 7(2): 1–6.

Sherman, Justin. 2021. 'Digital Authoritarianism and Implications for U.S. National Security,' *The Cyber Defense Review* 6(1): 107–118.

Sherman, Justin. 2022. 'Europe's Spyware Scandal Is a Global Wakeup Call,' *Slate*. Available at https://slate.com/technology/2022/11/europe-spyware-scandal-pegasus-report.html?via=rss.

Shihab-Edlin, Ahmed. 2023. 'How Egyptian Police Hunt LGBT People on Dating Apps,' *BBC News*. Available at www.bbc.co.uk/news/world-middle-east-64390817.

Shue, Henry. 1993. 'Subsistence Emissions and Luxury Emissions,' *Law & Policy* 15(1): 39–60.

Shue, Henry. 2020. *Basic Rights: Subsistence, Affluence & U.S. Foreign Policy. 40th Anniversary Edition* (Princeton: Princeton University Press).

Silva, Patricia, Alice Delerue Matos, Roberto Martinez-Pecino. 2022. 'Can the Internet Reduce the Loneliness of 50+ Living Alone?' *Information, Communication & Society* 25(1): 17–33.

Similarweb. 2023. *Top Websites Ranking*. Available at www.similarweb.com/top-websites/.

Skepys, Brian 2012. Is There a Human Right to the Internet? *Journal of Politics and Law* 5(4): 15–29.

Skidelsky, William. 2010. 'Ha-Joon Chang: The Net is Not as Important as We Think,' *The Guardian*. Available at www.theguardian.com/technology/2010/aug/29/my-bright-idea-ha-joon-chang.

Smith Galer, Sophia. 2020. 'How Tik-Tok Changes the World in 2020,' *BBC Culture*. Available at www.bbc.com/culture/article/20201216-how-tiktok-changed-the-world-in-2020/.

Smith, Justin E. H. 2022. *The Internet Is Not What You Think It Is: A History, A Philosophy, A Warning* (Princeton: Princeton University Press).

Smith, Leonie, Fay Niker. 2021. 'What Social Media Facilitates, Social Media Should Regulate: Duties in the New Public Sphere,' *The Political Quarterly* 92(4): 613–620.

Song, Jiewuh. 2019. 'Human Rights and Inequality,' *Philosophy & Public Affairs* 47(4): 347–377.

Sørensen, Frode. 2016. 'Specialised Services and the Net Neutrality Service Model' in Luca Belli, Primavera De Filippi (eds.), *Net Neutrality Compendium: Human Rights, Free Competition and the Future of the Internet* (Cham: Springer): 99–107.

Stahl, Titus. 2016. 'Indiscriminate Mass Surveillance and the Public Sphere,' *Ethics & Information Technology* 18(1): 33–39.

Stark, Birgit, Daniel Stegmann. 2020. 'Are Algorithms a Threat to Democracy? The Rise of Intermediaries: A Challenge For Public Discourse,' *AlgorithmWatch*. Available at https://algorithmwatch.org/en/governing-platforms/.

State of Connecticut. 2021. *Unemployment Benefits*. Available at https://portal.ct.gov/Services/Jobs-and-Employment/Unemployment/Unemployment-Benefits.

State of Iowa. 2021. *Iowa Workforce Development*. Available at www.iowaworkforcedevelopment.gov/file-claim-unemployment-insurance-benefits.

Statista. 2023. *Global Social Network Penetration Rate as of January 2023, by Region*. Available at www.statista.com/statistics/269615/social-network-penetration-by-region/.

Steinhubl, Steven, Mark Marriott, Stephan Wegerich. 2015. 'Remote Sensing of Vital Signs: A Wearable, Wireless "Band-Aid" Sensor with Personalized Analytics for Improved Ebola Patient Care and Worker Safety,' *Global Health: Science and Practice* 3(3): 516–519.

Stewart, Alexander J., Joshua B. Plotkin, Nolan McCarty. 2021. 'Inequality, Identity, and Partisanship: How Redistribution Can Stem the Tide of Mass Polarization,' *Proceedings of the National Academy of Science* 118(50): e2102140118.

Stockwell Stephanie, Brendon Stubbs, Sarah E. Jackson, Abi Fisher, Lin Yang, Lee Smith. 2021. 'Internet Use, Social Isolation and Loneliness in Older Adults,' *Ageing & Society* 41(12): 2723–2746.

Summers, Kelly H., Timothy D. Baird, Emily Woodhouse, Maria Elisa Christie, J. Terrence McCabe, Felista Terta, Naomi Peter. 2020. 'Mobile Phones and Women's Empowerment in Maasai Communities: How Men Shape Women's Social Relations and Access to Phones,' *Journal of Rural Studies* 77: 126–137.

Sunstein, Cass. 2017. *#Republic: Divided Democracy in the Age of Social Media* (Princeton: Princeton University Press).

Sutel. 2017. *Statistics from the Telecommunications Sector Costa Rica 2017*. Available at www.sutel.go.cr/sites/default/files/sutel_informe-eng_18_junio_ver_baja1_0.pdf.

Sutel. 2020. *Telecommunications Sector Statistics 2020 Costa Rica*. Available at www.sutel.go.cr/sites/default/files/estadisticas_sector_de_telecomunicaciones_2020_ingles.pdf.

TalkTalk. 2020. *3 in 4 Parents Rely on The Internet to Help Kids with Homework*. Available at www.talktalkgroup.com/article/talktalkgroup/2020/3-in-4-parents-rely-on-the-internet-to-help-kids-with-homework.

Tasioulas, John. 2017a. 'Exiting the Hall of Mirrors: Morality and Law in Human Rights' in Tom Campbell, Kylie Bourne (eds.), *Political and Legal Approaches to Human Rights* (New York: Routledge): 73–89.

Tasioulas, John. 2017b. 'Minimum Core Obligations: Human Rights in the Here and Now,' *World Bank*. Available at https://openknowledge.worldbank.org/handle/10986/29144.

Tasioulas, John. 2021. 'The Inflation of Concepts. Human Rights, Health, and the Rule of Law. Why Are These Concepts Inflated to the Status of Totalising, Secular Religions?' *Aeon*. Available at https://aeon.co/essays/conceptual-overreach-threatens-the-quality-of-public-reason.

Thakur, Neeta, Stephanie Lovinsky-Desir, Christian Bime, Juan P. Wisnivesky. 2020. 'The Structural and Social Determinants of the Racial/Ethnic Disparities in the U.S. COVID-19 Pandemic. What Is Our Role?' *American Journal of Respiratory and Critical Care Medicine* 202(7): 943–949.

Theilen, Jens T. 2021. 'The Inflation of Human Rights: A Deconstruction,' *Leiden Journal of International Law* 34(4): 831–854.

The Shift Project. 2019. *'Climate Crisis: The Unsustainable Use of Online Video': Our New Report on the Environmental Impact of ICT*. Available at https://theshiftproject.org/en/article/unsustainable-use-online-video/.

Thumfart, Johannes. 2024. 'Digital Rights and the State of Exception. Internet Shutdowns from the Perspective of Just Securitization Theory,' *Journal of Global Security Studies* 9(1): ogad024.

Timms, Henry, Jeremy Heimans. 2018. *New Power. How It's Changing the 21st Century – And Why You Need to Know* (London: Macmillan).

Tirole, Jean. 2021. 'Digital Dystopia,' *American Economic Review* 111(6): 2007–2048.

Tocqueville, Alexis de. 2009. *Democracy in America Volumes I & II*, trans. Henry Reeve (Auckland: The Floating Press).

Tomalty, Jesse. 2017. 'Is There a Human Right to Internet Access?' *Philosophy Now* 118. Available at https://philosophynow.org/issues/118/Is_There_A_Human_Right_To_Internet_Access.

Toya, Hideki, Mark Skidmore. 2018. 'Cellular Phones and Natural Disaster Vulnerability,' *Sustainability* 10(9): 2970.

Trengrove, Markus, Emre Kazim, Denise Almeida, Airlie Hilliard, Sara Zannone, Elizabeth Lomas. 2022. 'A Crucial Analysis of the Online Safety Bill,' *Patterns* 3(8): 100544.
UK Department for Digital, Culture, Media & Sport. 2018. *Culture Is Digital*. Available at www.gov.uk/government/publications/culture-is-digital.
UK Department for Work & Pensions. 2020. *Universal Credit and You*. Available at www.gov.uk/government/publications/universal-credit-and-you/draft-uc-and-you.
UK Government. 2012. *Digital Efficiency Report*. Available at www.gov.uk/government/publications/digital-efficiency-report.
UK Government. 2020a. *Get Help with Technology During Coronavirus (Covid-19)*. Available at www.gov.uk/guidance/get-help-with-technology-for-remote-education-during-coronavirus-covid-19.
UK Government. 2020b. *One Million Laptops and Tablets for Disadvantaged Children and Young People*. Available at www.gov.uk/government/news/one-million-laptops-and-tablets-for-disadvantaged-children-and-young-people.
UK Government. 2023. *Sustainability of Local Journalism. Seventh Report of Session 2022–23*. Available at https://committees.parliament.uk/publications/33635/documents/183838/default/.
UK Parliament. 2021. *Postnote Number 643: Developing Essential Digital Skills*. Available at https://researchbriefings.files.parliament.uk/documents/POST-PN-0643/POST-PN-0643.pdf.
UK Parliament. 2022. *The Universal Service Obligation (USO) for Broadband*. Available at https://commonslibrary.parliament.uk/research-briefings/cbp-8146/.
UK Parliament. 2023. *Petitions*. Available at https://petition.parliament.uk/.
UN. 1948. *Universal Declaration of Human Rights*. Available at www.un.org/en/about-us/universal-declaration-of-human-rights.
UN. 1966a. *International Covenant on Economic, Social and Cultural Rights*. Available at www.ohchr.org/en/professionalinterest/pages/cescr.aspx.
UN. 1966b. *International Covenant on Civil and Political Rights*. Available at www.ohchr.org/en/instruments-mechanisms/instruments/international-covenant-civil-and-political-rights.
UN. 2011a. *Report of the Special Rapporteur on the Promotion and Protection of the Right to Freedom of Opinion and Expression, Frank LaRue*. Available at https://digitallibrary.un.org/record/706331?ln=en&v=pdf.
UN. 2011b. *Guiding Principles on Business and Human Rights*. Available at https://digitallibrary.un.org/record/720245?ln=en&v=pdf.
UN. 2014. *The Right to Privacy in the Digital Age*. Available at https://digitallibrary.un.org/record/777869?ln=en&v=pdf.
UN. 2015. *Report of the Special Rapporteur on the Promotion and Protection of the Right to Freedom of Opinion and Expression, David Kaye*. Available at https://digitallibrary.un.org/record/798709?ln=en&v=pdf.
UN. 2016. *The Promotion, Protection and Enjoyment of Human Rights on the Internet*. Available at https://digitallibrary.un.org/record/845727?ln=en&v=pdf.
UN. 2017. *OL DEU 1/2017*. Available at www.ohchr.org/sites/default/files/Documents/Issues/Opinion/Legislation/OL-DEU-1-2017.pdf.
UN. 2022. *ICTs as a Catalyst for Sustainable Development*. Available at https://sustainabledevelopment.un.org/index.php?page=view&type=20000&nr=579&menu=2993.

UN. 2023a. *Sustainable Development Goals*. Available at https://sdgs.un.org/goals.
UN. 2023b. *Goal 9: Build Resilient Infrastructure, Promote Sustainable Industrialization and Foster Innovation*. Available at https://unric.org/en/sdg-9/.
UN Department of Economic and Social Affairs. 2022. *Pipol Konek. Free Wi-Fi for All*. Available at https://sdgs.un.org/partnerships/pipol-konek-free-wi-fi-all.
UNESCO. 1997. *Adult Education: The Hamburg Declaration; The Agenda for the Future*. Available at https://unesdoc.unesco.org/ark:/48223/pf0000116114.
UNESCO. 2015. *Mobile Phones and Literacy. Empowerment in Women's Hands*. Available at https://unesdoc.unesco.org/ark:/48223/pf0000234325.
UNESCO. 2016a. *School Resources and Learning Environment in Africa*. Available at http://uis.unesco.org/en/topic/education-africa.
UNESCO. 2016b. *Closing the Teacher Gap: Almost 69 Million Teachers Needed*. Available at http://uis.unesco.org/en/blog/closing-teacher-gap-almost-69-million-teachers-needed.
UNESCO. 2017a. *Global Education Monitoring Report 2017/18: Accountability in Education*. Available at https://digitallibrary.un.org/record/4028113?ln=en&v=pdf.
UNESCO. 2017b. *More Than One-Half of Children and Adolescents are Not Learning Worldwide*. Available at https://unesdoc.unesco.org/ark:/48223/pf0000261556.
UNESCO. 2019. *World Teachers Day 2019 Fact Sheet*. Available at http://uis.unesco.org/en/news/world-teachers-day-2019.
UNESCO. 2020a. *Education in Africa*. Available at http://uis.unesco.org/en/topic/education-africa.
UNESCO. 2020b. *Global Education Coalition Facilitates Free Internet Access for Distance Education in Several Countries*. Available at www.unesco.org/en/articles/global-education-coalition-facilitates-free-internet-access-distance-education-several-countries.
UNESCO. 2020c. *Giraffe: South African Automated Job Matching Platform*. Available at www.unicef.org/innovation/innovation-fund-giraffe.
UNESCO 2023. *An Ed-Tech Tragedy? Educational Technologies and School Closures in the Time of COVID-19*. Available at www.unesco.org/en/digital-education/ed-tech-tragedy.
UNICEF. 2022. *Giga Annual Report: 1 Million Students Connected to the Internet*. Available at https://giga.global/annual-report-2021/.
US Census Bureau. 2021. *Computer and Internet Use in the United States: 2018*. Available at www.census.gov/library/publications/2021/acs/acs-49.html.
US Congress. 1791. *Fourth Amendment*. Available at https://constitution.congress.gov/constitution/amendment-4/.
US Department of Commerce. 2021. *Fact Sheet: Department of Commerce's Use of Bipartisan Infrastructure Deal Funding to Help Close the Digital Divide*. Available at www.commerce.gov/news/fact-sheets/2021/11/fact-sheet-department-commerces-use-bipartisan-infrastructure-deal-funding.
Uscinski, Joseph E., Adam Enders, Casey Klofstad, Michelle Seelig, Hugo Drochon, Kamal Premaratne, Manohar Murthi. 2022. 'Have Conspiracy Beliefs Changed Over Time?' *PLoS One* 17(7): e0270429.
Uscinski, Joseph E., Joseph M. Parent. 2014. *American Conspiracy Theories* (Oxford: Oxford University Press).

Uswitch. 2018. *Digital Poverty Line: Poor Broadband Services See 1.2 Million Children Falling Behind*. Available at www.uswitch.com/media-centre/2018/03/digital-poverty-line-poor-broadband-services-see-1-2-million-children-falling-behind/.

Valentini, Laura. 2014. 'No Global Demos, No Global Democracy? A Systematization and Critique,' *Perspectives on Politics* 12(4): 789–807.

Vallence, Chris. 2023. 'Meta Fined €390m over Use of Data for Targeted Ads,' *BBC News*. Available at www.bbc.co.uk/news/technology-64153383.

Van den Broek, Tijs, David Langley, Tobias Hornig. 2017. 'The Effect of Online Protests and Firm Responses on Shareholder and Consumer Evaluation,' *Journal of Business Ethics* 146(2): 279–294.

Van den Hoven, Jeroen. 2009. 'Distributive Justice and the Value of Information: A (broadly) Rawlsian Approach' in Jeroen van den Hoven, John Weckert (eds.), *Information Technology and Moral Philosophy* (Cambridge: Cambridge University Press): 376–396.

Van Dijcke, David, Austin Wright, Mark Polyak. 2023. 'Public Response to Government Alerts Saves Lives during Russian Invasion of Ukraine,' *Proceedings of the National Academy of Science* 120(18): e2220160120.

Van Parijs, Philippe. 1995. *Real Freedom for All: What If Anything Can Justify Capitalism?* (Oxford: Oxford University Press).

Véliz, Carissa. 2019. 'Online Masquerade: Redesigning the Internet for Free Speech Through the Use of Pseudonyms,' *Journal of Applied Philosophy* 36(4): 643–658.

Véliz, Carissa. 2020. *Privacy Is Power. Why You How You Should Take Back Control of Your Data* (London: Penguin Random House).

Véliz, Carissa. 2024. 'The Surveillance Delusion' in Carissa Véliz (ed.), *The Oxford Handbook of Digital Ethics* (Oxford: Oxford University Press): 555–574.

Vergerio, Claire. 2021. 'Beyond the Nation State,' *Boston Review*. Available at www.bostonreview.net/articles/beyond-the-nation-state/.

Verizon. 2018. *How Much Is 4GB Per Month?* Available at www.verizon.com/about/news/what-can-you-do-4-gb-wireless-data-month.

Verma, Ravi K., Nalini V. Khurana. 2023. 'Healthy Masculinities and the Wellbeing of Young Boys and Men,' *BMJ* 380: p. 385.

Virtualcity. 2023. *AgriManagr*. Available at www.virtualcity.co.ke/our-products/agrimanagr/.

Vogels, Emily A. 2021. 'The State of Online Harassment,' *Pew Research Center*. Available at www.pewresearch.org/internet/2021/01/13/the-state-of-online-harassment/.

Wagner, Ben. 2012. 'After the Arab Spring: New Paths for Human Rights and the Internet in European Foreign Policy,' *European Parliament – Directorate-General for External Policies*. Available at www.europarl.europa.eu/thinktank/en/document/EXPO-DROI_NT(2012)457102.

Walsh, Declan, Mark Tran. 2009. 'Pakistan Claims 700 Taliban Killed in Swat Valley Strikes,' *The Guardian*. Available at www.theguardian.com/world/2009/may/11/pakistan-swat-taliban-army-refugees.

Walsh, Declan. 2009. 'Video of Girl's Flogging as Taliban Hand Out Justice,' *The Guardian*. Available at www.theguardian.com/world/2009/apr/02/taliban-pakistan-justice-women-flogging.

Weinberg, Samantha. 2012. 'What's the Greatest Invention of All Time?' *The Economist*. Available at www.economist.com/1843/2012/08/17/whats-the-greatest-invention-of-all-time.

Wenar, Leif. 2023. 'Rights,' *Standford Encyclopedia of Philosophy*. Available at https://plato.stanford.edu/archives/spr2023/entries/rights/.

West Cape Government. 2022. *Switching on Public WiFi Hotspots Across the Western Cape*. Available at www.westerncape.gov.za/general-publication/switching-public-wi-fi-hotspots-across-western-cape.

WHO. 2016. *Global Diffusion of eHealth: Making Universal Health Coverage Achievable*. Available at www.who.int/publications/i/item/9789241511780.

Widdows, Heather. 2018. *Perfect Me. Beauty As An Ethical Ideal* (Princeton: Princeton University Press).

Wikipedia. 2021. *Wikipedia*. Available at https://en.wikipedia.org/wiki/Wikipedia.

Wikipedia. 2023a. *Internet*. Available at https://en.wikipedia.org/wiki/Internet.

Wikipedia. 2023b. *Panopticon*. Available at https://en.wikipedia.org/wiki/Panopticon.

Wikipedia. 2023c. *Network Enforcement Act*. Available at https://en.wikipedia.org/wiki/Network_Enforcement_Act.

Wikipedia. 2024a. *LTE (telecommunication)*. Available at https://en.wikipedia.org/wiki/LTE_(telecommunication).

Wikipedia. 2024b. *Dunning-Kruger Effect*. Available at https://en.wikipedia.org/wiki/Dunning%E2%80%93Kruger_effect.

Williams, Alexander, Raul Raekstad. 2022. 'Surveillance Capitalism or Information Republic?' *Journal of Applied Philosophy* 39(3): 421–440.

Williamson, Elizabeth. 2021. 'Alex Jones Loses by Default in Remaining Sandy Hook Defamation Suits,' *New York Times*. Available at www.nytimes.com/2021/11/15/us/politics/alex-jones-sandy-hook.html.

Wittrock, Jon. 2022. 'A Human Right to Friendship? Dignity, Autonomy, and Social Deprivation,' *International Journal of Human Rights* 26(9): 1590–1607.

Wolff, Jonathan, Avner de-Shalit. 2007. *Disadvantage* (Oxford: Oxford University Press).

Wolff, Jonathan. 2015. 'The Content of the Human Right to Health' in Rowan Cruft, S. Matthew Liao, Massimo Renzo (eds.), *Philosophical Foundations of Human Rights* (Oxford: Oxford University Press): 491–501.

Wong, Stan Hok-Wui, Jiachen Liang. 2021. 'Dubious until Officially Censored: Effects of Online Censorship Exposure on Viewers' Attitudes in Authoritarian Regimes,' *Journal of Information Technology & Politics* 18(3): 310–323.

Woolley, Samuel C., Douglas R. Guilbeault. 2017. 'Computational Propaganda in the United States of American: Manufacturing Consensus Online,' *Computational Propaganda Research Project*, Working Paper No. 2017.5.

Woolley, Samuel C., Philip Howard. 2017. 'Computational Propaganda Worldwide: Executive Summary,' *Computational Propaganda Research Project*, Working Paper No. 2017.11.

Woolley, Samuel C., Philip Howard. 2018. *Computational Propaganda: Political Parties, Politicians and Political Manipulation on Social Media* (Oxford: Oxford University Press).

World Bank. 2017. *The Global Findex Database 2017. Measuring Financial Inclusion and the Fintech Revolution*. Available at https://openknowledge.worldbank.org/entities/publication/ed800062-e062-5a05-acdd-90429d8a5a07.

World Bank. 2018a. *Facing Forward: Schooling for Learning in Africa*. Available at www.worldbank.org/en/region/afr/publication/facing-forward-schooling-for-learning-in-africa.
World Bank. 2018b. *Where Do the World's Poorest People Live Today?* Available at https://datatopics.worldbank.org/world-development-indicators/stories/where-do-the-worlds-poorest-people-live-today.html.
World Bank. 2023. *Connecting for Inclusion: Broadband Access for All*. Available at www.worldbank.org/en/topic/digitaldevelopment/brief/connecting-for-inclusion-broadband-access-for-all.
World Economic Forum. 2019. *We Must Treat Cybersecurity as a Public Good. Here's Why*. Available at www.weforum.org/agenda/2019/08/we-must-treat-cybersecurity-like-public-good/.
World Economic Forum. 2020. *These Are the Countries Where Internet Access Is the Lowest*. Available at www.weforum.org/agenda/2020/08/internet-users-usage-countries-change-demographics/.
World Economic Forum. 2021. *Repairing – Not Recycling – Is the First Step to Tackling E-Waste from Smartphones. Here's Why*. Available at www.weforum.org/agenda/2021/07/repair-not-recycle-tackle-ewaste-circular-economy-smartphones/.
World Inequality Database. 2022. *World Inequality Report 2022. Executive Summary*. Available at https://wir2022.wid.world/executive-summary/.
Worldreader. 2023. *Worldreader*. Available at www.worldreader.org/.
WTO. 2023. *Information Technology Agreement – An Explanation*. Available at www.wto.org/english/tratop_e/inftec_e/itaintro_e.htm.
Wu, Xiaoping, Richard Fitzgerald. 2021. '"Hidden in Plain Sight": Expressing Political Criticism on Chinese Social Media,' *Discourse Studies* 23(3): 365–385.
Wyrębska-Đermanović, Ewa. 2019. 'The World Republic, The State of States or The League of Nations? Kant's Global Order Revisited,' *Con-Textos Kantianos* 10: 27–42.
Xiao, Muyi, Paul Mozur. 2022. 'A Digital Manhunt: How Chinese Police Track Critics on Twitter and Facebook,' *New York Times*. Available at www.nytimes.com/2021/12/31/technology/china-internet-police-twitter.html.
Xu, Xu, Genia Kostka, Xun Cao. 2022. 'Information Control and Public Support for Social Credit Systems in China,' *Journal of Politics* 84(4): 2230–2245.
Xu, Xu. 2020. 'To Repress or Co-Opt? Authoritarian Control in the Age of Digital Surveillance,' *American Journal of Political Science* 65(2): 309–325.
Youyou, Wu, Michal Kosinski, David Stillwell. 2015. 'Computer-Based Personality Judgments Are More Accurate Than Those Made by Humans,' *Proceedings of the National Academy of Science* 112(4): 1036–1040.
Yu Kexin, Shinyi Wu, Iris Chi. 2021. 'Internet Use and Loneliness of Older Adults Over Time: The Mediating Effect of Social Contact,' *Journal of Gerontology: Social Sciences* 76(3): 541–550.
Yuan, Li. 2019. 'Learning China's Forbidden History, So They Can Censor It,' *New York Times*. Available at www.nytimes.com/2019/01/02/business/china-internet-censor.html.
ZHIN. 2023. *Zentralstelle zur Bekämpfung der Hasskriminalität im Internet – Niedersachsen*. Available at https://staatsanwaltschaft-goettingen.niedersachsen.de/zhin/zhin-195737.html.

ZIT. 2023. *Zentralstelle zur Bekämpfung der Internet- und Computerkriminalität.* Available at https://staatsanwaltschaften.hessen.de/staatsanwaltschaften/generalstaatsanwaltschaft-frankfurt-am-main/aufgabengebiete/zentralstelle-zur-bekaempfung-der-internet-und-computerkriminalitaet-zit.

Zuboff, Shoshana. 2019. *The Age of Surveillance Capitalism: The Fight for a Human Future at the New Frontier of Power* (London: Profile Books).

Zwilling, Moti, Galit Klien, Dusan Lesjak, Lukasz Wiechetek, Fatih Cetin, Hamdullah Nejat Basim. 2022. 'Cyber Security Awareness, Knowledge and Behaviour: A Comparative Study,' *Journal of Computer Information Systems* 62(1): 82–97.

Index

A4AI. *See* Alliance for Affordable Internet (global digital connectivity coalition)
Access Now (nonprofit organisation), 7, 101, 195
affective polarisation. *See* political polarisation
Akamai (content delivery network service), 230
algorithms
    automated serendipity, 301
    definition of, 234
    and extremist content suggestions, 302
    and filter bubbles, 300
    inferences through use of, 234
    and informational power, 252
    online content removal, 226
    user engagement maximisation, 234, 301
Alibaba (e-commerce platform), 200
Alliance for Affordable Internet (global digital connectivity coalition), 156, 157, 159, 161, 163–165, 167, 174, 181, 182
Amazon (e-commerce platform), 200, 230, 234, 245, 269, 274
anonymity (online). *See* privacy
Apple, 104, 168, 210, 230
Arab Spring, 74–75
Argentina, 166
Article 19 (NGO), 282, 283
AT&T (Internet backbone operator), 230
Australia, 95, 134, 160, 177
    regional broadband scheme, 171
Austria, 177

Baidu (search engine), 200
Bangladesh, 149
basic digital skills. *See* Internet access
basic rights. *See* rights
BBC. *See* British Broadcasting Corporation (BBC)
Beitz, Charles, 24, 32, 36, 40, 46
Bellingcat (open-source intelligence), 75
BEREC. *See* European Union

Bild (newspaper), 292
Bill & Melinda Gates Foundation (charity), 89, 179
Black Lives Matter (social movement), 77, 96
Brazil, 96, 248, 256
Brecht, Bertolt, 189
British Broadcasting Corporation (BBC), 7, 293, 294
    BBC Bitesize (online learning resource), 111
Broadband Commission, 7, 126, 145, 164–166, 173, 175, 180–183
    2025 Broadband Advocacy Targets, 181
    affordability target, 155
BT Group (Internet service provider), 230

Canada, 117, 170, 225
censorship, 192
    definition of, 193
    porous censorship, 201
    through distraction, 200
    through information control, 200
    through website speed throttling, 200
Cerf, Vinton, 39, 42, 49
ChatGPT, 103, 316
child pornography, 12, 256, 278–284
Chile, 76, 179
China, 5, 48, 134, 149, 195, 201, 205, 197–209, 225, 266, 281, 286, 330
    cybersecurity law, 197
    Fifty Cent Party (paid government agitators), 200
    Golden Shield Project, 197, 198
    Great Firewall of China, 200, 201, 208, 330
    social credit scores system, 201–206
China Telecom (Internet backbone operator), 230
Christiano, Thomas, 29, 76, 189, 192, 210, 252, 310, 311
Citizens Online (digital inclusion charity), 115, 179

climate change, 304, 308, 322–324
climate change denial, 298
Cloudflare (content delivery network service), 230
Colombia, 165
  Internet access centres ('puntos digitales'), 172, 179, 182
  Internet Móvil Social para la Gente programme, 158, 166
  Vive Digital (2010–2014) national broadband plan, 182
  Vive Digital Para la Gente (2015–2018) national broadband plan, 182
Comcast (Internet service provider), 230
conspiracy narratives, 247–249, 278, 281, 289, 290, 304–308, 313, 314, 319, 320
conspiracy theories. *See* conspiracy narratives
Costa Rica
  Connected Homes ('hogares connectados') programme, 167
  National Telecommunication Development Plan 2015-2021 (PNDT), 162, 166, 182
Council of Europe, 119
COVID-19 pandemic, 97, 111, 117–119, 125, 156, 197
  lockdowns, 24, 37, 108, 111, 146
  misinformation, 101, 118, 247, 305
  vaccines, 43
Craigslist (advertisements website), 116
CrowdJustice (crowdfunding platform), 82
cyberbullying, 278, 281
cybersecurity, 223
cyber-sovereignty, 209
cyber-utopianism, 4

D64–Centre for Digital Progress (nonprofit civil society association), 286
Daily Mail, 292
dangerous speech, 278
darknet, 283
deep packet inspection, 266
democracy
  e-democracy, 95
  participatory, 94
  as political expression of moral equality, 191, 310
  tyranny of the majority, 189
Deutsche Telekom (Internet backbone operator), 230
dictator's dilemma, 193
digital authoritarianism, 188, 191, 194, 206, 208
Digital Inclusion (charity), 167, 168
Digital Markets Act. *See* European Union
digital poverty, 143, 145–149
Digital Services Act. *See* European Union
Douyin (social media platform), 200
doxing, 278

echo chambers, 7, 258, 289, 290, 299–304, 313, 319
Ecuador, 159
e-democracy, 95. *See* democracy
e-government, 113–115, 183
eHealth, 126, 127, 135, 270
electricity, 4, 102, 123, 135, 173, 180
Electronic Frontier Foundation (digital rights nonprofit organisation), 223
Emmaüs Connect (digital inclusion charity), 179
epistemic anarchy, 207, 248
Ethiopia, 93, 127, 128, 130
European Commission, 7, 94, 146, 170, 177–178, 274
  Digital Education Plan (2021–2027), 178
  WiFi4EU initiative, 161
European Court of Human Rights, 43, 101, 221, 228
European Court of Justice, 219, 227, 228, 244
European Parliament, 82, 211, 212, 225, 228
European Union
  Body of European Regulators for Electronic Communications (BEREC), 268
  Digital Markets Act, 259, 274
  gatekeepers, 274
  Digital Services Act, 265, 281
  General Data Protection Regulation (GDPR), 235, 241, 244
European Union (EU), 44, 94, 119, 169, 224
Eurostat, 148
e-waste, 168
extreme speech, 247

Facebook, 48, 75, 77, 81, 90, 104, 206–208, 210, 230, 234, 235, 242, 245–247, 249, 252, 259–261, 269, 274, 330
fake news, 102, 186, 207, 226, 247, 249, 278, 281, 289, 290, 299, 302–304, 311, 313, 314, 319
Fastly (content delivery network service), 230
FCC (Federal Communications Commission). *See* USA
filter bubbles, 289, 290, 299–301
financial inclusion
  crowdfunding, 132
  FinTech, 133, 134
  Internet banking, 132
Finland, 170
Floyd, George, 77
Flusser, Vilem, 73, 74
Fox News, 292, 307
France, 179
free Internet access as a human right
  digital sufficiency, 143, 334
  formal argument for, 53, 69, 98

Index 369

free for those unable to afford it, 159, 160, 167, 185, 333, 335
free from arbitrary interference, 2, 143, 187, 229, 241, 266, 273, 279, 335
   legitimate restrictions of, 331
   minimum core obligations of, 183
   reasons for standalone right, 100–104
   responses to violations of, 329–30
   statement of, 335
Freedom House (NGO), 2, 5, 7, 191, 194, 197, 199, 208, 229, 247, 256

gatekeepers. *See* European Union
General Data Protection Regulation (GDPR). *See* European Union
German Democratic Republic, 190
Germany, 24, 87, 148, 283, 285, 287, 292, 294
   Bundesnetzagentur, 171
   cybercrime law enforcement agencies, 283
   DigitalPakt Schule, 177
   Initiative Digitale Bildung, 177
   Network Enforcement Act, 281–83
GetUp! (political activist group), 95, 96
Ghana, 125, 173
Global System for Mobile Communications Association (lobby organisation), 163, 166, 173
Good Things Foundation (digital connectivity charity), 7, 118
   DeviceDotNow campaign, 167
   future digital inclusion programme, 179
   national device bank, 168
   online centres network, 179
Google, 48, 104, 158, 200, 210, 230, 233–235, 242, 268, 269, 274, 330
great replacement conspiracy, 307
Griffin, James, 32, 217
GSMA. *See* Global System for Mobile Communications Association (lobby organisation)
Guiding Principles on Business and Human Rights. *See* United Nations Guiding Principles on Business and Human Rights

HarassMap (nonprofit organisation), 79
human right to
   adequate standard of living, 108
   housing, 66, 115, 116
   subsistence farming, 133
   cultural participation, 108, 119–120
   education, 60, 61, 108, 110–113, 123–126, 280
      free primary education, 60
      free secondary and vocational education, 60
      higher education, 61
   free association/assembly, 90, 101, 249
   free information, 43, 51, 52, 54, 86
   free speech/free expression, 52, 81, 101, 251, 256, 257, 281
   health/health care, 8, 25, 28, 34, 36, 63, 108, 117–118, 126–129, 151, 153, 182
      General Comment 14, 63, 153
      Internet as super-determinant of, 118
      social determinants of, 118
   literacy, 54, 103
   press freedom, 43, 51, 52, 54, 66, 67, 99, 293
   privacy, 22, 204, 212, 214
   social security and insurance, 43, 107, 113
   work, 67, 107, 116, 131
human rights
   3-part test for legitimately restricting, 219, 256, 335
   and humanitarian intervention, 24, 25, 46
   dignity as basis of, 27–28
   feasible for majority of countries, 9, 151, 152, 334
   inequality critiques of, 38
   inflation of category of, 18, 68, 100
   interdependence of, 109
   as matters of international concern, 25, 26, 32, 45, 48, 136, 150, 173, 329
   minimum core obligations of, 152–153
   as moral rights, 23, 25, 26, 34, 50
   neo-imperialist and neo-colonialist critiques of, 37
   political conceptions of, 40
   progressive realisation of, 153, 154
   as protections of minimally decent lives, 26–28, 31–33
   strict criteria of, 9, 331
   technology and, 44
   temporariness of, 44–45
   universality of, 39–42
Human Rights Watch (NGO), 75
Hungary, 212, 293, 294

ICCPR. *See* International Covenant on Civil and Political Rights (ICCPR)
ICESCR. *See* International Covenant on Economic, Social and Cultural Rights (ICESCR)
identity theft, 278
IMF. *See* International Monetary Fund (IMF)
incels, 328
India, 113, 128, 149, 165, 167, 173, 177
   PM-WANI scheme, 173
indispensability
   practical, 53, 56, 69, 97
   systemic, 54–56, 118, 135
individual digital harms, 278, 279, 281
Indonesia, 149, 172
informational autocracy, 188, 199, 200

informational power, 310–312, 315, 317, 318
Instagram, 48, 206, 207, 230, 233, 245, 246, 260
International Broadband Development Fund (IBDF), 175, 183
International Covenant on Civil and Political Rights (ICCPR), 43, 100, 101, 214, 219, 255, 256, 258, 266, 276, 281–283
International Covenant on Economic, Social and Cultural Rights (ICESCR), 57, 60–63, 66, 107
International Monetary Fund (IMF), 91, 286
International Telecommunication Union (ITU), 2, 145–147, 149, 155–157, 162, 163, 168, 169, 171, 176, 178–179
EQUALS (digital skills initiative), 178
Internet
  amphitheatre discourses, and, 73
  ARPANET, 230
  basic utility/necessity, 11, 122, 138, 139, 143, 156, 174, 334
  definition, 3
  different impact in developed and developing countries, 107, 122
  gateway technology, 102, 103
  influence on beauty norms, 328
  Internet addiction/problematic Internet use, 324–326
  number of global mobile broadband users, 163
  number of non-users globally, 2, 146
  Online misogyny, 328
  public broadband ownership, 274
  repression technology, as a, 187, 194, 210, 224
  shutdowns, 105, 128, 186, 195, 196, 226, 329, 330
  submarine cables, 130
  user attention and ability to focus, reduction of, 324–326
Internet access
  basic digital skills, 176
  costs of universal, 149, 171
  coverage gap, 147, 169–170
  gender digital divide, 147, 164, 181
  global 4G broadband coverage, 169
  global fixed broadband traffic, 156
  global mobile broadband coverage, 169
  global standard of connectivity, 155, 163, 169, 176, 184
  good quality broadband, 168
  homeless people and, 161
  meaningful connectivity, 163
  new human right to, 331–336
  as part of the socio-cultural minimum level of subsistence, 159
  people with disabilities and, 97, 120, 164, 172
  universal service guarantees, 170

usage gap, 145–146
virtual private networks (VPN), 200, 225, 287, 315
world price for mobile data, 156
Internet skills
  algorithmic awareness, 315
  critical privacy literacy, 314
  cybersecurity awareness, 312
  Internet search skills, 313
  news media literacy, 313
Iran, 76, 208, 225
Israel, 88, 90
ITU. See International Telecommunication Union (ITU)

Jio Phone, 165

Kant, Immanuel, 27, 44, 53
Kenya, 125, 127, 134, 165

Latin America, 178, 209
login trap, 286–287
Luxemburg, 167

Malaysia, 166, 172, 179, 182
MeToo (social movement), 77, 78, 96
Mexico, 256, 293
Microsoft, 103, 210, 230
misinformation. See social media platforms
moral philosophy, 5, 7, 8, 329
Mozambique, 128
Mozorov, Evgeny, 4

national broadband plan, 156
net neutrality, 266–267
Netflix, 165, 230, 274
New York Times, 7, 49, 283
Nickel, James, 9, 11, 18, 26, 27, 33, 34, 38, 53–56, 69, 72, 98, 137, 151, 152, 331, 332, 334
Nigeria, 128, 149
Norway, 177, 304, 317
NSA. See USA
Nussbaum, Martha, 30, 32

OECD. See Organization for Economic Co-operation and Development (OECD)
online harassment, 258, 289
Open Observatory of Network Interference (non-profit software project), 227
Open Society Foundations (grantmaking network), 223
open-source intelligence. See Bellingcat
Organization for Economic Co-operation and Development (OECD), 159, 177, 178
Oxfam, 93, 150
Oxford Internet Survey, 82, 87

Pakistan, 74, 149, 167
Patients Like Me (social networking service), 118
Pegasus (spyware), 211, 212, 218, 228, 293
Philippines, 161
Poland, 212, 293, 294
political legitimacy, 25, 222
political polarisation
  affective polarisation, 297
  as aim of foreign political interference, 207
  increased political sorting as driver of, 298
  issue polarisation, 297
  political elites as drivers of, 298
  and political violence, 298
  socio-economic inequality as driver of, 298
Portugal, 177
practical indispensability. *See* indispensability
preventive repression, 194
privacy, 210, 215–218
  encryption, 210, 225, 285
  end-user choice model of, 238
  fiduciary model of, 242
  legitimate violations of, 219–220
  of emails, search history, hard drives, 215
  online anonymity, 284–285
  paradox of, 239
  personal value of, 212–213
  privacy and security, 218
  privacy policies and terms of service, 237, 238
  privacy settings, 176, 177
  public/political value of, 213, 214
proportionality, 220, 224, 256, 329
pseudonyms databank, 285–287
public libraries, 52, 54, 87, 88, 89, 113, 161, 179, 180, 182
public service broadcast, 293–296, 302, 309, 320

QAnon (conspiracy narrative), 305, 307

Rawls, John, 6, 27, 64, 66, 103, 322
Raz, Joseph, 21, 40, 52, 57, 58
revenge pornography, 12, 247, 278–282, 284
right to be forgotten, 224
rights
  3 general conditions of the enjoyment of, 279
  adequate opportunities for enjoying and exercising, 64–68
  anchor rights, 52, 53, 55
  basic rights, 34, 35, 46, 52, 108, 281
  derived/derivative rights, 51–53, 55, 71
  due process rights, 53, 54
  duties to respect, protect, aid, 35, 46, 231
  Hohfeldian rights incidents, 22
  legal rights, 21–23
  linkage arguments for, 52–57
  minimal vs medium vs maximal interpretations of, 59
  moral rights, 20–23
  negative vs positive rights, 33–35
  as social guarantees against standard threats, 9, 36, 51, 73, 76, 139, 280, 332
  standard threats to, 11, 36, 46, 332
  types of costs of corresponding duties, 58
Roberts, Margaret E., 193, 200–201, 266, 268
Russia, 5, 75, 87, 190, 195, 196–201, 206–209, 225, 286
  blocklists, 199
  Internet Research Agency (IRA), 206, 243
  Roskomnadzor (media regulator), 199, 225
  SORM (System for Operative Investigative Activities) surveillance hardware, 196, 209
Rwanda, 179

Saudi Arabia, 208
Save Heart Kashmir (medical initiative), 128
Sen, Amartya, 29, 74
Shue, Henry, 8, 29, 33–36, 46, 51, 52, 76, 80, 108, 139, 231, 281, 332
Sierra Leone, 127
Sky (Internet service provider), 230
Skype, 81, 158
Snowden, Edward, 188, 210, 215–218, 221, 229
social media platforms
  bottom floor of permissible speech for, 255
  breaking up of, 259–263
  community rules of, 249, 256, 262
  decline of local journalism, 249
  editorial rights of, 250, 251, 260
  intermediary vs publisher liability of, 264
  misinformation spreading via, 249
  network effects of, 245
  power to exclude, 249, 252, 253
  virtual public sphere, 246, 250, 260, 261
South Africa, 127, 130, 162, 172, 177
South Korea, 225
spyware. *See* Pegasus (spyware)
Sri Lanka, 179
standard threats. *See* rights
Sub-Saharan Africa, 123–124, 126, 132, 137, 147, 163, 166, 171, 173, 175, 177
Sudan, 132
surveillance capitalism, 232–235, 237, 239–241, 244, 275, 277, 281, 309, 311, 312, 315
Sweden, 157, 177
systemic indispensability. *See* indispensability

Tasioulas, John, 17, 18, 34, 153
techno-determinism, 4
Thailand, 131
  village broadband project (Net Pracharat), 161, 172, 182
The Guardian, 7, 210
The Shift Project (nonprofit organisation), 323
TikTok, 119, 200, 230, 233, 235, 245, 246, 274
Transatlantic Trade and Investment Partnership (TTIP), 92, 93, 246
trolling, 258, 278, 281
TTIP. *See* Transatlantic Trade and Investment Partnership (TTIP)
Twitter. *See* X (formerly Twitter)
Twitter revolutions, 75

Uber, 165
Uganda, 127, 128, 180
Ukraine, 75, 87, 190, 195
UN Women, 178
UNESCO, 111, 123–125, 130, 164
  Giraffe (job matching platform), 130
  Global Education Coalition, 125
UNICEF, 7, 178
  Giga initiative, 178
United Kingdom (UK), 87, 111, 119, 167, 177, 179, 209, 235, 293, 297
  Brexit referendum, 206
  General Communications Headquarters (GCHQ), 211, 216, 218–221, 274
  House of Lords, 295
  Ofcom, 110, 148, 159, 169
  UK Parliament, 82, 171, 177, 250
  UK Supreme Court, 82
  Universal Credit, 114
  universal service obligation, 171
United Nations (UN), 2, 5, 25, 42, 91, 120, 187, 255
United Nations Committee on Economic, Social, and Cultural Rights (CESCR), 152, 153
United Nations General Assembly, 2, 25, 187, 279
United Nations Guiding Principles on Business and Human Rights, 35, 231, 245, 258, 330
United Nations Human Rights Council, 2, 7, 211, 219
United Nations Security Council, 91
United Nations Sustainable Development Goals, 122, 149, 152, 223
  SDG 9.c, 173
United States. *See* USA
Universal Declaration of Human Rights, 18–19, 24, 27, 28, 86, 107, 116, 191, 214
universal service funds, 159, 160, 170

upskirting, 8
USA, 24, 77, 78, 87, 101, 110, 114, 117, 148, 161, 177, 209, 230, 256, 281, 286, 289, 293, 294, 297, 300, 301, 321
  1996 Communications Decency Act, 265
  2016 US Presidential Election, 206
  2020 Presidential Election, 305, 307
  Federal Communications Commission (FCC), 159, 170
    Affordable Connectivity Program, 159, 166
    E-rate program, 160
    Lifeline program, 159, 160
  Infrastructure Investment and Jobs Act, 170
  National Security Agency (NSA), 210–211, 216, 218–221, 238, 274
  US Congress, 159, 170, 214, 229
  US Supreme Court, 85, 103, 225, 236

Véliz, Carissa, 213, 214, 234–236, 239, 240, 285, 286
Verizon, 157, 210, 230
Vietnam, 133
virtual Internet user profiles, 190
Vodafone (Internet service provider), 230
VPN. *See* Internet access

WeChat (instant messaging service), 200
Weibo (microblogging website), 200
WhatsApp, 128, 137, 158, 200, 230, 245, 248, 260
WHO. *See* World Health Organization (WHO)
Wikipedia, 3, 270
World Bank, 91, 123, 132, 133, 147, 174–175
World Economic Forum, 147, 168, 223
World Health Organization (WHO), 7, 127, 153, 175, 324
World Trade Organization (WTO), 91, 286
  information technology agreement, 165
Worldreader (nonprofit organisation), 124, 125
wrongful exploitation, 310, 311
WTO. *See* World Trade Organization (WTO)

X (formerly Twitter), 75, 77, 81, 82, 93, 200, 206–207, 245, 247, 249, 303

YouTube, 48, 93, 111, 119, 158, 207, 230, 245, 252, 301, 302, 307

zero-rating, 268, 272, 273
Zoom, 81
Zuboff, Shoshana, 4, 233–234, 237